T0405599

THE PRINCIPALITY OF ANTIOCH AND ITS
FRONTIERS IN THE TWELFTH CENTURY

THE PRINCIPALITY OF ANTIOCH AND ITS FRONTIERS IN THE TWELFTH CENTURY

ANDREW D. BUCK

THE BOYDELL PRESS

First published 2017
The Boydell Press, Woodbridge

ISBN 978 1 78327 173 3

The Boydell Press is an imprint of Boydell & Brewer Ltd
PO Box 9, Woodbridge, Suffolk IP12 3DF, UK
and of Boydell & Brewer Inc.
668 Mt Hope Avenue, Rochester, NY 14620–2731, USA
website: www.boydellandbrewer.com

A catalogue record for this book is available
from the British Library

Contents

List of Maps   vi

Acknowledgements   vii

Abbreviations   ix

Introduction   1

1. The Extent of the Principality   21

2. The Rulers of Antioch   62

3. Central Governance and Military Service   86

    Appendix 1: The Officers of the Principality, 1127–1201   123

4. Lordship in the Principality   128

    Appendix 2: The Noble Families   160

5. A Frontier Society? The Nature of Intercultural Relations   164

6. Relations with Byzantium   189

7. Antioch and the Latin East   218

Conclusion   245

Bibliography   253

Index   277

Maps

Map 1. Northern Syria and Cilicia   2

Map 2. Northern Syria and Cilicia, 1130   23

Map 3. Northern Syria and Cilicia, 1135   28

Map 4. Northern Syria and Cilicia, early summer, 1138   32

Map 5. Northern Syria and Cilicia, 1149   40

Map 6. Northern Syria and Cilicia, 1165   47

Map 7. Northern Syria and Cilicia, 1193   58

Acknowledgements

The creation of this book has incurred a great many debts. None more so than to my former PhD supervisor, Tom Asbridge, whose guidance, knowledge, fierce questioning and mutual enthusiasm for the history of the principality of Antioch made the handling of its difficult history both possible and enjoyable. Without his support this book would not exist. I would also like to express my gratitude to Peter Edbury and Andrew Jotischky, for their important suggestions on how to better my work and to further my ideas, as well as for their continued support; to Susan Edgington, for her feedback and for easing the burden of medieval Latin for me and many others; and to Bernard Hamilton, for his unfailing kindness, erudite criticism and guidance. I also wish to make known my thanks to Stephen Church and Nicholas Vincent, who first introduced me to medieval history as an undergraduate and cultivated a passion and interest for the period that continues unabated. I must also express a vast debt of appreciation to Stephen Spencer. A friend, drinking buddy and comrade in arms, I cannot imagine a better colleague. The products of his generous support and advice can be seen throughout this book.

I am also grateful for the advice and help offered over the years by Phil Baldwin, David Bates, Stephen Bennett, Betty Binysh, Jochen Burgtorf, Paul Cobb, Taef El-Azhari, Catherine Hanley, Jonathan Harris, Martin Hall, Konrad Hirschler, Melissa Julian-Jones, Ioanna Karakatsani, Hubert Kaufhold, Benjamin Kedar, Max Lau, Kevin Lewis, Rickelt Lutz, Balazs Major, Alex Mallett, Jean-Marie Martin, Benjamin Michaudel, Alan Murray, Agnès Ouzounian, David Parnell, Simon Parsons, Mathias Piana, Jonathan Phillips, Eyal Poleg, Yossef Rapoport, Dan Roach, Catherine Rose, Miri Rubin, Antonella Liuzzo Scorpo, Carol Sweetenham, Steven Tibble, Klaus-Peter Todt, Ian Wilson, James Wilson and Sam Wilson. I would also like to thank the staff at the libraries of Queen Mary University of London, the University of New York, Senate House, the Institute of Historical Research, the Warburg Institute, the School of Oriental and African Studies, the British Library, as well as Philip Skingley and the Spink Numismatic Society, who very kindly answered and fulfilled requests for obscure texts. The Isobel Thornley Bequest to the University of London provided invaluable financial support for this publication and its maps. Likewise, my thanks go to Cath d'Alton for creating the maps, to Caroline Palmer, Rob Kinsey and Nick Bingham at Boydell for so patiently guiding me through the publication process and to the anonymous reader for their useful suggestions.

Also, to my friends who have provided laughs, alcohol, patience, food and their time. I cannot truly express the extent of my gratitude for having put up with me over the last few years. Perhaps the most significant thanks, however, is owed to my family: my parents, my Nan, my brother, my great aunt Silvy and my grandparents, some of whom are sadly no longer with us. Through their unfailing enthusiasm and support, I have incurred debts I will never truly be able to repay. It is to them that this book is dedicated.

Abbreviations

1234	*Anonymi auctoris Chronicon ad A. C. 1234 pertinens*, ed. and trans. A. Abouna, J.-M. Fiey and J.-B. Chabot, 4 vols (Louvain, 1916–74)
Al-Azimi	Monot, F., 'La chronique abrégée d'al-Azimi années 518–538/1124–1144', *Revue des études islamique* 59 (1991), 101–64
AOL	*Archives de l'orient latin*
AS	Abu Shama, 'Le livre des deux jardins', *RHC Or.* IV, 3–522; V, 3–206
BD	Baha al-Din Ibn Shaddad, *The Rare and Excellent History of Saladin*, trans. D. S. Richards (Aldershot, 2002)
CCSSJ	*Le cartulaire du chapitre du Saint-Sépulchre de Jérusalem*, ed. G. Bresc-Bautier (Paris, 1984)
CGOH	*Cartulaire général de l'ordre des hospitaliers de S. Jean de Jérusalem (1100–1300)*, ed. J. Delaville Le Roulx, 4 vols (Paris, 1894–1906)
CGT	*Continuation de Guillaume de Tyr (1184–1197)*, ed. M. R. Morgan (Paris, 1982)
Chartes Josaphat	*Chartes de Terre Sainte provenant de l'Abbaye de N.-D de Josaphat*, ed. H.-F. Delaborde (Paris, 1880)
Constantine Manasses	Aerts, W., 'A Byzantine Traveller to one of the Crusader States', *East and West in the Crusader States: Context–Contacts–Confrontations III*, ed. K. Ciggaar and H. Teule (Leuven, 2003), pp. 165–221
Deeds Done Beyond the Sea	Edgington, S., and H. Nicholson (ed.), *Deeds Done Beyond the Sea: Essays on William of Tyre, Cyprus and the Military Orders Presented to Peter Edbury* (Farnham, 2014)
DOP	*Dumbarton Oaks Papers*

Documenti Toscane	*Documenti sulle Relazione delle citta Toscane: Coll' Oriente Cristiano e coi Turchi fino all'anno MDXXI*, ed. G. Müller (Rome, 1966)
East and West I	Ciggaar, K., and M. Metcalf (ed.), *East and West in the Medieval Eastern Mediterranean I: Antioch from the Byzantine Reconquest until the End of the Crusader Principality* (Leuven, 2006)
East and West II	Ciggaar, K., and V. van Aalst (ed.), *East and West in the Medieval Eastern Mediterranean II: Antioch from the Byzantine Reconquest Until the End of the Crusader Principality* (Leuven, 2013)
EHR	*The English Historical Review*
Eracles	'L'estoire de Eracles empereur et la conqueste de la terre d'Outremer', ed. M. Paulin Paris, *Guillaume de Tyr et ses continuateurs*, 2 vols (1879–80)
'Eracles'	'L'estoire de Eracles empereur et la conqueste de la terre d'Outremer', *RHC Occ.* II, 1–638
Ernoul	*Chronique d'Ernoul et de Bernard le Trésorier*, ed. L. de Mas Latrie (Paris, 1871)
GBE	Gregory Bar Ebroyo, *The Chronography: Being the First Part of his Political History of the World*, trans. E. A. Wallis Budge, 2 vols (London, 1932)
GP	'Gregory the Priest: Continuation of Matthew of Edessa', trans. A. E. Dostourian, *Armenia and the Crusades: Tenth to Twelfth Centuries* (New York, 1993), pp. 241–80
IA	Ibn al-Athir, *The Chronicle of Ibn al-Athir for the Crusading Period from al-Kamil fi'l-Ta'rikh*, ed. and trans. D. S. Richards, 3 vols (Aldershot, 2005–08)
ID	Imad al-Din al-Isfahani, *Conquête de la Syrie et de la Palestine par Saladin*, trans. H. Massé (Paris, 1972)
Libri Iurium	*I Libri iurium della Repubblica di Genova*, ed. D. Puncuh, 8 vols (Rome, 1992–2002)
Inventaire du Jébel Baricha	Peña, I., P. Castellana and R. Fernández, *Inventaire du Jébel Baricha: Recherches archéologiques dans la région des Villes Mortes de la Syrie du Nord* (Milan, 1987)
Inventaire du Jebel el-A'la	Peña, I., P. Castellana and R. Fernández, *Inventaire du Jebel el-A'la: Recherches archéologiques dans la région des Villes Mortes de la Syrie du Nord* (Milan, 1990)

Inventaire du Jébel Wastani	Peña, I., P. Castellana and R. Fernández, *Inventaire du Jébel Wastani: Recherches archéologiques dans la région des Villes Mortes de la Syrie du Nord* (Milan, 1999)
Inventaire du Jébel Douelli	Peña, I., P. Castellana and R. Fernández, *Inventaire du Jébel Doueili: Recherches archéologiques dans la région des Villes Mortes de la Syrie du Nord* (Milan, 2003)
IQ	Ibn al-Qalanisi, *The Damascus Chronicle of the Crusades*, trans. H. A. R. Gibb (London, 1932)
IS	Izz al-Din ibn Shaddad, *Description de la Syrie du Nord*, trans. A.-M. Eddé-Terrasse (Damascus, 1984)
JK	John Kinnamos, *Deeds of John and Manuel Comnenus*, trans. C. M. Brand (New York, 1976)
JMH	*Journal of Medieval History*
KD	Kemal al-Din, 'La chronique d'Alep', *RHC Or.* III, 577–690; E. Blochet, 'L'histoire d'Alep', *ROL* 3 (1895), 509–65; 4 (1896), 145–225; 5 (1897), 37–107; 6 (1898), 1–49
Manganeios Prodromos	Jeffreys, E., and M. Jeffreys, 'A Constantinopolitan Poet Views Frankish Antioch', *Crusades* 14 (2015), 49–152
ME	'Matthew of Edessa: Chronicle', trans. A. E. Dostourian, *Armenia and the Crusades: Tenth to Twelfth Centuries* (New York, 1993), pp. 1–239
MGH SS	*Monumenta Germaniae Historica Scriptores*, 39 vols (Hannover, 1826–)
MS	Michael the Syrian, *Chronique de Michel le Syrien, patriarche jacobite d'Antioche (1166-1199)*, ed. and trans. J.-B. Chabot, 4 vols (Paris, 1916–1920)
NC	Niketas Choniates, *O City of Byzantium, Annals of Niketas Choniates*, trans. H. J. Magoulias (Detroit, MI, 1984)
RHC Arm.	*Recueil des historiens des croisades: documents arméniens*, 2 vols (Paris, 1869–1906)
RHC Occ.	*Recueil des historiens des croisades: historiens occidentaux*, 5 vols (Paris, 1844–1895)
RHC Or.	*Recueil des historiens des croisades: historiens orientaux*, 5 vols (Paris, 1872–1906)
RHGF	*Recueil des historiens des Gaules et de la France*, 24 vols (Paris, 1738–1904)
ROL	*Revue de l'orient latin*

RRH	*Regesta Regni Hierosolymitani* (MCVII–MCCXCI), ed. R. Röhricht, 2 vols (Innsbruck, 1893–1904)
Sempad	Sempad the Constable, 'Chronique du royaume de la Petite Armenie', *RHC Arm.* I, 605–80
Sempad, 'Armenian Chronicle'	Der Nersessian, S., 'The Armenian Chronicle of the Constable Smpad or of the "Royal Historian"', *DOP* 13 (1959), 141–68
Sempad, *Chronique*	Sempad the Constable, *La chronique attribuée au connétable Smbat*, trans. G. Dédéyan (Paris, 1980)
Tabulae Theutonici	*Tabulae Ordinis Theutonici*, ed. E. Strehlke (Berlin, 1869, rep. 1975)
TRHS	*Transactions of the Royal Historical Society*
Urkunden Jerusalem	*Die Urkunden der lateinischen Könige von Jerusalem*, ed. H. E. Mayer and J. Richard, 4 vols (Hannover, 2010)
Urkunden Venedig	*Urkunden zur älteren Handels- und Staatsgeschichte der Republik Venedig: mit besonderer Beziehung auf Byzanz und die Levante vom neunten bis zum Ausgang des fünfzehnten Jahrhunderts*, ed. G. Tafel and G. Thomas, 2 vols (Vienna, 1856)
WC	Walter the Chancellor, *Bella Antiochena*, ed. H. Hagenmeyer (Innsbruck, 1896)
WT	William of Tyre, *Chronicon*, ed. R. B. C. Huygens, 2 vols (Turnhout, 1986)

Introduction

Situated at the easternmost edge of Latin Christendom, the principality of Antioch offered profound challenges to its inhabitants. Founded in 1098 by the Norman adventurer and First Crusade leader, Bohemond of Taranto, its territorial extent – based largely on a former duchy of the Byzantine Empire – acted as a meeting point between Asia Minor, Syria and Mesopotamia.[1] This brought the newly arrived Latin Christians – described more generally as Franks – into contact with a nearly incomparable wealth of religious and political groups, both internally and externally.[2] Incorporated within this were numerous Eastern Christian communities and powers, such as Byzantium and the Greek Orthodox Church, the Armenians, including the independent warlords of Cilicia, the Syriac Jacobites and the Melkites, the latter of whom were liturgically Greek but spoke Arabic. Likewise, there were Sunni Muslim peoples and potentates theoretically linked to the Abbasid Caliphs of Baghdad, such as those of Aleppo, Mosul and the Seljuk and Danishmend Turks of Asia Minor, as well as Shi'a Muslims, including the enigmatic Isma'ili sect, famously known as the Assassins. Finally, there were other Latin powers to contend with, including Western kings and states, the papacy, the military orders and even the other Crusader States.[3] In addition to this were numerous topographical challenges, such as the various mountain ranges and limestone massifs which dotted the region and hampered easy settlement and movement, as well as the Orontes River that bisected the principality. The maintenance of Antioch's authority thus demanded a delicate balance of diplomacy, warfare and political reactivity in order to counter the political and geographical demands placed upon its ruling elites.

One result of this, is that the boundaries of the Frankish polity waxed and waned to an unheralded degree during the twelfth century. Despite severe fluctuations, particularly after defeats at Harran in 1104 and *Ager Sanguinis* in 1119, the princi-

---

[1]   J.-C. Cheynet, 'The Duchy of Antioch during the Second Period of Byzantine Rule', *East and West I*, pp. 1–16.
[2]   The kingdom of Hungary had a similarly diverse wealth of peoples, but has distinct differences with Antioch; namely, as Nora Berend has noted, it was a 'society ... not formed by Christians conquering a population of different religious adherence ... [rather] they migrated into the kingdom voluntarily'. See *At the Gate of Christendom: Jews, Muslims and 'Pagans' in Medieval Hungary, c. 1000–c.1300* (Cambridge, 2001), p. 41. For the term 'Frank', see A. V. Murray, 'Ethnic identity in the crusader states: the Frankish race and the settlement of Outremer', *Concepts of National Identity in the Middle Ages*, ed. S. Forde, L. Johnson and A. V. Murray (Leeds, 1995), pp. 59–73.
[3]   For an overview of the wider demography of the Near East, see C. MacEvitt, *The Crusades and the Christian World of the East: Rough Tolerance* (Philadelphia, PA, 2008), pp. 7–12.

I

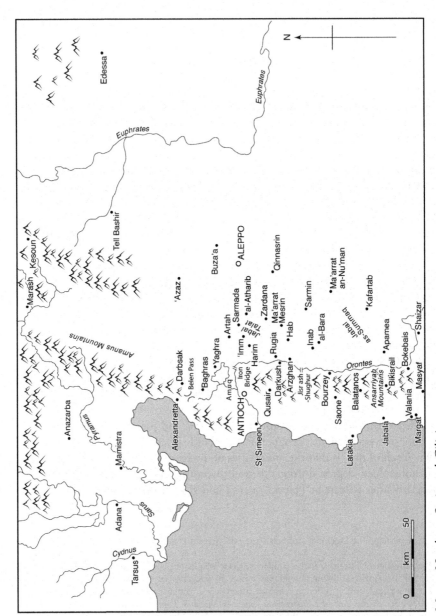

Map 1: Northern Syria and Cilicia

2

pality reached its zenith under Prince Bohemond II in around 1130. However, in this year the young ruler – son of the principality's founder – died, and from this date onwards Antioch faced major disasters and losses in 1149, 1164 and finally, in 1188, Saladin's capture of all but the city of Antioch. This was a complex and convoluted process, in which the struggle for key sites, particularly those guarding river crossings or major road confluences and mountain passages, had a strong influence over the aims and tactics of the Antiochene Franks and those powers who sought to intervene in the region. The growing military demands this placed upon the principality's ruling elites ensured the fluid imposition of governmental structures, while the courting of potential external overlords was required to prevent collapse and allowed powerful figures, such as the Byzantine Emperors or the kings of Jerusalem, to vie for influence. This book argues that, as a result of this, the processes of administration, as well as the negotiating and politicking which surrounded diplomatic ties, were often dynamic, and delicately and deliberately manipulated to ensure their terms benefitted Antioch and contributed to its survival. Given that the extent of external scrutiny placed upon the principality was unparalleled in the medieval world, a thorough examination of its military, social, political and administrative history can therefore offer a crucial insight into the nature of cross-cultural interaction and the practice of power in the Middle Ages.

* * *

To date, only three major monographs have been dedicated to the principality's history. The earliest, and still most influential, is Claude Cahen's *La Syrie du nord a l'époque des croisades et la principauté Franque d'Antioche*, published in 1940.[4] Offering a largely chronological overview of northern Syria from the mid-eleventh century to the end of the 'crusader period' in 1291, Cahen's mastery of Arabic and personal topographical knowledge makes his work a vital repository of detail. Despite this, its commentaries on the principality's internal frameworks of power and Latin relations with indigenous communities are now rather dated in their approach, while the critical analysis of key moments is often overlooked in favour of pure narrative. His work thus stands in need of revision and updating, a fact Cahen himself accepted in the foreword to an unrealised new edition.[5] Hans Mayer seemingly did not share this pessimism, however, noting in his own monograph on the principality – *Varia Antiochena: Studien zum Kreuzfahrerfürstentum Antiochia im 12. und frühen 13. Jarhundert* – that Cahen's work left little need or room on which to improve.[6] Nonetheless, this did not deter Mayer from offering his own

---

4   C. Cahen, *La Syrie du nord a l'époque des croisades et la principauté Franque d'Antioche* (Paris, 1940).
5   F. Micheau, 'De l'Occident a l'orient: Claude Cahen, historien des croisades', *Arabica* 43:1 (1996), 85–8.
6   H. E. Mayer, *Varia Antiochena: Studien zum Kreuzfahrerfürstentum Antiochia im 12. und frühen 13. Jarhundert* (Hannover, 1993), pp. 1–7.

thoughts on a number of technical aspects of Antioch's history, such as its chancery, charter material (including valuable editions of previously unknown documents) and certain key political events. A highly valuable contribution to modern understanding of the principality, Mayer's uncompromising style did at times lead him to overlook or reject important factors which influenced Antiochene actions, while his decision to not challenge certain traditional themes of Cahen's work with any great rigour ensured that elements of his analysis can be questioned. The most recent study is Thomas Asbridge's *The Creation of the Principality of Antioch 1098–1130*, which focuses on the first three decades of Latin settlement, offering the first systematic re-evaluation of the principality's formation and various key aspects of its internal structures.[7] Of special importance are his discussions on the composition of Antioch's nobility, the powers of its prince and its administrative frameworks, for these took the first steps towards placing the principality within the context of modern scholarship of medieval authority and frontiers. Asbridge has also followed this with a number of articles on the principality's inter-cultural relations and its political and military history, including the career of Princess Alice of Antioch and the topographical pressure points of northern Syria; while his recent history of the crusades touches upon several events pertinent here.[8] Nevertheless, there is a need to advance from his foundations. Beyond these are two essay collections, both entitled *East and West in the Medieval Eastern Mediterranean: Antioch from the Byzantine Reconquest until the End of the Crusader Principality*, which emerged from a series of conferences dedicated to Antioch.[9] Contained within these are invaluable contributions on a variety of topics relating to the crusading period, including studies on the role of the military orders, the development and structures of the Latin Church, cross-cultural exchange, the position of indigenous communities, aspects of the principality's archaeological remains and its numismatic evidence.

A number of other works, primarily those on Byzantium, the Muslim world and the wider Latin East, likewise touch upon Antioch's history, albeit often only tangentially, and will be introduced and examined as they become relevant. Others have also provided shorter works examining specific aspects of the principality, some of which focus solely on the period examined by Asbridge, and will again be noted sporadically over the course of this book. However, a number are worthy of note here.[10] The first of these is Jean-Marie Martin's stimulating examination of

---

7   T. Asbridge, *The Creation of the Principality of Antioch 1098–1130* (Woodbridge, 2000).

8   T. Asbridge, 'The "Crusader" Community at Antioch: The Impact of Interaction with Byzantium and Islam', *TRHS 6th Series* 10 (1999), 305–25; 'Alice of Antioch: A Case Study of Female Power in the Twelfth Century', *The Experience of Crusading vol. 2: Defining the Crusader Kingdom*, ed. P. Edbury and J. Phillips (Cambridge, 2003), pp. 29–47; 'The Significance and Causes of the Battle of the Field of Blood', *JMH* 23 (1997), 301–16; *The Crusades: The War for the Holy Land* (London, 2010). See bibliography for further works.

9   *East and West I* and *East and West II*.

10   In addition to the present monograph, I have examined, in smaller, more-focused studies, some key events or aspects of the principality's history. While each of these topics appear here as well, they do not always do so in as direct a manner. See A. D. Buck, 'Between Byzantium and Jerusalem? The Principality of Antioch, Renaud of Châtillon, and the Penance of Mamistra in 1158', *Mediterranean*

Antioch's 'feudality' and governance, which refutes some of Cahen's key supposi-
tions regarding the imposition of Italo-Norman power structures.[11] Peter Edbury
has also recently discussed internal frameworks in an article on the composition
of, and influences upon, the thirteenth-century legal customs known as the *Assises
d'Antioche*.[12] Meanwhile, in addition to a seminal monograph on the Latin Church
in the crusader states, Bernard Hamilton has produced numerous works on aspects
of Antioch's ecclesiastical and political history.[13] Similarly, Rudolf Hiestand has
provided a series of useful articles on topics including an edition and discussion
of a text describing an Antiochene Church Council in 1140, Antioch's diplomatic
policy towards the West at the end of the twelfth century and its role in intellectual exchange.[14] In addition, George Beech has produced studies on Raymond of
Poitiers, prince of Antioch 1136–1149, and the Frankish lordship of Marash, while
Kristin Skottki has examined the principality's 'interculturality' and Scott Redford
its trade.[15] The role of the military orders has also attracted further scholarly interest,
in particular through works on the introduction of the Templars into the Amanus
Mountains and the Hospitallers' acquisition of Margat in 1187.[16] This book is also

---

Historical Review 30:2 (2015), 107–24; 'The Noble Rebellion at Antioch, 1180–82: A Case Study in
Medieval Frontier Politics', *Nottingham Medieval Studies* 60 (2016), 93–121; 'The Castle and Lordship
of Harim and the Frankish-Muslim Frontier of Northern Syria in the Twelfth Century', *Al-Masaq*
28:2 (2016), 113–31.

[11]   J.-M. Martin, 'Les structures féodale normanno-souabes et la Terre Sainte', *Il Mezzogiorno normanno-svevo e le Crociate: Atti delle quattordicesime giornate normanno-sveve Bari, 17-20 Octobre 2000*, ed. G.
Musca (Bari, 2002), pp. 225–50.

[12]   P. Edbury, 'The *Assises d'Antioche*: Law and Custom in the Principality of Antioch', *Norman Expansion: Connections, Continuities and Contrasts*, ed. K. Stringer and A. Jotischky (Farnham, 2013), pp.
241–8.

[13]   B. Hamilton, *The Latin Church in the Crusader States: The Secular Church* (London, 1980); 'Three
Patriarchs at Antioch, 1165-1170', *Dei gesta per Francos: études sur les croisades dédiées à Jean Richard*, ed.
M. Balard, B. Kedar and J. Riley-Smith (Aldershot, 2001), pp. 199–207; 'Ralph of Domfront, Patriarch
of Antioch (1135–1140), *Nottingham Medieval Studies* 18 (1984), 1–21; 'Aimery of Limoges, Patriarch of
Antioch: Ecumenist, Scholar and Patron of Hermits', *The Joy of Learning and the Love of God: Studies
in Honor of Jean Leclercq*, ed. E. R. Elder (Kalamazoo, MI, 1995), pp. 269–90.

[14]   R. Hiestand, 'Ein neuer Bericht über das Konzil von Antiochia 1140', *Annuarium historiae conciliorum* 20 (1988), 314–50; 'Antiochia, Sizilien und das Reich am Ende des 12. Jahrhunderts', *Quellen und
Forschungen aus italienischen Archiven und Bibliotheken* 73 (1993), 70–121; and 'Un centre intellectuel
en Syrie du Nord? Notes sur la personalité d'Aimery d'Antioche, Albert de Tarse et *Rorgo Fretellus*', *Le
Moyen Age* 100 (1994), 7–36.

[15]   G. Beech, 'The Ventures of the Dukes of Aquitaine into Spain and the Crusader East in the Early
Twelfth Century', *Haskins Society Journal* 5 (1993), 61–75; and 'The Crusader Lordship of Marash in
Armenian Cilicia, 1104–1149', *Viator* 27 (1996), 35–52; K. Skottki, 'Of 'Pious Traitors' and Dangerous
Encounters. Historiographical Notions of Interculturality in the Principality of Antioch', *Journal of
Transcultural Medieval Studies* 1:1 (2014), 75–115; S. Redford, 'Trade and Economy in Antioch and
Cilicia in the Twelfth and Thirteenth Centuries', *Trade and Markets in Byzantium*, ed. C. Morrisson
(Washington, DC, 2012), pp. 297–309.

[16]   J. Riley-Smith, 'The Templars and the Teutonic Knights in Cilician Armenia', *The Cilician Kingdom
of Armenia*, ed. T. Boase (London, 1978), pp. 92–117; M.-A. Chevalier, *Les ordres religieux-militaires en
Arménie cilicienne: Templiers, hospitaliers, teutoniques & Arméniens à l'époque des croisades* (Paris, 2010);
T. Riis, 'Die Übernahme Marqabs durch die Johanniter (1186)', *Werkstatt des Historikers der mittelalterlichen Ritterorden. Quellenkundliche, Probleme und Forschungsmethoden*, ed. Z. Nowak (Toruń, 1987),
pp. 151–6.

heavily indebted to existing archaeological and topographical works on northern Syria. The most seminal of these, alongside Cahen's, remain those of René Dussaud, Paul Deschamps and Hugh Kennedy, although further advances have recently been made.[17] This includes the findings detailed by Tasha Vorderstrasse, Sauro Gelichi, Balazs Major, Benjamin Michaudel, Jean Mesqui and others.[18] Supplementing this is the series *Recherches archéologiques dans la région des Villes Mortes de la Syrie du Nord*, a four-volume work examining the various limestone massifs (or 'Jabals') of the region.[19]

Given that this work examines the 'frontier' nature of the principality of Antioch and the form of its power structures, it is also reliant for its theoretical frameworks, and for comparative examples, on important studies made of other contemporary borderlands, as well on the general practice of medieval authority.[20] While comparisons are sought, in the interests of contextualisation, in various regions of inter-cultural contact in the Middle Ages, such as Iberia, the Baltic, Hungary and Byzantium, the primary focus here will be on the other crusader states as well as frontier regions whose roots also lay in a Norman conquest, for example the Anglo-Norman realm, including the Welsh Marches and the border with the kingdom of France, and southern Italy.[21] It is not argued that such comparative examples can necessarily fill gaps in our knowledge of Antiochene affairs, even though the wider span of *Outremer* and the Norman world offer the best chance at doing so given the

[17]   R. Dussaud, *Topographie historique de la Syrie antique et médiéval* (Paris, 1927); P. Deschamps, *Les châteaux des croisés 3: La défense du comté de Tripoli et de la principauté d'Antioche* (Paris, 1973); H. Kennedy, *Crusader Castles* (Cambridge, 1994).

[18]   See particularly, though not exclusively: T. Vorderstrasse, *Al-Mina: A Port of Antioch from Late Antiquity to the End of the Ottomans* (Oosten, 2005); S. Gelichi, 'The Citadel of Harim', *Muslim Military Architecture in Greater Syria: From the Coming of Islam to the Ottoman Period*, ed. H. Kennedy (Leiden, 2006), pp. 184–200; B. Major, *Medieval Rural Settlements in the Syrian Coastal Region (12th and 13th Centuries)* (Oxford, 2015); B. Michaudel, 'Le château de Saône/Sahyûn en Syrie, creuset de l'architecture médiévale en Orient', *Chronos* 23 (2011), 1–39; J. Mesqui, 'Bourzey, une forteresse anonyme de l'Oronte', *La fortification au temps des Croisades*, ed. N. Faucherre, J. Mesqui and N. Prouteau (Rennes, 2004), pp. 95–133; T. Grandin, 'Introduction to the Citadel of Salah al-Din', *Syria: Medieval Citadels Between East and West*, ed. S. Bianca (Turin, 2007), pp. 139–80; T. Riis, 'The Medieval Period', *Topographical Studies in the Gabla Plain*, ed. P. J. Riis *et al.* (Copenhagen, 2004), pp. 85–115; D. Kaniewski *et al.*, 'Medieval Coastal Syrian Vegetation Patterns in the Principality of Antioch', *The Holocene* 21 (2010), 251–62.

[19]   *Inventaire du Jébel Baricha*; *Inventaire du Jebel el-A'la*; *Inventaire du Jébel Wastani*; *Inventaire du Jébel Douelli*.

[20]   See for example: D. Abulafia, 'Introduction: Seven Types of Ambiguity, c.1100–c.1500', *Medieval Frontiers: Concepts and Practices*, ed. D. Abulafia and N. Berend (Aldershot, 2002), pp. 1–34; R. Burns, 'The Significance of the Frontier in the Middle Ages', *Medieval Frontier Societies*, ed. R. Bartlett and A. MacKay (Oxford, 1996), pp. 307–30; S. Reynolds, *Fiefs and Vassals: the Medieval Evidence Reinterpreted* (Oxford, 1994); T. Bisson, *The Crisis of the Twelfth Century: Power, Lordship, and the Origins of European Government* (Princeton, NJ, 2009).

[21]   See for example: S. Tibble, *Monarchy and Lordships in the Latin Kingdom of Jerusalem, 1099–1291* (Oxford, 1989); R. Davies, *The Age of Conquest: Wales, 1064–1415* (Oxford, 1991); M. Lieberman, *The Medieval March of Wales: The Creation and Perception of a Frontier, 1066–1283* (Cambridge, 2010); D. Power, *The Norman Frontier in the Twelfth and Early Thirteenth Centuries* (Cambridge, 2004); and the various essays in G. Loud and A. Metcalfe (ed.), *The Society of Norman Italy* (Leiden, 2002).

relative potential for similarities in formation and development. More importantly, they provide crucial context for the principality's surviving, and often intractable evidence, thus helping to pinpoint instances in which unique customs might have emerged in relation to the region's specific demands.

The Primary Sources

As might be expected from a polity which interacted with so many peoples and powers, the available primary source material stretches across numerous religions and languages. The core focus of this research is on narratives and documents in Latin or Old French, but use is also made of texts in Greek, Arabic, Syriac and Armenian, as well as numismatic, sigillographic and archaeological materials.[22]

Latin and Old French Narratives

For the period before 1130, two useful Antiochene Latin narratives survive: Ralph of Caen's *Gesta Tancredi* and Walter the Chancellor's *Bella Antiochena*.[23] However, the principality, like the wider Latin East, suffers from a dearth of Frankish textual sources after 1127, that being the end date of the Jerusalemite *Historia* of Fulcher of Chartres.[24] While use will be made of these and other earlier narratives, the present work is most greatly indebted to William of Tyre's *Chronicon*, composed in the kingdom of Jerusalem in the 1170s and 1180s, which covers the history of *Outremer* from its creation until 1184.[25] Born in Jerusalem *c.* 1130, William was educated in the West for some twenty years (*c.* 1146–*c.* 1165) and enjoyed prominence upon his return to the East as archbishop of Tyre and royal chancellor.[26] A vast corpus of work has emerged around William's chronicle, certainly too much to cover here, but some key aspects require comment.

Of initial interest are William's motives for writing and the factors which may have influenced the nature of his composition. Various plausible theories have been advanced, such as King Amalric of Jerusalem's patronage, William's desire to promote the Latin East's plight to the West and simply that he wanted to record

---

[22] For previous overviews, see Cahen, *Syrie*, pp. 1–104; Asbridge, *Creation*, pp. 5–13.

[23] Ralph of Caen, 'Gesta Tancredi in Expeditione Hierosolymitana', *RHC Occ.* III, 599–716; WC. On these, see B. Bachrach and D. Bachrach, *Ralph of Caen's Gesta Tancredi: A History of the Normans on the First Crusade* (Aldershot, 2005), pp. 1–18; T. Asbridge and S. Edgington, *Walter the Chancellor's The Antiochene Wars* (Aldershot, 1999), pp. 1–76.

[24] Fulcher of Chartres, *Historia Hierosolymitana*, ed. H. Hagenmeyer (Heidelberg, 1913).

[25] WT.

[26] P. Edbury and J. Rowe, *William of Tyre: Historian of the Latin East* (Cambridge, 1988), pp. 13–22; H. E. Mayer, 'Guillaume de Tyr á l'École', *Mémoires de l'Académie des sciences, arts et belles-lettres de Dijon* 127 (1988), 257–65.

the events of his homeland for posterity.[27] None can be truly ruled out, but what is certainly true is that William's chronicle has a notable Jerusalemite bias and a clear sense of the behavioural traits he considered correct. This often led him to suppress information relating to northern Syria in favour of matters associated with the kingdom – albeit not uniformly – and to negatively portray the actions of Antioch's ruling house, who often failed to meet his standards.[28] Likewise, his opinion of Antioch may have been influenced by the patriarch of Antioch's dispute with Jerusalem and the papacy regarding the right to jurisdiction over the See of Tyre.[29] Certain other underlying influences are also important to note, such as his promotion of Byzantine military involvement in *Outremer*, coupled with his reservations about their possession of territory, and his keen interest in power, law and administration.[30]

Another important debate relates to William's sources. As a Jerusalemite and an absentee from the East for almost two decades, the extent of his access to reliable information on the principality before 1165 is unclear. It is known that he had access to the works of Walter the Chancellor and Fulcher of Chartres, while Peter Edbury and John Rowe have posited that William used a now lost Antiochene narrative – a suggestion which remains possible, albeit subject to the same potential problems of misdirection that Susan Edgington has identified in relation to Albert of Aachen's relationship to the so-called 'lost Lotharingian chronicle'.[31] More secure is his reliance on oral testimony. Although it is generally assumed that such witnesses cannot be identified, there are some important clues which point towards potential sources of information.[32] First, William actually names one of his informants: Lady

[27] Edbury and Rowe, *William of Tyre*, pp. 23–31; D. Vessey, 'William of Tyre and the Art of Historiography', *Mediaeval Studies* 35 (1973), 433–55; B. Ebels-Hoving, 'William of Tyre and his patria', *Medi Latinitas: A Collection of Essays to Mark the Occasion of the Retirement of L. J. Engels*, ed. R. Nip, H. van Dijk *et al.* (Turnhout, 1996), pp. 211–16; B. Z. Kedar, 'Some New Light on the Composition Process of William of Tyre's *Historia*', *Deeds Done Beyond the Sea*, pp. 3–12.

[28] T. Asbridge, 'William of Tyre and the First Rulers of the Latin Principality of Antioch', *Deeds Done Beyond the Sea*, pp. 35–42 and 'Alice', pp. 29–47; P. Handyside, 'Differing Views of Renaud de Châtillon', *Deeds Done Beyond the Sea*, pp. 43–52.

[29] Hamilton, *Latin Church*, pp. 18–85.

[30] Edbury and Rowe, *William of Tyre*, pp. 61–108, 130–50; B. Hamilton, 'William of Tyre and the Byzantine Empire', *Porphyrogenita: Essays on the History and Literature of Byzantium and the Latin East in Honour of Julian Chrysostomides*, ed. C. Dendrinos, J. Harris *et al.* (Aldershot, 2003), pp. 219–33; J. Rubin, 'The Debate on Twelfth-Century Frankish Feudalism: Additional Evidence from William of Tyre's *Chronicon*', *Crusades* 8 (2009), 53–62; C. Kostick, 'William of Tyre, Livy, and the Vocabulary of Class', *Journal of the History of Ideas* 65:3 (2004), 353–68; M. R. Tessera, '*Prudentes homines...qui sensus habebant magis exercitos*: a Preliminary Inquiry in William of Tyre's Vocabulary of Power', *Crusades* 1 (2002), 63–71.

[31] Asbridge, 'William of Tyre', pp. 35–42; Edbury and Rowe, *William of Tyre*, pp. 46–60; S. Edgington, 'Albert of Aachen Reappraised', *From Clermont to Jerusalem: The Crusades and Crusader Societies 1095–1500*, ed. A. V. Murray (Turnhout, 1998), pp. 57–8.

[32] Edbury and Rowe, *William of Tyre*, pp. 46–60; S. John, 'Historical Truth and the Miraculous Past: The Use of Oral Evidence in Twelfth-Century Latin Historical Writing on the First Crusade', *EHR* 543 (2015), 274–5.

Stephany, abbess of the church of St Mary the Major in Jerusalem from *c.* 1174.[33] Born *c.* 1120, Stephany was the daughter of Count Joscelin I of Edessa and Maria of Salerno, sister to Prince Roger of Antioch.[34] She was therefore a likely eyewitness to much that was going on in northern Syria from the 1130s onwards, perhaps even spending time at Antioch following the county's sale to Byzantium in the early 1150s. Moreover, in commenting on his conversations with Stephany regarding her years in the north, William stressed that, although she was advanced in years, her memory was reliable for she was a witness to these events.[35] This suggests that he trusted her opinion and that he wanted his audience to do so as well.[36] In addition, there is a potential link to another source of information: Michael the Great, Jacobite Patriarch of Antioch, 1166–1199. Michael is most famous for his world chronicle of the period (on which, see below) and he travelled throughout the East – including to Jerusalem in 1178/1179, where he met King Baldwin IV at Acre. Significantly, charter evidence demonstrates that Baldwin was accompanied at Acre during this period by his chancellor, William of Tyre.[37] The Jacobite Patriarch may also have been in Antioch during 1180, at which point William was also visiting the city.[38] Michael was proficient enough in Latin to have written a treatise on the Cathar heresy to be delivered at the Third Lateran Council – an ecclesiastical meeting at which William was present – in 1179 and to have had a personal friendship with Aimery of Limoges, the patriarch of Antioch, meaning the two had a mutual language through which they could have conversed.[39] There are a number of occasions when their narratives uniquely converge, as well as instances of divergence of interest or explanation, which could indicate a shared narrative source used to different effect; but the potential for personal correspondence cannot, and should not, be ruled out. It is certainly almost impossible that they would have been unaware of each other.

Also useful to a study of the principality are those western chroniclers who detailed Antiochene events, particularly major defeats, crusading expeditions or the visits of Byzantine emperors. Authors like Orderic Vitalis, Otto of Freising, Odo of Deuil, Robert of Torigny and others, provide useful context to eastern Latin sources and help to show how events in *Outremer* were presented to, and perceived by Western audiences.[40] Attention must also be given to the Old French translation

---

33   *RRH*, 516.
34   WT, pp. 868–70; M. Amouroux-Mourad, *Le Comté d'Edesse 1098–1150* (Paris, 1988), appendix. On the dating of Joscelin and Maria's marriage, see MacEvitt, *Rough Tolerance*, pp. 77, 202.
35   WT, pp. 868–70.
36   On medieval authors' methods of establishing the trustworthiness of an oral source, see E. van Houts, 'Genre Aspects of the Use of Oral Information in Medieval Historiography', *Gattungen mittelalterlicher Schriftlichkeit*, ed. B. Frank, T. Haye and D. Tophinke (Tübingen, 1997), pp. 297–311; John, 'Historical Truth', pp. 263–301.
37   MS, I, ix–x; *Urkunden Jerusalem*, II, 704–10.
38   MS, III, 382; WT, p. 1011.
39   MS, I, x–xi, xviii, III, 334–5.
40   Orderic Vitalis, *The Ecclesiastical History of Orderic Vitalis*, ed. and trans. M. Chibnall, 6 vols (Oxford, 1969–1980); Otto of Freising, *Chronica sive Historia de Duabus Civitatibus*, ed. A. Hofmeister

of William of Tyre known as *Eracles*, produced at some point between the end of the twelfth century and the 1230s, as well as the various continuations which also appear under this name and which seemingly evolved from the earliest re-working of the *Chronicon*, the text known as the *Chronique d'Ernoul et de la Bernard Le Trésorier*.[41] The quality of *Eracles*' modern editions has been questioned, as has the extent to which its authors and those of the continuations had access to any unique information for the years before 1184 – although there are occasions when William of Tyre's text was clearly altered to suit a different audience.[42] Importantly, those divergences can help to pinpoint potential cases of bias in the *Chronicon* and also to signify how later writers interpreted earlier events. These texts, especially those produced in the East, also provide a useful perspective on *Outremer* for the events surrounding and following Saladin's conquest.

Other Narratives

The Frankish presence at Antioch also attracted the interest of Eastern Christian and Muslim authors. Texts produced by Byzantine chroniclers are of particular use given imperial involvement in northern Syria and Cilicia, with the most famous authors being John Kinnamos, who wrote his biographical work on Emperors John and Manuel Komnenos between 1180 and 1183, and Niketas Choniates, whose chronicle was composed from 1195 up to the 1210s.[43] These are seemingly linked, as Choniates is believed to have abridged and extended Kinnamos' text and both demonstrate a generally anti-Latin stance.[44] Kinnamos nevertheless often overlooks instances when the Franks undermined imperial successes and thus the reputations of his protagonists, while Choniates, who is generally more balanced in his assessment of Manuel, may have been influenced by a desire to show that the Byzantines, through their stance towards Latin Christendom, were not accountable for the events of

(Hannover, 1912); Odo of Deuil, *De Profectione Ludovici VII in Orientem*, ed. and trans. V. G. Berry (New York, 1948); Robert of Torigny, 'The Chronicle of Robert of Torigni, Abbot of the Monastery of St. Michael-in-Peril-of-the-Sea', ed. R. Howlett, *Chronicles of the Reigns of Stephen, Henry II, and Richard I*, 4 vols (London, 1884–89), IV, 81–315.

41   *Eracles*; *Ernoul*; *CGT*; 'Eracles', *RHC Occ*. II, 1–638.

42   P. Edbury, 'The French Translation of William of Tyre's *Historia*: the Manuscript Tradition', *Crusades* 6 (2007), 69–106; 'New Perspectives on the Old French Continuations of William of Tyre', *Crusades* 9 (2010), 107–14; and 'The Lyon *Eracles* and the Old French Continuations of William of Tyre', *Montjoie; Studies in Crusade History in Honour of Hans Eberhard Mayer*, ed. B. Kedar, J. Riley-Smith and R. Hiestand (Aldershot, 1997), pp. 139–54; B. Hamilton, 'The Old French Translation of William of Tyre as an Historical Source', *The Experience of Crusading vol. 2: Defining the Crusader Kingdom*, ed. P. Edbury and J. Phillips (Cambridge, 2003), pp. 93–12; Handyside, 'Differing Views', pp. 43–52.

43   John Kinnamos, *Epitome: Rerum ab Ioanne et Alexio Comnenis Gestarum*, ed. A. Meineke (Bonn, 1836) (for trans., see JK); Niketas Choniates, *Historia*, ed. I. van Dieten (Berlin, 1975), (for trans., see NC).

44   A. Simpson, *Niketas Choniates: A Historiographical Study* (Oxford, 2013), pp. 68–77, 214–24; V. Grecu, 'Nicétas Choniatès a-t-il connu l'histoire de Jean Cinnamos?', *Revue des Études Byzantines* 7 (1949), 194–204; A. Kazhdan and S. Franklin, *Studies on Byzantine Literature of the Eleventh and Twelfth Centuries* (Cambridge, 1984), pp. 256–86.

the Fourth Crusade.[45] Insights can also be gleaned from several travel accounts and poems which the chroniclers themselves perhaps also drew upon, most prominently Michael Italikos, Manganeios Prodromos and Constantine Manasses – although they are highly stylised and must be treated with caution.[46]

Also important are a number of texts composed by Jacobite Christians during a period which has been described as a 'Renaissance' in Syriac historiography.[47] The most famous of these is the chronicle of the aforementioned Michael the Great. Born *c.* 1126, Michael appears to have compiled his text, which ends in 1195, over the course of fifty years from the 1140s until his death in 1199, and Dorothea Weltecke has praised his ability to critically utilise the sources he addressed over the course of an immense period of research.[48] The modern translation by Jean-Baptiste Chabot has faced criticism due to the poor quality of his copy of the sole extant sixteenth-century manuscript, while lacunae in this meant that a number of extrapolations are taken from sources known to have used the chronicle, such as Gregory Bar Ebroyo and later translations into Armenian and Arabic.[49] Nevertheless, Michael's text remains crucial to the study of Antioch for its information gleaned from non-Latin sources, including the now lost twelfth-century chronicle of Basil, the Jacobite bishop of Edessa, and his own eyewitness observations.[50] Another Syriac source is the thirteenth-century *Anonymi auctoris Chronicon ad A. C. 1234 pertinens.*[51] This was likely produced in two phases – the first up to 1204 with additions later added up to 1237 – probably by a single author, who travelled widely and had ties to Edessa and the monastery of Bar Sawmo.[52] The text drew on a number of the Syriac and Arabic works also known to Michael the Syrian, such as Basil of Edessa and potentially another unknown narrative covering the rest

---

45 R.-J. Lilie, *Byzantium and the Crusader States 1096–1204*, trans. J. Morris and J. Ridings (Oxford, 1993), pp. 277–84; P. Stephenson, 'John Cinnamus, John II Komnenos and the Hungarian Campaign of 1127–1129', *Byzantion* 66 (1996), 177–87; Simpson, *Choniates*, pp. 214–24, 314–29.

46 Michael Italikos, *Lettres et Discours*, ed. and trans. P. Gautier (Paris, 1972); Manganeios Prodromos, pp. 49–152; Constantine Manasses, pp. 165–221. On their form and use, see B. Baldwin, 'Classicism, Content, and Contemporaneity in Michael Italicus', *Byzantion* 62 (1992), 109–17; M. Marcovich, 'The *Itinerary* of Constantine Manasses', *Illinois Classical Studies* 12:1 (1987), 277–91; K. Horna, 'Das Hodoiporikon des Konstantin Manasses', *Byzantinische zeitschrift* 13 (1904), 313–55; Simpson, *Choniates*, p. 230.

47 D. Weltecke, 'A Renaissance in Historiography? Patriarch Michael, the Anonymous Chronicle ad a. 1234, and Bar 'Ebroyo', *The Syriac Renaissance*, ed. H. Teule, T. Fotescu *et al.* (Leuven, 2010), pp. 95–111.

48 MS, I, i–lx; D. Weltecke, *Die "Beschreibung der Zeiten" von Mor Michael Dem Grossen (1126–1199): Eine Studie zu ihrem historischen und historiographiegeschichtlichen Kontext* (Leuven: Peeters, 2003), pp. 127–52.

49 Weltecke, *Michael Dem Grossen*, pp. 153–9; MS, I, p. i, xliii–l.

50 MS, III, 278–81.

51 *1234*.

52 W. Witakowski, 'Syriac Historiographical Sources', *Byzantines and Crusaders in Non-Greek Sources 1025–1204*, ed. M. Whitby (Oxford, 2007), pp. 261–4; A. Hilkens, 'The Anonymous Syriac Chronicle Up to the Year 1234 and its Sources' (Unpublished PhD thesis, Universiteit Gent, 2014), pp. 11–25; H. Kaufhold, 'Notizen zur Späten Geschichte des Barsaumo-Klosters', *Hugoye: Journal of Syriac Studies* 3:2 (2000), pp. 223–46.

of the twelfth century, but divergences in their texts show that these two sources were not immediately linked.[53] The *1234 Chronicle*, as it will be called here, thus provides an invaluable independent perspective, even if its narrative is not infallible.[54] Another thirteenth-century chronicler, Gregory Bar Ebroyo – otherwise known as Bar Hebraeus – is also useful, although his text is largely derived from Michael the Syrian's for the period up to 1195.[55]

Events related to the principality were also noted by Armenian chroniclers. The earliest of these is Matthew of Edessa, whose work ends in 1137.[56] While the modern translation of his text has been criticised, his chronicle remains useful.[57] As does its continuation up to the year 1162, written in Kesoun by Gregory the Priest.[58] Little has been done to chart the manuscript tradition of this text or its composition, yet it carries crucial eyewitness insights into the principality and its relations with Byzantium.[59] There are other important texts, in particular the late thirteenth-century chronicle of Sempad the Constable.[60] Although he was heavily reliant on Matthew and Gregory for the years before 1162, Sempad made some additions, and for the later twelfth century and beyond, he is an invaluable treasury of information, despite suggestions he utilised William of Tyre, Michael the Syrian and Niketas Choniates.[61] As Sempad was an important figure in the thirteenth century and would have been heavily influenced by the disputes which emerged between Antioch and Armenian Cilicia during this period, his text offers an insight into how twelfth-century events were interpreted in the wake of these divisions.[62]

The final group of narratives are those written in Arabic. Michael Köhler has expressed the importance of using such works, noting they 'provide … the possibility of analysing the history of the Frankish states as part of Syrian history', although Carole Hillenbrand has warned that they are 'couched in rigidly ideological terms where the enemy is irrevocably the enemy and where God is on the Muslim side' –

---

53 Hilkens, *Anonymous*, pp. 13–21, 399–412.

54 *Ibid.*, pp. 12–13.

55 GBE; Witakowski, 'Syriac', pp. 264–9.

56 ME, pp. 1–239.

57 Tara Andrews has urged against an uncritical use of Matthew's information: 'The New Age of Prophecy: The Chronicle of Matthew of Edessa and its Place in Armenian Historiography', *The Medieval Chronicle* 6 (2009), pp. 105–23; T. Greenwood, 'Armenian Sources', *Byzantines and Crusaders in Non-Greek Sources 1025–1204*, ed. M. Whitby (Oxford, 2007), pp. 221–35, 240–1.

58 GP, pp. 241–80.

59 Greenwood, 'Armenian', pp. 221–35, 240–1; G. Beech, 'A Little-Known Armenian Historian of the Crusading Period: Gregory the Priest (1136–1162)', *Truth as Gift: Studies in Medieval Cistercian History in Honor of John R. Sommerfeldt*, ed. M. Dutton, D. La Corte and P. Lockey (Kalamazoo, MI, 2004), pp. 119–43.

60 Three translations are used here: Sempad, *RHC Arm.* I, 605–80; Sempad, 'Armenian Chronicle', pp. 141–68; Sempad, *Chronique*.

61 Greenwood, 'Armenian', pp. 221–35, 247–9; Sempad, 'Armenian Chronicle', pp. 141–68.

62 See generally G. Dédéyan, 'Les listes "féodales" du pseudo-Smbat', *Cahiers de civilisation médiévale* 125 (1989), 25–42; J. Burgtorf, 'The Antiochene War of Succession', *The Crusader World*, ed. A. Boas (Abingdon, 2016), pp. 196–211.

an accusation which can of course be levelled at most sources for this period.[63]
Two early works are of particular use. The first is the Damascene chronicle of Ibn
al-Qalanisi, written in around 1160.[64] This text has been described as accurate and
objective, while Ibn al-Qalanisi's position as *rayyis* of Damascus during the 1140s
and 1150s granted him access to important documentary and eyewitness evidence.[65]
However, the chronicle's focus is largely on southern Syria, with Niall Christie
noting that the author was primarily influenced by his affinity for Damascus, the
jihad against the Franks and the promotion of Sunni Islam – thus meaning he
viewed Nur al-Din's rise to power there favourably.[66] Conversely, his contemporary,
the Aleppan chronicler al-Azimi, who also wrote *c.* 1160, predominantly detailed
events in northern Syria even though he appears to have drawn on Ibn al-Qalanisi's
text.[67] Hillenbrand has classified al-Azimi's style as laconic and relatively impartial
and he proves very important for an understanding of Antiochene relations with
Aleppo.[68] Nevertheless, as his text survives only in an abridged copy, some of its
content may have been altered or lost.[69] Also of use are the biographies of the
Ayyubid Sultan Saladin, produced in the decades after his death by two members
of his entourage, Baha al-Din ibn Shaddad and Imad al-Din al-Isfahani.[70] Unsurprisingly, both offer favourable representations of Saladin, but they do provide
otherwise unknown information on the Sultan's rise to power and invasion of the
principality in 1188.[71] Beyond this are three key thirteenth-century texts. The first is
that of Kemal al-Din, otherwise known as Ibn al-Adim, a prolific Aleppan scholar
whose focus was primarily on his home city.[72] There are hints that he was influenced by a desire to please his Ayyubid sponsors, but he remains valuable for his
access to now lost sources, including the full version of al-Azimi's chronicle.[73] The
second is Ibn al-Athir, a Zengid supporter from Mosul who wrote something of
a world history of Islam.[74] His text is well known for its more nuanced view of
the Ayyubids and has been praised by Françoise Michaeu for its objectivity and

[63]   M. Köhler, *Alliances and Treaties between Frankish and Muslim Rulers in the Middle East*, trans. P.
Holt and K. Hirschler (Leiden, 2013), p. 5; C. Hillenbrand, *The Crusades: Islamic Perspectives* (Edinburgh, 1999), pp. 9–10.
[64]   IQ.
[65]   N. Christie, 'Ibn al-Qalanisi', *Medieval Muslim Historians and the Franks in the Levant*, ed. A.
Mallett (Leiden, 2015), pp. 7–28.
[66]   *Ibid.*, pp. 16–28.
[67]   Al-Azimi, pp. 101–64; Christie, 'Ibn al-Qalanisi', p. 10.
[68]   C. Hillenbrand, 'Sources in Arabic', *Byzantines and Crusaders in Non-Greek Sources 1025–1204*, ed.
M. Whitby (Oxford, 2007), p. 312.
[69]   A.-M. Eddé, 'Kamal al-Din 'Umar Ibn al-'Adim', *Medieval Muslim Historians and the Franks in the
Levant*, ed. A. Mallett (Leiden, 2015), p. 129.
[70]   BD; ID.
[71]   Hillenbrand, 'Arabic', pp. 313–14, 331–2; L. Richter-Bernburg, ''Imad al-Din al-Isfahani', *Medieval
Muslim Historians and the Franks in the Levant*, ed. A. Mallett (Leiden, 2015), pp. 29–51.
[72]   KD, *RHC Or.* III, 577–690; *ROL* 3 (1895), 509–65; 4 (1896), 145–225; 5 (1897), 37–107; 6 (1898),
1–49.
[73]   Eddé, 'Kamal al-Din', pp. 109–35.
[74]   IA.

historical value.[75] Finally, Abu Shama, whose dual biography of Nur al-Din and Saladin drew on otherwise unknown texts and has been noted for its partisan, albeit generally accurate, presentation of events.[76] Alongside these, use can also be made of the autobiographical work of Usamah ibn Munqidh, despite its rather anachronistic style, and Izz al-Din ibn Shaddad's late thirteenth-century geographical text, which offers invaluable insights into the region's topography.[77]

Other Sources

This book also draws on other source materials. For example, observations can be made from the available numismatic and sigillographic evidence, as although the erratic survival rates for these types of source means wide-ranging conclusions are problematic, that historians have noted significant changes to Antioch's coinage after 1136, as well as the somewhat static style of the princely seal, means they can be used to help contextualise other materials.[78] There also exists a law code known as the *Assises d'Antioche*. This collection of customs is divided between the court of the barons and the court of the burgesses and now exists only as a translation made from the original Old French into Armenian by Sempad the Constable.[79] It was likely compiled within the first two decades of the thirteenth century, emerging in the context of the succession dispute between Bohemond IV of Antioch and his nephew, the half-Armenian Raymond-Rupen, which fragmented the principality's ruling elites after the death of Bohemond III in 1201.[80] Despite this, the exact reasons for its compilation are unclear. Cahen suggested the *Assises* were composed to educate Raymond-Rupen, who would have been less grounded in Antiochene custom than his uncle, while Peter Edbury has urged caution in this regard, noting the distinct lack of certainty.[81] Given that the *Assises* promote vassalic freedoms, much like the contemporary codes of the kingdom of Jerusalem, they may represent an effort to limit the powers of the ruler.[82] With an armed dispute raging over the succession this is not implausible, and the thoroughness of the stipulations

---

75   F. Michaeu, 'Ibn al-Athir', *Medieval Muslim Historians and the Franks in the Levant*, ed. A. Mallett (Leiden, 2015), pp. 52–84; A. Mallett, 'Islamic Historians of the Ayyubid Era and Muslim Rulers from the Early Crusading Period: A Study in the Use of History', *Al-Masaq* 24:3 (2012), 241–52.

76   AS, *RHC Or.* IV, 3–522, V, 3–206; Hillenbrand, 'Arabic', pp. 315–18; K. Hirschler, *Medieval Arabic Historiography: Authors as Actors* (London, 2006).

77   Usamah ibn Munqidh, *The Book of Contemplation: Islam and the Crusades*, trans. P. Cobb (London, 2008); IS.

78   D. Metcalf, *Coinage of the Crusades and the Latin East in the Ashmolean Museum* (Oxford, 1983) and 'Six Unresolved Problems in the Monetary History of Antioch, 969–1268', *East and West I*, pp. 283–318; G. Schlumberger, *Numismatique de l'Orient latin* (Paris, 1878); G. Schlumberger, F. Chalandon and A. Blanchet, *Sigillographie de l'Orient latin* (Paris, 1943); M. Rheinheimer, 'Tankred und das Siegel Boemunds', *Schweizerische Numismatische Rundschau* 70 (1991), 75–93.

79   *Assises d'Antioche*, ed. and trans. L. Alishan (Venice, 1876).

80   Cahen, *Syrie*, pp. 28–32, 582–643; Martin, 'Structures', pp. 239–50; Edbury, '*Assises*', pp. 241–8. On the crisis, see Burgtorf, 'War of Succession', pp. 196–211.

81   Cahen, *Syrie*, pp. 28–32; Edbury, '*Assises*', pp. 244–8.

82   John of Ibelin, *Le Livre des Assises*, ed. P. Edbury (Leiden, 2003), pp. 34–44.

included within this code at least suggest a lengthy period of debate.[83] Nevertheless, it can be questioned whether the *Assises* accurately reflect twelfth-century legal practice – for the nature of landholding, and thus the composition of the 'barony', was extremely divergent between the two centuries – or if they, again like their southern counterparts, represent more the aspirations of the thirteenth-century nobility.[84] Apparent instances of contiguity with earlier Norman or Anglo-Norman customs might imply implementation of Western customs soon after the conquest, but the lack of detailed corroborative material ensures the *Assises'* must be treated with care.[85]

As regards the documentary evidence for Antioch, historians are fairly well served, albeit not on the scale of the kingdom of Jerusalem or the administrative bastions of the West.[86] Indeed, for the period examined here, there are nearly one hundred known charters issued from within, or directly relating to the principality. These predominantly survive in the collections of the military orders or religious institutions, although there are also documents pertaining to the Italian city states of Venice, Pisa and Genoa.[87] A number of issues arise from these charters. First, not all survive as originals, rather as cartulary entries or later copies. That they have been subjected to scribal errors or deliberate alterations cannot, therefore, be ruled out; with Mayer noting that this is particularly prominent for Genoese documents.[88] Furthermore, the ravages of time mean that most administrative acts have been lost, meaning only an incomplete picture can be gleaned: which creates inherent difficulties.[89] However, as Nicholas Vincent has noted, charters remain an invaluable source of information for the composition of princely courts and internal structures of power and so use must be made of what remains, not what is lost.[90]

---

[83]   Martin, 'Structures', pp. 246–7.

[84]   On this, see generally J. Riley-Smith, *The Feudal Nobility and the Kingdom of Jerusalem, 1174–1277* (London, 1973).

[85]   Edbury, '*Assises*', pp. 241–8.

[86]   For Jerusalem, see *Urkunden Jerusalem*. For the West, see e.g. M. Clanchy, *From Memory to Written Record: England 1066–1307*, 2nd edn (Oxford, 1993), pp. 44–80.

[87]   *CGOH*; J. Delaville le Roulx, *Les archives la bibliothèque et le trésor de l'Ordre de Saint-Jean de Jérusalem a Malte* (Paris, 1883); and 'Inventaire de pièces de Terre Sainte de l'Ordre de l'Hopital', *ROL* 3 (1885), 36–106; C. Kohler, 'Chartes de l'abbaye de Notre-Dame de Josaphat', *ROL* 7 (1890), 108–222; *Chartes Josaphat*; *Codice diplomatico del Sacro Militare Ordine Gerosolimitano oggi di Malta*, ed. S. Paoli, 2 vols (Lucca, 1733–37); *Documenti Toscane*; Comté Marsy, 'Fragment d'un cartulaire de l'ordre de Saint Lazare, en Terre-Sainte', *AOL* 2B (1884), 121–57; *Libri Iurium*; *CCSSJ*; Mayer, *Varia*, pp. 110–22; *Memorie storico-diplomatiche dell'antica città e ducato di Amalfi*, ed. M. Camera (Salerno, 1876); E. Rey, *Recherches geographiques et historiques sur la donations des latins en Orient* (Paris, 1877); *Tabulae Theutonici*; *Urkunden Venedig*. For a register of most known charters, see *RRH*. Henceforth, unless stated, references to charters are given to document numbers rather than pages.

[88]   Mayer, *Varia*, pp. 203–17. See M. Hall and J. Phillips, *Caffaro, Genoa and the Twelfth-Century Crusades* (Aldershot, 2013), pp. 23–26. More generally, see C. R. Cheney and B. Jones, *English Episcopal Acta II: Canterbury 1162–1190* (London, 1986), pp. xxix–xxxiii.

[89]   This is particularly relevant for the Templars, whose central archive is now lost. See R. Hiestand, 'Zum Problem des Templerzentralarchiv', *Archivalische Zeitschrift* 76 (1980), 17–37.

[90]   N. Vincent, 'The Court of Henry II', *Henry II: New Interpretations*, ed. C. Harper-Bill and N. Vincent (Woodbridge, 2007), pp. 284–8.

There are also a number of surviving letters, dispatched to the West either by figures within Antioch or on the principality's behalf.[91] Even more so than administrative documents, these rarely survive in the original and so may have been subject to copyist errors or later alterations. These letters nonetheless highlight the aims and concerns of *Outremer*'s leaders, as well as the internal impact of major disasters.[92]

The Scope of this Book

While this book makes use of materials pertaining to the entire twelfth century, and even at times beyond, the primary focus is on the period 1130–1193. It does so, first, as 1130 marks the end point of Asbridge's study, with which there is little need for revision, and also because that year saw the death of Bohemond II of Antioch. This event, it will be argued, proved a major turning point in the principality's history. Likewise, 1193 marks a convenient point of termination, for it was in this year that Prince Bohemond III was taken captive by the Armenian warlord Leon II, which sparked the aforementioned succession crisis and created deep internal fractures that persisted long into the thirteenth century. Such vast changes require separate examination and go beyond the remit of this book. Therefore, this monograph looks instead to significantly advance our understanding of the principality up to this point. It does so not through a simple narrative of events – for which purpose Cahen's study still remains the most useful for its scope – but by tackling a number of key questions and themes in the hope of challenging a series of crucial assumptions which have directed modern historiography.[93] Perhaps the most important of these relates to the need to explain how the principality was able to survive in the face of unparalleled territorial losses and how its frameworks of government and administration were adapted to suit changing circumstances, both centrally and on a local level. This is attempted not just through an investigation of the Antiochene evidence, but also, as noted earlier, via comparative studies with other contemporary states, particularly those similarly situated on frontiers. This allows for a better understanding of what made the principality unique or distinctive and opens the way for a discussion on the question: 'what was the principality of Antioch?' Importantly, renewed examination of the relationships of power reveals that traditional historical conceptions of the Frankish presence in northern Syria

---

[91] 'Epistolae A. Dapiferi Militiae Templi', *RHGF* XV, 540–1; Hiestand, 'Antiochia', pp. 115–19; Suger of Saint Denis, 'Epistolae', *RHGF* XV, 496, Louis VII, 'Epistolae', *RHGF* XVI, 14–15, 27–8, 38–9, 61–2; H. E. Mayer, 'Das syrische Erdbeben von 1170: Ein unedierter Brief König Amalrichs von Jerusalem', *Deutsches Archiv* 45 (1989), 474–84.

[92] M. Barber and K. Bate, *Letters from the East: Crusaders, Pilgrims and Settlers in the 12th–13th Centuries* (Farnham, 2013), pp. 1–10.

[93] Cahen, *Syrie*, pp. 347–434, 579–81. For other good narrative overviews, see N. Elisséeff, *Nur ad-Din: un grande prince musulman de Syrie au temps des croisades*, 3 vols (Damascus, 1967), II, 277–699; Köhler, *Alliances and Treaties*, pp. 127–266; M. Barber, *The Crusader States* (New Haven, CT, 2012), pp. 149–357.

offer a misleading picture of what it meant to live and rule on the eastern frontier of Latin Christendom. Such conclusions contribute not only towards modern
understanding of the nature and diversity of the Latin East, but also of the wider
divergences and individualities of the medieval world.

To set the scene for this, Chapter 1 examines the principality's territorial extent,
identifying the major topographical and strategic areas and discussing the key
events which surrounded these regions. It demonstrates the territorial fluctuations
and military disasters that can be seen to have had a profound influence on the
military, diplomatic and political activities of Antioch's ruling elites. Indeed, on top
of the great internal changes heralded by Bohemond II's death, the fragility caused
by the Armenian, Turkish and Byzantine presence in Cilicia deeply affected the
actions of the Antiochene Franks, especially towards their Eastern Christian neighbours and the Templars. Furthermore, the fierce contest for control with nearby
Aleppo over the crossings of the River Orontes, which came to mark something
of a linear border between these two powers after 1149, as well as sites like Harim,
al-Atharib and the fortresses of the Ansarriyah Mountains, helped to shape relations
with both Muslim powers and the Hospitallers, which thus dictated the balance of
power in northern Syria. In turn, these problems impacted upon the development
of Frankish diplomatic and political tactics towards other foreign and neighbouring
powers, particularly Byzantium and Jerusalem.

Chapters 2, 3 and 4 discuss whether these fluctuations, as well as the setbacks
caused by the frequent deaths or incarcerations of Antiochene rulers, impinged
upon the implementation of princely, noble and ecclesiastical authority. Chapter 2
considers the use of the princely title and the nature of succession, while Chapter 3
examines the exercise and composition of central governance, as well as the exaction
of military service. These thematically related chapters therefore assess the validity
of the traditional historiographical opinion of strong princely power and demonstrates the unique facets of administration which the Franks adopted in reaction
to political and territorial changes. It is argued that, contrary to belief in a stringently autocratic 'feudal' state, Antioch was as varied and fluid as western frontiers,
perhaps even more so. Although the princes had control of many aspects of government, the nobles appear to have taken a stronger position over matters of succession, diplomacy and 'feudo-vassalic' services than has been imagined – seemingly at
the expense of Church influence, which appears to have diminished severely after
1140. Chapter 4 develops this theme further by examining Antiochene lordships
and the extent to which power was devolved to the aristocracy on a local level.
It tests existing opinion, which has been polarised between belief in a weak aristocracy and notions of marcher style seigneuries, noting that noble independence
was highly varied. Through discussions on lordly titles, the creation of households
and retainers, as well as the formalisation of inheritance rights, it will be argued
that, despite suggestions of aristocratic freedoms, princely efforts to retain rights
of interference endured, albeit not always successfully. Above all, what becomes
apparent is that power was a fluid and challenging process, not one governed by

strict convention or obdurate regulation – a reality almost certainly influenced, if not always through a clearly defined pattern, by the region's military pressures.

Chapter 5 continues from this by addressing the issue of inter-cultural relations between the Franks and the indigenous communities who populated northern Syria. A place of great diversity and exchange, the extent to which peoples of different faiths and denominations interacted can help to shape modern understanding of cross-cultural interaction during the era of the crusades. This chapter thus outlines the various groups who can be identified, and where they were found, before examining the levels of religious, social and political freedoms they were granted, as well as the extent to which indigenous peoples were involved in Frankish governance. It is argued that, while the difficulties which surround the fragmentary evidence preclude firm conclusions, the available sources point towards a level of distrust and suspicion born from the Frankish inability to ever truly control such divergent and unevenly dispersed populations. While this was evidently not enough to prevent interaction, it suggests relations were not always cordial or overtly tolerant.

Chapter 6 turns to relations with Byzantium. This has attracted a great amount of scholarship, but little has been done to systematically discuss the Antiochene perspective, a reality this chapter rectifies. It is argued that the principality's ruling house and aristocracy exhibited far less opposition to the notion of imperial overlordship than has previously been assumed. Beginning in the early 1130s, a form of *détente* with Byzantium was regularly used as a method of limiting Jerusalemite incursions, while the growing difficulties in Cilicia and Syria meant Greek support became increasingly favourable. This culminated in 1158 with the implementation of secure imperial overlordship during the reign of Emperor Manuel Komnenos. Contact was still fraught with problems, but historians have frequently overlooked the nuances and delicate subtleties of Antioch's diplomatic policy, which often appears to have preserved Frankish independence of action and engineered situations in its favour.

Finally, Chapter 7 examines Antioch's place within the Latin East. It first discusses the notion of Jerusalemite regency, showing that, whereas historians have attributed the kings with strong powers over the principality – including the ability to call on military services, lead administration and dictate over issues of succession and foreign policy – the period in question instead witnessed a growing diminution in royal influence in favour of Byzantine support, even during times of crisis. Moreover, it challenges the notion that the kingdom of Jerusalem was accepted as head of an association of crusader states in *Outremer*, demonstrating that, whether successfully or not, the principality extended its own influence over the counties of Edessa and Tripoli and even interfered in Jerusalem during the 1170s and 1180s. Finally, it is argued that, with the exception of a brief period in the 1140s and other isolated events, Antioch was nevertheless keenly involved in securing the wider safety of the Latin East, through its military and political participation in what has been, and perhaps can still be called a 'confraternity'.

This book therefore provides a picture of a highly complex medieval state. Far from being browbeaten into inaction or unimportance, the principality of Antioch appears to have demonstrated a level of both proactivity and reactivity which allowed for its survival, and its continued role in the politics of the Near East, for much of the twelfth century. It will become clear that this was not always successful, and as time progressed it became harder for Antioch's Frankish elites to make their influence felt, but it would be wrong to suggest that this was inevitable. Whether through a distinct sensitivity to the region's topographical pressure points, the astute managing of diplomatic and military alliances, or the forging of internal frameworks of power, the frequency with which the Antiochenes demonstrated their adaptability to emerging situations is testament to the need for historians to recognise the principality's place within the wider context of medieval frontiers. A place of fluid and dynamic custom, Antioch's rich history is worthy of greater interest and knowledge – a gap this book seeks to fill.

I

The Extent of the Principality

The twelfth century was a period of profound territorial change for the principality of Antioch. From its very inception, the principality had emerged within a complicated patchwork of Islamic mini-states – classified by Michael Köhler as a system of 'Syrian autonomous lordships' – subject to external interests and influences. According to Köhler, this engendered a 'no place doctrine', in which northern Syria's Muslim elites opposed the hegemony of outside forces in favour of preserving their own independence.[1] The opening decades of Frankish control saw the principality largely able to slot into this framework, and through martial dominance and crafty politicking, particularly under the energetic leadership of Tancred of Hauteville, the Antiochenes were able to assert control over much of Cilicia and northern Syria. Most importantly, this was done not only by opposing Byzantine interference, but also by isolating Antioch's nearest military threat and greatest rival for power in the region, the city state of Aleppo, to such a degree that it was forced to pay financial tribute to the Franks. The principality's fortunes still waxed and waned in response to military and political changes, and defeats against Muslim forces at Harran in 1104 and *Ager Sanguinis* in 1119 were followed by significant land losses.[2] Nevertheless, by 1130 Antioch had reached its greatest territorial extent. In the decades which followed, however, successive disasters reduced the principality to little more than the capital city and its immediate environs, but the Franks endured. To survive such fluctuations as the Antiochenes did was almost entirely unknown elsewhere in the medieval world, especially in the Latin East, as although Jerusalem and Tripoli experienced territorial changes, before 1187 these were far less profound than in the principality. Meanwhile, Edessa's fall in 1144 quickly heralded the county's total demise. As will become evident throughout this study, such territorial changes prompted the creation of a fluid and responsive state, one whose existence sparked the attention of various nearby powers and was predicated on an ability to manage these interventions. By charting the principality's territorial

---

[1] Köhler, *Alliances and Treaties*, pp. 7–20.
[2] Asbridge, *Creation*, pp. 47–91. See also his works: 'Field of Blood', pp. 301–16; 'How the Crusades Could Have Been Won: King Baldwin II of Jerusalem's Campaigns against Aleppo (1124–5) and Damascus (1129)', *Journal of Medieval Military History* 11 (2013), 73–86; and 'The Principality of Antioch and the Jabal as-Summaq', *The First Crusade: Origins and Impact*, ed. J. Phillips (Manchester, 1997), pp. 142–52.

extent from 1130 to 1201, as well as the main events which governed it, this chapter looks to provide suitable context for an understanding of the region's power relationships. More significantly, it also seeks to demonstrate, for the first time, the influence of the region's strategic topographical pressure points on the aims and policies of the Antiochene Franks and their interactions with other invested powers.

1130–1135: Crisis and Contraction

In early 1130, an event occurred which brought the inherent instability of this region sharply into focus, and served as a turning point in the principality's history. While raiding in Cilicia, Prince Bohemond II of Antioch, son of the principality's founder, came across a group of Danishmend Turks and was killed along with his small retinue.[3] His death had a significant immediate impact, as it gave Antioch's enemies the opportunity to strike and left Bohemond's infant daughter, Constance, as sole heir – thus leading to a six-year interregnum. Moreover, when King Baldwin II of Jerusalem came to Antioch soon afterwards to attempt to secure its safety, he faced open opposition, perhaps led by the prince's widow, Alice, and it took some time before he could gain entrance into the city and the dispute was settled.[4] Bohemond's death and its aftermath thus created political upheaval and served to influence the long-term political tactics of the Frankish ruling elites.

To the north, particularly on the Cilician plain and around the region of Marash, the difficulties were intense. In 1129, even before Bohemond II's death, the Armenian warlord Leon I had captured the fortress of Anazarba and he soon demonstrated his continued willingness to oppose the Latins.[5] Such was the danger of this threat, it is said to have been the impetus for the prince's fateful campaign in 1130.[6] Leon soon inflicted further damage, seizing the cities of Tarsus and Mamistra. The exact date of these conquests in unclear. Michael the Syrian confirmed Armenian possession of the region in 1136, but as Sempad the Constable alluded to a failed Antiochene attempt to recover lost territory in 1132, it would seem 1130 or 1131 is most likely.[7] This severely dented Antioch's northern defences, as both of these cities housed archbishoprics and were bastions of Latin power, which pushed Frankish control back to the Amanus Mountains and divided Syria from Cilicia.[8] It also facilitated Turkish raiding incursions from Asia Minor, such as the devastating attacks by the Danishmends – now allies to the Armenians – in 1133.[9] With Latin

---

3   WT, pp. 623–5; Orderic Vitalis, VI, 108, 134–6; Suger of Saint Denis, *La Vie de Louis le Gros*, ed. A. Molinier (Paris, 1887), pp. 23–4; al-Azimi, p. 123; IA, I, 284; MS, III, 227; *1234*, II, 76–7.
4   WT, pp. 623–5; MS, III, 320; al-Azimi, pp. 125–6; KD, *RHC Or.* III, 660–1. See also pp. 221–2 of this book.
5   Cahen, *Syrie*, pp. 152, 349–50; Asbridge, *Creation*, p. 147.
6   WT, pp. 623–5; Orderic Vitalis, VI, pp. 108, 134–6; MS, III, 227.
7   MS, III, 244; Sempad, *RHC Arm.* I, 615. See also *1234*, II, 81.
8   Cahen, *Syrie*, pp. 150–2, 349–50; Asbridge, *Creation*, p. 147; Hamilton, *Latin Church*, pp. 18–26.
9   IA, I, 304. See also Cahen, *Syrie*, pp. 354–5.

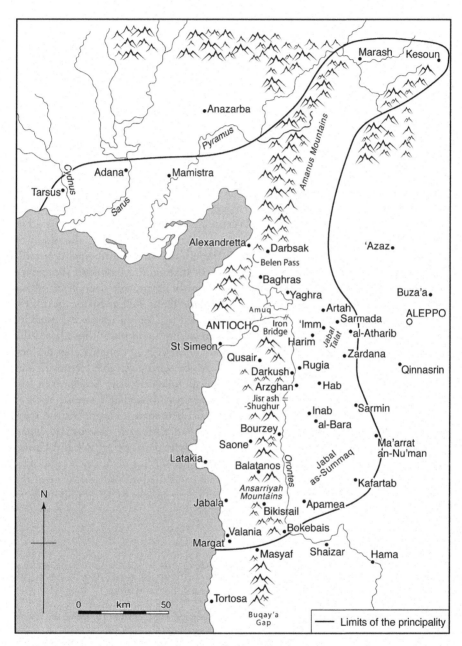

Map 2: Northern Syria and Cilicia, 1130

control in Cilicia deteriorating, it is perhaps of no surprise that, as will be explored later, the Franks now decided to broach renewed contact with Byzantium through a proposed marriage alliance between Constance and Emperor John II Komnenos' son, Manuel.[10]

Matters also changed to the east. By the late 1120s, a powerful new neighbour had emerged for the Latins in the form of the Turkish *atabeg* of Mosul, Zengi. Having grown up in a dangerous political climate, by the time he took personal control of Aleppo in June 1128, Zengi was a hardened and dangerous general.[11] Although his status as *jihad* leader was not yet recognised by the Caliph of Baghdad, in fact Taef El-Azhari has posited that Zengi may have moved on Aleppo in order to forge a base of power should he be stripped of Mosul, he was quick to cement himself here by marrying the daughter of its former ruler, Ridwan, and to look to extend his authority over two other important cities, Hama and Homs.[12] Although both Köhler and El-Azhari have argued that this did not have an immediate initial territorial impact on the Franks because the *atabeg*'s power was still emerging and because he was preoccupied with his eastern heartlands in Mesopotamia, his influence was soon felt.[13] Primarily, the union of Mosul and Aleppo now greatly damaged the efficacy of the principality's traditional policy, explored in depth by Asbridge, of maintaining Frankish supremacy by isolating and subjugating Aleppo through control of strategic sites on the plains to the west of the city, like the fortress of al-Atharib, as well as further south on the Jabal as-Summaq.[14] With the city now backed by Zengid resources, encirclement was improbable. This increase to Muslim strength and unity thus altered the balance of power in a way not previously seen. Moreover, although Zengi did not take immediate advantage of Bohemond's death by seizing sizeable territories – as his predecessor Il-Ghazi had temporarily achieved following *Ager Sanguinis* in 1119 and Leon did in Cilicia – attacks were made against important fortresses such as al-Atharib and Ma'arrat Mesrin, probably by his lieutenant, Sawar.[15] As the 1130s progressed, Muslim aggression intensified. The chance for gain arose in 1132, when the Latin East was disrupted by a civil war as Count Pons of Tripoli and Count Joscelin II of Edessa, perhaps in alliance with Princess Alice of Antioch (who now governed the coastal cities of Latakia and Jabala) and the lord of Saone (one of the principality's main fortresses), opposed the influence sought by King Fulk of Jeru-

---

[10] On this, see pp. 191–2.

[11] C. Hillenbrand, '"Abominable Acts": The Career of Zengi', *The Second Crusade: Scope and Consequences*, ed. J. Phillips and M. Hoch (Manchester, 2001), pp. 111–32; T. El-Azhari, *Zengi and the Muslim Response to the Crusades: The Politics of Jihad* (Abingdon, 2016), pp. 10–23, 62–5.

[12] El-Azhari, *Zengi*, pp. 65–7.

[13] Köhler, *Alliances and Treaties*, pp. 127–3; El-Azhari, *Zengi*, pp. 67–8. See also Hillenbrand, '"Abominable Acts"', pp. 116–17.

[14] Asbridge, 'Field of Blood', pp. 301–16; 'How the Crusades Could Have Been Won', pp. 73–86; and 'The Principality of Antioch and the Jabal as-Summaq', pp. 142–52. See also Abu'l Fida, 'Tire des Annales d'Abou'l-Feda', *RHC Or.* I, 18–19.

[15] Al-Azimi, pp. 124–6; KD, *RHC Or.* III, 661; MS, III, 230.

salem after Bohemond II's death.[16] As such, nomadic Turcoman forces, perhaps allied to the Zengids, attacked Kafartab and Ma'arrat an-Nu'man, which both lay in the territorially significant Jabal as-Summaq and overlooked an important road south towards Shaizar and southern Syria.[17] There are some suggestions that these fortresses were captured, but this was seemingly only temporary, as al-Azimi reported that they were again assaulted in 1134, along with other fortified sites, including Zardana, Ma'arrat Mesrin and Harim.[18] Zardana, whose strategic value derived from its proximity to Aleppo, became vulnerable after the apparent assassination of its lord, William of Saone, in 1133.[19] Harim, meanwhile, was integral to monitoring movements across the Jabal Talat, a hilly region separating the Aleppan plain from the Orontes River, through which passed the main road to Antioch.[20] The defences either side of this massif, including forward posts like al-Atharib and positions further back at Harim and Artah, acted in a similar fashion to lines of defence identified in Iberia, for they helped to screen the principality from surprise attacks.[21] Control of this region therefore helped to dictate the balance of power between the two cities. Zengi had perhaps taken a little while to focus on northern Syria, but his rise to power was a much stronger long-term threat than his predecessors, and his attacks now probed at the very heart of Latin power on the Aleppan frontier.

There were some setbacks for Zengi, with defeats inflicted on his armies near to Aleppo by Joscelin I of Edessa in 1131 and, more importantly, at Qinnasrin by King Fulk in 1133.[22] This latter victory for the Franks was followed by their capture of Qusair, a fortress to the south of Antioch which overlooked an important mountain road between the capital and the Jisr ash-Shughur crossing over the Orontes, and appears to have been handed to the patriarch.[23] Muslim pressure continued, however, and resulted in another wave of attacks in 1135 – which El-Azhari suggests marks the point at which Zengi truly turned his attention onto Syria.[24] As such, the Latins suffered severe territorial losses at al-Atharib, Zardana, Tell Aghda, Ma'arrat an-Nu'man and Kafartab.[25] This not only dented Antiochene dominance over

---

[16]   Asbridge, 'Alice', pp. 37–9. See also pp. 222–4 of this book.

[17]   Al-Azimi, p. 130; IQ, p. 215; KD, *RHC Or.* III, 664–5; MS, III, 233.

[18]   Al-Azimi, pp. 130, 133–4; KD, *RHC Or.* III, 667.

[19]   IQ, p. 215. See also pp. 130, 223 of this book.

[20]   Asbridge, 'Field of Blood', pp. 301–16. The history of Harim, particularly in relation to the period examined in this chapter, is also discussed in depth in Buck, 'Castle and Lordship of Harim', pp. 113–31.

[21]   M. Jiménez, 'Frontier and Settlement in the Kingdom of Castile (1085–1350)', *Medieval Frontier Societies*, ed. R. Bartlett and A. MacKay (Oxford, 1996), p. 74.

[22]   WT, pp. 638–9; al-Azimi, pp. 126, 132; IQ, pp. 222–3; IA, I, 299–300; KD, *RHC Or.* III, 665; MS, III, 233–4.

[23]   MS, III, 234. It is unknown from whom Fulk took Qusair, but it could either have been held by a local non-Latin tribal leader or may have been captured by Zengi in the early 1130s. See also Hamilton, *Latin Church*, pp. 154–8, 232–3.

[24]   El-Azhari, *Zengi*, pp. 71–3.

[25]   KD, *RHC Or.* III, 670–1; MS, III, 238. Ibn al-Athir (I, 336–7) detailed that Ma'arrat an-Nu'man and Kafartab were taken alongside Montferrand in 1137, while the *1234 Chronicle* (II, 80–1) suggested al-Atharib and Zardana were taken during that attack. The silence of contemporaries like Ibn al-Qala-

the Aleppan frontier by pushing the border back to the castle of Sarmada, it also placed greater pressure on the remaining Latin possessions in and around the Jabal as-Summaq and Jabal Talat. Likewise, these gains granted Zengi easy access to the major route leading as far south as Damascus, a city the *atabeg* had quickly coveted and had even laid siege to in 1133. This pushed the Damascenes into an alliance with Jerusalem, but of greater significance for Antioch is that it further prevented hopes of proactively managing the threat of Aleppo through territorial dominance.[26] By the end of 1135, therefore, the eastern frontier had become highly unstable. Surprise incursions into the heart of the principality were prevented through retention of essential sites like Harim and perhaps also Sarmada and Sarmin, yet Zengi had forged a strong barrier against direct Antiochene aggression and forced the Franks into a reactive position.

These difficulties were compounded by the emergence of another Muslim threat in the form of the Shi'a Isma'ili sect most famously known as the Assassins. This group enjoyed a certain level of prominence in Syria at the time of the First Crusade, but had successively been expelled from Aleppo and Damascus for their 'unorthodox' beliefs. By the 1130s, they had forged a more permanent base in the Ansarriyah Mountains, a massif which dissected the principality and the county of Tripoli, with Masyaf becoming their headquarters after 1140.[27] The Isma'ilis caused various problems for the Franks in this area, with al-Azimi reporting that in 1131 they helped to lead an uprising at Bikisrail, an important castle guarding a route from the Orontes Valley to the port of Jabala. Subsequently, 'al-Mazuir' (Renaud I Masoir, lord of Margat), the constable of Antioch, was forced to come south to the capital and settle the conflict.[28] The Isma'ilis' rise could not be halted for long, and in 1133 they expelled the Latin lord of the mountain fortress of Qadmus, a site which overlooked an ancient road leading from Hama all the way to Saone and had been in Antiochene hands since its capture by Bohemond II in 1129.[29] Its loss was an acute threat to security. A further internal Muslim uprising by the 'people of the mountains' then occurred in 1135/1136 at Balatanos, a fortress connected to the lordship of Saone, with an attempt made to support the rebels by a Turcoman lord, Mankujuk, who had reportedly since taken control of Bikisrail. The lord of Saone was able to forestall the threat through armed intervention (perhaps even recovering Bikisrail in the process), but it is clear that the principality's southern frontier had become highly fragile, with Isma'ili power even threatening to compel

nisi and al-Azimi on this means precision is difficult, but 1135 is more probable given that Zengi organised matters at Aleppo and departed for Baalbek very soon after Montferrand, making a widespread campaign unlikely. See also El-Azhari, *Zengi*, pp. 73–6.

26 Köhler, *Alliances and Treaties*, p. 173; El-Azhari, *Zengi*, pp. 66–72; Elisséeff, *Nur ad-Din*, II, 355–6.
27 F. Daftary, *The Isma'ilis: Their History and Doctrines*, 2nd edn (Cambridge, 2007), pp. 331–55; B. Smarandache, 'The Franks and the Nizari Isma'ilis in the Early Crusader Period, *Al-Masaq* 24:3 (2012), 221–40.
28 Al-Azimi, p. 127.
29 Al-Azimi, p. 121; KD, *RHC Or.* III, 665; Abu'l Fida, *RHC Or.* I, 21. Based on Kemal al-Din's text, El-Azhari (*Zengi*, pp. 68–9) suggests that the Isma'ili lord of Qadmus aided the Franks at Qinnasrin, but this is not altogether clear. See also Daftary, *Isma'ilis*, p. 349.

local communities to oppose their Frankish overlords.[30] This emergence of a hostile internal power perhaps offers similarities to the difficulties faced by Norman Dukes in maintaining the complicity of ambitious nobles whose lands straddled the frontier with Capetian France.[31] As will be demonstrated below, like the Norman Dukes, the Antiochenes appear to have recognised the value of adopting a conciliatory approach when the situation required.

The period 1130–1135 was thus one of great difficulty for those leading Antioch's defences. Facing an unparalleled diversity of threats from internal and external powers, and without the leadership of a prince, the Franks were pushed back to the Amanus Mountains by the Armenians in the north, while Zengi weakened hopes of containing Aleppan aggression to the east by forging a strong foothold in the Jabal as-Summaq and seizing key sites such as al-Atharib. Isma'ili incursions to the south also damaged the hold over the mountain passes leading from the Orontes Valley into the heart of the principality. Bohemond II's death may not have been as damaging to resources as Harran or *Ager Sanguinis* given his smaller retinue, while the lack of cohesion between the various antagonistic groups perhaps prevented total capitulation, but the unification of Mosul and Aleppo, coupled with the growth of the Armenians and Isma'ilis, offered a far greater long-term menace – one compounded by the lack of a male heir. As will be explored later, such instability impacted upon diplomatic policy, as the increased interest of Jerusalem and Byzantium helped to shape the future direction of Antiochene political interests.

1136–1138: A Temporary Recovery

The six-year interregnum at Antioch was finally ended with the arrival of the western nobleman, Raymond of Poitiers, who married Constance and became prince in 1136.[32] Seen as a whole, the period of his reign was to have an important impact on Near Eastern politics and Antioch's status, for it helped to signify how traditional policies could be merged with, and adapted to, new relationships.

One of Raymond's first acts in 1136 was to attack Cilicia, invading the region and capturing Leon, possibly with the help of his relative, Baldwin (now lord of Marash), and Count Joscelin II of Edessa.[33] Although the sources do not offer precise evidence regarding those lands recovered, reports that Emperor John II Komnenos of Byzantium 'ejected ... those faithful to the lord prince of the Antiochenes' from Tarsus, as well as from Adana, Mamistra and Anazarba, in 1137, indicates that Latin control

30 Bikisrail's capture is not noted but it does appear to have returned to Frankish possession before 1180. See Ibn al-Furat, *Ayyubids, Mamlukes and Crusaders*, trans. U. Lyons, M. Lyons and J. Riley-Smith, 2 vols (Cambridge, 1987), II, 134–5; and pp. 141–2 of this book.
31 Power, *Norman Frontier*, pp. 338–54.
32 Cahen, *Syrie*, pp. 356–58.
33 MS, III, 244; *1234*, pp. 81–2; Sempad, *RHC Arm.* I, 616.

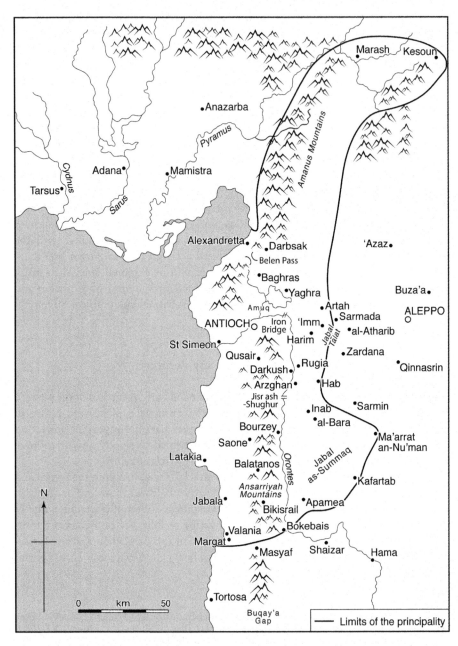

Map 3: Northern Syria and Cilicia, 1135

28

had been restored there.[34] Ralph-Johannes Lilie has urged caution in exaggerating the extent to which Frankish power was actually re-implemented, but the decision to strike so immediately at Cilicia is an important signifier of Antioch's priorities.[35] Rather than face Zengi, the most pressing concern had been the Armenians, which perhaps explains why one of the new prince's kinsmen had been chosen to govern the isolated city of Marash.[36] The underlying reasons for prioritising Cilicia are not stated by the sources, although the influence of relations with Byzantium may have had an impact. Indeed, Bohemond II's death and the rise of Armenian influence had heralded a move towards a potentially closer union between Antioch and the Greeks, although the aforementioned proposed marriage alliance had not come to fruition.[37] As such, it is possible that the Latins felt control over Cilicia was of vital importance given the increased likelihood of imperial intervention, either in retaliation or in support of the Latins. This has parallels with other medieval frontiers, as Daniel Power has noted, in relation to the Norman border with France, that 'even minor protests in the frontier regions could be fanned into a dangerous threat … by [provoking] external interference'.[38] The Antiochene need to balance the difficulties created by rival Orthodox Christian powers was nevertheless a unique concern in *Outremer* and helps to demonstrate the distinct problems faced by the principality when compared to the other crusader states.

If the Franks had hoped that control over Cilicia would hamper the emperor, such an allusion was shattered when John Komnenos seized the region, along with Leon, in 1137.[39] Latin power here was now ended – returning only briefly in the 1180s – and the instability created by the Greeks allowed the resumption of the Danishmend Turk threat, as they attacked Marash and Kesoun.[40] This is a clear indication of Cilicia's fragility, as any reduction in control dangerously exposed the various routes into the principality via the Amanus Mountains. Byzantine occupation of the fortress of Baghras – which lay just 25 km to the north of Antioch and guarded one of the major mountain passes linking Cilicia and northern Syria – would only have exacerbated the situation, as it had been considered vital to the protection of the city since the tenth century.[41] The early history of this castle is extremely vague. Jonathan Riley-Smith has posited that, by 1137, it was held by the Templars, who had been introduced as a result of Leon's incursions, whereas

---

34 WT, pp. 662–3 (here 663): eiectis … ea domini principis Antiocheni fidelibus; Odo of Deuil, pp. 69–71.
35 Lilie, *Byzantium*, pp. 105–9.
36 Beech, 'Marash', pp. 35–52. See also pp. 142–3 of this book.
37 See pp. 191–2.
38 Power, *Norman Frontier*, p. 354.
39 WT, pp. 662–3; al-Azimi, pp. 137–8; IQ, pp. 240–1; KD, *RHC Or.* III, 673–4; JK, pp. 22–3; NC, pp. 14–16; Michael Italikos, pp. 239–40; MS, III, 245; *1234*, II, 81–2; ME, p. 239; GP, p. 241; Sempad, *RHC Arm.* I, 616–17.
40 MS, III, 245–6; *1234*, II, 84–5; NC, p. 18; ME, pp. 238–9; GP, pp. 241–2.
41 KD, *RHC Or.* III, 674; Michael Italikos, p. 241. See also C. Holmes, 'Byzantium's Eastern Frontier in the Tenth and Eleventh Centuries', *Medieval Frontiers: Concepts and Practices*, ed. D. Abulafia and N. Berend (Aldershot, 2002), p. 97.

Marie-Anna Chevalier dates the sale to the 1150s and credits the Armenians with a prominent role in this move.[42] Precision is difficult without a donation charter, but although Riley-Smith is seemingly supported by John Kinnamos' comment that the 'Frères' – a clear reference to the military orders – aided the Antiochenes in their discussions with John Komnenos, the silence on the Templars of a papal letter, most likely sent to censure the emperor for his actions in 1137, lends weight to Chevalier's hypothesis, for the pope was the Order's protector.[43] Moreover, given Cilicia's central importance, as well as the interregnum, it is unlikely that strategically important sites would, or indeed could have been surrendered so early, which makes the 1150s more probable – especially as relations with the Armenians had improved by this point. There can be no doubt, however, that the lack of Latin presence in Cilicia left Antioch's northern frontier zones extremely vulnerable and increased the potential value of the military orders.

Matters were to some extent more positive to the east. No further losses were inflicted on the principality, albeit a powerful Zengid raid reached as far as the port of Latakia in late 1135 or early 1136.[44] This relative lack of activity was influenced by the *atabeg*'s need to maintain his grip over Mosul and Mesopotamia, while the agreement of a truce with Prince Raymond probably freed the latter to intervene in Cilicia.[45] Zengi's capture of the Tripolitan fortress of Montferrand in 1137, despite an Antiochene effort to relieve the Latin forces of Jerusalem and Tripoli who were besieged there, perhaps offset this, because it increased Muslim access to southern Syria and further weakened the principality's southern frontier, which had already been damaged by the Isma'ilis.[46] With the arrival of John Komnenos, though, the opportunity arose for a Christian counter-attack, despite an initial attempt to besiege Antioch and to capture it by force. As part of a treaty concluded between John and Raymond, which also saw the prince pay homage to the emperor, a joint campaign was thus launched against Muslim Syria with the aim of capturing Aleppo, Shaizar, Hama and Homs (which would be swapped for Antioch). This reveals that Aleppo remained the region's major city and continued to lie at the very heart of Antiochene military policy, for it was almost certainly to form the capital of a newly proposed crusader state. In this regard, however, the campaign was a failure, for Aleppo easily withstood a short siege, as did Shaizar – where a dispute may even have arisen between the Christian factions. Despite this, important conquests were made, including al-Atharib, Ma'arrat an-Nu'man, Kafartab, al-Bab and Buza'a – the latter two of which, lying north-east of Aleppo, were

---

[42] Riley-Smith, 'Templars and Theutonic Knights', pp. 92–117; Chevalier, *Ordres*, pp. 56–68.
[43] JK, p. 24; R. Hiestand, *Papsturkunden für kirchen im Heiligen Lande* (Göttingen, 1985), pp. 168–9.
[44] IQ, pp. 238–9; IA, I, 327; KD, *RHC Or.* III, 672; MS, III, 245.
[45] MS, III, 236–7; al-Azimi p. 141. Köhler (*Alliances and Treaties*, p. 138) argues al-Azimi referred to an agreement made at Montferrand, but Raymond was uninvolved in those talks. See also El-Azhari, *Zengi*, pp. 30–3.
[46] WT, pp. 663–6, 669–70; Orderic Vitalis, VI, 497–503; IQ, pp. 242–3; al-Azimi, pp. 138–41; IA, I, 335–6; KD, *RHC Or.* III, 671–5; JK, p. 23; MS, III, p. 246; *1234*, II, 80.

significant for their part in controlling a key line of communication with Mosul.[47] If these could be retained, then the potency of the Aleppan threat could perhaps once again be contained, with the monitoring of key road networks a prominent tactic on many medieval frontiers.[48] In fact, the extension of the campaign to al-Bab and Buza'a perhaps reflects an attempt to overcome the added difficulties provided by Zengid possessions in Mesopotamia. This is indicated by al-Azimi's comment that the Latins immediately renewed their use of nearby al-Atharib as a hub of activity, with control over the plain again ensuring effective surveillance over Aleppo.[49] However, John's subsequent decision to reject Latin requests to meet Zengi in battle proved crucial, as it ensured that the latter's martial resources were not significantly weakened. Control of Buza'a and al-Bab might help to monitor movements; yet, like any fortified site, they could do little to hamper the progress of an army.[50] Therefore, while the frontier with Aleppo had largely been restored to Frankish hands, when the emperor departed the East in 1138 after falling into dispute with the Latins (probably as a result of an attempt to seize Antioch), the general security of the principality remained vulnerable.[51]

The years 1136–1138 were an important phase in the principality's territorial history. Raymond of Poitiers' arrival had reinvigorated Latin martial activity by immediately combatting the Armenians until John Komnenos' intervention precluded further Frankish control in Cilicia and provided the Turks with a renewed opportunity to attack. Imperial support against Zengi had restored the eastern frontier, but the failure to defeat the *atabeg* in the field prevented durable stability. Cilicia was perhaps more secure, so long as the emperor preferred diplomacy over warfare with the Latins, but geographical supremacy could not oppose numerical superiority in northern Syria.

---

[47] WT, pp. 670–6; al-Azimi, pp. 141–3; IQ, pp. 249–52; KD, *RHC Or.* III, 673–8; *IA*, I, 337–41; JK, pp. 24–5; NC, pp. 16–18; MS, III, 245.
[48] Lieberman, *March of Wales*, pp. 351–2.
[49] Al-Azimi, p. 144.
[50] R. Ellenblum, *Crusader Castles and Modern Histories* (Cambridge, 2007), pp. 103–86.
[51] The plight of Zardana and Ma'arrat Mesrin went unreported. On John's dispute with the Latins, see pp. 196–8.

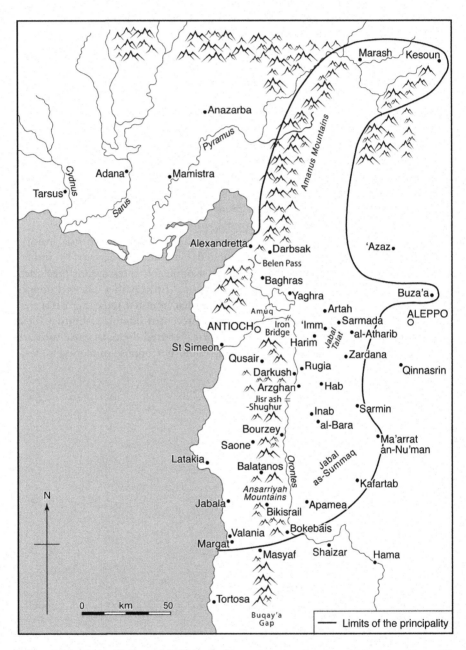

Map 4: Northern Syria and Cilicia, early summer, 1138

32

1138–1144: From the Zengid Counter-Attack to the Fall of Edessa

Over the following years, the failure to eliminate Zengi was to place severe strain on the principality. Muslim counter-attacks, earthquakes, near-continuous raiding and the breakdown of relations with Byzantium, all took their toll. By the end of 1144, the *atabeg* was left all but free to capture Edessa. This dangerous and damaging period had notable long-term ramifications for the Latin presence in northern Syria.

In the final months of 1138 and into early 1139, Zengi reacted fiercely to the Christian conquests, recovering Buza'a, Ma'arrat an-Nu'man, Kafartab and al-Atharib.[52] This eased the pressure on Aleppo by pushing back the frontier to the Jabal Talat and securing the road south towards Damascus. The folly of capturing strategic sites without combating the underlying menace of Zengid numerical supremacy was thus made apparent, as positions could not be maintained with the Latins' inferior resources. As well as continuing to strengthen ties between Jerusalem and Damascus, the *atabeg*'s gains allowed him to strike further west against the principality.[53] Kemal al-Din reported that Zengi now laid siege to 'Jisr', or 'the bridge'.[54] This could be the northern-most Orontes crossing of the Iron Bridge, otherwise known as Jisr al-Hadid, but, because Zengi was active to the south of the principality, it is more likely to refer to Jisr ash-Shughur, which is close to the river port of Arzghan and was defended by the double fortress of Shughur-Bakas.[55] Such a reality is made all the more likely by reports that 'Jisr' was defended by Latin refugees who had fled from Bokebais, a southern mountain fortress which guarded routes to Bourzey and Sarmin – the loss of which further destabilised the area.[56] Zengi's retaliation to 1138 was ferocious. The recovery of sites central to any attempt to contain Aleppo, as well as the capture of Bokebais, renewed the pressure on the principality and lessened the Franks' ability to retaliate.

Fortunately for the Antiochenes, Zengi did not then seek to push further west. This was undoubtedly a result of his preoccupation with Damascus, but also because an earthquake struck northern Syria in 1139, destroying long-contested fortifications such as al-Atharib, Tell Khalid (on the borders of the county of Edessa) and Zardana.[57] While this all but ended Latin hopes of recovering these fortresses – it would have been very hard to secure them for long enough to rebuild – it also prevented their immediate use by the Muslims as forward operating posts against the principality. As far as can be discerned, Zardana and al-Atharib were at this point Zengi's western-most fortifications, and it would have been difficult, albeit

---

52 Al-Azimi, pp. 143–5; IQ, pp. 251, 256; KD, *RHC Or.* III, 678–9; *1234*, II, 86.

53 Asbridge, *Crusades*, pp. 190–3.

54 KD, *RHC Or.* III, 678–9.

55 *Ibid.*

56 *Ibid.* It is unclear whether Bokebais fell to Zengi or the Isma'ilis, although the former is more likely given the good relations enjoyed between them and the Latins in the 1140s.

57 Al-Azimi, p. 145; IQ, p. 256; KD, *RHC Or.* III, 679; *1234*, II, 86. See also El-Azhari, *Zengi*, pp. 82–6.

not impossible, for him to strike from Aleppo into Antiochene territory without the protection they afforded over the Aleppan plain. Indeed, the Franks' maintenance of key sites in the Jabal Talat, like Harim, allowed for the monitoring of the border region through which any attack would have to pass. When Sawar, Zengi's lieutenant in Aleppo, entered the principality in 1139, Raymond was therefore able to ambush the Muslim force and take a great many prisoners.[58] Conversely, Latin hopes of raiding undetected through enemy territory increased, for Harim and other nearby fortifications provided useful staging points from which to attack. This increased the prominence of castles in this area, as well as the aforementioned river crossings, and it can be of little surprise that this was to become the battleground on which Raymond of Poitiers and his successors were to face their greatest challenges.[59] Not only does the emergence of strategic hotspots raise certain parallels with the West, such as the castle of Carreghofa – described as 'the fulcrum' of the Shropshire region of the Anglo-Welsh marches – or the Norman Vexin, it also adds support to Ronnie Ellenblum's argument that centres of authority could be more important to maintaining control than linear borders.[60] Denys Pringle is perhaps correct that castles could not defend a frontier, but they could certainly help to define the balance of power.[61]

Full-scale conflict was delayed during the early 1140s, though, and a temporary period of truce may have been agreed.[62] Raymond definitely felt secure enough to aid King Fulk's defence of Banyas in the kingdom of Jerusalem in 1140, which was probably a joint effort to oppose Zengi's interest in Damascus.[63] Even when hostilities did occur, they were largely confined to raiding expeditions. In 1140/1141, nomadic Turcoman forces devastated areas of the principality, and Antiochene forces retaliated with similar vigour by launching counter-raids as far south as Shaizar.[64] This continued throughout 1141, as the Latins attacked Sarmin – thus suggesting it had earlier fallen to Zengi – which provoked Sawar and his Turcoman allies to ride to the gates of Antioch itself.[65] 1142 marked something of a peak in hostilities, as an Aleppan assault on the principality routed an Antiochene force of 700 men, which had gathered to meet them, and Muslim forces were able to raid Harim unopposed. A further defeat was then inflicted on the Latins, who had gathered

---

[58] KD, *RHC Or.* III, 680.

[59] The Iron Bridge seems to have acted as a rallying point for Antiochene forces. Both al-Azimi (p. 150) and Kemal al-Din (*RHC Or.* III, 684) reported Raymond gathered his forces there in 1142, and Raymond's charter for the Holy Sepulchre of 1140 (*CCSSJ*, 77) referred to the prince's presence at the Iron Bridge at the time of the ambush of Sawar.

[60] Lieberman, *March of Wales*, pp. 164–5; Power, *Norman Frontier*, pp. 338–47; Ellenblum, *Castles*, pp. 127–43.

[61] D. Pringle, 'Castles and Frontiers in the Latin East', *Norman Expansion: Connections, Continuities and Contrasts*, ed. K. Stringer and A. Jotischky (Farnham, 2013), pp. 238–9.

[62] No source outwardly confirms this, but Kemal al-Din's (*RHC Or.* III, 683) report of an Antiochene envoy, sent to Zengi to complain about the Turcoman raids of 1140/1141, suggests this violence contravened an earlier agreement.

[63] WT, pp. 685–8; IQ, p. 261; KD, *RHC Or.* III, 682; IA, I, 353.

[64] Al-Azimi, p. 148; KD, *RHC Or.* III, 683.

[65] Al-Azimi, pp. 148–9; KD, *RHC Or.* III, 683.

at the Iron Bridge to face another invasion.[66] The lack of territorial supremacy on either side nevertheless appears to have prevented a decisive outcome.

John Komnenos' return to Syria in 1142 provided an appropriate subtext for the cessation of conflict, although he failed to reignite his earlier attacks on Muslim authority. Indeed, he instead seemingly fell into dispute with the Franks, first marching on Tell Bashir to prevent Joscelin II from intervening, and then moving to Antioch, which he now demanded. His success was probably only prevented by his death in a Cilician hunting accident in 1143.[67] Soon after this, Raymond sought to take advantage of the fact that Zengi's attention had once more been drawn away by matters in Mesopotamia by striking at Buza'a.[68] The decision to attempt to recapture this site further demonstrates that control over the Jabal as-Summaq and the castles of the Aleppan plain was no longer considered enough to neutralise the Muslims, especially after the earthquake of 1139. Raymond's ability to move a force so far into Muslim territory without detection, moreover, supports the belief that the retention of Harim and the Jabal Talat could still be of great use to Antioch. However, the subsequent failure to capture Buza'a suggests that Latin military power was limited, while martial weakness also decreased the impact of raiding, as the Frankish governor of Barsutah, a castle 35 km north-west of Aleppo, is said to have launched raids on sites like Kafarbasil in 1143 and 1144, only to be defeated and captured.[69] A caravan travelling from Antioch was also seized by Sawar and its armed escort killed.[70] Then, on Christmas Day 1144, after a short siege, Zengi violently captured Edessa, whose count, Joscelin II, was away at Tell Bashir.[71] The first major city to come under crusader control was lost, and the principality's northern frontier was left dangerously exposed.

Up until this point, though, while the eastern regions of the principality suffered, Greek control over Cilicia seems to have ensured that the north remained largely peaceful. Al-Azimi suggested that the Danishmends brutally captured Marash in 1141, and while this is seemingly inaccurate – for Gregory the Priest, an inhabitant of nearby Kesoun, did not report this, and because Baldwin of Marash issued a charter here in around 1143 – a temporary occupation or attack is possible.[72] This demonstrates an important consequence of Cilicia's loss. Greek power had elimi-nated the Armenian problem, but the deterioration of Frankish control accentuated the fragility of isolated northern possessions like Marash and Kesoun, which would

[66]   Al-Azimi, pp. 149–50; IQ, p. 263; KD, *RHC Or.* III, 684; IA, I, 365; MS, III, 253.

[67]   WT, pp. 700–2. See also pp. 97–8, 198 of this book.

[68]   Al-Azimi, p. 151; IQ, p. 264; KD, *RHC Or.* III, 684. On Zengi's affairs in Mesopotamia, see IA, I, 368–9.

[69]   Al-Azimi, p. 152–4. Kafarbasil's site is unknown, although the Greek connotations of its name suggest it corresponds to Kafar Rum, a site south of Ma'arrat an-Nu'man. See Cahen, *Syrie*, p. 162.

[70]   IQ, pp. 265–6; KD, *RHC Or.* III, 685. This may be connected to the Barsutah raid of 1143, as al-Azimi suggested the Latins were defeated in Damascene territory, which is unlikely in the context of a raid given its distance from Barsutah, but is plausible for the escort of a caravan.

[71]   El-Azhari, *Zengi*, pp. 91–106.

[72]   Al-Azimi, p. 147; *CGOH*, I, 313.

only have come into sharper focus after Edessa's fall.[73] Despite this, the only other recorded threat came in 1144, when John Komnenos' son, Manuel, now emperor, ordered an attack on the northern Syrian coast and other Antiochene lands due to an apparent slight made against him by Raymond in 1143.[74] It is unlikely that this altered the territorial extent of the principality, yet Jonathan Phillips is correct that it weakened Raymond at a time of growing Zengid strength.[75]

The period 1138–1144 was thus one in which the principality of Antioch failed to take advantage of the potentially strong position afforded them by John Komnenos' campaign. Having avoided a reverse in the field, Zengi soon recaptured lost possessions, and a war of attrition, characterised by raids and counter-raids, eroded Antiochene manpower and increased the military pressures placed on the Latins. Retention of sites like Harim, as well as the destruction of al-Atharib and Zardana in an earthquake, potentially precluded a surprise invasion. However, the Antiochene ability to go on the offensive was severely diminished. The breakdown of relations with Byzantium also precluded their support, while an imperial assault on the principality again brought the potential problems caused by the lack of Latin power in Cilicia to the fore. As Zengi laid siege to Edessa in late 1144, Raymond was in no position to offer effective support to the city or its count (with whom he is said to have fallen into open dispute), especially without the promise of Greek reinforcements.[76] It swiftly fell.

1145–1152: The Rise of Nur al-Din

The growing pressure came to a head between 1145 and 1152, as the Latins failed to provide an adequate counter offensive to the fall of Edessa, or to react with strength to Zengi's death in 1146. Aleppo's new governor, the *atabeg*'s son, Nur al-Din, was thus able to inflict disaster on the principality, leading to territorial losses on a level only surpassed by Harran in 1104 and, as will be seen below, Saladin's conquests of 1188.

One of the lasting consequences of Edessa's loss was that it left the principality perilously exposed to the north and east, a situation that was underlined by the ease with which Zengi defeated a Latin relief force gathered at Antioch.[77] Raymond departed for Constantinople to seek aid from Byzantium, but immediate imperial military intervention was not to be forthcoming.[78] The *atabeg*'s death at Qal'at

---

73 Amouroux-Mourad, *Edesse*, pp. 16–18.
74 JK, pp. 35–6; NC, p. 31.
75 J. Phillips, *Defenders of the Holy Land: Relations between the Latin East and the West, 1119–1187* (Oxford, 1996), pp. 73–4.
76 Asbridge, *Crusades*, pp. 193–6. On Joscelin and Raymond, see WT, pp. 718–20; and pp. 231–3 of this book.
77 IQ, p. 269. William of Tyre's evidence (pp. 718–20) suggests Raymond may have been awaiting reinforcements from Jerusalem.
78 JK, p. 36; MS, III, 267.

Ja'bar in 1146 temporarily delayed any move to conquer Antiochene territory and Raymond was able to direct raids against Aleppo, Hama and Salda. Yet, his forces were defeated near to Artah, which was followed by a damaging Muslim counter-attack.[79] Abu Shama's report that the prince's response was delayed by the slow dissemination of the news of Zengi's demise has caused Alex Mallett to doubt the adequacy of Antiochene spy networks. While this may not be entirely unfair given the Latins' continued presence in areas of the Jabal as-Summaq, such as al-Bara and Apamea, Antioch was in an undoubtedly delicate position and attacks would have required careful planning.[80] Moreover, the Muslims would likely have gone to great lengths to conceal news of Zengi's death from the Franks until the issue of his succession was settled – which would have been made all the more achievable given that Qal'at Ja'bar lies around 120 km east of Aleppo. The elevation of his sons, Saif al-Din and Nur al-Din, at Mosul and Aleppo respectively, was certainly carried out with haste, and so the threat to the principality's eastern frontier endured.[81]

This was confirmed in 1146/1147, when Nur al-Din launched heavy raids against sites in and around the Jabal Talat, including Artah, Basarfut, Mabula (or Mamulah), Hab and Kafarlatha – with the possibility remaining that he captured these sites.[82] Nur al-Din's actions represent a concerted effort to push the entire length of Antioch's eastern border further west, with Latin protection of the nearest areas of the eastern frontier now reduced to Harim. To the south, Frankish authority centred on al-Bara and Apamea: both heavily fortified sites which presided over a key network of routes linking northern and southern Syria and allowed access into the heart of the principality via the Orontes Valley and the Ansarriyah Mountains.[83] Crucially, this may have helped to initiate a coalition between Raymond and the Isma'ilis. Upon his accession in Aleppo, Nur al-Din had abolished Shi'a practices there, which Farhad Daftary has argued 'amounted to an open declaration of war on the Isma'ilis'.[84] Their status on the south-eastern frontier of the principality was thus of great interest to both rulers, with Nur al-Din keen to remove them and, as will be seen below, Raymond open to the opportunity for an alliance. Meanwhile, the loss of Hab opened a central corridor for Nur al-Din to strike at Jisr ash-Shughur, a benefit that was to be enhanced by the subsequent failure of the Second Crusade. Launched in the West in response to the fall of Edessa, crusader forces under

---

79 AS, *RHC Or.* IV, 48–9; GBE, II, pp. 272–3. The site of Salda is unknown, although it could refer either to Sarmada or Zardana, with the former more likely given its proximity to Artah (see Cahen, *Syrie*, pp. 134–8).

80 A. Mallett, 'The Battle of Inab', *JMH* 39:1 (2013), 48–60.

81 Elisséeff, *Nur ad-Din*, II, 389–95.

82 KD, *ROL* 3, 515–16; IA, II, 15; MS, III, 282. It is unclear if these sites were captured, although it seems likely they were given that only Artah was mentioned as being seized later (after Inab).

83 J.-P. Fourdrin, 'La fortification de la seigneurie épiscopale latine d'El Bara dans le patriarcat d'Antioche (1098–1148)', *Pèlerinages et Croisades*, ed. L. Pressouyre (Paris, 1995), pp. 351–406; P. Dangles, 'Afamiya – Qal'at al-Mudiq. Die Mittelalterliche Wiederbefestigung der Antiken Zitadelle von Apamea am Ende des 12. bis Mitte des 13. Jahrhunderts', *Burgen und Städte der Kreuzzugszeit*, ed. M. Piana (Petersberg, 2008), pp. 221–33.

84 Daftary, *Isma'ilis*, p. 352.

Conrad III of Germany and Louis VII of France had both come unstuck during the march through Asia Minor. As such, while French forces made it to northern Syria in March 1148, Raymond was unable to convince Louis to support him in an attack upon Aleppo, as the king preferred instead to unite with Conrad, who had since travelled to Acre in the kingdom of Jerusalem, and to launch an eventually abortive siege of Damascus in concordance with Baldwin III of Jerusalem.[85] Coupled with the unlikelihood of immediate Byzantine military intervention due to Manuel's pre-occupation with dealing with the passage of the crusade through his lands, the path was laid clear for Muslim aggression.[86] Thus, later in 1148, Apamea and Yaghra were assaulted, at which point al-Bara may well have been captured, further weakening this area.[87] Raymond responded by inflicting one, perhaps even two defeats upon Nur al-Din, but the young Muslim ruler had tested Antioch's pressure points and succeeded in opening a gap.[88]

This fragmentation of the principality's eastern defences gave the sultan ample room to strike at the central elements of this border zone. It was into this corridor, therefore, that he drew Raymond – who had been raiding Muslim territory with the help of the Isma'ilis under the leadership of Ali ibn Wafa – after a brief siege of Harim in 1149. Battle was joined at Inab, just to the east of Jisr ash-Shughur, with defeat leaving the prince dead, along with his Isma'ili allies and probably also Renaud, lord of Marash.[89] Nur al-Din followed this by raiding the principality at will, seizing Harim, Apamea and potentially al-Bara and Artah (if they were not already his). It was likely only a Jerusalemite-Templar relief force, as well as Antioch's formidable walls, that prevented a successful siege of the Latin capital.[90] Antiochene resistance on the eastern bank of the Orontes had been removed. Mallett has attributed these successes to luck, asserting that the inexperienced Nur al-Din simply sought to defend his lands from Latin aggression.[91] However, while it is correct that the young Zengid was still emerging as a leader, the events surrounding Inab appear instead to be the result of a concerted plan, in which a series of targets

---

[85] J. Phillips, *The Second Crusade: Extending the Frontiers of Christendom* (New Haven, CT, 2007), pp. 168–227. This is also examined on p. 242 of this book.

[86] Lilie, *Byzantium*, pp. 145–63.

[87] IQ, pp. 288–9; AS, *RHC Or.* IV, 60; KD, *ROL* 3, 517–18; IA, II, 24–5; MS, III, p. 288; *1234*, II, 115. For al-Bara see Ibn al-Furat, II, 227. Mallett ('Inab', p. 53) readily accepts the evidence of this late fourteenth-century compilation, but it remains possible that al-Bara was actually captured in the wake of Inab.

[88] Mallett, 'Inab', pp. 53–5; Asbridge, *Crusades*, pp. 239–45.

[89] WT, pp. 770–4; William of Newburgh, 'Historia Rerum Anglicarum', ed. R. Howlett, *Chronicles of the Reigns of Stephen, Henry II, and Richard I*, 4 vols (London, 1884–1889), I, 67–8; IQ, pp. 292–4; KD, *ROL* 3, 521–2; IA, II, p. 31; AS, *RHC Or.* IV, 61–4; MS, III, 289–90; *1234*, II, 115–16; GP, p. 257.

[90] WT, pp. 770–4; William of Newburgh, I, 290; 'Epistolae A. Dapiferi Militiae Templi', *RHGF* XV, 540–41; IQ, pp. 292–4; KD, *ROL* 3, 521–3; IA, II, 31, 36; AS, *RHC Or.* IV, 61–4; MS, III, 289–90; *1234*, II, 115–16; GP, p. 257. On the walls, see C. Brasse, 'Von der Stadtmauer zur Stadtgeschichte. Das Befestigungssystem von Antiochia am Orontes', *Neue Forschungen zu antiken Stadtbefestigungen im östlichen Mittelmeerraum und im Vorderen Orient (Byzas 10)*, ed. J. Lorentzen, F. Pirson, *et al.* (Istanbul, 2010), pp. 261–82.

[91] Mallett, 'Inab', pp. 48–60.

were carefully chosen, thereby opening a large central corridor on the principality's eastern frontier. It was into this area that he drew Raymond, deploying his superior numbers to achieve victory.[92] The losses of Harim and Apamea were of particular importance, as this eliminated surveillance of Muslim movements from the Jabal Talat and afforded Nur al-Din control over the major road confluences of the Jabal as-Summaq; thus offering him easier access into the southern regions of the principality and on towards Damascus. Hopes of preventing a surprise invasion from any point along the Orontes, or opposing the unification of northern and southern Syria, were now severely damaged.

The loss of Edessa also greatly impacted on matters to the north, as Nur al-Din now had largely unchallenged access to the region. Meanwhile, as already noted, the distraction caused to Byzantium by the passage of the Second Crusade precluded any imperial support, particularly in securing their aid against Danishmend or Seljuk raids. This compounded the dangers to the already fragile lordship of Marash, especially in the wake of the death of its lord, Baldwin, during a disastrous attempt at recovering Edessa along with Count Joscelin II in 1146 – a venture which Raymond of Poitiers seemingly refused to support.[93] The presence of his brother, Renaud, perhaps compensated for this, at least until he also died in battle. While there is some confusion over whether Renaud perished at Inab or if Michael the Syrian was correct to suggest he was killed defending Kesoun in 1150, it is nevertheless clear that the Seljuks had seized the lordship of Marash by 1150, thus eliminating the final elements of the principality's northern-most defences.[94] The Turks then attacked the Edessan fortress of Tell Bashir and entered the principality.[95] By 1151, moreover, Nur al-Din had completed the annexation of the county of Edessa, despite its sale to Manuel Komnenos and a relief effort of launched by Baldwin III of Jerusalem, with the support of Antiochene nobles.[96]

The period 1145–1152 was thus one of significant territorial loss. To the east, the Orontes River became Antioch's border with Muslim Syria, and so the defences of its crossings now took on a particularly high level of importance. Significantly, this reliance on a river to denote a border or a limit of jurisdiction was known in the West, such as the River Epte in Normandy, which acted as a frontier zone with Capetian France, and also in Iberia, as its confluences have been seen to define the various stages of re-conquest.[97] The principality had also lost the majority of its northern defences, with the fortresses of the passes through the Amanus Mountains – perhaps soon to be placed under Templar control – as well as the marshy Amuq

92 As such, I follow more closely the arguments set out in Asbridge, *Crusades*, pp. 239–45.
93 WT, pp. 734–8; IQ, pp. 274–5; KD, *ROL* 3, 514–15; IA, II, 8; MS, III, 270–1; *1234*, II, 104–9; GP, pp. 244–5.
94 MS, III, 293–7; GP, pp. 257–9.
95 IQ, pp. 300–1; MS, III, 293–4.
96 WT, pp. 782–5; IQ, pp. 300–1; AS, *RHC Or.* IV, pp. 73–6; IA, II, 39–40, 45–6, 72–3; KD, *ROL* 3, 523–6; MS, III, 297.
97 Power, *Norman Frontier*, pp. 43, 102–3; B. Reilly, *The Medieval Spains* (Cambridge, 1993), pp. 90–2.

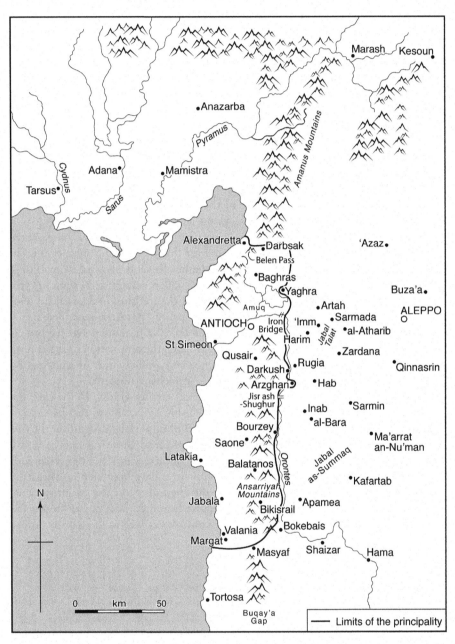

Map 5: Northern Syria and Cilicia, 1149

region north-east of Antioch the only remaining barriers to aggression.[98] Meanwhile, the Second Crusade had singularly failed to halt, or even to combat, the rise of the Zengids in northern Syria. Indeed, while Martin Hoch has played down the extent to which the crusade was a turning point in the East, it is undoubted that the failed attack on Damascus increased Nur al-Din's hopes of incorporating the city into his empire.[99] More significant here, though, is that the decision to ignore Aleppo meant that the growing pressure on the principality's eastern frontier had not been alleviated, which helped to facilitate the disaster at Inab. Had Nur al-Din not then prioritised efforts to seize Damascus, the very future of the principality may have been in doubt.

1153–1161: A Tense Frontier

During 1153–1161, the fevered pace of military action seen in the previous decade made way for a more static border zone, for the most part along the Orontes River; with conflict focused largely on specific strategic pressure points. However, the political dynamic was complicated by the renewal of Byzantine interest and the re-emergence of Armenian power under the warlord Thoros. As such, the Latins seemingly prioritised securing the vital river crossings over the Orontes, rather than contemplating a full-scale counter-offensive against Nur al-Din.

Crucially for Antioch, Nur al-Din seems to have been content with the status quo in the immediate aftermath of his victory, with the capture of the small fortress of Afis in 1153 marking his only Antiochene conquest.[100] His decision to refrain from seizing Antioch, or to embark on widespread conquests, has been interpreted either as a recognition of the city's strong defences or fears of imperial intervention.[101] Asbridge and Mallett have also argued that it reflects Nur al-Din's desire to secure his borders, to consolidate his position in Aleppo and to allow him to move on Damascus.[102] Seizing Antioch and taking responsibility for its defences during the inevitable backlash from the West and Byzantium would have certainly stretched his resources. This represented a greater risk than leaving the principality too weak

---

[98]   As well as Baghras, this included Darbsak, La Roche Guillaume and La Roche de Roissel. See Cahen, *Syrie*, pp. 140–8.

[99]   M. Hoch, 'The Price of Failure: the Second Crusade as a Turning-Point in the History of the Latin East?', *The Second Crusade: Scope and Consequences*, ed. J. Phillips and M. Hoch (Manchester, 2001), pp. 180–200; S. Mourad and J. Lindsay, 'A Muslim Response to the Second Crusade: Ibn Asakir of Damascus as a Propagandist of Jihad', *The Second Crusade: Holy War on the Periphery of Latin Christendom*, ed. J. Roche and J. Møller Jensen (Turnhout, 2015), pp. 91–111.

[100]   IQ, p. 315; AS, *RHC Or.* IV, 76–7. This is likely modern-day Afis, a site to the north-east of Ma'arrat an-Nu'man on the main route to Aleppo.

[101]   Elisséeff, *Nur ad-Din*, II, 434–5; Cahen, *Syrie*, p. 384; Köhler, *Alliances and Treaties*, pp. 145–6; Asbridge, *Crusades*, p. 244.

[102]   Asbridge, *Crusades*, p. 244; Mallett, 'Inab', pp. 59–60. See also Elisséeff, *Nur ad-Din*, II, 463–88; Barber, *Crusader States*, pp. 194–5.

to react. Moreover, in the context of Köhler's belief in the system of 'autonomous Syrian lordships' and the anti-hegemonic 'no-place doctrine' this engendered, it is possible that such a monumental rise could have elicited an alliance between Mosul and Baghdad, and perhaps also Damascus, to prevent Nur al-Din from too overtly altering the balance of power.[103] For now, Zengid interests were better served by a diminished, but extant, principality. Although militarily weakened, this gave the Antiochenes some political influence.

Nur al-Din's preoccupation with issues in the Muslim world also allowed the new prince of Antioch, Constance's second husband, the western migrant Renaud of Châtillon, to strike back. Indeed, according to the Norman chronicler Robert of Torigny, Renaud immediately attacked Aleppan territory upon his accession in 1153 and captured three fortresses.[104] The names of these sites were not recorded, but it is possible that they included Harim, which became an increasingly central hub of military activity. This belief stems not only from the castle's inherent significance, but also because Nur al-Din laid siege to it in 1156, seemingly in retaliation for Latin raids on Aleppo – an act which would have been unnecessary had the sultan still possessed it.[105] Interestingly, having failed to recapture Harim, Nur al-Din reportedly settled for the creation of a condominium; although, given that a further, successful Latin siege of the castle was initiated in 1157 following an earthquake and the arrival of the news that the Zengid ruler had fallen gravely ill, it seems that the sultan had at some point captured it.[106] Harim's rather confusing chronology during this period – in which it may have changed hands three times – attests to its growing significance.[107] Lying to the south of the major road between Antioch and Aleppo, it provided an advanced defence against Muslim attacks aimed at the Iron Bridge. As noted above, it also offered the Latins a crucial forward operating position for launching raids – such as those enacted in 1156, 1158 and 1159/1160 – and monitoring enemy movements across the Jabal Talat.[108] With the river crossings of the principality now of premium importance following the loss of all other territories to the east of the Orontes, retention of this fortress was paramount to the frontier's security.[109]

---

[103] Köhler, *Alliances and Treaties*, pp. 7–19.
[104] Robert of Torigny, p. 180. Renaud's accession is discussed on pp. 77–80 of this book.
[105] For Latin attacks, see IQ, p. 325; AS, *RHC Or.* IV, 83. For Harim, see KD, *ROL* 3, 528; IA, II, 79.
[106] For the condominium, see IA, II, p. 79; Köhler, *Alliances and Treaties*, pp. 312–20. For 1157, see WT, pp. 838–40; Robert of Torigny, pp. 199–200; IQ, p. 326, 338, 344; AS, *RHC Or.* IV, 92–3, 96; KD, *ROL* 3, 530; IA, II, 87; MS, III, 315–16; *1234*, II, 117–19.
[107] It also had an impact on its lordship. See pp. 143–7; and Buck, 'Castle and Lordship of Harim', pp. 121–9.
[108] IQ, pp. 325, 344; AS, *RHC Or.* IV, 83, 96; KD, *ROL* 3, 528, 533; IA, II, 79; MS, III, 316; *1234*, II, 119; GP, p. 277.
[109] In this, it was perhaps similar to the castle of Banyas in the kingdom of Jerusalem, which helped to govern the frontier with Damascus. See Ellenblum, *Castles*, pp. 142–3; J. Schenk, 'Nomadic Violence in the First Latin Kingdom of Jerusalem and the Military Orders', *Reading Medieval Studies* 36 (2010), 39–55.

Despite the demonstrable intent of retaining Harim, the Antiochenes appear to have lacked a desire to make any further conquests to the east. Before Harim's capture in 1157, a joint venture was launched against Shaizar – a fortress overlooking the Orontes from which the route towards Damascus could be monitored – in conjunction with Baldwin III of Jerusalem, Count Thierry of Flanders and Thoros of Armenia.[110] Formerly a target for Latin aggression and the exaction of financial tribute, it had been badly damaged in the earthquake – which had killed most of the ruling Banu Munqidh family – and was taken by Nur al-Din soon after the Latin withdrawal.[111] William of Tyre recorded that the attack failed due to a demand made by Renaud that Thierry do homage to him should he govern the fortress, and while Phillips has suggested that the prince simply baulked at the idea of a rival power emerging in northern Syria, it must also be taken into account that the castle was probably indefensible.[112] The Latins no longer controlled the Aleppan road, having lost Kafartab and Ma'arrat an-Nu'man, and with other nearby fortifications such as Apamea and Bokebais also in enemy hands, any garrison placed at Shaizar would have been dangerously exposed. This would have been compounded by the shifting alliance with the Isma'ilis, who controlled nearby Bokebais and Masyaf and were listed amongst the Muslim forces defending Shaizar.[113] Moreover, as Thierry is unlikely to have envisaged settling in northern Syria, Renaud would probably have been called upon to contribute to the fortress' defences, a price he was undoubtedly unable to pay.[114] With the Antiochene Franks seemingly acutely aware of the difficulties posed by the topography and political composition of the region, and surrounded by hostile groups on almost all sides, they were apparently content to maintain Harim and the defences of the Orontes River, rather than risk a large-scale reaction from Nur al-Din. The validity of such a policy was to be proved in 1159 when Manuel Komnenos, who had come to Antioch to establish his authority there and over Cilicia, failed to fulfil a promise to campaign against the Muslim Sultan, as it demonstrated that widespread territorial recovery was unlikely.[115]

This afforded the situation in Cilicia a great level of significance. Indeed, it was during this period that the principality became embroiled in a military dispute between Byzantium and the Armenians after Leon I's son, Thoros, had escaped from Constantinople and threatened Greek power. When Manuel Komnenos visited the region in 1158 he was able to settle this and secure his overlordship over the principality, but not before Renaud used an imperially sponsored campaign against Thoros in 1154 to cement, or even to introduce, a Templar presence in the

---

[110] WT, pp. 834–40; Robert of Torigny, pp. 199–200; IQ, pp. 341–2; AS, *RHC Or.* IV, 93; *1234*, II, 118–19. An unlikely account of Apamea's capture is found in 'Sigeberti Gemblacensis, Auctarium Affligemense', *MGH SS* VI, 403.

[111] IA, II, pp. 87–9; KD, *ROL* 3, 530. See also Asbridge, '"Crusader" Community', 305–25.

[112] Phillips, *Defenders*, p. 280.

[113] IQ, pp. 341–2; AS, *RHC Or.* IV, 93.

[114] On the military capabilities of the princes, see pp. 110–22.

[115] WT, pp. 848–9; JK, p. 144; MS, III, 316; *1234*, II, 119; GP, pp. 274–5; Sempad, *Chronique*, p. 149. See also Buck, 'Between Byzantium and Jerusalem?', pp. 109–14; and pp. 202–8 of this book.

Amanus Mountains, as well as to launch an assault on the Byzantine island of Cyprus in conjunction with the Armenian warlord in 1156.[116] The former venture was significant as it placed the principality's remaining northern defences into the hands of the Templars, who were most prominently provided with Baghras, but at some point also received the mountain fortresses of Darbsak, La Roche de Roissel and La Roche Guillaume.[117] The value of this was to be demonstrated in 1157, as Gregory the Priest reported that the Templars, with Thoros' aid, defeated a Seljuk army on its way to raid the principality.[118] Arabic sources suggest that the Turks still managed to attack Antioch, which perhaps means the Templar ambush occurred as the Seljuks withdrew through the mountains, but their ability to strike at invading forces nevertheless attests to the great worth of their presence. Meanwhile, the assault on Cyprus, which appears to have been sparked by Manuel's failure to pay Renaud for the 1154 campaign, demonstrates how quickly matters in Cilicia could change, especially now that Armenian and Greek powers vied for influence with the Antiochene Franks.

During the first half of the 1150s, therefore, the principality of Antioch was a polity on the edge of collapse. The eastern frontier had been pushed back to the Orontes River and the northern lands were now entirely in Muslim hands. That the Latins prioritised the recapture of Harim over other potential conquests, suggests it was a crucial pressure point, on a par with the sites which lay in and around the vital river crossings, such as the Iron Bridge and Jisr ash-Shughur. This implies that the Antiochene Franks considered a static border zone along the Orontes, coupled with the surveillance benefits of Harim, the best hope for the principality's long-term security, as it largely prevented surprise attacks by Nur al-Din. Manuel Komnenos' arrival in 1158 was to change the political dynamic of the Near East, for he secured confirmation of his overlordship, stabilised relations between Greek, Latin and Armenian rulers, and the looming threat of his intervention perhaps provided a deterrent to extensive Muslim aggression. Just as Harim was integral to Antiochene survival to the east, a strong Eastern Christian presence in Cilicia, coupled with increased Templar involvement, prevented any further collapse to the north.

1162–1168: The Final Loss of the Eastern Frontier

The importance of the river crossings and their nearby defences continued to have a prominent influence over the balance of power between Antioch and its Muslim neighbours throughout the 1160s. It was during this period that, with the ultimate

---

[116] WT, pp. 823–5; MS, III, 314; JK, pp. 143–4; MS, III, 314–15; GP, p. 272–5; Sempad, *RHC Arm.* I, 621. The attack on Cyprus is discussed in greater depth on pp. 121–2, 201–2 of this book.
[117] Riley-Smith, 'Templars and Theutonic Knights', pp. 92–17; Chevalier, *Ordres*, pp. 56–68.
[118] IQ, p. 339; AS, *RHC Or.* IV, 92; GP, p. 283.

loss of Harim, the final, damaging blows were inflicted on Antiochene territorial interests to the east of the Orontes. Perhaps the only remaining factors preventing further extensive territorial losses were Byzantium, the sale of the central eastern corridor to the Hospitallers and the growing strength of the Armenians, each of whom their offered military support to the principality.

As already noted, the Antiochenes went to great lengths to capture and maintain Harim, in part due to its strategic role in screening attacks on the Iron Bridge and also because it acted as an advanced post from which to monitor, and even to enter Muslim territory. Harim's pivotal strategic importance was re-emphasised in early 1162, when Nur al-Din enacted a siege there in the wake of Renaud of Châtillon's capture during a raiding expedition to the north in November 1161.[119] The sultan's efforts were thwarted by the size of the Frankish garrison, however, which had evidently been heavily strengthened to ensure its protection – thus showing its significance.[120] The growing fear for this area's security also led the principality's ruling elite, temporarily in charge of Antioch, to refortify the Iron Bridge with the support of Baldwin III of Jerusalem; perhaps in the hope that it could offer greater resistance to the Muslims should Harim fall.[121] It is evident that the long-term hopes for the security of Antioch were now heavily invested in maintaining possession of this river crossing.

This was made especially pertinent in 1162/1163 by Nur al-Din's capture of the river port of Arzghan, near to Jisr ash-Shughur.[122] As argued above, the sultan had placed pressure on the central corridor leading to this site in 1149 in order to draw Raymond into battle at Inab, and this likely represented a continuation of such a policy.[123] Indeed, any weakness here provided Nur al-Din with easy access into the heart of the principality and it is probably of no coincidence that Michael the Syrian reported a Muslim raid striking as far east as Latakia at around the same time as the loss of Arzghan.[124] The ability to attack so deep into Latin lands would potentially have also required the movement of military resources away from Harim and towards Jisr ash-Shughur, perhaps supported by seigneurial forces from nearby Saone. This may have weakened, or at least isolated, Harim's garrison, which offered Nur al-Din an easier opportunity to strike. That these attacks formed part of a coherent Zengid strategy has been overlooked by historians, despite their evident significance.

Even though the loss of Arzghan was only recorded by Gregory the Priest and not Arabic authors, there is reason to trust in his account, or at least the reality of

---

[119] Louis VII, 'Epistolae', *RHGF* XVI, 27–8; WT, pp. 851–2; Robert of Torigny, p. 214; KD, *ROL* 3, 533; MS, III, 319; *1234*, II, 119; GP, pp. 278–9. See also Mayer, *Varia*, pp. 45–54.

[120] IA, II, p. 134; KD, *ROL* 3, 534; AS, *RHC Or.* IV, 105; GP, p. 279.

[121] WT, p. 858.

[122] GP, p. 279.

[123] Cahen (*Syrie*, p. 404), citing Ibn al-Furat, argued Arzghan was captured in 1149/1150 and recovered in 1157, whereas Elisséeff (*Nur ad-Din*, II, p. 551), who provides no source, suggests it was retaken in 1160. Whatever the case, this only adds further to belief in this area's central importance.

[124] MS, III, p. 320.

fears for Jisr ash-Shughur's security. In 1168, Bohemond III made a sizable sale to the Hospitallers, largely comprising a concentration of sites in this central corridor.[125] These included Arzghan itself, which would have been unlikely had the prince still held it, the nearby fortifications of Basarfut and Farmith, the prince's half of the highly prized Rugia estate in the Ruj valley, which probably centred on the fortress also known as *Chastel Rouge*, as well as *Caveam*, which is believed to be the cave fortress above Darkush on the western bank of the river.[126] Meanwhile, the presence of two further sites of importance within this charter, the more southerly Bokebais and Apamea, was perhaps facilitated by Nur al-Din's interest in the Buqay'a Gap – a plain in the county of Tripoli which offered access to the coast and was the site of a famous defeat at the hands of Tripolitan, Antiochene, military order, Byzantine and Armenian forces, near to the formidable castle of Krak des Chevaliers in 1163.[127] The surrendering of lost sites to the military orders in the hope that they may recover them was not unique to the principality – it was a tactic utilised throughout the Latin East and West, such as in Iberia and Hungary – and it cannot be doubted that it was carried out with the hope of limiting the threat to the southern mountain passes, especially as no evidence survives to suggest that positive relations existed with the Isma'ilis at this time.[128]

That the sultan hoped to weaken Harim's protection by placing pressure on the central crossing of the Orontes was demonstrated in 1164, as he now laid siege to the castle. Muslim authors considered this attack as revenge for the reverse at Buqay'a Gap, which helps to demonstrate what a rich prize Harim was considered.[129] In reaction, Prince Bohemond III gathered a force of allies of unparalleled size, including Tripolitan, military order, Byzantine, and Armenian soldiers, but Nur al-Din was victorious, defeating and capturing the Latin and Greek leaders at Artah before inflicting the definitive loss of Harim.[130] It has been argued that the Muslim ruler again refrained from laying siege to Antioch, despite the ease of access to the city, for fears that Manuel Komnenos would intervene and because a weakened Latin buffer state better served Zengid interests.[131] The influence of imperial interest over his actions is certainly confirmed by both William of Tyre and Ibn al-Athir.[132] Moreover, with control over Harim and Arzghan, Nur al-Din had so crippled the advanced defensive positions of the principality that there was

---

[125] *CGOH*, I, 391.

[126] P. Castellana and E. Hybsch, 'Il castello del Roudj o Chastel de Ruge dei Crociati', *Studia Orientalia Christiana Collectanea* 23 (1990), 309–23; Deschamps, *Châteaux*, pp. 61, 78; *Inventaire du Jébel Wastani*, pp. 171–81; B. Major, 'The Fortified Caves of the Jabal Wastani Region', *Château Gaillard* 22 (2006), 251–7.

[127] WT, pp. 873–4; IA, II, 141–2; KD, *ROL* 3, 534–6; AS, *RHC Or.* IV, 109; MS, III, 324.

[128] N. Morton, *The Medieval Military Orders, 1120–1314* (Harlow, 2013), pp. 24–7, 36–41; Berend, *Gates of Christendom*, p. 28.

[129] IA, II, pp. 144–9; KD, *ROL* 3, 538–40; AS, *RHC Or.* IV, 108–9.

[130] WT, pp. 874–5; Robert of Torigny, p. 224; IA, II, 144–9; KD, *ROL* 3, 538–40; AS, *RHC Or.* IV, 108–9; MS, III, 324–5; *1234*, II, 121–2.

[131] Cahen, *Syrie*, pp. 409–11; Elisséeff, *Nur ad-Din*, II, 593–4; Asbridge, *Crusades*, p. 260.

[132] WT, pp. 874–5; IA, II, 148.

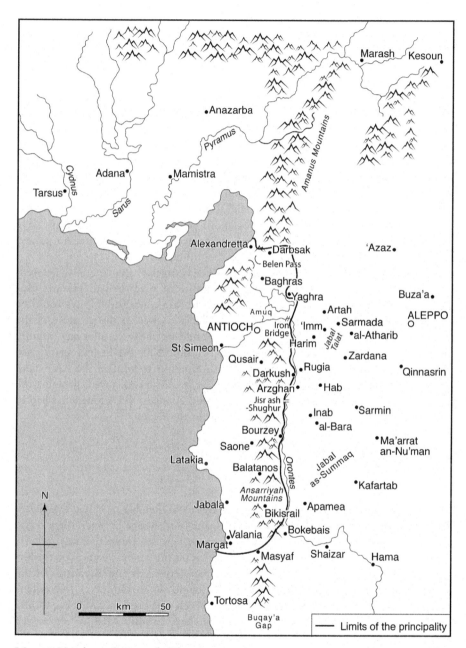

Map 6: Northern Syria and Cilicia, 1165

47

realistically no need to push any further west. This was made especially pertinent given that, as will be explored below, conflict with the kingdom of Jerusalem over control of Egypt demanded his attention.

To the north, matters were calmer. Renaud of Châtillon was even able to target the region around Marash and Duluk for raiding: although, as already noted, he was captured on his return journey from this expedition and imprisoned at Aleppo. Importantly, Greek and Armenian forces now began to provide regular support to Antioch. With an imperial *dux* of Cilicia resident at Tarsus, and Thoros peacefully settled in his lands, both could enter northern Syria and seek to contribute militarily in the struggle against Nur al-Din – which they did at Buqay'a Gap in 1163 and Artah in 1164. Both Manuel – who had married Raymond and Constance's daughter, Maria, in 1162 – and Thoros were even said to have contributed to Bohemond III's release in 1165 (with the former doing so in return for securing the return of a Greek patriarch to Antioch).[133] In comparison to the instabilities of the early 1130s and 1150s, Cilicia had steadied, and although repossession of this region by the Antiochene Franks remained impossible if positive ties with Byzantium were to be maintained, it was during the early 1160s that the Eastern Christian powers of this region were of their greatest use to the principality.

This was a period, therefore, in which the last vestiges of security on the eastern frontier were wiped away by Nur al-Din's capture of Arzghan and Harim's ultimate loss. While it may have been hoped that full-scale territorial losses could be prevented by support from Byzantium and Cilicia, as well as the presence of the military orders on troubled borders, Antioch could not hope to offer any military pressure on Aleppo without first recovering Harim. Nur al-Din had again used the central territorial corridor around Jisr ash-Shughur to weaken the Latins and inflict a chastening defeat. Once more, however, his hand was stayed; meaning the principality's endurance continued to retain value. As such, the Antiochenes had to find more varied ways to secure influence within the region.

1169–1174: Cilicia in Crisis

Although the principality's eastern frontier was as vulnerable as it had ever been, the years 1168–1174 were relatively calm, with the border zone between Aleppo and Antioch remaining static. For Köhler, northern Syria was no longer a lively military frontier, rather it served as a pressure point, becoming an active zone of conflict only when the Zengid ruler wanted to distract Jerusalem and Byzantium from an alliance to seize Egypt before Nur al-Din could do so himself.[134] The sultan's efforts to break the inter-Christian coalition, which had been so damaging to him at Buqay'a Gap, by allying with Thoros' aggressive brother Mleh – who seized

---

133   WT, pp. 877–9; MS, III, 324–6. See also pp. 212–3, 229–30 of this book.
134   Köhler, *Alliances and Treaties*, p. 199. See also Lilie, *Byzantium*, pp. 189–93, 198–202.

power following his sibling's death – and thus isolating the Armenians from the Franks and Byzantium, appear to substantiate this. Nevertheless, this in turn added political value to the principality's endurance, as its full-scale destruction was not considered profitable.

Perhaps the clearest indication of this is that, in the years before his death in 1174, Nur al-Din made only sporadic, small-scale attacks on Antiochene territory, with greater pressure exerted instead on the now leaderless county of Tripoli, which was governed by King Amalric of Jerusalem after Count Raymond III's capture at Artah in 1164.[135] Even when another devastating earthquake struck in 1170, the sultan did not attempt to take advantage of Latin weakness caused by damage to Antioch, Latakia and Jabala, preferring to concentrate on his own repairs and not to provoke imperial intervention.[136] Nur al-Din did still send raiding parties into Syria while campaigning in Mesopotamia in 1171, perhaps to draw Latin attention away from the anti-Latin Mleh's rise to power; while he was quick to launch reprisals when Bohemond III seized Egyptian ships at Latakia in 1172.[137] The Zengid ruler was evidently keen to remind the Antiochenes of his military supremacy, even if there are no suggestions that he sought to continue the territorial acquisitions of the early 1160s. Events in Cilicia nonetheless demonstrate that he was not entirely disinterested in weakening the principality.

When Thoros died in 1168, he left his son, Rupen II, to govern Cilicia under the tutelage of a certain Thomas. However, soon after this, Thoros' brother Mleh seized power from his nephew with the support of Nur al-Din, with Thomas fleeing to Antioch.[138] With Zengid support, Mleh demonstrated an opposition to ties with Byzantium and even expelled the Templars from the Amanus Mountains. At this moment, the coalition was dead. The Armenian-Zengid alliance was seemingly short-lived, though, as Mleh had reportedly ended his association with Nur al-Din by 1172, but the damage had been done.[139] The direct danger to Latin authority was eventually terminated in around 1171/1172 through a joint campaign led by Amalric and Bohemond III (who had earlier tried to combat Mleh himself), and possibly with Manuel Komnenos' support.[140] Magdalino has commented that the activities of the Armenian warlord, who he regarded as Nur al-Din's 'client prince', helped 'to bind Antioch to Constantinople'; and it is undoubtedly true that renewed instability in Cilicia would have been as alarming to the Antiochene Franks as it had been in the 1130s.[141] Interestingly, one fourteenth-century Muslim author, al-Dahabi, considered this ultimately doomed coalition 'a rare error of judgement' in Nur al-Din's

[135] Elisséeff, *Nur ad-Din*, II, 615; Köhler, *Alliances and Treaties*, pp. 203–4; J. Richard, *Le comté de Tripoli sous la dynastie toulousaine* (Paris, 1945), pp. 33–8.

[136] WT, pp. 934–6; IA, II, 185–6; AS, *RHC Or.* IV, 150; MS, III, 339; *1234*, II, 127; Sempad, *Chronique*, p. 53; Mayer, 'Das syrische Erdbeben', pp. 474–84.

[137] KD, *ROL* 3, 550; IA, II, 200.

[138] Sempad, *Chronique*, pp. 52–3. See also Elisséeff, *Nur ad-Din*, II, 655–6, 675–6, 691–2.

[139] WT, pp. 948–50; IA, II, 210; KD, *ROL* 3, 553–4; JK, pp. 214–17; MS, III, 331; Sempad, *Chronique*, pp. 53–4.

[140] WT, pp. 948–50; JK, p. 217.

[141] P. Magdalino, *The Empire of Manuel I Komnenos 1143–1180* (Cambridge, 1993), pp. 75, 107.

foreign policy.[142] However, Chevalier has argued that the union emanated from the Zengid ruler's desire to engineer a further buffer zone with Byzantium, which is certainly plausible; although, conversely, such actions also threatened to initiate a fresh imperial visit to the region.[143] It is also possible that Nur al-Din's efforts here reflected a need to distract Jerusalem and Byzantium from an alliance against Egypt, or even a hope that, by fostering inter-Christian tensions, he would destroy a once profitable allegiance and also block Amalric's reported attempt to promote mass Armenian migration into the kingdom at the expense of the Muslim populace.[144] For the most part, the *détente* proved a failure, as Mleh's loyalty was often in question and he was deposed in 1174; yet the long-term implications of these events may have been greater.[145] Indeed, as will be demonstrated below, although good relations were temporarily restored between Antioch and Armenia under Rupen III, it was not long until tensions re-emerged. The alliance between Nur al-Din and Mleh may thus have sown the seeds for the conflict which erupted at the end of the twelfth century and created the succession crisis which fractured the principality in the first decades of the thirteenth century.[146]

When compared to the previous decade, the period leading to Nur al-Din's death was one of relative calm for the principality. The eastern frontier was weak, and the sultan seems to have been content to use the Antiochene Franks as a distraction to events in Egypt rather than to eliminate its existence. This helps to explain the attempt to create a Cilician buffer zone through an alliance with Mleh, as it drew Jerusalemite and Byzantine attention away from North Africa and represented a clear attempt to break the emerging Christian coalition which, as Augé has noted, was beginning to offer a strong challenge to Muslim supremacy.[147] Furthermore, it raises certain questions over the efficacy of the deterrent now offered by Manuel Komnenos, especially after the failure of joint ventures with the Franks in Egypt. Nur al-Din nevertheless continued to favour peace over destruction, even after Sunni power was established at Cairo in 1169, preferring to spend the next five years seeking the support of the caliph of Baghdad for conquests against the Turks, as well as his position as leader of the *jihad*.[148] This indicates that the principality's presence in the political world of northern Syria remained more favourable than

[142]   Al-Dahabi, *Kitab Duwal al-Islam (Les Dynasties de l'Islam)*, trans. A. Nègre (Damascus, 1979), p. 228.

[143]   Chevalier, *Ordres*, pp. 106–11; C. Mutafian, 'The Brilliant Diplomacy of Cilician Armenia', *Armenian Cilicia*, ed. R. Hovannisian and S. Payaslian (Costa Meza, CA, 2008), pp. 96–7.

[144]   Lilie, *Byzantium*, pp. 189–211; I. Augé, *Byzantins, Arméniens et Francs au temps de la croisade. Politique religieuse et reconquête en Orient sous la dynastie des Comnènes (1081–1185)* (Paris, 2007), pp. 250–307; G. Dédéyan, 'Un projet de colonisation Arménienne dans le Royaume Latin de Jérusalem sous Amaury Ier (1162–1174)', *Le Partage du Monde: Échanges et Colonisation dans la Méditerranée Médiévale*, ed. M. Balard and A. Ducellier (Paris, 1998), pp. 101–40.

[145]   MS, III, 361; *1234*, II, 133; Sempad, *Chronique*, p. 55.

[146]   Cahen, *Syrie*, pp. 579–631; Burgtorf, 'War of Succession', pp. 196–211.

[147]   Augé, *Byzantins*, pp. 277–95, 306–7.

[148]   E. Sivan, *L'Islam et la Croisade: idéologie et propagande dans les réactions musulmanes aux Croisades* (Paris, 1968) pp. 85–7; Köhler, *Alliances and Treaties*, pp. 202–12; Elisséeff, *Nur ad-Din*, II, 638–93.

its disappearance, particularly given the added difficulties offered by the growing influence of the Kurdish general Saladin, who had himself declared Sultan of Egypt and had begun to break away from Zengid control with the support of his family, known as the Ayyubids.[149] However, despite the relative lack of martial activity and the swift breakdown of ties between Mleh and Nur al-Din, lasting damage had been done to the relationship between the Antiochene Franks and Cilicia, which undermined the principality's long-term security.

1175–1187: The Rise of Saladin and Recovery in Cilicia

The situation changed with Nur al-Din's death in 1174. With Aleppo now controlled by his child heir, al-Salih, a fierce battle raged between the Zengid ruler's advisors and relatives – particularly Izz al-Din of Mosul – on the one hand, and on the other Saladin, who had used this instability to swiftly assert independent control over Damascus and now called on the caliph of Baghdad to recognise his status as leader of the *jihad*.[150] The relationship between Nur al-Din and Saladin had begun to fragment even before 1174, but the discord the latter's actions engendered in the years which followed the former's death resembled the disunited territories which the armies of the First Crusade had witnessed and exploited in the late 1090s.[151] The Antiochenes were thus offered an important opportunity to recover their influence. This was hampered, however, by Manuel Komnenos' death in 1180, and by Bohemond III's decision to immediately divorce his Greek wife, Theodora Komnena, in order to marry an Antiochene woman, Sybil. This act incited Antioch's patriarch, Aimery of Limoges, to excommunicate the prince and place the principality under an interdict, and Bohemond to violently attack Church property. It also caused a noble rebellion led by the lord of Margat, Renaud II Masoir, the effects of which appear to have lasted until 1182 and were such a source for concern that King Baldwin IV of Jerusalem sent a delegation to attempt to settle the dispute.[152] As this was happening, anti-Latin riots were sparked in Constantinople by the usurpation of power by Manuel's relative, Andronikos Komnenos, who had Maria of Antioch and her son, Alexios II, murdered.[153] This permanently removed the safety net of future Byzantine intervention, although it also opened the way for the potential recovery of Cilicia.

Conflict on the eastern frontier again revolved around Harim and the Iron Bridge. From 1174 to 1187, no fewer than four attempts were made to recover Harim, often with the complicity of its Muslim governors. The first such occasion occurred sometime between 1175 and 1177. During this time, Harim's Muslim

[149] M. Lyons and D. Jackson, *Saladin: The Politics of the Holy War* (Cambridge, 1982), pp. 47–70.
[150] *Ibid.*, pp. 81–200; Sivan, *L'Islam*, pp. 93–130.
[151] Köhler, *Alliances and Treaties*, pp. 7–58.
[152] See also Buck, 'Noble Rebellion', pp. 93–121; and pp. 99–100, 214–15, 236 of this book.
[153] Lilie, *Byzantium*, pp. 222–9.

governor, Gumushtegin, who had previously been a powerful figure in Aleppo but had lost al-Salih's support over an attempt to assassinate one of the sultan's trusted allies, now offered to surrender the fortress to Bohemond III in return for money or protection.[154] In response, al-Salih had Gumushtegin executed. However, the threat of an Antioch–Aleppo alliance, which had not happened since the 1110s, sparked Saladin into action, as he raided the principality and took control of Kafartab and Ma'arrat an-Nu'man.[155] This was a calculated move, as it allowed him to monitor movements across the Jabal as-Summaq. That Saladin did not look to capitalise further on these gains perhaps reflected a hope that Aleppan weakness might spur the Franks into action and thus allow him to further promote his aptitude as leader of the *jihad*. These events certainly demonstrate the fragile nature of Muslim politics, for a troubled succession now threatened to reawaken the divisions which had allowed the Latins to first consolidate their place in the Near East. Moreover, as Saladin may have hoped, the Antiochenes were indeed drawn into action, as, undeterred by Gumushtegin's demise, they attempted to recover Harim in late 1177 with the support of Count Philip of Flanders. Despite perhaps having initially been spurred on by its Muslim garrison, angered by their leader's execution, the castle was not relinquished. Therefore, as the siege dragged on over the harsh northern Syrian winter, which also witnessed a famine, a pay-off was eventually agreed with al-Salih, as both sides evidently recognised the benefits of preventing Saladin's intervention.[156] Attentions then turned further south, with a raiding expedition launched against Shaizar in 1179, probably in conjunction with its sale to the Templars and the Hospitallers, and a joint venture with Raymond III of Tripoli into the kingdom of Jerusalem, perhaps with the intention of intervening in the succession crisis surrounding the reign of the leprous king, Baldwin IV.[157] Nur al-Din's death had sparked the Antiochenes into action, although the need to show sensitivity to the emerging political fracture between the Zengids and Ayyubids appears to have limited the scope for territorial success. Instead, by acquiescing to al-Salih's requests for peace, the Latins could both gain financial rewards similar to those exacted from Aleppo in the opening decades of the twelfth century, and also help to prevent Saladin uniting Muslim Syria to the vast resources of Egypt: a dangerous prospect for the entire Latin East.

Following this, Bohemond III sought to further strengthen the south-eastern frontier in 1180 by selling Bokebais, Bikisrail (now in Frankish hands) and other fortified sites to the Spanish Military Order of Santiago di Compostella, with whom ties may have been facilitated by Patriarch Aimery, who had earlier spent time in Iberia.[158] The charter of donation for these lands included the stipulation that the Order could 'have in fief and by perpetual hereditary right those lands

[154] BD, p. 54; KD, *ROL* 4, 149–50; IA, II, 255–6; AS, *RHC Or.* IV, 163; IS, p. 38; MS, III, 375–6; *1234*, II, 142.
[155] BD, p. 52; KD, *ROL* 3, 563–4; AS, *RHC Or.* IV, 182–3. See also Asbridge, *Creation*, pp. 47–80.
[156] WT, pp. 984–7; BD, p. 54; IA, II, 54–60; AS, *RHC Or.* IV, 189–92; MS, III, 373–6; *1234*, II, 142–3.
[157] *CGOH*, I, 559; IA, II, p. 262; AS, *RHC Or.* IV, 198; WT, p. 1007. See also p. 238 of this book.
[158] Mayer, *Varia*, pp. 114–17; Hamilton, 'Ecumenist', p. 271.

which were granted to them by us if they are able to come and conquer them within one year'.[159] This suggests Bohemond – who may have been boosted by a recent truce with Saladin, who had travelled north to bring the Seljuks under his sway – actively hoped to stimulate a renewed series of conquests, especially given the limited time frame offered.[160] The likely context for this, and potentially also the aforementioned move on Shaizar with the Templars and Hospitallers, may have been al-Salih's decision to pursue an antagonistic stance towards the Isma'ilis. With their strong powerbase in the mountains, and despite being listed as land-holders in Bohemond's 1180 charter, the Isma'ilis proved their danger when, in reaction to al-Salih's actions, they opened diplomatic channels with Saladin.[161] Fear of such an alliance could certainly have forced the prince into seeking further help in defending the southern frontier. Nevertheless, in spite of these hopes, the Order do not appear to have taken up the offer. Moreover, the arrival of news of Manuel Komnenos' death soon after, as well as the disruption of the ensuing noble rebellion, probably put paid to any hopes of Antiochene military action in support of such conquests. It may even have led Patriarch Aimery to advise the Iberian Order not to come to the East.

Yet, with al-Salih's death in 1181, Antioch was offered the chance to take a more prominent position in northern Syria, as the Zengids desperately sought allies against Saladin. That same year, perhaps before the noble rebellion had fully emerged, the Latins reportedly used the confusion of a conflict between Izz al-Din and Saladin to attack Harim.[162] Abu Shama believed that the Antiochenes were convinced to retire by the Zengids' offer of an eleven-year truce and an alliance, perhaps with territorial concessions.[163] Malcolm Lyons and David Jackson have suggested that news of this threat to Harim, as well as the truce – which contravened Islamic law in its length – were fabricated by Saladin in order to diminish Izz al-Din's suitability as leader.[164] Even if this is so, that Harim, and the principality more generally, could be used in this way is testament to their combined significance to the region's wider political framework. This is also demonstrated by the fact that another attempt was made to capture Harim in 1183, perhaps again with the complicity of its governor, a *mamluk* named Surhak.[165] The Latins failed, and Bohemond then travelled south to aid Jerusalem against Saladin, but the Ayyubid capture of Aleppo later that year only served to intensify interest, for Gregory Bar Ebroyo reported that in 1184 Bohemond III attacked Harim and recovered the Iron Bridge, the latter of which having seemingly fallen into Muslim hands.[166] This level of activity was similar to

---

[159] *Ibid.*, p. 117: venerint ... terram sibi a nobis concessam ... possint conquirere, habeant eam in feodum et hereditatem iure perpetuo ... usque ad annum unum.

[160] IA, II, 271–3; AS, *RHC Or.* IV, 211–12. See also Lyons and Jackson, *Saladin*, pp. 147–9.

[161] Daftary, *Isma'ilis*, pp. 369–70.

[162] IA, II, 277–9; BD, pp. 55–6; KD, *ROL* 4, 154–60; AS, *RHC Or.* IV, 213–14, 222–7; GBE, II, 311–12.

[163] AS, *RHC Or.* IV, 222–7. See also KD, *ROL* 4, 157–60; GBE, II, 311–12.

[164] Lyons and Jackson, *Saladin*, pp. 161–3.

[165] IA, II, 295; AS, *RHC Or.* IV, 235–6; KD, *ROL* 4, 167–68; IS, pp. 40–1.

[166] WT, pp. 1046–8; GBE, II, 317; AS, *RHC Or.* IV, 236–7.

the 1150s; yet, whereas the Latins had tangible success in the earlier period, the looming threat of Saladin ensured the 1170s and 1180s were less fruitful.

By 1187, it may even have been felt that Saladin's rise would be too difficult to halt. The extremity of Andronikos Komnenos' actions in Constantinople now precluded co-operation with Byzantium, even beyond his death in 1185, with the lack of external support making it difficult to hinder Muslim activities even if Harim was recovered.[167] Consequently, further sales were now made to the Hospitallers, most prominently Margat and the entire Masoir lordship in February 1187, which some have argued reflected Bohemond III's desire to form a southern buffer zone similar to the Templar march in the Amanus Mountains.[168] This is plausible given the continued insecurities caused by the Isma'ilis and their *détente* with Saladin (which explains the inclusion of Qadmus in the sale), as similar difficulties had heralded earlier donations to the military orders to the north and east. However, the sale of Margat was made not by Bohemond (although he did later confirm it), but by its lord, Bertrand Masoir, who noted his inability to maintain the defences. More importantly, this also represented the largest voluntary surrender of land seen in the principality, as it relinquished the entire southern half of the polity, not just spatially dispersed fortresses. This demonstrates the surmounting pressure placed on Antioch by the inability to properly combat Saladin. It also, perhaps, denotes the limits of princely power: while he was able to send forces to support Jerusalem at the fateful battle of Hattin in 1187, and to combat Muslim and Turcoman forces at around this time, Bohemond was unable to simply subsume the Margat lordship into his own *demesne*.[169]

Meanwhile, events in Cilicia were also to be heavily impacted by the death of Manuel Komnenos. As already noted, Bohemond III had reacted to this news by divorcing his Greek wife, but he also sought to open the way for intervention in Cilicia. Indeed, the prince responded to the breakdown of imperial power by recapturing key cities in this region, perhaps aided by a campaign launched by Saladin against the Armenians in 1180 following his move on the Seljuks.[170] Bohemond's ambitions were initially limited to Tarsus, however, although in 1183 this was sold to the Armenian ruler, Rupen III – with whom ties appear to have initially been strong, as demonstrated by the move there of some of the prince's closest advisors, who were exiled as a result of the noble rebellion.[171] Yet, this was not to last, as a more concerted effort to subject Cilicia to Antiochene rule in 1185 brought Tarsus, Adana and Mamistra back under the prince's sway once Rupen had been taken pris-

[167] WT, pp. 1020–5; NC, pp. 124–49; MS, III, 388–90.
[168] *CGOH*, I, 783; Riis, 'Übernahme', pp. 151–6; Mayer, *Varia*, pp. 162–83.
[169] *Ernoul*, pp. 153–4; *CGT*, p. 42; BD, p. 71; AS, *RHC Or.* IV, 281; GBE, p. 328; Robert of Auxerre, 'Chronicon', *MGH SS* XXVI, 251. Michael the Syrian (III, 400–2) and Sempad the Constable (*Chronique*, pp. 63–4) also mentioned the Turcomans, but not Bohemond III's presence. See also pp. 157–8 of this book.
[170] IA, II, 272–3; AS, *RHC Or.* IV, 211–13.
[171] William of Tyre (pp. 1046–8) noted that those who went to Armenia were exiled by the prince because they opposed him. This is opposed in Buck, 'Noble Rebellion', pp. 109–14.

oner during a visit to Antioch. Despite Rupen agreeing to recognise Latin power and the Armenians' subject status, his brother, Leon II, retaliated violently to these actions and had succeeded in recovering all of these cities by 1187.[172] Bohemond III had thus attempted to fill the power vacuum left by Manuel's death and failed. He had also created a lasting fracture with the Armenians, as Leon never forgave the prince for his treatment of Rupen and actively pursued revenge – which he finally achieved at Baghras in 1193 (see below). Coupled with the return of Turkish raiding parties to the principality in 1187, the northern frontier was again under threat.[173]

Therefore, while the deaths al-Salih and Manuel Komnenos had provided Antioch with the chance to recover territories and political prominence, this had been largely unsuccessful. In the east, an attempt was made to utilise the instability of Saladin's rise to power to renew the tactics of the 1150s and 1160s, perhaps in the hope that control over Harim would provide a barrier against surprise attacks. The ramifications of the failure to achieve territorial growth were temporarily mitigated by the Zengids' willingness to come to terms, but as Saladin gradually secured the compliance of northern Syria's Muslim lords, and relations with Cilicia were soured by Bohemond III's activities, territorial concessions to the military orders emerged as the only remaining hope.

1188–1201: Northern Syria Re-forged

The stark reality of Antioch's vulnerability was demonstrated when Saladin followed up a decisive victory over the kingdom of Jerusalem at Hattin in 1187, which also saw the loss of the Holy City itself, by launching a full invasion of the principality in 1188.[174] The ease with which he wiped away all but a few of the Latin possessions in northern Syria highlights the fact that large-scale territorial losses could no longer be prevented.

When the Ayyubid ruler entered the principality, he did so at Margat. The sale of this fortress appears to have been vindicated, as it withstood his siege with the support of a Sicilian fleet.[175] However, the Hospitallers' focus on defending their own possessions, rather than helping those of neighbouring Antiochene lords or castellans, alongside Bohemond III's decision to refrain from meeting Saladin in the field, allowed the sultan to sweep up most of the principality. This included the economically vital ports of Jabala and Latakia, which were poorly fortified and swiftly fell – perhaps with the aid of a local Muslim *qadi*, Mansur ibn Nabil, who also seems to have negotiated the Frankish surrender of Bikisrail, which had

[172] MS, III, 396–7; Sempad, *Chronique*, pp. 267–8; R. Thompson, 'The Historical Compilation of Vardan Arewelts'i', *DOP* 43 (1989), 209. See also Burgtorf, 'War of Succession', pp. 198–200.
[173] Robert of Auxerre, 'Chronicon', *MGH SS* XXVI, 251; MS, III, 400–2; Sempad, *Chronique*, pp. 63–4.
[174] Asbridge, *Crusades*, pp. 342–64.
[175] ID, pp. 125–6; IA, II, 345; AS, *RHC Or.* IV, 356.

not been claimed by the Order of Santiago.[176] Saladin then captured Saone, an imposing site guarding one of the major routes into the principality from Jisr ash-Shughur, and its dependent castle of Balatanos, as well as the double fortress of Shughur-Bakas and even Bourzey, near to the western bank of the Orontes.[177] The southern and central regions of the principality were now in Saladin's hands. Having completed these attacks, he seized the Iron Bridge, thus giving him unfettered access to the north. The Templar held castles at Baghras, Darbsak, La Roche Guillaume and La Roche de Roissel were also soon captured, as their garrisons were reportedly diminished.[178] This was a surprisingly poor effort, which could reflect the fact that most of their resources had been lost at the battles of Cresson and Hattin in 1187.[179] An attempt was also made to lay siege to Antioch – the lone surviving Latin possession along with the patriarchal castle of Qusair – but a truce was agreed instead. The reasons for this and the apparent survival of Qusair are not definitively known. Little knowledge exists for the latter's fortifications before it was rebuilt with papal funds in the thirteenth century, and so it is possible that it was simply considered too inconsequential to besiege or to record its demise.[180] Regarding Antioch, Saladin appears to have faced internal pressure to allow his forces to return home, and Lyons and Jackson have posited that certain of his allies, particularly those from the former Zengid heartlands of northern Syria and Mesopotamia, feared control of the city would give the sultan too much power and so opposed his efforts – an interesting potential recurrence of Köhler's 'no place doctrine'.[181] Whatever the case may be, the principality had been reduced to its capital, and perhaps one outlying fortress, in a startlingly short space of time.

Bohemond III's apparent inactivity, as well as his limited involvement in the subsequent Western effort to recover the Holy Land known as the Third Crusade, has prompted some modern criticism of his leadership, with René Grousset's suggesting that the prince proved himself an inactive coward.[182] Yet, given the magnitude of this disaster, it would have been very difficult for Bohemond III to act in any other way than to ensure Antioch itself was retained.[183] The dramatic diminishing of the principality's territories also limited the scope for future military involvement in the region, even if it did not spell the end of princely efforts to influence matters. Saladin certainly seems to have feared Bohemond would strike against his interests in northern Syria, ordering a large force to monitor the principality once the period

[176] BD, pp. 83–4; ID, pp. 122, 127–31; IA, II, 345–6; KD, *ROL* 4, 186–7; AS, *RHC Or.* IV, 355–63. See also pp. 176–9 of this book.

[177] BD, pp. 84–6; ID, pp. 132–40; IA, II, 347–52; KD, *ROL* 4, 187–9; AS, *RHC Or.* IV, 364–74.

[178] BD, p. 87; ID, pp. 141–3; IA, II, 352–3; KD, *ROL* 4, 189–90; AS, *RHC Or.* IV, 375–9.

[179] M. Barber, *The New Knighthood: A History of the Order of the Temple* (Cambridge, 2004), pp. 110–14.

[180] Deschamps, *Châteaux*, pp. 351–7.

[181] BD, p. 87; ID, pp. 144–5; IA, II, 353–4; KD, *ROL* 4, 189–90; AS, *RHC Or.* IV, p. 380; Lyons and Jackson, *Saladin*, pp. 290–1; Köhler, *Alliances and Treaties*, pp. 1–19.

[182] R. Grousset, *Histoire des Croisades et du Royaume Franc de Jérusalem*, 3 vols (Paris, 1934–1936, new edn 2006), III, 155.

[183] Particularly given the apparent limitations to military services. For this, see pp. 110–22.

of truce came to an end in 1189.[184] In spite of this, the Antiochene ruler launched a moderately successful raid on Harim, perhaps aided by the fact that the Muslim forces were stationed at Jabala, rather than on the eastern frontier.[185] A further attack met with failure, though, and the prince was forced to seek refuge at Shih al-Hadid, at the north-eastern corner of the Amuq.[186] With Saladin distracted by the events of the Third Crusade, as Richard I of England secured the recovery of Acre and then inflicted a chastening defeat on the Ayyubid Sultan at Arsuf, Bohemond reportedly attempted to recover Jabala and Latakia in September or October 1191. However, it seems these sites had been so badly damaged by Saladin that they could not be retained and the Latins were also ambushed on their return to Antioch.[187] Such reverses showed Bohemond's limited martial strength, but his efforts brought some political success. In October 1192, with the crusade now over, Saladin – exhausted and no doubt keen to secure peace in northern Syria – agreed to provide Bohemond with Arzghan and the Amuq in order to sustain himself and his people.[188] The prince's raiding expeditions had failed to directly recover lost territory, and in reality these sites offered little in the way of actual power, but the pressure exerted on Saladin during the Third Crusade had ensured that rather generous terms were extracted. This suggests a level of political acumen few historians have acknowledged, with the notable exception of Malcolm Barber, who described Bohemond as 'the great survivor'.[189] It also shows that, by this point, the political motivations of the principality did not converge with those of Western crusading powers. Bohemond had initially approached King William II of Sicily to look for help in 1187, while he had also offered to do homage to Frederick of Swabia, the *de facto* leader of the German crusading forces who reached Antioch in 1190 after Emperor Frederick Barbarossa had died in Cilicia, and had also held low-level discussions with Richard while he was in Cyprus.[190] Yet none of these unions came to fruition, with the Antiochene prince even accused of robbing the Germans (albeit not by German sources), and he certainly did not offer his support as Richard's venture faltered during 1192.[191] It is likewise significant that the prince's negotiations at Beirut were entirely separate to the peace which the English King had secured with Saladin at Jaffa in September 1192.[192]

The prince's aptitude for endurance took a blow, though, when a further dispute arose between himself and Leon regarding control of the fortress of Baghras, with

[184] ID, p. 231; IA, II, 367; KD, *ROL* 4, 191.

[185] GBE, II, 330.

[186] BD, p. 132; ID, pp. 242–3, 258; AS, *RHC Or.* IV, 467, 486–7.

[187] BD, p. 185; *CGT*, p. 98. On the Third Crusade, see Asbridge, *Crusades*, pp. 430–76.

[188] BD, pp. 35, 237; ID, pp. 399–400; AS, *RHC Or.* V, 89; Sempad, *Chronique*, pp. 67–8.

[189] Barber, *Crusader States*, p. 354.

[190] Hiestand, 'Antiochia', pp. 94–119; *CGT*, pp. 89–90; Roger of Howden, *Gesta Regis Henrici Secundi*, ed. W. Stubbs, 2 vols (London, 1867), II, 165; IA, II, 374–6; BD, pp. 117, 121, 125; AS, *RHC Or.* IV, 458–9; ID, pp. 232, 250; NC, pp. 228–9; *1234*, II, 151.

[191] G. Loud, *The Crusade of Frederick Barbarossa: The History of the Expedition of the Emperor Frederick and Related Texts* (Farnham, 2013), pp. 164–5, 180–1.

[192] Asbridge, *Crusades*, pp. 477–513.

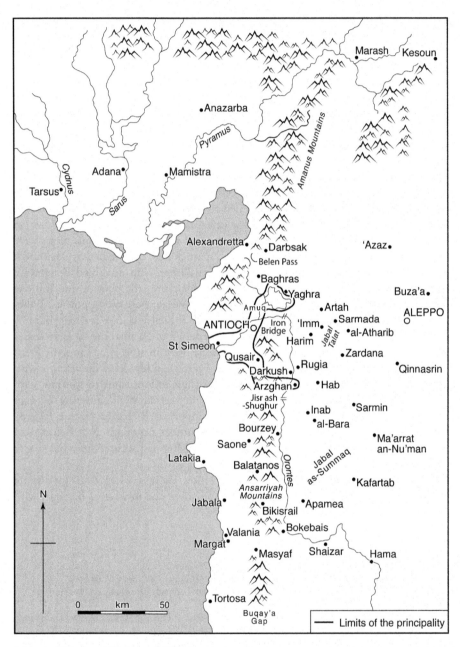

Map 7: Northern Syria and Cilicia, 1193

58

the Armenian having provoked princely ire by occupying the castle following the withdrawal of its Muslim governor in 1189. The ensuing conflict, the roots of which can be found in Bohemond's earlier attempt to influence matters in Cilicia, even led Leon to capture the prince in 1193 – perhaps with the aid of Princess Sybil – and to attempt to launch a coup to seize Antioch. Leon's attempt failed, not least because of the creation of a city-wide commune that opposed him, but he was able to secure a marriage alliance in return for Bohemond's release in 1195. This placed the Rupenids within the princely succession as the union of Bohemond's son, Raymond II, to Leon's niece, Alice, begat an heir to the Antiochene throne, Raymond-Rupen, and thus indefinitely altered the dynamic of Latin–Armenian relations.[193] Significantly, after two gruelling years of imprisonment, the Antiochene prince also appears to have lost some of his former vigour.

Despite this, there was some activity against Antioch's Muslim neighbours following his release. Writing about events in 1196, Kemal al-Din noted the revolt of Frankish prisoners held at Darbsak, which implies that an earlier venture had occurred during which they had been taken captive.[194] Moreover, in 1197, Bohemond is said to have planned renewed ventures against Latakia and Jabala, probably with the aid of German crusaders who had come to the East at the instigation of Emperor Henry VI. Western sources suggest that this led to the temporary Latin re-occupation of these cities, although Muslim sources suggest instead that it prompted the region's Muslim governor to further destroy their fortifications.[195] Whatever the case, in the following year the Antiochene prince appears to have considered aggression less profitable, reportedly counselling the nearby Muslims not to destroy Latakia given that the Franks controlled the coast further south: a move which seemingly resulted in a strong programme of Islamic refortification in the area.[196] In the final years leading up to Bohemond's death in his early fifties in 1201, there were seemingly no further engagements, with the prince perhaps now more focused on organising his succession following the death of Raymond II in around 1197, as he used this opportunity to expel Raymond-Rupen and to promote the claim of his younger son, Bohemond IV, instead.[197]

The years 1188–1201 thus marked the greatest period of territorial loss ever inflicted on the principality. Saladin's campaign wiped away almost all vestiges of Latin resistance, including many of the military order fortifications sold in the hope of greater security. Despite Bohemond's raiding activities and Saladin's generous donation of Arzghan and Amuq, Antioch's power had been largely broken, or at the very least re-aligned. In this period, the political climate of its former territorial extent changed dramatically, with the extension of the Ayyubid Empire and the rise

---

[193] *CGT*, pp. 96, 165–72; *Ernoul*, pp. 318–24; 'Eracles', *RHC Occ.* II, 213–15; AS, *RHC Or.* IV, 379; IS, pp. 256–7, 264; MS, III, 411; Sempad, *Chronique*, pp. 68, 71–2.
[194] KD, *ROL* 4, 212–13.
[195] Roger of Howden, *Chronica magistri Rogeri de Houedene*, ed. W. Stubbs, 4 vols (London, 1868–1871), IV, 28; Arnold of Lübeck, 'Chronica Slavorum', *MGH SS* XXI, 207; KD, *ROL* 4, 214–15.
[196] KD, *ROL* 4, 215–16.
[197] Cahen, *Syrie*, pp. 590–5.

of the Armenians, whose Cilician lands were to be recognised as an independent kingdom by the German Emperor in 1198.[198] There were enduring signs that a continued Latin presence was preferred by certain Muslim powers, but relations with the Armenians were now a severe threat to Frankish control. As the twelfth century passed into the thirteenth, the principality of Antioch's future existence was delicately poised.

Conclusion

The period of the principality's history examined here was bookended by its territorial zenith and its geographic nadir. At the start, Bohemond II ruled a polity which retained power over Cilicia and ensured Aleppo's weakness through control of the Jabal as-Summaq and the Jabal Talat. The death of this young prince coincided with – or perhaps stimulated – the revival of Byzantine interest, as well as the emergence of the Rupenids and Zengids, and resulted in the gradual deterioration of territorial dominance. Various strategic pressure points were to emerge, which had a significant impact on Antiochene aims and security. Indeed, the principality's endurance, and the tactics it pursued, suggests that the Franks had a keen understanding of the value of their topographical surroundings.

In Cilicia, attempts to maintain control were swiftly brushed aside by the Byzantine emperors, although for the most part this, and the growth of friendly relations with the Armenians, ensured a greater level of security. Latin authority would never recover there, however, despite Bohemond III's ambitions in the 1180s, and so the strategic passes of the Amanus Mountains were handed to the Templars. Attempts were also made to renew pressure on Aleppo through the tactic of geographical dominance, but an inability to counter Muslim numerical superiority through the promotion of western migration or extensive conquests ensured that Zengid resources continually undermined Frankish efforts. Harim and the Orontes River crossings thus emerged as key strategic hubs, forming the basis of Antiochene hopes at retaining a presence on the eastern bank of the river. Their efforts failed in the face of the tactical skill of Nur al-Din, who continually destabilised the central corridor around Jisr ash-Shughur and Arzghan, using the instability this created to capture Harim definitively in 1164. This stimulated military order donations in the Orontes Valley, but Nur al-Din was able to unite northern and southern Syria, and in so doing permanently alter the balance of power in the Near East, largely unopposed. Further challenges to authority were provided by the Isma'ilis, as although they proved useful allies in the 1140s, they also frequently undermined Latin control over the south-eastern frontier in the Ansarriyah Mountains, and even created difficulties by fostering ties to Saladin in the 1180s.

---

[198] Burgtorf, 'War of Succession', pp. 198–200.

As the pressure mounted, it took guile and careful diplomatic manoeuvring – as opposed to the military force which had often characterised the careers of Antioch's early rulers – to prevent total collapse, with Frankish princes displaying more political acuity than has hitherto been imagined. This was undoubtedly aided by Byzantine overlordship, although Muslim rulers also seem to have preferred to preserve the principality, either for use as an effective tool to distract Christian interest in Egypt or in order to maintain the balance of power in northern Syria. For many, the principality was evidently of greater use in Latin hands. Its collapse could only be prevented for so long, though, especially once Byzantine interest had crumbled and Bohemond III's clumsy efforts in Cilicia had alienated the Armenians. This allowed for Saladin's success and set Antioch on a long-term collision course with the Rupenids.

It is also important to note that, unlike most other medieval frontiers, the principality was forged within distinct existing political frameworks. The centres of power used by the Latins were the very ones that had defined the balance of power before their arrival.[199] Thus, whereas new castles were established to promote settlement and growth in previously unsettled sites on other frontiers, such as Iberia, the Anglo-Welsh Marches and even the kingdom of Jerusalem, Antioch was tied, to a much greater extent, to the patchwork of northern Syrian politics and to the actions of their neighbours.[200] Proactivity could be demonstrated – as can be seen in the region around the Jabal Talat and at times in Cilicia – but it proved difficult, perhaps even impossible, to utilise tactics similar to the defensive screen of fortresses built around Ascalon by the kings of Jerusalem in the 1130s and 1140s.[201] This ensured that efforts to maintain security focused on relatively small areas of hotly contested land, upon which the general balance of power hinged. As Daniel Power has commented in relation to Ducal Normandy's frontiers, 'even small shifts in the range or intensity of territorial control could have a much broader impact upon the surrounding region'.[202] The keen understanding of the nuances of northern Syria's topography demonstrated by the principality's ruling elites in response to this, was to prove an essential component of their ability to survive, at least until Saladin's conquest and the rise of the Rupenids irrevocably altered matters. As will be seen in the following chapters, it also helped to promote a fluid and dynamic approach to governance, one which could endure even in the face of military disaster.

---

[199] Köhler, *Alliances and Treaties*, pp. 7–20.
[200] Jimenez, 'Frontier', pp. 49–76; Lieberman, *March of Wales*, pp. 34–6; Ellenblum, *Castles*, p. 135.
[201] Ellenblum, *Castles*, pp. 170–7.
[202] Power, *Norman Frontier*, pp. 471–2.

2

The Rulers of Antioch

The princes and ruling elites of Antioch thus faced an array of territorial and political challenges, perhaps more so than in any other contemporary polity. For Claude
Cahen, this created a vigorous, top-down 'feudal' regime, with the prince in full
control of governance and able to extract unlimited service from all fief-holders –
a view largely shared by Hans Mayer.[1] Cahen did admit that the prince was not
the master of administration, insofar as 'legislatively or judicially, the principality
was served in common by the prince and the court'; but this referred more to
notions of delegation, rather than a belief that non-princely factions could keep
the ruler in check.[2] Thomas Asbridge has since argued that a prince's power may
have varied according to personality, while Jean-Marie Martin has posited that the
Antiochene *haute cour* may have increased in authority, which led to a reduction
in the mundane administration of lordly dues through the office of the *secreta*
(a position of Byzantine origins that recorded and maintained the landholding
and financial dues of the region).[3] Yet, no historian has so far truly challenged
Cahen's original thesis. Therefore, the princes of Antioch have been considered
de facto monarchs, exercising the same breadth of authority traditionally – if not
accurately – ascribed to the great kings of the West, and perhaps even more than
the rulers of Jerusalem.[4] Just as modern research has reassessed Western and Jerusalemite 'feudalism', however, arguing for its varied and non-uniform application,
as well as the clear limitations to centralised authority, particularly on contested
frontiers, there is a similar need to re-evaluate the principality's political structures.[5] This is made especially pertinent by the fact that, in leaving behind an

---

[1] Cahen, *Syrie*, pp. 435–52, 527–43. For Mayer, see in particular his discussions on the strength of
Cahen's work and Bohemond III's interaction with the Masoirs in *Varia*, pp. 7–8, 174–83.

[2] Cahen, *Syrie*, pp. 440–1.

[3] Asbridge, *Creation*, pp. 148–68; Martin, 'Structures', pp. 245–7. On the *secreta*, see Cahen, *Syrie*,
p. 454; H. E. Mayer, 'Die Register der Secrète des Königreichs Jerusalem', *Deutsches Archiv* 57 (2001),
165–70.

[4] For the West and Jerusalem, see Bisson, *Crisis of the Twelfth Century*, pp. 1–12; Tibble, *Monarchy
and Lordships*.

[5] Reynolds, *Fiefs and Vassals*, pp. 475–82; and 'Fiefs and Vassals in Twelfth-Century Jerusalem: A
View From the West', *Crusades* 1 (2002), 29–48; Ellenblum, *Castles*, pp. 105–45; P. Edbury, 'Fiefs and
Vassals in the Kingdom of Jerusalem: from the Twelfth Century to the Thirteenth', *Crusades* 1 (2002),

infant daughter in Constance, Bohemond II's death in 1130 – perhaps more immediately politically significant than it was militarily – created the opportunity for the rise of a new ruling dynasty and offered the nobility charged with the task of choosing the new prince the chance to re-negotiate Antioch's relationships of power. Through a careful and critical re-examination of the surviving source material, and the principality's various internal workings, the following chapters therefore seek to examine the prestige and power of Antioch's rulers and the part played by other elements of the ruling elite, particularly the nobility and the Church. It will be argued that, while the prince was no aristocratic pawn, belief in a supreme and uncontested head of state is no longer sustainable. What emerges instead, is the picture of a polity which had to evolve and adapt in the face of the great territorial fluctuations outlined in Chapter 1. While it is not always possible to match internal changes to specific events, due in large part to the survival rate of the sources, it is nevertheless clear that, in response to these military challenges, the ability to exercise authority had to become both fluid and responsive.

The Sources

Before examining the processes of central authority, certain matters pertaining to the documentary and narrative source material must be addressed. The first is that, although the survival rate for charters is notably poorer than in the West or Jerusalem, there remains roughly 100 documents, as well as the thirteenth-century law code known as the *Assises d'Antioche*, from which information can be mined. Caution must be exercised, largely because charters sometimes only survive in later copies or registers, and as such may have been altered, while, as noted in the Introduction, the extent to which the *Assises* actually reflect twelfth-century custom remains questionable. If used carefully, though, both provide an important entry-point into Antioch's internal power structures and legal practices.

Another pertinent issue relating to the documentary evidence is the existence of language which denotes distinct 'feudal' or governmental structures or hierarchies. Interestingly, only five terms appear in the charters to describe the nature of the relationship between the ruler and the other elements of society: *baro*, *homo*, *vir*, *optimas* and *hominio ligio*. These terms mostly appear with possessive prefixes, such as *meum* or *nostrum* ('my' or 'our'), which demonstrates that such figures had a recognised and subordinate connection to the prince. Nevertheless, there is a noticeable lack of definition for the form of these ties. There are occasional references to social hierarchies, such as Bohemond III's allusion to 'barons [and] other of our men' (*baronibus ... ceteris hominibus nostris*) in 1180, but the exact connotations of *baro* or *optimas*, both terms traditionally associated with nobility, as compared to a simple 'man' (*vir* or *hominio*), are unclear.[6] The most frequent term, *baro*, certainly had varied uses in the medieval world. In areas of France it denoted nobility, especially when used to differentiate from a *vavassor* – a term meaning vassal which is absent from Antiochene documents of this period. Elsewhere, *baro* simply meant one involved in governance.[7] As such, terminology may have been used on an ad hoc basis, rather than according to fixed status, perhaps even assuming different meanings in different contexts. This creates difficulties in distinguishing between the aristocratic classes and other groups, like the princely household, retainer knights or officers of state. Thus, when Princess Constance described the *Laodicensium baronum*, or 'the barons of Latakia', in 1151, it is unlikely that she referred only to the great noble families, of whom only the Sourdevals had a known vested interest here. Rather, it alluded more generally to those involved in administration.[8]

Similar problems surround another term: *hominio ligio*. This refers to liege homage, traditionally considered a specific form of social contract whereby a vassal owed a level service to one overlord which superseded any similar agreements made with other lords – thus making it particularly prevalent in frontier lands which traversed more than one sphere of influence.[9] Recently, though, Susan Reynolds has argued that the term denoted allegiance only in the broadest possible sense and lacked rigid definition.[10] Without discernible proof, Cahen believed *ligio* first appeared in the principality before 1149 and related to all fiefs held directly from the prince.[11] Martin has gone further, contending that it denoted all vassals, whether directly or sub-enfeoffed, citing as evidence for this the three apparent types of identifiable landholding in Antiochene charters: the *propria*, or princely lands; the *dominationes*, meaning those possessions reserved by the prince; and the *liggiancias*, enfeoffed lands.[12] However, as the description of such a hierarchy of possessions is found in only a very small number of documents within the principality, and not before 1168, it is likely that these arguments also stem from liege homage's prominence in the *Assises d'Antioche*, where it is seemingly the foremost term used for vassals.[13] Yet, even in this text there are problems, for not all versions of the

6   Mayer, *Varia*, pp. 116–17. Rubin ('Feudalism', pp. 57–8) argued that William of Tyre used *hominium* as a synonym for *homagium*, and thus denoted one who has sworn fealty.
7   D. Barthélemy, 'Castles, Barons and Vavassors in the Vendômois and Neighboring Regions in the Eleventh and Twelfth Centuries', *Cultures of Power: Lordship, Status, and Process in Twelfth-Century Europe*, ed. T. Bisson (Philadelphia, PA, 1995), pp. 58–61; Asbridge, *Creation*, p. 151; P. van Luyn, 'Milites et Barones', *Cahiers de Civilisation Médiévale 36e année* 143 (1993), 281–95; Z. Hunyadi, '*Maiores, Optimates, Nobiles*: Semantic Questions in the Early History of the Hungarian Nobility', *Annual of Medieval Studies at the CEU* 4 (1996/1997), 204–11.
8   *CGOH*, I, 198. For the Sourdevals, see p. 131 of this book.
9   F. Ganshof, *Feudalism* (London, 1952), pp. 93–5.
10 Reynolds, *Fiefs and Vassals*, p. 214; and 'Fiefs and Vassals', p. 38.
11 Cahen, *Syrie*, pp. 527–8.
12 Martin, 'Structures', pp. 240–1.
13 CGOH, I, 391, 783; *Assises d'Antioche*, pp. 8–42.

Assises carry this term, and its modern translator, Leon Alishan, at times utilises 'liege' when the Armenian instead reads *djord*, a word for servant.[14] Belief that *ligio* was so codified, widespread and indelibly tied to the prince, is thus difficult to substantiate, at least for the twelfth century. This is made all the more pertinent by the fact that Bertrand Masoir, lord of Margat, claimed to have his own *liggiancias* in a charter of 1187 – a document Bohemond III himself re-confirmed.[15] Moreover, when large groups of vassals were described in the charters, the preferred term was not *homini ligii*, as might be expected if it related to all fief-holders, rather it was *barones*. This raises important questions regarding William of Tyre's comment that, when Bohemond II first arrived at Antioch in 1126, 'all of the nobles and great men of the region exhibited liege fealty [to him]' – a statement which appears to be an expansion from Fulcher of Chartres' comment that they had agreed to 'the submissive fealty of human nature' – as well as the similar 'liege' oath the archbishop suggested Raymond of Poitiers provided to John Komnenos in 1137.[16] Even if true, that such an oath was seemingly not repeated for or by any other prince, with the apparent exception of Raymond to Manuel Komnenos in 1145, raises the possibility that imperial instances reflected Byzantine perceptions of this term, not its actual use in the principality.[17]

In fact, there are only four documentary references to individuals who owed liege homage in this period, and it is unclear whether it referred to all of their assets or merely those listed in the charters. The earliest is Guy Falsart, a relative of Duke Geoffrey of Antioch, who appeared in a charter 1168. In this, he received a wasteland on the road to the Iron Bridge, along with the revenue of a ninth part of a former debt of assize owed at Antioch.[18] Unfortunately, it is not noted whether his *ligence* encompassed all or just some of these possessions. Likewise, while Walter II of Sourdeval belonged to one of Antioch's great families, his appearance as *hominio ligio* in 1179 related only to revenues at Jabala and Latakia, not his ancestral holdings at Laitor.[19] It is also highly unlikely that Bohemond III claimed homage for all of Count Joscelin III of Edessa's estates, especially those in the kingdom of Jerusalem, on top of those which were presented to the latter, as a princely liegeman, near to Arzghan and Darkush in 1179.[20] Finally, there is very little information for

---

14   A. Ouzounian, 'Les Assises d'Antioche ou la langue en usage: remarques à propos du texte arménien des Assises d'Antioche', *La Méditerranée Arméniens: XII–XV siècle*, ed. C. Mutafian (Paris, 2014), pp. 143–7.

15   CGOH, I, 783.

16   WT, pp. 613–14 (here 613): universi proceres et magnates regionis ... fidelitatem ligiam ... exhibuerent; and 671; Fulcher of Chartres, pp. 821–2 (here 822): humanitatis subditam fidelitatem. See also pp. 194–5 of this book.

17   JK, p. 36. On the Byzantine use of this term, see A. Kazhdan, *The Oxford Dictionary of Byzantium*, 3 vols (Oxford, 1991), III, 1243.

18   CGOH, I, 390.

19   Delaville Le Roulx, *Archives*, pp. 142–4.

20   *Tabulae Theutonici*, 9. See also H. E. Mayer, 'Die Seigneurie de Joscelin und der Deutsche Orden', *Die geistlichen Ritterorden Europas*, ed. J. Fleckenstein and M. Hellman (Sigmaringen, 1980), pp. 171–216.

Peter of Amalfi, the viscount of Antioch who appeared as *hominio ligio* in 1175, beyond his receipt of revenues from the prince.[21] The only common factors to provide clues on the exact nature of Antiochene liege homage, therefore, are that in each example the possessions were within the prince's own lands (or *demesne*) and that they were almost exclusively financial. It is thus difficult to accept Cahen and Martin's conclusions regarding the extent of liege homage. Likewise, Jonathan Rubin's assertion that in William of Tyre there is a sense that 'the term *ligius* was used to indicate a particularly strong bond created by a specific kind of oath', thus implying the existence of a hierarchy of oaths similar to traditional Western models, cannot be firmly attributed here.[22] This is again suggested by the example of a charter, discussed in greater depth in Chapter 4, in which a certain Thomas of Jabala donated a fief, held from Renaud II Masoir, in the presence of Bohemond III in 1178.[23] From this document, it is evident that Thomas had ties to both the lord of Margat and the prince of Antioch, so the absence of the term *ligio* demonstrates that this term was not the relevant form for the multi-layered social contracts traditionally described as liege homage. Indeed, the only argument which can be presented with any confidence is that, for this period at least, liege homage at times related to money fiefs and perhaps, albeit not exclusively given Bertrand Masoir's 1187 charter, the partitioning of the princely *demesne*. This helps to explain why the earliest documentary examples for *hominio ligio* and *liggiancias* are from 1168, just four years after the final loss of Harim and the eastern frontier. The waning of the ruler's domains, and the principality as a whole, would have ensured revenues became the prevalent form of patronage and may also have spurred the introduction of this form of 'feudo-vassalic' relationship.[24] Saladin's conquests of 1188 would have accelerated this process, which might account for liege homage's apparent prominence in the *Assises*. This conclusion, while complementing Reynolds' belief in this term's ambiguity in the West, demonstrates the influence that territorial losses could have on administration, and also breaks from traditional historical opinion for Antioch. It even betrays unique differences to Jerusalem, where this form of homage is said to have been exclusively used to tie rear vassals to the king.[25]

Another issue for an examination of authority relates to the narrative source base. As no internal chronicle to rival that of Walter the Chancellor survives for the period after the 1120s, any investigation into the principality's internal workings is reliant on external texts, above all William of Tyre's *Chronicon*. There are certain problems in relying too strongly on this account, given the date and place of its composition, as well as confusion over William's access to reliable Antiochene information – which is highlighted by the aforementioned discussion on his use of liege homage. Nonetheless, William was well educated, having been trained

21 Rey, *Recherches*, pp. 22–3.
22 Rubin, 'Feudalism', pp. 55–7.
23 *CGOH*, I, 545. See also pp. 155–6 of this book.
24 This undermines the accuracy of William of Tyre's aforementioned account of Bohemond II's arrival.
25 Edbury, 'Fiefs', p. 56; Rubin, 'Feudalism', pp. 55–7.

in law at Bologna, and was an experienced member of Jerusalemite governance. Peter Edbury and John Rowe have noted that this manifested in a clear dislike of those who illegally laid claim to titles and positions, for he had a distinct idea of how '[legal] transactions were done, or were supposed to be done'.[26] In response to this, Rubin has remarked that, while William had clear perceptions of legal frameworks, these 'do not necessarily mean that it was perceived that way by the parties involved'.[27] Yet, although the *Chronicon* is a challenging source, there is reason to believe that William would have shown sensitivity to the legal implications of social titles, with Conor Kostick even describing him as 'an extraordinarily attentive scholar … one who far surpasses his contemporaries in his awareness of social distinctions and [who] advanced sociological concepts'.[28]

One way in which William's value can be established is by examining his lexicon for Antioch's social frameworks. Importantly, such an analysis yields a complex array of terms, even if limited to his narrative of affairs in the principality for the period after 1127 (that is once he could no longer rely on other known narratives for his information). For the major men, there is: *maiores, magnates, potentiores, principes, nobili, proceres, primores, potens, optimes* and *prudentes*; and for the lesser men: *populi maiores, comitatu, fidelium, honesto comitatu, magis familiares* and *domesticorum*.[29] The absence of *baro* in this list is of interest because, as was established above, it remained a somewhat ambiguous term, one which had ultimately not yet achieved definitive meaning. William's reluctance to use *baro*, just as he did not include *feodum* ('fief'), may thus represent a certain amount of linguistic refinement, with neologisms overlooked for terms which had a more classical tradition, secure meaning or, perhaps in the case of *ligio*, were relevant to the kingdom of Jerusalem.[30] The extent of the list William was prepared to utilise nevertheless suggests an author with a keen awareness of, and interest in, the right order of things. It thus remains pertinent to compare the *Chronicon* with the other Latin narratives of the crusader states, to establish whether he lifted terminology from earlier texts or developed a lexicon which more accurately reflected the realities of Antioch's structures of governance, or at least his perceptions of them.

The most important of these is, of course, the *Bella Antiochena* of Walter the Chancellor, an author with unparalleled knowledge of the principality's social structures.[31] In his text, a few key terms for high-ranking men can be identified: *maiores, primates, proceres, barones, senatores* and *domini*; as well as those for retainers or members of the household: *minores, domestica familia, domesticis, curialibus, familiares* and *generis nobilitate*.[32] While there are some common words, such as *proceres*,

26 Edbury and Rowe, *William of Tyre*, pp. 33, 38, 49, 65–9. See also Rubin, 'Feudalism', pp. 53–62.
27 Rubin, 'Feudalism', p. 55.
28 Kostick, 'William', pp. 353–68. This view is generally shared by Rubin ('Feudalism', pp. 53–62).
29 WT, pp. 613–14, 623–5, 635–7, 658–9, 666, 671, 677–80, 702, 754, 754–5, 771–2, 782, 784–6, 833, 836–7, 844–5, 848, 857, 875, 878–9, 948–50, 1014–16, 1047.
30 Edbury and Rowe, *William of Tyre*, pp. 32–43.
31 Asbridge and Edgington, *The Antiochene Wars*, pp. 43–9.
32 WC, pp. 65, 71, 76, 80, 82–7, 90, 98–9, 103.

maiores and *familiares*, and Walter was prepared to use *baro*, it is evident that William's vocabulary was far more extensive. However, another internal Antiochene source, Ralph of Caen's *Gesta Tancredi*, included only one term: *proceres*.[33] Meanwhile, external authors either displayed a more limited range of terminology – Fulcher of Chartres used *proceres*, *gentes* and *optimes* – or demonstrated little overlap with William.[34] For instance, Albert of Aachen utilised *manu*, *societas*, *maioribus domus*, *optimes*, *comitatus*, *sociis* and *satellicio*, reserving *magnates* for figures such as King Baldwin I of Jerusalem.[35]

William's social lexicon was therefore not demonstrably copied from contemporary sources for *Outremer*, but instead reflects his own understanding, or at least perception, of the principality's social structures. The most likely explanation for this is that William's legal education in the West, as well as his experience as chancellor of Jerusalem, provided him with detailed knowledge of social terminology. It is true that this, as well as his own political leanings, could have led William to utilise terms designed to distort reality, with the absence of neologisms certainly denoting a certain amount of linguistic refinement, or that were more suited to Western or Jerusalemite models than they were for Antioch. Nevertheless, it is clear that he held a deep interest in social and political hierarchies, and as an Eastern native well versed in Latin law and governance, his chronicle remains invaluable.

Consequently, while problems exist with the surviving source base, enough remains for an examination of Antioch's political structures. Through this evidence, moreover, as well as comparative studies with the other crusader states and medieval frontiers, it is possible to say more about the relationships of power which underpinned the principality's existence.

The Legitimacy of Princely Authority

Perhaps the most immediate issue relates to how princes were appointed and how their power was then expressed and legitimised in their documents, coins and seals. For any medieval ruler, assignations like emperor, king or prince helped to denote authority and increased their prestige by tapping into wider biblical, or even classical, connotations of supremacy and legitimacy.[36] In this regard, the situation at Antioch before 1130 is of interest. During this period, the princely succession at Antioch appears to have protected the status of Bohemond I's male successor, Bohemond II, as he reached maturity in the West, with stability maintained through the

---

33 Ralph of Caen, *RHC Occ.* III, 312–13.
34 Fulcher of Chartres, p. 621, 633–5, 805–9, 819–22. See also V. Epp, *Fulcher von Chartres: Studien zur Geschichtsschreibung des ersten Kreuzzuges* (Düsseldorf, 1990), pp. 251–87.
35 Albert of Aachen, *Historia Hierosolimitana*, ed. and trans. S. Edgington (Oxford, 2007), pp. 482, 524, 552, 694–8, 738, 818–20, 822.
36 E. Kuehn, 'Melchizedek as Exemplar for Kingship in Twelfth-Century Political Thought', *History of Political Thought* 31:4 (2010), 557–75.

leadership or regency of the nearest male Norman relative or the king of Jerusalem. Yet, the exact political status of Bohemond I's successors, Tancred of Hauteville, Roger of Salerno and Baldwin II of Jerusalem, is unclear, as each acted as sovereign in their own right, even describing themselves as *princeps Antiochenus*.[37] That this is even so for Baldwin II, who styled himself prince of Antioch in a letter sent to the West and on coinage during an interregnum from 1119 to 1126, demonstrates the complexities of princely authority.[38] Gaps in our understanding remain, such as whether an incumbent Norman 'regent' would have actually moved aside for Bohemond II as Baldwin II did in 1126, with Tancred a figure unlikely to have willingly relinquished power. Moreover, it is uncertain whether Walter the Chancellor's description of a decree, issued following *Ager Sanguinis* in 1119 and stipulating that noble landholdings could no longer be altered by a ruler, related to Bohemond II, as well as to the king of Jerusalem, and thus acted as a proviso to their recognition of his right to be prince.[39]

What is evident is that, although the princely title remained a constant for whoever ruled Antioch, the situation regarding the succession, and the methods by which power was legitimised, was irrevocably altered by Bohemond II's death in 1130. Moves to strengthen the nobles' position perhaps began earlier, but they were crystallised by the novel challenge which emerged around the future of the infant heiress, Constance, as a husband was required to co-rule, rather than to act as temporary regent. The events which underpinned the Antiochene reaction to this, and the subsequent impact it had on the nature of the princely succession, offer a crucial insight into the balance of power within Antioch. Indeed, in this moment, the principality's nobles were able to assert a considerable amount of influence over the decision-making processes of designating Constance's husband, which perhaps continued into the 1150s. This alteration to the traditional dynamic also had potential long-term implications for the principality's identity and for the unchallenged, hereditary progression of its ruling house.

Raymond of Poitiers

In 1136, only a year after being invited to northern Syria, Raymond of Poitiers, son of Duke William IX of Aquitaine, arrived in Antioch to become prince.[40] The dynastic situation which had faced Antioch following Bohemond II's death, and had led to Raymond's migration, was unique to *Outremer*. It is true that Fulk of Anjou had come to Jerusalem in 1128 to marry its heiress, Melisende, and eventually to become king, but the decision to approach him had been made, for the most part, by the incumbent king, Baldwin II, not the aristocracy.[41] There are some parallels here with the succession crisis which followed King Henry I of England's death in

---

37   Asbridge, *Creation*, pp. 126–47.
38   See pp. 220–1.
39   WC, pp. 98–9. See also Asbridge and Edgington, *The Antiochene Wars*, p. 145, n. 169.
40   WT, pp. 640–1, 657–9; Orderic Vitalis, VI, 504–6; JK, p. 22.
41   Phillips, *Defenders*, pp. 19–43.

1135, as the nobles there took a prominent role in appointing his nephew, Stephen of Blois, as king. However, the notion of legitimacy still revolved around familial ties, and it is of note that, unlike in Antioch, the decision-making processes of this appointment led to a prolonged civil war.[42] To assign a new ruler without the guidance of an existing figurehead thus placed an unparalleled amount of authority and responsibility into the hands of the Antiochene nobility – a fact largely overlooked by historians. This is especially important given that no patriarchal involvement is mentioned in the sources. It is possible that Patriarch Bernard of Valence, an influential figure before his death in 1135, could have been involved, but the actions of his successor, Ralph of Domfront, upon Raymond's arrival in the East, during which he demanded the new prince pay him homage, suggest that the Church had not been party to negotiations.[43] As demonstrated in Chapter 1, this also came at a time of great instability, due to the important territorial losses inflicted by Zengi and the Armenians. The situation facing the nobles was therefore both delicate and crucial. With this established, the decision to select Raymond of Poitiers, although already subject to a certain amount of historiographical debate, is worth re-examining.

Primarily, historians have argued that the search for a suitor led to a deep internal fracture. The one side, led by Constance's mother, Alice, favoured a Byzantine alliance, and so dispatched an envoy to John Komnenos offering a marriage union, probably as a rival to that sent to Raymond in the West in 1135. The other, headed by King Fulk – who acted as bailiff of the principality – but with the complicity of Antioch's nobility and Church, sought instead to break the so-called Norman hegemony over northern Syria by installing a Western candidate with ties to his Angevin background.[44] Asbridge has since challenged one key aspect of this, demonstrating that Alice did not lack aristocratic or ecclesiastical support when she opposed Baldwin II of Jerusalem's attempt to assert his influence in the immediate aftermath of Bohemond II's death in 1130.[45] Moreover, it is crucial to note that the only source for the Latin envoy to Byzantium, John Kinnamos, cited only the involvement of the 'nobles' of the principality, not the princess.[46] If this is correct, the envoy almost certainly represented the entirety of Antioch's aristocracy, not an isolated faction, and would have been dispatched very soon after Bohemond's death, when Jerusalem's power had been challenged, or at least long before a similar message was sent to Raymond.[47] Nevertheless, there does appear to have been some difficulty upon the Poitevin's arrival in 1136. Indeed, if William of Tyre is to be believed, Alice eventually opposed Raymond's accession, while Patriarch Ralph

---

[42] D. Crouch, *The Reign of King Stephen 1135–1154* (Harlow, 2000), pp. 9–49.

[43] On Bernard, see Asbridge, *Creation*, pp. 200–8. See also pp. 101–3 of this book.

[44] Cahen, *Syrie*, pp. 350, 356–7; Beech, 'Ventures', pp. 69–71; Phillips, *Defenders*, pp. 51–72; Hamilton, 'Ralph of Domfront', pp. 5–8; Lilie, *Byzantium*, pp. 103–4. On Anjou and Poitiers, see B. Bachrach, 'A Study in Feudal Politics: Relations between Fulk Nerra and William the Great, 995–1030', *Viator* 7 (1976), 111–22. See also pp. 222–6 of this book.

[45] Asbridge, 'Alice', pp. 32–6.

[46] Kinnamos, *Epitome*, p. 16 (JK, p. 22): προύχοντες.

[47] See also pp. 191–2, 221–2.

used this opportunity to extract an oath of homage from the new prince before agreeing to perform the marriage ceremony.[48] However, although Alice's actions in 1136 have been taken as corroboration for her preference for a Byzantine alliance, if they are representative of reality, her obstruction, rather than relating – as has been assumed – to a personal desire for power, is more likely to have centred on the fact that, at only eight years old, Constance was not yet of marriageable age.[49] Likewise, although Ralph's ability to forestall the union could indicate certain limitations to noble authority, in truth neither the nobles nor Raymond would have wished to face accusations of an uncanonical marriage. It is also possible that the Antiochenes, mindful of Constance's youth, had not even originally envisaged inviting Raymond in 1135, but had been pushed into accelerating their plans by the Zengid assault on the eastern frontier during that year, as Fulk had initially been too pre-occupied to offer any military support because he was dealing with the aftermath of a rebellion by Count Hugh of Jaffa in 1134.[50] This may have brought forward the wedding and thus provided Ralph with a chance he would not otherwise have had; for there was no precedence for Antioch's princes owing fealty to the patriarch – as had been attempted by Daibert of Pisa as patriarch of Jerusalem in 1100.[51]

In relation to Fulk's supposed attempt to break Norman influence in the East, Phillips has noted that as regent the king had 'effectively recommended to the Antiochenes that they ignore both the Greek and the Sicilian interest in the succession'.[52] This relates, of course, to Byzantium, but also to the apparent interest in Antioch of King Roger II of Sicily, who, as Constance's closest male relative, may have harboured designs on forging an eastern satellite state.[53] The extent of Fulk's influence is seemingly supported by the Norman chronicler Orderic Vitalis, who suggested that Raymond had told John Komnenos in 1137 that Constance had been 'given to him in matrimony *by* Fulk, her kinsman', an assertion also put forth by John Kinnamos, and that he had 'sworn fealty' to the king in doing so.[54] Marc Carrier has dismissed Orderic's account as fantasy; yet, even if it did occur, Lilie is probably correct that it was simply a delaying tactic designed to allow the prince to play for time by sending an envoy to Jerusalem.[55] Caution must certainly be urged in accepting that Fulk had such power within Antioch. Indeed, whereas

---

[48] WT, pp. 657–9.

[49] H. Leyser, *Medieval Women: A Social History of Women in England 450–1500* (London, 1996), pp. 106–22; N. Hodgson, *Women, Crusading and the Holy Land in Historical Narrative* (Woodbridge, 2007), pp. 103–6.

[50] H. E. Mayer, 'Angevins *versus* Normans: The New Men of King Fulk of Jerusalem', *Proceedings of the American Philosophical Society* 133:1 (1989), 1–25.

[51] Hamilton, *Latin Church*, pp. 52–75. See also pp. 102–3 of this book.

[52] Phillips, *Defenders*, pp. 51–2.

[53] G. Loud, 'Norman Italy and the Holy Land', *The Horns of Hattin: Proceedings of the Second Conference of the Society for the Study of the Crusades and the Latin East*, ed. B. Kedar (Jerusalem, 1992), pp. 51–2.

[54] Orderic Vitalis, VI, 504–6: dono Fulconis consobrini sui sibi datam coniugem duxit ... promisi fidem; JK, p. 22.

[55] M. Carrier, 'Ordéric Vital sur les rapports entre Latins et Grecs à la veille de la deuxième croisade', *Memini: Travaux et documents* 11 (2007), 131–50; Lilie, *Byzantium*, pp. 298–308.

charter evidence shows that the king was 'governor and bailiff of the principality of Antioch and of the daughter of Bohemond the younger' in 1134, the clause relating to his influence over Constance had been removed by the time the king issued a charter at Antioch in August 1135, the year in which the decision to send an envoy to Raymond seemingly took place.[56] While the latter document likely post-dates this choice (for it was issued right at the end of sailing season), thus meaning Fulk's influence was not entirely void, this alteration in title still undermines scholarly belief in the extent of his authority.[57] Even the staunchly pro-Jerusalem William of Tyre recorded that the eventual decision was made by 'the common consent of all [the nobles of Antioch]', and that the only oaths of homage Raymond carried out were to Patriarch Ralph and John Komnenos, not to Fulk.[58]

However, it cannot be denied that the king's status in Europe carried a weight which the Antiochene nobility alone did not, and meant he could provide important access to suitable candidates. Some fascination for Antioch's place in the crusading past endured in the West, which can be seen by the growth of the traditions which surrounded the *Chanson d'Antioche*, but patriarchal disputes with the papacy over the primacy of Tyre, which was claimed instead by the Church of Jerusalem, as well as the complications of Greek and Sicilian interests, may have deterred some suitors.[59] Fulk would, therefore, have played an essential role. This does not mean his authority was supreme. The idea that he acted to break the 'Norman hegemony' of northern Syria is thus questionable, even if, as will be explored below, allusions to Antioch's Norman heritage did decline. Moreover, while changes occurred in the ruling house, the principality's nobility remained largely of Norman descent, and there is no evidence for a wholesale attempt to oust internal figures of power, such as Fulk had attempted in Jerusalem during the early 1130s.[60] Although the aristocracy may have feared that Roger of Sicily would seek to supplant their influence by promoting a fresh wave of Norman migration into northern Syria, and so call in to play old social hierarches which had existed in the West, there is little reason to believe they were driven in this impulse by Fulk.

Phillips has suggested that another major factor behind Raymond's appointment was that, as son of William IX of Aquitaine, he came from a distinguished lineage with powerful Western connections, a crusading background and ties to the ruling house of Tripoli.[61] Asbridge has even argued that it was expected Raymond would

---

[56] CCSSJ, 73–4 (here 73): rector et baiulus Antiocheni principatus filieque Boamundi iunioris.

[57] For the sailing seasons, see J. Pryor, *Geography, Technology and War: Studies in the Maritime History of the Mediterranean, 649–1571* (Cambridge, 1988), pp. 87–8.

[58] WT, pp. 640–1 (here 640): communi eorum omnium consilio; and pp. 657–9, 671, 691–2.

[59] S. Edgington and C. Sweetenham, *The Chanson d'Antioche: An Old French Account of the First Crusade* (Farnham, 2011), pp. 44–6; Hamilton, *Latin Church*, pp. 18–51.

[60] Mayer, 'Angevins', pp. 1–25. On Antioch's Norman nobility, see A. V. Murray, 'How Norman was the Principality of Antioch? Prolegomena to a Study of the Origins of a Crusader State', *Family Trees and the Roots of Politics: The Prosopography of Britain and France from the Tenth to the Twelfth Century*, ed. K. Keats-Rohan (Woodbridge, 1997), pp. 349–59; Martin, 'Structures', pp. 232–7.

[61] Phillips, *Defenders*, pp. 53–7.

'bring new wealth and manpower' to the East.[62] Despite Raymond's undeniable pedigree, it should be remembered that he was a non-inheriting heir, reduced to training as a *iuvenis* under Henry I of England, and so the extent to which he had access to large reserves of financial or military resources is uncertain.[63] Having spent time at the Anglo-Norman court, Raymond would have gained experience in the Norman forms of warfare and governance with which the aristocracy were probably also well versed, thus making him an attractive candidate. Nevertheless, although Raymond was able to introduce new figures into princely administration and fief-holding, it is significant that the composition of the surviving aristocracy remained predominantly unchallenged.[64] As such, he represented a choice which, as Phillips noted, was less threatening to the nobles as regards the survival of Antioch's existing power structures.[65] Given the instability caused by Bohemond II's death and the troubles experienced by Fulk in Jerusalem, the desire to prevent internal upheaval would have undoubtedly influenced noble actions – an impulse which, as noted above, may have its roots in the aftermath of *Ager Sanguinis*. This would also have proved a factor behind the decision to overlook the more powerful Byzantium and Sicily, and to instead approach Raymond.

An examination into how Raymond subsequently sought to legitimise his authority adds further complexities to the situation. The most valuable insight comes in the form of the title clause, or *Intitulatio*, of his charters.[66] Indeed, whereas the use of the princely title appears constant throughout the twelfth century, the lack of propagation of familial ties to the founding Norman dynasty as a source of legitimacy after 1130 is revealing. Evoking the great importance of lineage elsewhere in the medieval world, it is certainly clear that ancestral pedigree had earlier been of significance at Antioch, for Bohemond II styled himself 'son of Bohemond the great', while his wife, and later widow, Alice, perpetuated her own Eastern pedigree, as well as that of her husband, by issuing documents as 'daughter of Baldwin, second king of the Latins of Jerusalem, [and] formerly wife of the lord Bohemond, son of Bohemond the Great, the most excellent prince of the Antiochenes'.[67] This appears to support the views of a number of historians who argue for the influence of 'Norman' identity during the early years of Frankish settlement, imparted in the

---

[62] Asbridge, *Crusades*, p. 173. See also Beech, 'Ventures', pp. 69–71; Cahen, *Syrie*, pp. 356–7.
[63] J. Phillips, 'A Note on the Origins of Raymond of Poitiers', *EHR* 418 (1991), 66–7; J. Green, *Henry I: King of England and Duke of Normandy* (Cambridge, 2009), pp. 285–9.
[64] See p. 90.
[65] Phillips, *Defenders*, p. 52.
[66] On the form of charters, see L. Boyle, 'Diplomatics', *Medieval Studies: An Introduction*, 2nd edn, ed. J. Powell (New York, 1992), pp. 82–113.
[67] *Libri Iurium*, I/2, 337: magni Boamundi filius; Mayer, *Varia*, pp. 110–14 (here 113): Adelicia Balduini regis Hiersolymitani Latinorum secundi filia, uxor quondam domini Boamundi, Magni Boamundi filii, excellentissimi Antiochenorum principis. On the importance of lineage in the West, see e.g. N. Paul, *To Follow in their Footsteps: The Crusades and Family Memory in the High Middle Ages* (Ithaca, NY and London, 2012), pp. 21–53.

aftermath of Antioch's conquest.[68] This is most expressly noted in relation to the ruling house's ties to Robert Guiscard, although Timo Kirschberger has recently contended that the ruling elites of the principality created a new, distinctly 'Antiochene' identity – a view with some interest given the express absence of the term 'Norman' in the charters, even if many held on to their Western family names.[69] Before 1136, therefore, a line of descent was being presented leading all the way back to the principality's foundation. This tactic was not unique, as the kings of Jerusalem were sequentially numbered from the conquest – thereby ensuring a sense of continuity – even though the succession rarely passed from father to son and departed the male line after Baldwin II.[70] The situation was more complex in the counties of Edessa and Tripoli as, with some exceptions, there were no allusions to dynastic forebears.[71] Nevertheless, while Antioch's succession more closely resembled Jerusalem's, as both welcomed a Western ruler when the throne passed to a royal daughter, it is revealing that a numbering system did not develop, beyond occasional references to Bohemonds *primi et secundi*.[72]

What did appear during Raymond of Poitiers' reign is the inclusion of novel *Intitulatio* clauses that recognised that a donation was made alongside 'the lady Constance, my illustrious wife' (*domina Constantia, mea uxor illustrissima*). These, and other variants, were used in four of Raymond's eight surviving charters.[73] Significantly, however, while Constance and her dynastic heritage were occasionally recognised, they do not go so far as to say that the princess' permission was required. Comparatively, Fulk of Anjou, whose position as king of Jerusalem was predicated on his marriage to Jerusalem's heiress and so provides a valuable comparison, issued almost all of his charters 'with the assent' (*cum assensu*) of Queen Melisende.[74] Even Bohemond III (examined below) and the counts of Tripoli included such phrases, despite claiming rule through birth.[75] This changed slightly at the end of Raymond's reign for, in a charter confirming Hospitaller possessions in 1149, he stated that it was done '[by] the concession and assertion of my wife Constance, only daughter

---

[68] Murray, 'How Norman was the Principality of Antioch?', pp. 349–59; L. Russo, *I Normanni del Mezzogiorno e il movimento crociato* (Bari, 2014), pp. 155–72. More generally, see also E. Albu, 'Antioch and the Normans', *Crusading and Pilgrimage in the Norman World*, ed. K. Hurlock and P. Oldfield (Woodbridge, 2015), pp. 159–76.

[69] T. Kirschberger, *Erster Kreuzzug und Ethnogenese: In novam formam commutatus – Ethnogenetische Prozesse im Fürstentum Antiochia und im Königreich Jerusalem* (Göttingen, 2015), pp. 351–5.

[70] For example, Fulk of Anjou described himself as *Fulco dei gratia tercius rex Latinorum Iherusalem*, and Baldwin III was styled *Balduinus per gratia dei in sancta civitate Iherusalem Latinorum rex quartus* (*Urkunden Jerusalem*, I, 132, 227). See also Paul, *To Follow in their Footsteps*, pp. 29–30.

[71] *RRH*, 58, 151, 191, 212, 219, 380. For those without allusions in the *Intitulatio*, see 84, 108, 118, 193, 198, 206, 217, 218, 233, 236, 389, 549, 583, 585, 602, 605, 637, 662. On enduring Provençal identity in Tripoli, see K. Lewis, 'Rule and Identity in a Diverse Mediterranean Society: Aspects of the County of Tripoli during the Twelfth Century' (unpublished PhD thesis, University of Oxford, 2014), pp. 137–212.

[72] See e.g. *CCSSJ*, 74.

[73] *CCSSJ*, 76–7; *Libri Iurium*, I/2, 338; *CGOH*, I, 127.

[74] *Urkunden Jerusalem*, I, 131–2, 134–5, 138–9, 141, 146

[75] *CGOH*, I, 472; *Codice Diplomatico*, I, p. 19.

of Bohemond the younger'.[76] The strongest affirmation of the princess' rights yet seen, it may be that, aged twenty-one, she had finally enforced her position, which is seemingly supported by William of Tyre's claim that Constance was happy to rule independently after Raymond's death at Inab.[77] Nonetheless, the issue is further complicated by two other problematic pieces of evidence. First, in his confirmation of Venetian rights in 1144, Raymond was described as 'by God's grace prince of Antioch', with no allusion made to Constance.[78] Further, in an eighteenth-century description of a charter issued in favour of the Hospitallers in March 1139, he was styled 'prince of Antioch, son-in-law and heir of Bohemond'.[79] Regarding the former, the copy which survives is an extrapolation of a later deed, which may explain the anomaly. Yet the latter, if based upon the original Latin, implies that Raymond did not simply claim the princely title without reference to his wife: he designated himself the rightful, independent heir. Given the instability of this time, in addition to the evident desire to look elsewhere than Sicily for leadership, it is unsurprising that the nobles might agree to this. By not perpetuating ties to the Norman foundation, it weakened the ability for Roger to claim any form of legitimate power, for a recognition of Raymond as heir (theoretically) ruled out the possibility for later external challenges to the dynastic legitimacy of his children. The evidence presented here also raises doubts over the accuracy of William of Tyre's report that, when John Komnenos demanded that Raymond surrender 'the city with the citadel and all the other fortifications of the city' in 1142, the Antiochene nobles blocked this because it was 'his wife's inheritance'.[80] Lilie has argued that even the emperor recognised the 'feudal' legality of the aristocracy's assertions, but the charter evidence appears to suggest that such a stance does not accurately reflect Raymond's claim to the princely *demesne*.[81] If the aforementioned 'other fortifications' included aristocratic possessions, which is unclear, then this stance may have had at least some grounding in Antioch's legal practice, for princely control over noble landholdings was not so extensive.[82] As it is, Raymond's hold over Antioch, and the attendant status of the princely title, is likely to have been solid, even if noble influence had been strengthened by their role in his appointment.

Another way in which sovereigns could demonstrate their authority was through their coins and seals. Indeed, the right to mint money, or to use a ruler's impression, were fiercely guarded prerogatives in the West, with abuses of royal or imperial monopolies often met with strict punishment.[83] There is nothing to suggest that Antioch's princes did not hold similar control, which ensures that it is significant

---

76   *CGOH*, I, 183: concessione et assertione uxoris mee Constancie, Buamundi iunioris unice filie.
77   WT, pp. 785–6. See also pp. 226–8 of this book.
78   *Urkunden Venedig*, I, 46: dei gratia Antiochie princeps.
79   *CGOH*, I, 129.
80   WT, pp. 700–2 (here 701–2): urbem ei cum urbis presidio et omnibus indifferenter civitatis munitionibus … uxoris hereditatem.
81   Lilie, *Byzantium*, p. 137.
82   See pp. 150–9.
83   J. Green, *The Government of England Under Henry I* (Cambridge, 1986), pp. 88–91.

that upon Raymond's accession changes also came into effect in the numismatic, and perhaps also sigillographic evidence. Before 1130, Antiochene coins largely used Greek text and included representations of Christ, Saint Peter (the founder of the Church at Antioch) or even Saint George.[84] This ensured a sense of continuity with pre-Latin authority, useful for trading and interaction with indigenous communities, while the inclusion of Saint George was probably also an allusion to the reported appearance of warrior saints alongside the crusaders during the battle of Antioch in 1098.[85] The title of prince was rare, only first appearing in the Greek form, *ΠΡΙΓΚΙΠΟC*, under Roger, which again shows that apparent regent status was not a barrier to the use of the title.[86] Conversely, the coins issued in Raymond's reign, although rarely attested, carried a bareheaded bust on the obverse along with the Latin inscription *RAIMUNDUS*, with *ANTIOCHIE* and a cross on the reverse.[87] The continued absence of *princeps* was not unique, yet gone was the use of Greek text, as well as potential allusions to events of the First Crusade: another symbol of the shifting nature of 'Antiochene' identity. It is harder to discern the evolution of the princely seal as, without secure sigillographic evidence for the period before 1130, adequate context cannot be provided. Therefore, although Gustav Schlumberger has posited that an impression previously attributed to Bohemond III, which carries a mounted figure with a lance over his shoulder and the princely title on the obverse and Saints Peter and Paul on the reverse, could in fact date to the time of Bohemond I or Bohemond II, his arguments remain speculative.[88] If he is correct, then this would indicate a level of continuity throughout the twelfth century, for this style has clear similarities with the surviving sigillographic evidence for Raymond, Renaud and Bohemond III, with the exception that they held their lance couched as if ready to face an unseen enemy.[89] However, one might instead expect changes similar to those identified in the charters and on the coinage.

These developments have important implications for historiographical belief in the nature of authority at Antioch. Indeed, they suggest a significant shift in the way power was legitimised and how it was bestowed. The choice of Raymond, and the processes which led to his selection, reveal that the nobles' decision came following a period of careful discussion, in which a number of options were seemingly explored, including opening diplomatic channels with Byzantium. Raymond's subsequent appointment implies that the Antiochenes favoured a Latin with military and administrative experience, who had suitable, albeit not overwhelming, dynastic prestige. The most prevalent factor behind his selection, however, appears to be that it would not herald widespread change, which implies

---

[84] Metcalf, *Coinage*, pp. 7–8; R. Pesant, 'St. George and the Dragon on the Coinage of Roger of Antioch', *Spink Numismatic Circular* 100:3 (1992), 79.

[85] T. Asbridge, *The First Crusade: A New History* (London, 2004), pp. 239–40.

[86] Metcalf, *Coinage*, pp. 7–8.

[87] *Ibid.*, pp. 32–3.

[88] Schlumberger, *Sigillographie*, pp. 31–5.

[89] *Codice Diplomatico*, I, Plate II; G. Schlumberger, 'Monnaies et sceaux des Croisades', *Mélanges Numismatiques* 2 (1877), plate VIII, no. 10.

an aristocracy concerned with self-preservation. Likewise, although Raymond's authority within Antioch should not be doubted, there are clear signs that his elevation engendered a clean break in the form in which power was legitimised, for a new dynasty had been formed and the dynamics of power between the prince and the nobility had been altered. He was prince through their hand, not through conquest or birth-right, with the lack of references to the principality's foundation both strengthening Raymond's independent position but also serving as a reminder of his debt to the aristocracy. In this regard, it is significant that, whereas the nobles had reportedly sworn submissive fealty to Bohemond II in 1126, no apparent repeat of this ritual can be found in 1136, even if an agreement to safeguard the inheritance rights of the new prince's children – by recognising him as heir – was probably made.[90] Attempts to preserve aristocratic rights may have begun through their post-*Ager Sanguinis* decree, but they certainly found greater crystallisation and strength after 1130.[91]

Renaud of Châtillon

When Antioch was again robbed of its prince by Raymond's death at Inab in 1149, the need to choose a ruler arose once more. The existence of an infant male heir, Bohemond III, evoked similarities with the situation experienced during Bohemond II's minority, although complications were added by the continued presence of Constance, who was evidently prepared to take power for herself.[92] This likewise raises parallels with the circumstances in Jerusalem after Fulk's demise in 1142, as a succession dispute had grown between Queen Melisende, through whom the dynastic bloodline passed, and her son, the heir-apparent Baldwin III – albeit the immediacy of concern was perhaps less pressing in Antioch because Bohemond III was younger.[93] The process by which a minor French nobleman, Renaud of Châtillon, was then chosen as Constance's husband, and thus prince, is unfortunately less well documented than Raymond's elevation. Nevertheless, similar themes are identifiable, such as the involvement of Byzantium and Jerusalem, and, more significantly, a willingness to ensure the preservation of existing internal power structures.

In the direct aftermath of Inab, it was Baldwin III who sought to exert a strong influence over the principality's future, taking apparent responsibility for governance and the search for a new prince. Baldwin eventually failed in this regard, not least because Constance was unwilling to take direction. This was most aptly demonstrated at a council of the crusader states at Tripoli in 1151, during which Baldwin tried to impose upon the princess a decision to marry a suitor taken from three Jerusalemite candidates.[94] In contrast, she appears instead to have preferred

---

90 Fulcher of Chartres, pp. 821–2; WT, pp. 613–14.
91 WC, pp. 98–9.
92 *CGOH*, I, 190, 198; WT, pp. 789–90, 795–7.
93 H. E. Mayer, 'Studies in the History of Queen Melisende of Jerusalem', *DOP* 26 (1972), 93–182.
94 WT, pp. 789–90, 795–7.

to request a suitor from Byzantium; although, having eventually rejected a candidate proposed by Manuel Komnenos, seemingly on age grounds, Constance then,
according to William of Tyre, secretly decided to marry Renaud, albeit only after
first receiving the king's authorisation.[95] The nature of Baldwin's influence at this
point is uncertain, with the need for his permission more likely to relate to Renaud's
pre-existing relationship with the king, for whom he had seemingly acted as a military vassal, than Jerusalem's status within Antioch.[96] Perhaps of greater interest here
is that William of Tyre's account has led some to believe that, unlike in the 1130s,
the aristocracy were not consulted over the union and were thus angered.[97] This
stems in part from William's comment that it was 'not without amazement on the
part of many that so powerful and illustrious a lady and wife of so excellent a man
[i.e. Raymond] should deign to marry, as it were, a common soldier'.[98] Bernard
Hamilton has accordingly described it as 'the misalliance of the century', while
Asbridge has argued that Renaud, in contrast to Raymond, 'brought neither wealth
nor power to the match'.[99] However, William's account was undoubtedly influenced
by his dislike for Renaud, which stemmed from the latter's role in the factionalism
of Jerusalem during the 1170s and 1180s, in which the author himself was also
embroiled. This is suggested by the text of *Eracles*, which has been noted for its
greater interest in French crusaders than the Latin original, whose author actually
praised the new prince's martial skill.[100] Likewise, the marriage went unmentioned
in Western chronicles. Criticism of the match, therefore, was not universal, which
supports Jean Richard's suggestion that Renaud had at least some recognisable
dynastic credibility.[101] Moreover, in contrast to belief in aristocratic opposition, all
of the principality's major fief-holders – the Masoirs, Sourdevals, Fresnels and the
lords of Saone – witnessed Renaud's inaugural charter as prince in 1153.[102] Given
that such widespread noble involvement is rare for Antiochene documents, and
the nature of the gift – a confirmation of Venetian rights – was not overwhelmingly prestigious, their presence almost certainly related to Renaud's coronation.[103]
Although this does not go so far as to prove active aristocratic involvement in
Constance's decision, it at least undermines suggestions of their angry opposition.

---

[95] JK, pp. 96–8; WT, pp. 795–7. For this period, see also pp. 201, 226–8 of this book.
[96] B. Hamilton, 'The Elephant of Christ: Reynald de Châtillon', *Studies in Church History* 15 (1978),
97–108.
[97] Phillips, *Defenders*, pp. 126–9.
[98] WT, p. 796: non sine multorum admiratione quod tam preclara, potens et illustris femina et tam
excellentis uxor viri militi quasi gregario nubere dignaretur.
[99] Hamilton, 'Elephant', pp. 97–108; Asbridge, *Crusades*, p. 252; G. Schlumberger, *Renaud de
Châtillon, prince d'Antioche, seigneur de la terre d'Outre-Jourdain* (Paris, 1923), pp. 5–30; Cahen, *Syrie*,
p. 391.
[100] Handyside, 'Differing Views', pp. 43–52.
[101] J. Richard, 'Aux origines d'un grand lignage: des Paladii à Renaud de Châtillon', *Recueil de melanges
offerts a Karl Ferdinand Werner à l'occasion de son 65e anniversaire* (Maulévrier, 1989), pp. 409–18.
[102] *Urkunden Venedig*, I, 55.
[103] On noble involvement in princely charters, see also pp. 95–101.

This is further demonstrated through a comparison of the factors which may lay behind the choices of Raymond and Renaud, for the same themes which characterised noble involvement in the 1130s – stability and military leadership – remained prevalent. Like Raymond, Renaud was famed for his martial prowess, even gaining first-hand experience of Eastern warfare during the Second Crusade and the siege of Ascalon in 1153.[104] Meanwhile, although William of Tyre and modern historians have criticised Renaud's low birth, which, despite Richard's arguments, was certainly inferior to that of his predecessor, this actually made him the ideal candidate. The situation facing Antioch after 1149 was different to 1130: Bohemond III's survival ensured that whoever became prince would likely have been considered a regent, perhaps even more so than Tancred or Roger had been, given that the heir was in Antioch, not the West. As such, he would have been expected to eventually step aside. This would explain why the charter and numismatic material for Renaud's tenure suggests that he enjoyed a somewhat lower status than either Raymond or Bohemond III. Whereas recognition of Constance's position appeared in only around half of Raymond's charters, all of Renaud's carry clauses such as 'along with my lady Constance, princess of the same honour [and] daughter of Bohemond the younger' (*una cum domina mea Constantia eiusdem honoris Principissa ... Boemundi iunioris filia*).[105] It was noted above that Constance perhaps demanded a more active role by 1149, and the consistent presence of the *una cum* clause, along with the recognition of her greater heritage, certainly supports this. It is perhaps also significant that no coins survive for Renaud's reign, because there are numismatic survivals for all other princes, even those of a relatively comparative status, like Roger.[106] There is even narrative evidence to support belief in Renaud's reduced status. Alongside William of Tyre's comment that Renaud 'administered the principality' while Bohemond 'hoped to become prince in the near future' in 1157, even Ibn al-Athir noted that Constance had 'married a second prince to rule the land until her son grew up'.[107] Although Ibn al-Athir wrote in the thirteenth century, and William was prone to undermining Renaud's position, it is noteworthy that both arrived at the same conclusion. Renaud should, therefore, be considered more a prince-regent than a prince.

The decision to appoint Renaud thus appears to reflect a desire to ensure military leadership without causing internal disruption. In line with the aforementioned belief in the recognition of Raymond's dynastic line, Bohemond III's future legitimacy was seemingly not disputed, but Antioch now had a ruler who could govern the principality until the heir could emerge, or maintain power should the latter die. As such, Andrew Jotischky is surely correct that it 'made good political sense' within Antioch to have 'a western lord of good pedigree and military experience, yet

---

104 Hamilton, 'Elephant', pp. 97–108.

105 *Urkunden Venedig*, I, 55; *Documenti Toscane*, 4; *CGOH*, I, 222, 231, 280; *Codice Diplomatico*, I, pp. 206–7.

106 Metcalf, *Coinage*, pp. 33–9; and 'Six Unresolved Problems', pp. 283–318.

107 WT, p. 837: administrabat principatum ... in proximo sperabatur princeps futurus; IA, II, 31. See also KD, *ROL* 3, 522.

without a potential destabilising entourage'.[108] Constance was probably given some freedom to decide, as is demonstrated by the forlorn efforts of the king of Jerusalem and the envoy to Byzantium, but the underlying factors behind Renaud's selection suggest that the aristocracy were involved, or at least that she was sensitive to their concerns. This has to some extent been recognised by Hodgson, who argued that 'perhaps the most persuasive interpretation is that [the] marriage to Renaud was … a necessary act of reassurance for disgruntled vassals who feared submission to a Byzantine overlord'.[109] Although aristocratic views towards the Greeks were not so clear-cut, as is shown by their involvement in the envoy to John Komnenos in the early 1130s and in other diplomatic ties to Byzantium, an underlying sympathy for maintaining existing power structures can certainly be identified.[110] Consequently, the different examples of Raymond and Renaud suggest that, on the two occasions when a husband was sought for Constance, the nobles had their position within the principality protected.

Bohemond III

This shift in the balance of power continued to have an important impact when Bohemond III finally sought to come into his inheritance after Renaud was captured while raiding in November 1161 and Antioch was left without an incumbent male ruler for the fifth time since its foundation. In the context of his father and stepfather's statuses, that Bohemond III was now close to his majority – he is likely to have come of age (fifteen years old) in 1163 – should have led to a fairly smooth transition.[111] The situation was complicated, however, by the growing demands of leading the principality, which now involved balancing the interests of Manuel Komnenos, Nur al-Din and Baldwin III of Jerusalem, as well as the fact that, due to Renaud's survival, Constance could not simply take a new husband. This left something of a power vacuum in which the princess, the young heir and the nobility all seemingly vied for influence, with distinct similarities to the earlier dispute between Melisende and Baldwin III.

The most contemporaneous source for these events is Michael the Syrian. He detailed that, by 1163, a fracture had emerged between Constance, who sought to retain power, and the nobility, who favoured Bohemond. Apparently fearing that she would offer Manuel Komnenos increased powers in return for his support, the aristocracy are said to have turned to Thoros of Armenia and had together 'driven the queen [sic] from the city and confirmed her son on the throne'.[112] Mayer has accepted Michael's account as fact, arguing, not unfairly, that the patri-

108 A. Jotischky, *Crusading and the Crusader States* (Harlow, 2004), pp. 91–2.
109 Hodgson, *Women*, pp. 223–4.
110 On the nobles and Byzantium, see pp. 97–100.
111 WT, pp. 855–7. See also Mayer, *Varia*, pp. 57–8; *Assises d'Antioche*, p. 16.
112 MS, III, 324.

arch was 'excellently informed'.[113] Nevertheless, this is undermined by the other major account of these events, the *1234 Chronicle*, whose author, despite perhaps drawing on a similar source to Michael, overlooked noble, Armenian and Greek involvement, merely noting that 'the first son of Raymond ruled at Antioch after chasing his mother out, who went to Latakia'.[114] In this regard, the silence of the Armenian chronicler Sempad the Constable on an event which afforded his countrymen great political influence within Antioch is also somewhat surprising, given the retention of this story in the Armenian translation of Michael the Syrian and the Rupenids' later attempts at intervening in the principality's succession.[115] Equally unexpected is the taciturnity of William of Tyre given his usual disdain for the political activities of Antioch's princesses, although he may well have sought to prevent awkward parallels with Melisende and Baldwin. That Amalric of Nesle, the patriarch of Jerusalem, in a letter sent to the West *c.*1165, noted simply that 'Bohemond acceded to the principality after Renaud', means narrative precision remains difficult.[116]

This is further demonstrated by other contemporary evidence. First, when Bohemond III sent a letter reporting Renaud's capture to King Louis VII of France *c.*1162, he described himself not as prince, rather as the 'son of Raymond', and did not seek royal support for a power bid.[117] Bohemond also issued two charters at Latakia in 1163, initially maintaining the same title, but later claiming to have 'dominium over Latakia and Jabala' – which Mayer has argued marked the first stage in a coup given these lands traditionally formed part of the princess's dowry.[118] In spite of this, these documents made no allusion to tension with Constance. In fact, in the earlier of these two gifts, Bohemond stated that he made it 'for the salvation of my parents'.[119] Moreover, it is unclear whether the area of Latakia-Jabala continued to form a separate element away from the princely *demesne*.[120] Significantly, there is also a distinct lack of aristocratic involvement in these two documents, with the exception of Robert II of Sourdeval, whose family held a number of interests in Latakia and Jabala.[121] Mayer has plausibly suggested that this was the result of fears of imperial reprisals, yet important doubts nonetheless emerge regarding Michael the Syrian's belief that Bohemond's succession created a schism between Constance and the aristocracy, even though any pre-agreement made with Raymond in 1136 would have provided a suitable subtext for their intervention.[122] While the Jacobite

---

[113] Mayer, *Varia*, p. 56. See also Cahen, *Syrie*, p. 407; Barber, *Crusader States*, p. 215; Hodgson, *Women*, pp. 223–4.

[114] *1234*, II, 119.

[115] Michael the Syrian, 'Extrait de la Chronique de Michel Syrien, traduit de l'arménien', *RHC Arm.* I, 358. On later events, see Burgtorf, 'War of Succession', pp. 196–211.

[116] *CGOH*, I, 404: Boamundus post Rainaldum ad principatum accesserat.

[117] Louis VII, 'Epistolae', *RHGF* XVI, 27–8: Raimundi ... filius.

[118] *CGOH*, I, 311; *Memorie Storico*, I, p. 202: dominium Laodicee et Galadi; Mayer, *Varia*, pp. 59–61.

[119] *CGOH*, I, 311: pro salute ... parentum ... meorum.

[120] See p. 141.

[121] On this see also p. 131.

[122] Mayer, *Varia*, pp. 61–2.

patriarch appears to have been largely well informed, and generally critical in his use of sources, he is unlikely to have been an eyewitness. Furthermore, Weltecke's comment that Michael often sought to show the difficulties of successions, when coupled with his palpable dislike of the Greeks, could indicate that he altered the narrative for moralistic purposes or to show the negative consequences of closer ties to Byzantium.[123]

It cannot be ruled out that some tension existed, though, and these events can still potentially provide an insight into the developing nature of the princely succession. Doubts over Michael's testimony are important to this; for, by challenging his account, our perceptions of the dynamics of power within the principality are altered. That Bohemond does not seem to have initially enjoyed the overt support of a number of the great families, or perhaps even his own mother, suggests that the simple matter of genealogical legitimacy was not a definitive route to power, regardless of the apparent agreement made with Raymond. In addition, although fear of Manuel Komnenos cannot be entirely ruled out as a factor behind noble absence from Latakia, the more likely impetus is that they, and Constance, feared a fifteen-year-old was not the most suitable figure to lead Antioch's armies against Nur al-Din, or to maintain the delicate diplomatic balance behind managing the external interference of Byzantium and Jerusalem. In this context, even if Bohemond's legitimacy was unquestioned, it is likely his abilities were. As such, it is possible that Bohemond's presence at Latakia-Jabala, rather than a coup, actually reflected an attempt to provide him with valuable experience in governance before eventually taking the throne – a recognised practice in the West, as can be seen by the example of Richard I of England's tenure as count of Poitou.[124] Michael the Syrian's conviction in a polarisation between the princess and the great landholders over Bohemond III's succession is therefore difficult to sustain, especially given that the prince appears to have enjoyed a tenuous relationship with the aristocracy from the very start of his reign.[125] If a dispute occurred, it is probable that, as the *1234 Chronicle* suggests, Bohemond acted independently from the noble elites, perhaps having decided he was ready to take the reins of power.

That a recognised heir could not simply come into his inheritance without first having to placate or battle existing internal forces, just as Baldwin III had faced in Jerusalem, demonstrates the dynamic realities of power on the eastern frontier of Latin Christendom. Why this occurred is less clear. The quest for stability had evidently had a strong influence over the succession since 1130: hence the nobles appear to have acquiesced to an agreement which safeguarded Raymond's dynasty by, at least theoretically, protecting the inheritance of *his* progeny, not simply those of Constance. This would have ensured that, in the event of his early death, Raymond's children could not simply be usurped from their inheritance

123   D. Weltecke, 'Originality and Function of Formal Structures in the Chronicle of Michael the Great', *Hugoye: Journal of Syriac Studies* 3:2 (2000), 196.
124   J. Gillingham, *Richard I* (New Haven, CT, 1999), pp. 24–100.
125   See pp. 117–18.

by those of a second husband, or even by a claim from Constance's nearest male relative, King Roger II of Sicily – though it does not appear to have precluded some noble powers of intervention. With this established, it is easier to understand Renaud's status, and also why Baldwin, the princess' son by this second marriage, was considered so separate from the succession that he was allowed to seek his fortune in the Varangian Guard at Constantinople in the 1170s.[126] This emigration was possibly engineered by Bohemond III to protect his infant heirs, born from his marriage to Orgeuillse of Harim, should he die in battle (a pressing concern for any Antiochene prince!), but it is unlikely Baldwin, or the other ruling elites, would have countenanced this had he any rightful claim to the throne. It is also noteworthy that Bohemond chose to signify the legitimacy of his power through his Poitevin father, not his Norman mother. Indeed, in all but six of the forty-five documents which survive for his reign, the prince presented himself as neither the son of Constance nor of Norman descent, but rather as the 'son of Prince Raymond, by the grace of God prince of Antioch' (*principis Raimundi filius, dei gratia princeps Antiochenus*).[127] Unlike the kings of Jerusalem, moreover, he did not recall his polity's foundation, or even style himself the 'third' of his name. Bohemond also perpetuated his Poitevin heritage by maintaining his father's style of coinage – with the exception that he later added armour and a helmet to the figure – and by naming his eldest son Raymond.[128] The forename Bohemond, up to this point so prominent, was reserved instead for his second-born son. Given the importance of dynastic memory to power and elite identity in the medieval West, the significance of such a shift should not be overlooked.[129] This corroborates the notion that an agreement was made to recognise the creation of a new dynasty in 1136, as well as supporting the suggestion that some form of tension had emerged with Constance over the succession in 1163. Importantly, it also demonstrates the long-term difficulties in supporting the aforementioned arguments presented by Kirschberger, because whatever 'Antiochene' identity was in the opening decades of Frankish rule, it appears to have been altered after 1136.

This all serves to suggest that, even if the problems of 1163 revolved around Bohemond's age and not the legitimacy of his birth, the latter was no longer an infallible route to power in Antioch. Furthermore, that skill could take precedence

---

[126] NC, pp. 96, 102.

[127] *CGOH*, I, 311, 367, 390, 391, 414, 437, 472, 475, 522, 545, 546, 614, 648, 655, 782, 783, 827, 891, 906, 948, 966, II, appendix XXIII; *Urkunden Venedig*, I, 61, 68; Mayer, *Varia*, pp. 114–22; *Libri Iurium*, I/2, 340–3; Le Roulx, *Archives*, pp. 134–5, 142–4; Le Roulx, 'Inventaire', *ROL* 3, 159; *Documenti Toscane*, 13, 50; *Memorie Storico*, I, p. 202; *Tabulae Theutonici*, 9; Rey, *Recherches*, pp. 22–3, 25; Louis VII, 'Epistolae', *RHGF* XVI, 27–8.

[128] Metcalf, *Coinage*, pp. 33–9 and 'Six Unresolved Problems', pp. 283–318.

[129] As Nicholas Paul has noted for the West, '"lineage" ... was not a fixed social structure, but a way for the family to talk about their shared past, and thus their collective identity. Conceptions of the family were fluid, reflecting both changes in attitude ... and situational – often politically motivated – choices. Seen not as passive reflections of a new social structure, but as active statements of a lineage that was deliberately constructed, dynastic histories were clearly important statements of identity.' See *To Follow in their Footsteps*, p. 16.

over legal rights is testament to the complicated nature of frontier governance. As shown by the processes which had underpinned Raymond and Renaud's appointments, the ruling elites of the principality had, above all else, protected the political status quo. Therefore, although Jochen Burgtorf has noted his surprise at the outbreak of the Antiochene War of Succession after Bohemond III's death in 1201, given that the nature of the princely succession had been formalised during the twelfth century, it appears instead that such conflict was deeply rooted in the principality's dynamic balance of power.[130] Thus, having witnessed the early death or incarceration of many of its princes, Antioch's nobility, almost certainly in alliance with Constance (now a veteran of governance), probably hoped in 1163 to provide the youthful Bohemond with the requisite experience to govern before handing him full control. That he successfully opposed them is testament to his formidable spirit, as is the fact his reign lasted until 1201; although his capture at Artah in 1164 is a sign that they may have been right.

Conclusion

During the period of this study, the methods by which princely authority was secured and legitimised changed. Facing a situation of unparalleled difficulty after Bohemond II's death, the Frankish nobles were afforded a far stronger position in determining who ruled than had previously been the case, with the right to lead the principality now stemming from election by their hands. The eventual choices of Raymond of Poitiers as prince and Renaud of Châtillon as prince-regent, as well as the difficulties faced by Bohemond III upon his accession, demonstrate the aristocracy's desire, and willingness, to retain a guiding hand over the succession. The Frankish nobles showed a great deal of caution in choosing suitors who could take on the mantle of political and military leadership but would not destabilise existing structures of landholding and power. Through this, Raymond appears to have secured the endurance of his dynastic legitimacy, even if Bohemond III still had to force his way onto the throne. More significantly, this also led to a diminution in the significance of the Norman heritage of Antioch's ruling house, with a move away from allusions to the principality's foundation in the documentary and numismatic evidence, and even, to some extent, in the naming patterns of the princely family. The memory of the Frankish conquest did not completely lose its value, as Constance still alluded to her Norman heritage and the name Bohemond continued to hold political significance into the thirteenth century, just as Raymond and Baldwin had become synonymous with Tripoli and Jerusalem in the twelfth century.[131] Yet, it is evident that Antioch's princes were no longer distinctly Norman, rather they were Poitevin, with the legitimacy of the princely house here-

---

[130] Burgtorf, 'War of Succession', pp. 203–4. See also Cahen, *Syrie*, pp. 579–643.
[131] *CGOH*, I, 190, 198.

tofore based solely on the deal to bring Raymond from the West. Consequently, the succession and authority of Antioch's ruling house was now the subject of an intricate mix of dynastic legitimacy and delicate aristocratic discussion, even if Raymond's line had been recognised. This had long-term ramifications for the dynamics of power within Antioch.

3

Central Governance and Military Service

Now we have established the ways in which princely power was bestowed and legit-imised, it is also important to outline how it was physically manifested. As already noted, historians have primarily seen the princes of Antioch as supreme rulers, able to exercise near-complete authority and to demand unrestricted services from fief-holders. In the context of the previous chapter and the realisation that the internal balance of power altered after 1130, this requires further examination. Due to the difficulties of the source material, however, it is impossible to cover all potential avenues. For example, little is known of the ruler's income. It is almost certain that the prince was the single largest landholder, and so the ruler's *demesne*, in addition to ensuring his military superiority over the other major landholders, would also have formed the basis of princely finances.[1] Monies would have been gathered from landholding rents and taxes, such as the ninth-part of revenues the princes appear to have retained over some fiefs, the payments made on harvests, and even the income from fishing rights at the Lake of Antioch (situated on the Amuq). Of greater significance, though, would have been places along the coast, mainly St Simeon, Latakia and Jabala, as well as river ports like Arzghan, as these would have allowed for trade exactions – an important boon for any ruler.[2] Yet, despite charter evidence which demonstrates that money and commerce were being trafficked through these sites, like the confirmation of a money-fief of two-thousand bezants to Walter II of Sourdeval at Jabala in 1179 and the granting of trade rights to the Italian states of Venice, Genoa and Pisa, there is little specific evidence for exact figures.[3] Therefore, although a severe economic disparity emerged between the prince and the Church at Antioch, which proved a source of great friction throughout this period, it was not recorded how or why this occurred.[4] Scott Redford has suggested that it stemmed in part from the decision to focus trade along the coast of Syria, not Cilicia (where Byzantine trade had once thrived), and while this does not

[1]   Cahen, *Syrie*, pp. 439–41; Asbridge, *Creation*, pp. 148–9; Martin, 'Structures', pp. 244–7.
[2]   Cahen, *Syrie*, pp. 465–7, 472–80, 532, 555–60; Martin, 'Structures', pp. 242–5.
[3]   Le Roulx, *Archives*, pp. 142–4; *Urkunden Venedig*, 46, 55; *Libri Iurium*, I/2, 337–8, 340–3; *Documenti Toscane*, 4, 13, 50. On the Italian states in the principality, see Cahen, *Syrie*, pp. 487–500; M.-L. Favreau-Lilie, *Die Italiener im Heiligen Land vom Ersten Kreuzzug bis zum Tode Heinrichs von Champagne 1098–1197* (Amsterdam, 1999), pp. 152–60, 165–77, 214–29, 327–381, 421–4, 455–61, 486–96.
[4]   See pp. 101–9.

adequately take into account the potential destabilising factors of Greek, Armenian and Turkish military activities in the latter region, there is reason to believe that trade was not so extensive as it was elsewhere in the Latin East.[5] In addition to this, it might also be that the fulfilment of taxes and rents varied considerably due to the territorial fluctuations and military pressures outlined in Chapter 1, while the independence of noble lordships (to be demonstrated in Chapter 4) may have limited income from these holdings. Beyond this, however, not a great deal more can be said. Conversely, an examination of Antioch's central administration, as well as the extent of the provision of military service to the ruler, proves a more fruitful avenue for understanding the exact extent of princely authority.

Antioch's Central Governance

Antioch's central governance would have been divided into a number of institutions. The office of the *secreta* was seemingly responsible for the financial, land-holding and 'feudal' service records (and is perhaps synonymous with the 'statistical map' of fiefs described in the *Assises d'Antioche*), while Antioch's central judiciary was split into two bodies: the *haute cour*, or high court, in which sat the prince, the officers of state and the great fief-holders; and the *cour de bourgeois*, or the burgess court, which dealt with matters of lesser importance.[6] In the case of the *secreta*, despite its apparent mention in the *Assises*, the fact that there is no known holder of this office after 1140 suggests Martin may be correct that it declined in importance in the second half of the twelfth century, with the nobles of the *haute cour*, acting out of self-interest, perhaps able to push for a certain amount of weakening in the monitoring of 'feudal' landholdings and services owed.[7] Similar problems exist for identifying the workings of the *haute cour*, or at least the general assembly of most of its members, as this can only be discerned on three occasions in this period: when John Komnenos sought to extend the diplomatic agreement made with Raymond of Poitiers in 1138; when Raymond delayed his response to a claim made by representatives of the Holy Sepulchre in 1139/1140 so as to 'convoke the council of my nobles'; and, when that same prince, 'in the presence of us and our barons', confirmed a donation made by a certain Barutellus in 1149.[8] This demonstrates the court's existence, and that it could be called upon to aid the prince in decision-making; yet, it is difficult to distinguish the exact composition

---

[5]   Redford, 'Trade and Economy in Antioch', pp. 297–309. On Antiochene trade, see also pp. 185–7 of this book.

[6]   *Assises d'Antioche*, pp. 8–85. See also Cahen, *Syrie*, pp. 439–54; Asbridge, *Creation*, pp. 189–94; M. Nader, *Burgesses and Burgess Law in the Latin Kingdoms of Jerusalem and Cyprus (1099–1325)* (Aldershot, 2006).

[7]   Martin, 'Structures', pp. 245–7.

[8]   WT, pp. 677–81; *CCSSJ*, 77: meorum obtimatum consilium convocare; *CGOH*, I, 183: in presenti nostri baronumque nostrorum.

or powers of such a body, and whether participation was regulated or a more fluid, ad hoc affair. This raises parallels with Western examples, as Nicholas Vincent has described King Henry II of England's court as 'enigmatic' and 'ill defined', with even contemporaries proving 'incapable of explaining what, or more rightly who, the court might be'.[9] Nevertheless, whereas cases brought before the courts would have been solely judicial, it is also significant that their members would also have presided over issues of civil administration, the princely *demesne* and diplomacy.[10] Cahen recognised that these courts played an important role in administration and law, although he did not go so far as to argue for their overbearing influence – he certainly did not suggest that there was any aristocratic move to limit services owed to the prince.[11] This has for the most part been accepted by historians like Mayer, with the exception of Martin's aforementioned comments and the fact that Asbridge has maintained that the princes retained centralised control over 'an institutional framework largely to their own design'.[12]

Contrary to historical belief, which largely continues to propound the totality of princely power over governance and fief-holder services, the years following Bohemond II's death in 1130 instead saw a shift in the principality's balance of power and the nature of rulership. In light of this, and the evolving scholarly view on the nature of medieval governance, feudalism and frontiers, there is a need to re-examine the form of Antioch's central administration and its political structures. Therefore, through a discussion of the role and relative importance of the different groups who participated in governance – the officers of state, the *familiares*, the landed nobility and the Church – significant fresh insights can be made into the strengths and limitations of princely authority. Indeed, whereas the prince did enjoy powerful control over various aspects of rulership, important aristocratic checks were seemingly implemented in matters of diplomacy and marriage: a growing influence which seemingly came at the expense of the Church.

The Officers of State

There were a total of eleven known major offices attached to princely governance in this period: the constable, marshal, chamberlain, butler, seneschal, chancellor, castellan of Antioch, viscount, and the dukes (or *dux*) of Antioch, Latakia and Jabala.[13] Cahen believed that the duties of these offices would have followed Norman models imported from the West, although Asbridge has taken the adoption of formerly Byzantine positions, such as *dux*, as well as a number of minor civic roles, including a *praetor* (the chief judge for municipal matters), *praecones* (that is a

---

9   Vincent, 'Court', pp. 278–334.
10   On the division of judicial decisions and administration, such as tax regulation, see J. Riley-Smith, 'Some Lesser Officials in Latin Syria', *EHR* 87 (1972), 1–26.
11   Cahen, *Syrie*, pp. 439–52, 527–8.
12   Mayer, *Varia*, pp. 174–84; Martin, 'Structures', pp. 245–7; Asbridge, *Creation*, pp. 150–1, 181–2; Asbridge and Edgington, *The Antiochene Wars*, pp. 43–7.
13   For the full list of office-holders, along with details of their charter appearances, see Appendix 1.

messenger) and *iudex* (another form of judge), as a sign that some cross-fertilisation occurred with Eastern models.[14] Due to the lack of an internal Antiochene narrative after Walter the Chancellor, as well as the *Assises'* general silence on these positions, it is difficult to exactly pinpoint the officers' roles. It is clear that they were often called upon to accompany the prince on diplomatic missions, which is attested to by the presence of the constable, marshal and duke of Antioch in Bohemond III's entourage during a visit to kingdom of Jerusalem in 1179.[15] They may also have constituted the *domestici* who William of Tyre listed alongside Renaud of Châtillon at Shaizar in 1157.[16] Beyond this, though, it is not possible to either confirm or deny Cahen's hypothesis, even if some points of clarification can be offered. What proves more fruitful is an assessment of the prosoprographical details of these offices and what this reveals about princely authority and the dynamics of power.

Importantly, with the exception of Renaud I Masoir, who held the position of constable *c.*1127–1134, none of landed nobles were provided with an office during the twelfth century.[17] This is similar to Angevin England, but is in direct contrast to the kingdom of Jerusalem, where the members of the key noble lineages frequently held office.[18] There are some possible exceptions, as Walter I of Sourdeval was constable of Latakia in the 1130s, but this was only within Princess Alice's independent lordship at Latakia-Jabala and he never appeared as such when witnessing a princely charter.[19] Meanwhile, despite Cahen's belief that William Baufre, duke of Antioch in the 1160s, was a scion of Kafartab's ruling house, this stems from an apparent confusion between a 'Lord Bonable', mentioned in relation to a gift of lands at Kafartab to the Abbey of Josaphat in 1182, and Bonable Baufre, William's brother.[20] The 1182 charter in question was in fact a reconfirmation of a document originally issued by Roger of Salerno in 1118, in which a different Bonable did appear in relation to lands he held near to Kafartab.[21] As such, there is nothing to link Bonable Baufre (and by consequence his brother) to Kafartab, or to the earlier Bonable, excepting their first names. Finally, while a number of officers carry toponymic surnames linking them to sites in northern Syria – such as the seneschals Schivard and Gervaise of Sarmenia (a site near to Bourzey) and William *de Cavea* (Darkush), who was the marshal and also a temporary duke of Latakia – it cannot even be demonstrably proven that they were fief-holders. As will be argued below, they are more likely to have been members of the princely *familiares*, initially charged with governing parts of the *demesne* and later elevated to office, perhaps as a result of the loss of those sites to the Muslims. Therefore, despite the shift

---

14 Cahen, *Syrie*, pp. 452–62; Asbridge, *Creation*, pp. 181–94. See also Mayer, *Varia*, pp. 75–109.
15 *CGOH*, I, 559; *Tabulae Theutonici*, 9.
16 WT, pp. 833, 839.
17 Appendix 1. For before 1130, see Cahen, *Syrie*, p. 545; Asbridge, *Creation*, p. 182.
18 Vincent, 'Court', pp. 284–304; J. L. La Monte, *Feudal Monarchy in the Latin Kingdom of Jerusalem, 1100–1291* (Baltimore, MD, 1932), pp. 114–37, 252–6.
19 Asbridge, 'Alice', p. 40; *CCSSJ*, 76–7.
20 Mayer, *Varia*, pp. 118–21.
21 *Chartes Josaphat*, 4.

in the balance of power after 1130, Antioch's princes filled the offices of state not with nobles, as might be expected if it were to be assumed that this led to greater surveillance of princely authority, but with those whose elevation would have made them more dependent on the sovereign for their status.

In addition to this, each new ruler installed a number of their own officers rather than simply maintaining existing personnel. For example, Raymond of Poitiers appears to have only retained two of Bohemond II's officers: Leo Maiopoli, the duke of Antioch, who may have been appointed by Fulk having attested princely documents without title in 1127, and Thomas the viscount.[22] Raymond thus appointed an array of new individuals, probably drawn from the 'companions' and *familiares* who accompanied him to the East.[23] This included figures of possible southern French origin, such as the castellan, Peter Armoin, and the marshals, Raymond and Garinus *Malmut*; while the constable, Roger *de Montibus*, was potentially, due to his likely Norman heritage, a fellow *iuvenis* from Henry I's court.[24] This supports Hamilton's conviction that 'Raymond was concerned to give office to men from his native Aquitaine', although his belief that this represented an attempt 'to counter the power of the Normans' is undermined by the general lack of impact on the established noble classes.[25] Moreover, the long-term implications of these appointments would have been limited by Renaud of Châtillon's installation of his own men. With central administration having perhaps been robbed of numbers by the defeat at Inab, the prince-regent replaced most official positions, despite temporarily retaining Leo Maiopoli as duke, Garinus Malmut as marshal and Schivard of Sarmenia as seneschal.[26] Again, the new men appear to carry geographical links to the ruler's earlier career. Geoffrey Falsard, the duke of Antioch appointed in 1154, was likely of French origin, and the constable, Geoffrey *Jordanis*, probably accompanied Renaud from Jerusalem.[27] That Renaud held strong powers over the offices of the principality, despite his reduced status, is also suggested by William Tirel's position as marshal during this time. It has been argued that the Tirels, who were probably Norman, held one of Antioch's two marshalcies by hereditary right, having first appeared in this role at the end of Raymond's reign.[28] However, this is challenged by William's appearance without office throughout Renaud's reign, only recovering his title under Bohemond III.[29] This not only suggests that Cahen is wrong that the marshal was a military position (for William is unlikely to have survived of Inab had he been there), it also demonstrates further that, rather than

---

[22] Appendix 1.

[23] WT, pp. 657–9 (here 657): socii … familia.

[24] Appendix 1. Mayer (*Varia*, p. 170) argued Roger was actually from Mons in Hainault, although this is unclear.

[25] Hamilton, 'Ecumenist', pp. 271–2. See also Cahen, *Syrie*, p. 536; and pp. 129–33 of this book.

[26] Appendix 1.

[27] *Ibid.*

[28] Cahen, *Syrie*, pp. 30, 535–6; Mayer, *Varia*, p. 172.

[29] *CGOH*, I, 390–1; *Urkunden Venedig*, I, 61; *Libri Iurium*, I/2, 340.

being the Tirels' inheritance, the prince was able to re-assign their positions, and all others, as he saw fit.

The situation was slightly different during Bohemond III's reign as, unlike his immediate predecessors, he was not an outsider. Nevertheless, his difficult rise to power may have alienated some of the existing officers, especially those who had supported Constance and the nobles. Consequently, Bohemond installed a new constable (Guiscard *de Insula*), a marshal (William *de Cavea*), a duke (William Baufre – albeit only temporarily), a butler (William *de Monci*) and a viscount (Vasilius – who was soon replaced by Peter of Amalfi).[30] Interestingly, Vasilius – whose name suggests Greek heritage – made his one and only appearance in 1166/1167, thus just a short time after Bohemond had agreed to certain concessions in response to Manuel Komnenos paying his ransom following the battle of Artah. This could imply he was imposed upon the prince, just as a Greek patriarch was.[31] In addition to these new men, a number of Raymond and Renaud's officers were retained. This included his father's seneschal, Schivard of Sarmenia, the return as marshal of the aforementioned William Tirel, as well as the retention of Renaud's chamberlain, Peter, and his castellan at Antioch, Payen *de Castellud*.[32] This probably represented an attempt by Bohemond to provide a sense of continuity and legitimacy following his troubled accession. Yet, the control he wielded over this group is undoubted, given that Guiscard *de Insula* remained at court until the 1180s (despite losing his position as constable after 1172) and, in 1183, William *de Cavea* was moved from his position as marshal to that of duke of Latakia.[33] The sole exception to this relates to those who were exiled as a result of the noble rebellion of 1180–1182 (which included Baldwin the constable and Oliver the chamberlain). In his account of this, William of Tyre described their expulsion as resulting from their role in challenging the prince over his divorce of Theodora Komnena.[34] However, given that those who departed only returned once the leader of the rebellion, Renaud II Masoir, was dead, it appears instead that they had been removed by the nobles, almost certainly for their part in influencing Bohemond's actions.[35] Thus, while the composition of the offices of state could be impacted upon by diplomatic circumstance, it remained for the most part the prince's inalienable right, with those who filled these roles subject to removal or transferral. Importantly, this was seemingly as dependent upon the desires and aims of the ruler as it was in Jerusalem or in the West.[36] More significantly, the nobles were almost entirely absent. It is unclear whether this was prompted by a desire to ensure aristocratic holdings remained

---

[30] Appendix 1.

[31] See pp. 212–13.

[32] Appendix 1.

[33] For Gusicard, see *CGOH*, I, 472, 475, 522, 614; Rey, *Recherches*, pp. 22–3; Le Roulx, *Archives*, pp. 142–4; Mayer, *Varia*, p. 117; WT, pp. 1015–17. For William, see Appendix 1.

[34] WT, pp. 1015–17.

[35] This argument and the events of the rebellion are set out in greater depth in Buck, 'Noble Rebellion', pp. 109–14.

[36] H. E. Mayer, 'The Wheel of Fortune: Seignorial Vicissitudes under Kings Fulk and Baldwin III of Jerusalem', *Speculum* 65 (1990), 860–77; Vincent, 'Court', pp. 278–303; M. Prestwich, 'The Military

guarded, or if it reflected an attempt to limit noble influence over central admin-istration. Regardless, it demonstrates the need to be alive to the complexities of Antioch's political structures.

The Familiares

Perhaps the closest group to the prince were the *familiares*. This band largely comprised the ruler's military retinue, which ensured they were afforded a great deal of trust. It also meant they were often provided with offices of state or dispatched to administer territorially vulnerable estates – even if, once in office, these indi-viduals were set apart from the *familiares*, a trend which Asbridge has identified within the principality as early as the 1110s.[37] As the prince's closest advisers and the most immediate military support, their importance to central administration is self-evident. Despite this, an effort to chart the exact composition of this group has never been attempted.

A primary reason for this is that they were not differentiated from the *barones* in the documentary sources. Figures like Guiterius of Moceon and Richard of Belmont, who petitioned Raymond of Poitiers on behalf of the Holy Sepulchre in 1140, were therefore listed as *barones* in the princely charters, despite not being discernible members of the landed nobility – another indication of the adaptability of *baro*. Indeed, the description of the presence of these men alongside the prince at the Iron Bridge almost certainly precludes their membership of the *optimatum*, or great nobles, who were subsequently called once it had been agreed to hold a tribunal.[38] That Muslim reports recorded that Raymond was at the river crossing in preparation for a military venture, suggests rather that they were members of the knightly retinue, and thus *familiares*.[39] Another difficulty concerns the matter of toponymic surnames. As already noted, there are a number of individuals carrying names which link them to sites in northern Syria, who have traditionally been assigned to the aristocracy, but appear instead to have been members of the *familiares*, perhaps designated castellans of key sites in the princely *demesne*. These include the aforementioned William *de Cavea* and Schivard of Sarmenia, John of Salqin (close to Harim), Walter of Arzghan, Richier of Armenaz (a small forti-fied town south of Harim), Geoffrey and Adam of Quorchiya (which sat upon a road confluence linking Latakia and Saone), Leonard of La Roche de Roissel and William of Mt Hingron (a mountain probably to the north of Antioch).[40] Within

Household of the Norman Kings', *EHR* 378 (1981), 1–35; H. Takayama, 'Familiares Regis and the Royal Inner Council in Twelfth-Century Sicily', *EHR* 441 (1989), 357–72.

37   J. Prestwich, 'The Military Household of the Norman Kings', *Anglo-Norman Warfare: Studies in Late Anglo-Saxon and Anglo-Norman Military Organization and Warfare*, ed. M. Strickland (Wood-bridge, 1992), pp. 93–127; Asbridge and Edgington, *The Antiochene Wars*, pp. 43–4.

38   *CCSSJ*, 77.

39   Al-Azimi, p. 148; KD, *RHC Or.* III, 683.

40   For William *de Cavea* and Schivard of Sarmenia, see Appendix 1. For John of Salqin, see *Codice Diplomatico*, I, pp. 206–7; *CGOH*, I, 391, 427, 472, 475, 522, 948; *Libri Iurium*, I/2, 340; *Documenti Toscane*, 13, 50; Rey, *Recherches*, pp. 22–3. For Walter of Arzghan, see Mayer, *Varia*, pp. 121–2; *CGOH*,

this list might also be included William Bucellus, who was allowed to retain lands near to the castle of Bikisrail, which he appears to have governed – despite historical belief that it was a Masoir possession – before it was offered to the Order of Santiago in 1180.[41]

It must first be noted that the terms *castellanus*, and its likely synonym *praefectus*, do not appear in the sources, at least not outside Antioch itself. As such, this status cannot be so securely affiliated as it can for earlier figures like Joseph, castellan of Artah, or Engelrand, *praefectus* of Apamea.[42] Nevertheless, there are certain clues which indicate that these men should be considered *familiares* acting in this role, rather than as independent fief-holders. First, a number of them were attached to possessions of vital strategic importance, particularly in the Orontes Valley, including Arzghan, Salqin, Darkush and Armenaz. Given that, as will be seen below, the great families rarely absented themselves from their lordships, it must be assumed that these men had a stronger relationship with the prince. The most likely explanation for this is that they were instead *familiares*. More indicative of this is the realisation that a sizeable proportion of these individuals, including William *de Cavea*, Walter of Arzghan and Leonard of La Roche de Roissel, maintained their presence at court even after the lands to which they were linked had been sold to the military orders. In contrast to demonstrable fief-holders, they even received important offices, like that of duke of Latakia or marshal of Antioch, and were never ascribed the title of *dominus*, or lord. The possible exception to this is *dominus Leonardus*, who appeared in an Antiochene charter of 1154 and may be synonymous with Leonard of La Roche de Roissel.[43] However, given that the latter first appeared in a document of 1183, it is unlikely that they are the same person, while the title of *dominus*, although predominantly a signifier of noble status, was used by Eastern Christians and household officers in the lordship of Margat to simply denote knighthood.[44] Additionally, incumbent lords were not referred to in the charters confirming the alienation of the lands in question, thus suggesting that they were sold through the prince's authority alone. This did not occur in relation to noble fiefs, which denotes that they were instead elements of the ruler's own *demesne*.[45] The same can be said for Bikisrail, for although Mayer has interpreted the comment, contained within the charter detailing its sale, that William Bucellus 'returned' (*reddidit*) the castle to Bohemond III as evidence it was held in fief, William was not actually described as its lord.[46] As such, he is more likely to have

---

I, 782–3, II, 23; *Urkunden Venedig*, I, 68. For Richier of Armenaz, see *CGOH*, I, 522, 546, 559, 782–3, 906, 948, 866; *Tabulae Theutonici*, 9; Le Roulx, *Archives*, pp. 142–4; Mayer, *Varia*, pp. 118–22; *Documenti Toscane*, 50; *CGT*, pp. 165–71. For Geoffrey and Adam of Quorchiya, see *CCSSJ*, 77; *CGOH*, I, 183. For Leonard of La Roche de Roissel, see *CGOH*, II, 23 (and perhaps also *Documenti Toscane*, 4). For William of Mt Hingron, see Mayer, *Varia*. p. 121; *Urkunden Venedig*, I, 68.

41 Mayer, *Varia*, pp. 114–17. See also pp. 141–2 of this book.
42 Asbridge, *Creation*, pp. 148–50.
43 *Documenti Toscane*, 4.
44 *CGOH*, I, 783. See also pp. 134–5, 185 of this book.
45 On noble land alienation, see pp. 150–9.
46 Mayer, *Varia*, pp. 114–17 (here 116).

simply been unable to continue his role as castellan. That these men were *familiares*, as opposed to noble fief-holders, is also implied by the fact that many only first appeared in princely documents *after* the sale of their supposed sites, that being once their placement had ended. William *de Cavea* first acted as witness to a charter in 1175, seven years after Darkush's sale; Walter of Arzghan was not seen until 1182, fourteen years after the site was sold; and although the date of La Roche de Roissel's transference to the Templars is unknown (it first appeared under their control in Muslim accounts of its fall in 1188), Leonard's presence at Antioch in 1183 suggests it was around this date.[47] In all likelihood, therefore, these individuals were the prince's *familiares*, sent to administer outlying regions – a practice well known in Anglo-Norman England.[48] Consequently, it is unsurprising that most were linked to the Orontes Valley, particularly the central corridor which, as shown in Chapter 1, proved so vital to the balance of power between Antioch and Aleppo during Nur al-Din's reign. Any ruler would have wanted to entrust the defences of so significant a region to loyal individuals dependent on him for their status. This refutes Cahen's hypothesis that this duty would have fallen to various dukes or counts, like those seen at Jabala and Latakia, and argues instead for a more independent position, albeit not one demonstrably described in the charters.[49]

Questions nevertheless remain regarding this group's wider involvement in princely affairs. Charter evidence for Bohemond III's visits to the kingdom of Jerusalem in 1179, 1183 and 1185/1186, demonstrates that a number of household retainers, most probably also the *familiares*, were frequently amongst the princely entourage for journeys outside of the principality, which attests to a level of diplomatic use.[50] Likewise, when Manuel Komnenos arrived in Cilicia in 1158, it was the 'wise members of the *familiares*' who Renaud of Châtillon called upon to advise him on the best course of action, while the '*fideles* and friends' of Bohemond III worked to secure his release after Artah in 1164.[51] Their primary use, though, was almost certainly military, as alongside their apparent role as castellans, the martial role of the *familiares* (as will be examined below) is repeatedly mentioned in the narrative sources, with the *familiaribus* or *comitatu* often accompanying the princes during armed ventures. During one such campaign – the siege of Shaizar in 1157 – William of Tyre even designated two distinct groups accompanying Renaud of Châtillon: the *domestici*, or household officers, and the *familiares*, the military retinue.[52] This demonstrates a level of continuity from the earlier period, in which the prince's household played a key part in military action, while it is tempting to see in Orderic Vitalis' description of the *iuvenes* who died with Bohemond II in 1130, evidence of a system of patronage of young knights similar to that known

---

47 *CGOH*, I, 391, 472, II, 23; Mayer, *Varia*, p. 121.
48 S. Morillo, *Warfare under the Anglo-Norman Kings, 1066–1135* (Woodbridge, 1994), pp. 60–6.
49 Cahen, *Syrie*, pp. 457–60.
50 *CGOH*, I, 559; *Tabulae Theutonici*, 9; *Urkunden Venedig*, I, 68; Mayer, *Varia*, pp. 121–2.
51 WT, pp. 844–5 (here 845): magis familiaris; pp. 877–8 (here 878): fidelibus et amicis.
52 *Ibid.*, p. 833.

in Anglo-Norman England under Henry I.[53] It cannot even be ruled out that the nobles participated in this, as is shown by the example of Roger of Sourdeval, who spent a much greater amount of time at court than any other of his family, and, as demonstrated by a charter issued in favour of Walter II of Sourdeval in 1179, was clearly not considered part of the inheritance.[54] This perhaps indicates he was a *iuvenis*, or part of the wider *familiares*, and offers the – albeit far from secure – suggestion that the princely court acted as a hub for noble sons, just as the Anglo-Norman court did in the West.

Whatever the case may be, it is clear that these men formed a distinct group within princely governance. Like other medieval sovereigns, the princes of Antioch utilised a group of *familiares* to act as their closest core of military personnel and advisors. Similar to the officers of state, their composition was seemingly a princely prerogative, used to secure the ruler's power and influence, as well as the security of his *demesne*.

The Landed Nobility

The next group whose contribution to governance is worth examining is the landed nobility, who held the principality's great fiefs.[55] Given the rise in their influence after 1130, afforded to them by the need to find a husband for Constance, it might be assumed that their role in administration would also have increased. The prominence of the 'foremost nobles' in calming an anti-Greek riot which broke out at Antioch in response to John Komnenos' attempt to take the city in 1138 certainly suggests they held a certain amount of civic prestige within the capital.[56] By drawing on the *Assises d'Antioche*, Martin has therefore argued that the aristocracy formed a key element of the *haute cour*.[57] However, although – as noted above – there is some fragmentary evidence for the court's meeting to support this, it must be remembered that Antioch's law code related specifically to judicial matters, not everyday administration, and its stipulation that a call to perform service at the court could be challenged if not correctly delivered, demonstrates that checks to summonses existed.[58] Moreover, it has already been shown here that the nobles did not take up offices of state during this period. As such, whether the increased influence over key matters of the succession and diplomacy is also indicative of the wider surveillance of central governance, requires further analysis.

In this regard, it is significant that, alongside their non-appearance in offices of state, Antioch's great families, with the exception of the Sourdevals, were either

---

53 Orderic Vitalis, VI, 134–6.
54 In fact, Roger witnessed fourteen charters: *Urkunden Venedig*, I, 55; *CGOH*, I, 391, 475, 522, 546, 614, II, 23; *Libri Iurium*, I/2, 340; *Documenti Toscane.*, 13; Rey, *Recherches*, pp. 22–3; Le Roulx, *Archives*, pp. 142–4; Mayer, *Varia*, pp. 117, 121; *Codice Diplomatico*, I, p. 281. For Walter II Sourdeval, who appeared only twice, see Le Roulx, *Archives*, pp. 142–4; *CGOH*, I, 783.
55 For a fuller discussion, see Chapter 4.
56 WT, pp. 676–81 (here 680): nobilium primores.
57 Martin, 'Structures', pp. 239–48.
58 *Assises d'Antioche*, pp. 8–43.

largely infrequent attesters to princely charters in the case of the Masoirs, the lords of Saone and the Fresnels, or entirely absent, like the lords of Marash. Full-scale aristocratic involvement appears instead to have been reserved for occasions or matters of great importance, such as the confirmation of Holy Sepulchre possessions in 1140, Renaud of Châtillon's first charters as prince in 1153 or the sale of Margat in 1187.[59] This fits with similar patterns in Angevin England and Norman Italy, where noble turnout was at its most extensive during festivals or key discussions.[60] Cahen recognised this and argued that fief-holder presence was dictated by proximity – an explanation which could account for the non-participation of Marash's lords, but not the frequent absence of those closer to Antioch.[61] Indeed, between 1136 and 1201, the Masoir family of Margat (whose castle lay 120 km south of Antioch) and the lords of Saone (70 km south-east) each appeared in eight princely documents, whereas the Fresnel lords of Harim (30 km east) were only present on three occasions.[62] This might indicate that prestige was important, for the size of the castles at Margat and Saone suggests they were the principality's premier lordships, although this is undermined by the fact that the most regular attendees at the rulers' court, with twenty-two and seventeen appearances respectively, were the Sourdevals and the Loges', a minor landholding family from Latakia.[63] Neither of these families held assets comparable to the other fief-holders, although the Sourdevals had come over with the First Crusade.[64] Perhaps a more likely factor, therefore, is that of military vulnerability, as both the Sourdevals and Masoir held lands in areas of relative, albeit not complete security, while Saone, although on the eastern frontier, was not mentioned in a martial capacity in the narrative sources until its fall in 1188 and so is unlikely to have been a hugely active military hub. By contrast, Harim was subject to near-constant pressure until its definitive loss in 1164. Other considerations are also possible, with the Loges' and Sourdevals perhaps enjoying prominence under Bohemond III having been with him as he sought power at Latakia-Jabala in 1163.[65] It has even been argued that the lords of Saone suffered for their reported involvement in the civil war of 1132, although this did not preclude Garenton of Saone's privileged position in the

---

[59]   CCSSJ, 76–77; Urkunden Venedig, I, 55; CGOH, I, 783.

[60]   Vincent, 'Court', pp. 293–4; D. Matthew, The Norman Kingdom of Sicily (Cambridge, 1992), pp. 143–4.

[61]   Cahen, Syrie, pp. 440–1. See also Asbridge, Creation, p. 151.

[62]   For the Masoirs, see Urkunden Venedig, I, 55, 61; CGOH, I, 391, 559, 623; Le Roulx, Archives, 142–4; Tabulae Theutonici, 9; Mayer, Varia, pp. 114–17. For Saone, see CCSSJ, 76–7; Urkunden Venedig, I, 55; Documenti Toscane, 4, 50; CGOH, I, 231, 948, 966, II, 23. For the Fresnels, see CCSSJ, 76–7, Urkunden Venedig, I, 55; Codice Diplomatico, I, pp. 206–7.

[63]   For the Sourdevals, see CGOH, I, 222, 231, 311, 390–1, 475, 522, 546, 614, 782–3, II, 23; CCSSJ, 76–7; Urkunden Venedig, I, 55, 61; Documenti Toscane, 4, 13; Mayer, Varia, pp. 114–21; Memorie Storico, I, p. 202; Rey, Recherches, pp. 22–3; Le Roulx, Archives, pp. 142–4; Codice Diplomatico, I, p. 281. For the Loges', see CGOH, I, 133, 198, 311, 475, 576, 614, 648, 916, II, 23; Memorie Storico, I, p. 202; Documenti Toscane, 13; Le Roulx, Archives, pp. 142–4; Mayer, Varia, pp. 114–22; Libri Iurium, I/2, 343; Urkunden Venedig, I, 68.

[64]   See p. 131.

[65]   Memorie Storico, I, p. 202; CGOH, I, 311.

Holy Sepulchre documents of 1140, nor had ties to Princess Alice proved a barrier to the Sourdevals, who, unlike the holders of Saone, were heavily involved in her lordship at Latakia-Jabala.[66] Despite this, Jerusalem's nobles enjoyed similarly divergent fortunes during the reigns of Fulk and Baldwin III depending on who they had supported in periods of crisis.[67] Perhaps the most plausible explanation is that the decision to invoke the full *haute cour*, or the elite group of advisors – as opposed to isolated appearances (which may, indeed, have been influenced by proximity) – depended on the significance of the matter. It is also possible that, in a similar vein to Nicholas Vincent's comments on Henry II of England's court, the entrenched nature of the principality's aristocracy, and their non-involvement in the offices of state, meant that there was little need to appear at Antioch with any frequency in order to gain the ruler's favour.[68] By consequence, princely control over central administration must have been strong enough to deal with most issues independently, even if matters of great importance still appear to have required noble counsel.

There were areas of governance in which the Antiochene aristocracy did play an influential role: particularly, as already noted, the succession, but also in diplomatic dealings with foreign powers. When Raymond of Poitiers did homage to John II Komnenos outside Antioch in 1137, he was reportedly accompanied by 'his entire noble escort', and it may be that the nobles, who initially came to the city to discuss the relief of Montferrand, were the 'wise men' (*prudentioribus*) who earlier inter-vened to forge an agreement with the emperor in order to break his siege.[69] Their prominence continued when John returned to Antioch after the siege of Shaizar in 1138 and seemingly demanded the capital and its citadel. In response, Raymond secured a delay 'so that he could consider this fully with the counsel of his men', who consisted of Joscelin II of Edessa and the prince's *fideles*.[70] While William of Tyre's description of this lacks specifically noble connotations, he also noted that it was the 'nobles of the region' who both calmed a subsequent riot which forced the Greeks from the city and then led a delegation to restore the emperor's goodwill.[71] Thus, although the Byzantine accounts largely overlooked diplomatic proceedings, speaking only of 'other Latins', and 'all of the populace [of Antioch]', William certainly emphasised noble influence.[72] This continued with John's return to Antioch in 1142. As noted in the previous chapter, at this point Raymond is said

---

[66] On Saone/Garenton, see *CCSSJ*, 76–7; and pp. 222–4 of this book. On the Sourdevals at Lata-kia-Jabala, see Mayer, *Varia*, 113–14; *CGOH*, I, 109. See also Asbridge, 'Alice', p. 40; G. Saadé, 'Histoire du château de Saladin', *Studii Medievali 3rd Series* 9:2 (1968), 980–1016.

[67] Mayer, 'Wheel of Fortune', pp. 860–77.

[68] Vincent, 'Court', pp. 293–5.

[69] WT, pp. 670–1 (here 671): omni suorum nobilium comitatu.

[70] *Ibid.*, pp. 676–8 (here 678): oportet enim ut cum suorum … consilio super hoc plenius deliberet.

[71] *Ibid.*, pp. 678–81 (here 680): magnates regionis.

[72] Kinnamos, *Epitome*, p. 19 (JK, p. 24): λοιπαί Λατίνων; Choniates, *Historia*, p. 31 (NC, p. 18): του πλήθους παντός.

to have received an imperial demand that he should 'resign to him the city with the citadel and all the fortifications of the city'.[73] The Antiochene prince then:

> called together the powerful and foremost of the city and the whole region to undertake the role of deliberation, having asked for counsel … [Following this], they sent legates to the emperor from the nobles of the region … [and] signified that those [promises] which the prince had previously made should be considered entirely invalid, as the same prince should not be considered to have the right to make such a bargain in his wife's inheritance, or for either of them to have been altogether permitted the power or authority to injure the citizens or the leaders of the region by transferring it by right to another; because, if one or both should presume to obstinately persevere in this, it would happen that they would be ejected from the city and all of their lands, made exiles of their inheritance, which, to the detriment of their *fideles*, they had proposed to sell against the law.[74]

This represents a startlingly strong level of noble influence, certainly more than William would have dared to suggest at Jerusalem. That there is a lack of independent corroboration, means care must be exercised in taking this at face value, especially when compared to William's account of King Fulk's response to an envoy the emperor then sent to Jerusalem offering to come to the kingdom and provide military support. The king did take noble counsel on the best way to respond, but he controlled proceedings in a way that Raymond did not.[75] Perhaps this was a deliberate attempt to diminish princely authority in order to better demonstrate the strength of Jerusalem's monarchy, or it may represent William's disapproval of Greek possession over *Outremer* – a prominent theme of his text – by showing the breadth of popular opposition to its implementation.[76] Even if true, it is also possible that Lilie is correct to suggest that the Antiochene envoy was simply a ploy to force the emperor to back down – although for such a ploy to work, John would have needed to have recognised the validity of the nobility's influence.[77] Whatever the case may be, it is apparent that William of Tyre consistently presented the Antiochene aristocracy as highly powerful, particularly in matters of diplomacy. Perhaps the underlying motives behind his narrative might be questioned, as could the overarching legality of noble claims over *demesne* alienation (given the infrequency of their involvement in day-to-day administration), but

---

73 WT, p. 701: *urbem ei cum urbis presidio et omnibus indifferenter civitatis munitionibus.*

74 WT, pp. 701–2: *convocatisque maioribus et primoribus tam civitatis quam regionis universe, partes ingreditur deliberationis, consilium postulans … legatos dirigunt ad imperatorem de nobilioribus regionis … significentque se principis facta que precesserent rata omnino non habituros neque eundem principem sic paciscendi in uxoris hereditatem de iure habuisse vel habere omnino potestatem, aut auctoritatem in iniuriam civium vel principum regionis transigendi ullam aliquot iure alterutri illorum concessam: quod si in hoc vel uterque vel alter obstinate perseverare presumerent, futurum esse ut urbe et universis finibus illorum eiectos extorres faciant eius, quem cum detrimento fidelium suorum contra ius venalem proposuerant, hereditatis.*

75 *Ibid.*, pp. 702–4.

76 Edbury and Rowe, *William of Tyre*, pp. 130–50.

77 Lilie, *Byzantium*, p. 137.

his account remains a significant potential indicator of the principality's internal balance of power. This becomes clearer when the rest of the period of considered. Indeed, when Prince Raymond left Antioch to greet crusader forces under Louis VII of France in 1148, he was accompanied by the 'the nobles and major people of the entire region'.[78] Meanwhile, it was 'the nobles of the principality of Antioch', or, as Kinnamos described them, the 'nobles' or 'legitimate ones', who accompanied Manuel Komnenos during his procession into Antioch in 1158.[79] There are some exceptions, for the nobles were seemingly uninvolved in planning Renaud's initial response to Manuel's arrival in 1158, perhaps because of the emperor's speedy arrival, and there is no evidence that the aristocracy accompanied the prince on visits to foreign powers, beyond Renaud II Masoir's presence with Bohemond III in the kingdom of Jerusalem in 1179.[80] The latter probably resulted from a desire not to risk leaving fiefs undefended for extended periods, while the nobles' absence during the two visits of the counts of Flanders is likely explained by the fact that these were solely military ventures (in which, as will be outlined below, fief-holder involvement was a complicated matter).[81] Likewise, that they were not involved in diplomatic dealings with the leaders of the Third Crusade can be explained by the fact that Saladin's campaign of 1188 had wiped away all non-princely holdings.[82] For the most part, therefore, Antioch's nobility were at the forefront of proceedings when the principality interacted with major external powers.

Another significant element of noble participation relates to the marriages of the princely house. It was shown in Chapter 2 that the aristocracy took an active role in the succession of the throne after 1130, and it appears that this was not simply limited to deciding who acted as sovereign. Evidence for the ruling family's unions is mostly fragmentary, including the marriage of Maria of Antioch to Manuel Komnenos, that of Agnes of Antioch, daughter of Renaud and Constance, to Bela III of Hungary, as well as the circumstances surrounding Bohemond III's first two wives, Orgeuillse of Harim and Theodora Komnena.[83] Nonetheless, the events following Bohemond's rejection of Theodora in 1180 suggest that the aristocracy expected to be consulted over a new princess. As already noted, when Bohemond decided to wed Sybil – an Antiochene woman whose family had links to the castle of Bourzey and was accused of myriad offences ranging from prostitution, to witchcraft and even spying for Saladin – and attacked the Antiochene Church following his excommunication by the patriarch, a rebellion erupted led by Renaud II Masoir

78 WT, p. 754: nobilibus totius regionis et populi primoribus.

79 *Ibid.*, p. 848: Antiocheni principatus proceribus; Kinnamos, *Epitome*, p. 187 (JK, p. 143): γνησιωτάτων. See also Manganeios Prodromos (pp. 128–31), who referred to nobles or major peoples on this occasion using both 'προΰχονσι' and 'κέλητες', the latter of which relates to their position as horse riders.

80 WT, pp. 844–5; *Eracles*, II, 232; CGOH, I, 559.

81 WT, pp. 834–40, 984–7, 994–6.

82 CGT, p. 165; Roger of Howden, *Gesta Regis Henrici Secundi*, II, 165; BD, pp. 117–25.

83 For Maria, see WT, pp. 856–7; JK, pp. 158–60. For Agnes, see JK, p. 214; NC, p. 96; Alberic of Trois Fontaines, 'Chronica', *MGH SS* XXIII, 849–50. For Orgeuillse, see *Lignages d'Outremer*, ed. M.-A. Nielen (Paris, 2003), p. 83. For Theodora, see WT, p. 1012; MS, III, 389.

and 'the nobles of that region'.[84] Given that such internal conflict was unheard of in the principality, it is evident that the nobles felt a key element of their influence had been infringed upon. A number of reasons for this have been advanced. Cahen and Mayer described it as a reaction to anti-Church violence, but given that, as will be outlined below, all previous acts of aggression towards the patriarch had passed without noble intervention, there is perhaps more to it.[85] Hamilton has stated that 'whether they had political as well as personal reasons for objecting to Sybil is not clear', although Phillips has suggested that one such motive may have been fears of Byzantine reprisals.[86] The primary sources are vague in either regard: William of Tyre simply noted that the nobles felt the prince's behaviour was 'insane' (*insaniam*), Michael the Syrian withheld comment, and an Armenian colophon dated to 1181 implied that the Latin patriarch had fostered discontent.[87] In the context of aristocratic involvement in diplomatic relations with the empire, it seems likely that Phillips is to some extent correct, as the fact that Maria of Antioch was at that time still regent in Constantinople for her and Manuel's son, Alexios II, ensured that – at least until Andronikos seized power – the potential for support was great (a significant concern given the rise of Saladin).[88] Perhaps of deeper importance is that Bohemond's actions also threatened to have an influence over the princely succession. Should the prince's sons by Orgeuillse, Raymond II and Bohemond IV, die – like a number of their predecessors – early, then it was possible that any by Sybil, who was evidently not considered of suitable prestige, could suddenly have been thrust into power. The Antiochene succession was clearly a delicate process, one which could lead to tension if not properly governed (as became even more apparent after Bohemond III's death in 1201) and seen as very much within the noble purview. Concern over the lack of consultation over Sybil's marriage to the prince, when coupled with issues of diplomacy and the succession, is thus certainly enough to explain the noble reaction between 1180 and 1182.

The evidence is perhaps difficult, but there remain suggestions that certain elements of governance warranted strong noble involvement. This offers an important caveat to traditional historiography, as well as another useful indication that greater checks to princely power existed than has been envisaged. In part, this supports Martin's belief that the landed classes became more independent, but her view that this led to prominent self-interest, rather than a concern for the security of the wider principality, ignores key evidence to the contrary.[89] Central administration does appear to have been largely the preserve of the prince, and, as will be explored in the next chapter, local governance may well have been considerably

---

84 WT, pp. 1013–15 (here 1014): magnatibus regionis illius. See also Buck, 'Noble Rebellion', pp. 93–121.
85 Cahen, *Syrie*, pp. 422–3; Mayer, *Varia*, pp. 162–8. See also pp. 102–8 of this book.
86 B. Hamilton, *The Leper King and his Heirs: Baldwin IV and the Crusader Kingdom of Jerusalem* (Cambridge, 2005), pp. 164–5; Phillips, *Defenders*, p. 245.
87 WT, pp. 1013–15 (here 1014); MS, III, 388–9; M. E. Stone, 'A Notice about Patriarch Aimery of Antioch in an Armenian Colophon of 1181', *Crusades* 3 (2004), 125–9.
88 See also pp. 214–15.
89 Martin, 'Structures', pp. 246–7.

devolved, but it does not automatically follow that the nobles were entirely without influence over matters of state. Indeed, although aristocratic presence at Antioch was largely infrequent, and perhaps dictated by the importance of the occasion or their proximity, examples of noble involvement in the succession, as well as in diplomatic ventures and the events of 1180–1182, suggest that checks to the ruler's authority existed.

The Church

The final potential group to be discussed here is the Antiochene Church, which included the Latin patriarch, the archbishops of Tarsus, Mamistra and Apamea, as well as the bishops of Marash, Kesoun, Artah, Latakia, Jabala and Valania. From the early period, the Church was a prominent body within the principality, as although the emperors in Constantinople continued to appoint Greek patriarchs and, from as early as 1108 and the Treaty of Devol, to demand their restoration at Antioch, new Latin sees were created, or raised to the status of archbishopric, most likely with the aim of securing key military frontier zones such as Artah, Apamea and Cilicia.[90] Of additional significance is the fact that the patriarchate's sphere of influence was greater than the prince's, for – despite being based on smaller foundations than the earlier Greek Orthodox patriarchate – it stretched over the county of Edessa and even much of the county of Tripoli (despite a bitter dispute with the patriarchs of Jerusalem over the See of Tyre).[91] These factors allowed the first Latin patriarch, Bernard of Valence, and other figures like Peter of Narbonne, the archbishop of al-Bara and Apamea, to wield considerable military and governmental influence.[92] Indeed, in a polity formed through a holy enterprise, and one centred on a city so intrinsically linked to the early history of the Christian faith (its Church having been founded by Saint Peter), it might be assumed that Antioch's princes would have consistently made use of Church figures to cement and support secular authority. However, while Patriarch Bernard and the principality's other senior churchmen appeared in number of princely charters until the 1130s, and helped to secure Antioch's defences and governance in times of crisis, including after *Ager Sanguinis* in 1119 and Bohemond II's death in 1130, ecclesiastical influence appears to have diminished sharply after this patriarch's death in

---

[90]   Anna Komnene, *The Alexiad*, trans. E. Sewter and P. Frankopan (London, 2009), p. 392; K.-P. Todt, 'The Greek-Orthodox Patriarchate of Antioch in the Period of the Renewed Byzantine Rule and in the Time of the First Crusades (969–1204)', *The History of the Greek Orthodox Church. What Specificity? Papers Given at a Conference in the University of Balamand (Tripolis/Lebanon) 11–14 January 1999* (Balamand, 1999), pp. 33–53.
[91]   Hamilton, *Latin Church*, pp. 25–42, 393. See also J. Rowe, 'The Papacy and the Ecclesiastical Province of Tyre', *Bulletin of the John Rylands Library* 43 (1960–1), 160–89; M. R. Tessera, *Orientalis ecclesia: Papato, Chiesa e regno latino di Gerusalemme (1099–1187)* (Milan, 2010).
[92]   Cahen, *Syrie*, pp. 308–23, 439–40; Hamilton, *Latin Church*, pp. 18–30; Asbridge, *Creation*, pp. 188–207; Fourdrin, 'El Bara', pp. 351–406.

1135.[93] Bernard's successors and the other churchmen continued to seek to assert a position of power, particularly in times of tumult, but the efficacy of this was reduced. Perhaps as a result of increasingly fractious ties with Antioch's rulers, likely facilitated by issues of territorial fluctuation, money and the influence of Byzantium, ecclesiastical involvement in governance became severely limited, even if the Church's diplomatic and political prestige ensured it retained some value.[94]

Fulk of Anjou, in his capacity as bailiff of the principality, did allow for the involvement of Patriarch Bernard, Archbishop Ralph of Mamistra (Ralph of Domfront, later patriarch), Archbishop Stephen of Tarsus, Bishop S. of Artah and Osmund of Mt Garou, canon of St Peter's in Antioch, in his charters.[95] Archbishop Ralph also supported a sale made by William of Baronia to the abbey of Josaphat, which was witnessed by Hugh, canon of Mamistra, Hugh Blois, monk of St Paul's in Antioch and Walter, chaplain and priest of Baronia.[96] Yet, there is no sign that Bernard contributed to the decision to approach Raymond of Poitiers, and it is significant that tension emerged as soon as the new prince arrived in 1136, when Ralph of Domfront, now patriarch, demanded he perform an oath of homage in return for agreeing to allow the union with Constance.[97] Ralph appears to have initially gained his way and to have exerted the level of influence enjoyed by his predecessor, but this quickly led to a backlash. In 1137, Raymond reportedly used John Komnenos' appearance to arrest Ralph, perhaps with the excuse that a Greek Orthodox prelate was to take his place.[98] Interestingly, while diplomatic meetings usually engendered the ceremonial appearance of the Latin Church hierarchy, in this instance Ralph is not mentioned, perhaps due to his apparent incarceration or in protest at John's expulsion of the Frankish archbishops and churchmen from Tarsus, Adana and Mamistra.[99] The patriarch and clergy were in a position to accompany the emperor's ceremonial re-entrance into Antioch after the campaign of 1138, but it is noteworthy that they were not involved in the subsequent negotiations.[100] If a demand was made to restore an Orthodox patriarch, though, it was not fulfilled, and so Raymond's actions may instead represent an attempt to reassert the balance of power between himself and the Church.

It is certainly clear that relations between Raymond and Ralph never recovered, for although the patriarch issued an independent charter in 1140 – a sign of at least

---

93 See note above and *Carte dell'Archivio Capitolare di Pisa*, ed. M. T. Carli, 4 vols (Rome, 1969–1977), IV, 37–8; Kohler, 'Josaphat', *ROL* 7, 4, 21; *Italia Sacra*, ed. F. Ughelli, 10 vols (Venice, 1717–1722), IV, cols 846–8; *CGOH*, I, 43, 45, 102; *Libri Iurium*, I/2, 337; Hiestand, 'Ein unbekanntes Privileg', pp. 44–6; *CCSSJ*, 74.

94 For overviews of Antioch's Church in this period, see Cahen, *Syrie*, pp. 443–4, 501–10; Hamilton, *Latin Church*, pp. 30–50.

95 *CCSSJ*, 73–4.

96 Kohler, 'Josaphat', *ROL* 7, 21.

97 WT, pp. 657–9.

98 Al-Azimi, p. 141; IQ, p. 245.

99 WT, p. 663; Odo of Deuil, pp. 69–71.

100 WT, pp. 676–81.

some enduring authority – he did not appear in any princely documents.[101] Most significantly, this included Raymond's major donations to the Holy Sepulchre in 1140, which were witnessed by Archbishop Gaudinus of Mamistra, Bishop Hugh of Jabala, Aimery the deacon (Aimery of Limoges, later patriarch), three chaplains of the palace (Aimery, William Brachetus and William of Poitiers), as well as George and Thomas, cantor and sub-cantor of the Church of Saint Mary respectively.[102] Moreover, in 1140, Raymond was foremost amongst those who pushed a papal legate, Alberic of Ostia, to convene a Church Council in order to have the patriarch deposed on the grounds that his election, by popular acclaim rather than a vote, was uncanonical. Showing his usual indomitable spirit, Ralph refused to accept the summons to appear and was removed *in absentia*, yet he continued to fight his case in the West until his death there in 1142.[103] Ralph's actions in seeking to secure the submission of a secular power to the ecclesiastical are not entirely without prece-dence in this period: it was a major motivation of the reformist papacy and had also been seen in the kingdom of Jerusalem when Patriarch Daibert sort to impose ecclesiastical supremacy there in 1100.[104] Nevertheless, it had never been seen in Antioch (Bernard appears instead to have sought to work with the princes), and the changing nature of the principality's power structures, which saw the increased status of the nobility, as well as the loss of key archbishoprics in Cilicia, appears to have undermined the Church's political reach.

Ralph's successor, the Poitevin Aimery of Limoges, whose appointment was undoubtedly linked to Raymond's own elevation, probably enjoyed a more peaceful relationship with the prince, even if this did not equate to a prominent role in governance, for him or the wider Church. In fact, the only surviving evidence for ecclesiastical involvement in secular administration is from the lordship of Marash, as Geoffrey, chaplain of Cisson, witnessed a document of Baldwin of Marash in 1143.[105] The Church was still called upon for its ties to the papacy when military aid was sought after the fall of Edessa in 1144, with Bishop Hugh of Jabala visiting Rome and perhaps going on to France.[106] Likewise, when Louis VII of France reached Antioch as part of the Second Crusade, a procession accompanying the monarch into the city, which included the prince and the nobles, also encom-passed 'the entire [Latin] clergy'.[107] The symbolic prestige of the Latin Church thus retained value, even if its internal political influence waned. With Raymond's death at Inab, Aimery appears to have sought to recover some of this lost authority. Not only did the patriarch help to protect the city against Nur al-Din, paying

---

[101] *CGOH*, I, 108.

[102] *CCSSJ*, 76–7.

[103] WT, pp. 688–99; Hiestand, 'Ein neuer Bericht', pp. 314–50. See also Hamilton, 'Ralph of Domfront', pp. 1–21; Mayer, *Varia*, pp. 19–30.

[104] C. Morris, *The Papal Monarchy: The Western Church from 1050 to 1250* (Oxford, 1991); Hamilton, *Latin Church*, pp. 52–75.

[105] *CGOH*, I, 313.

[106] Otto of Freising, *Duabas Civitatibus*, pp. 363–5; *La Chronique de Morigny*, ed. L. Mirot (Paris, 1912), p. 85.

[107] WT, pp. 754–5 (here 754): universo clero.

for food and soldiers to secure its walls, he also reportedly exercised influence over governance and attempted to prolong his period of authority by advising Constance against taking a new husband.[108] The limited nature of the patriarch's abilities is demonstrated, however, by the princess' issuing of charters without the patriarch's involvement – albeit, in one instance, with the support of Bishop Gerard of Latakia – and by his apparent dismay at her choice of Renaud of Châtillon as spouse.[109] Indeed, so frustrated was Aimery, he is said to have vocally expressed his consternation at the unsuitability of the new prince.[110] This led to the resumption of conflict between Antioch's ruler and its patriarch as, in the summer of 1154, Renaud, perhaps goaded by Aimery's insults or out of frustration at the Church's apparent reluctance to furnish him with much needed funds to support military operations, had the patriarch arrested, placed atop the citadel with his head smeared in honey and left to face the torment of the heat and the insects.[111]

It remains a matter for debate quite why the Antiochene Church's financial resources were so much greater than the prince's, for while severe land losses and defeats in battle, as well as a lack of focus on trade, can partly account for secular money constraints, no specific contemporary evidence survives to account for ecclesiastical income in the twelfth century. Hamilton has correctly noted that, while the assimilation of former Byzantine Church endowments, particularly in the coastal trading sites like Latakia, Jabala and Valania, would have brought some income, the exact extent to which these were financial centres is unknown.[112] Moreover, while the tithe was a traditional source of money for the Church in Europe, evidence for its existence in the principality is unknown until the thirteenth century, and even then only in relation to monastic dues owed to the patriarch.[113] This would also have been impacted upon by the growing role of the military orders as landholders in northern Syria, because they were protected from ecclesiastical exactions like the tithe. It is unknown, therefore, how the patriarchs were able to pay for Antioch's defence in times of crisis, or how they could maintain (and perhaps expand) the patriarchal castle of Qusair, as the only evidence for the funding of its fortifications comes from papal efforts in the thirteenth century.[114] Whatever the case, this divergence in wealth evidently caused a deep fracture between the secular and ecclesiastical elements of the principality, for no one within Antioch came to Aimery's aid: instead it was Baldwin III of Jerusalem who stepped in and allowed the patriarch to go into exile in the kingdom.[115] Once in a position of safety, Aimery appears to have pursued his dislike of the prince, as he enacted the papal demand to lay a sentence of excommunication over Renaud regarding a dispute between

---

108 WT, pp. 772–4, 785–6; MS, III, 290.
109 *CGOH*, I, 190, 198.
110 WT, pp. 809–10.
111 WT, pp. 809–10; JK, p. 139.
112 Hamilton, *Latin Church*, pp. 137–40.
113 *Ibid.*, pp. 145–50; *Les registres de Grégoire IX*, ed. L. Auvray, 4 vols (Paris, 1896–1955), I, 1101.
114 Hamilton, *Latin Church*, pp. 154–8, 232–3.
115 WT, pp. 842–4.

Antioch and Genoa – albeit surprisingly no mention was made of his abuse of a senior churchman.[116] It is unclear how Renaud was able to elude punishment for his actions in 1154 when he could not do so in relation to his dispute with Genoa, although the continued unwillingness of Aimery (like his predecessors) to follow papal directives in the matter of Tyre could have contributed to this.[117] It is at least clear that relations remained sour, for Aimery is said to have offered to hand the prince over to Emperor Manuel Komnenos in 1158.[118] The Byzantine ruler rejected this, though, and although he allowed the Latin Church to play a lead role in his triumph into Antioch, Manuel also appears to have sought to supplant its hierarchy by demanding the installation of an Orthodox Patriarch.[119] Such a stipulation was not enacted, but it does appear Bishop Gerard of Latakia – who, in a demonstration of the Church's continued diplomatic value, had initially been sent as envoy to Mamistra to open dialogue with the emperor – was seemingly removed from office.[120] Thus, despite retaining his title, Gerard was never again seen in the principality, appearing instead in the kingdom of Jerusalem until 1161, after which point he disappeared.[121] This is a further sign that increased ties with Byzantium had an influence on the nature of relations between Antioch's secular ruling elites and the Church.

Despite this, Manuel's arrival actually allowed for Aimery's return to Antioch, even if it did little for his actual influence. Indeed, the only churchmen to appear in secular documents for the remainder of Renaud's reign were Renaud II Masoir's personal chaplain and Abbot Leuthbrand of St George's in Antioch, the latter of whom helped a secular figure, Hugh of Corbeil, to make a donation to the Order of St Lazarus in March 1160.[122] This level of absence also seemingly endured beyond Renaud's capture in November 1161, as although Baldwin III of Jerusalem sought to place Aimery in control of Antioch's administration, there is no overt evidence this was enforced – with Constance retaining power instead.[123] Moreover, there are no signs that the patriarch or the wider Church were involved in the princess' negotiations with Manuel for his marriage to Maria in 1161/1162, or in the dispute over Bohemond III's accession in 1163: no churchmen figure in either of the charters issued by the heir-apparent at Latakia-Jabala, or in the account of Michael the Syrian, who was usually sensitive to demonstrating the patriarch's status.[124] Matters did not improve for the Church, and perhaps became even worse, after Bohemond III secured power. In 1165, despite sending a letter to the West requesting aid, Aimery was expelled from Antioch by the prince as a result of Manuel's demand

[116] Hiestand, *Papsturkunden*, pp. 217–18.
[117] Hamilton, *Latin Church*, pp. 25–30, 36–42.
[118] JK, p. 139.
[119] WT, 847–9; JK, pp. 137–45; Manganeios Prodromos, pp. 129–37.
[120] WT, pp. 844–5; 'Eracles', II, 232.
[121] B. Kedar, 'Gerard of Nazareth, a Neglected Twelfth-Century Writer in the Latin East: A Contribution to the Intellectual and Monastic History of the Crusader States', DOP 37 (1983), 55–77.
[122] *Codice Diplomatico*, I, pp. 206–7; Kohler, 'Saint Lazare', *AOL* 2B, pp. 137–8.
[123] WT, pp. 854–7. See also pp. 211, 228–9 of this book.
[124] WT, pp. 856–7; *CGOH*, I, 311, 404; *Memorie Storico*, I, p. 202; MS, III, 324; *1234*, II, 119.

that an Orthodox Patriarch, Athanasius III, be installed in his stead in return for paying the prince's ransom following the defeat at Artah.[125] Whether or not Bohemond favoured this state of affairs is unclear, but the situation endured until the Greek prelate's death in the earthquake of 1170, after which Bohemond reportedly begged Aimery to return from his castle at Qusair and resume his position.[126] Without a Latin as head of the Antiochene Church in this period, there was little chance of it securing influence within secular governance, and it is even unclear whether the other senior Frankish churchmen continued to recognise Aimery's authority. Bishop Anterius of Valania was able to independently forge agreements with the Templars in 1163 and 1169, as did Abbot Peter of St Paul's in Antioch with the Hospitallers in 1168, with neither mentioning the Latin patriarch.[127] This perhaps indicates a lack of ecclesiastical unity.

It might be assumed that relations would have improved with the Latin patriarch's return to office, especially given Bohemond III's supposedly emotional request. Nevertheless, ecclesiastical involvement remained elusive, with the exception of Canon Alexander of Apamea, who drafted a charter for Bohemond III in 1174.[128] This period may even have witnessed a hardening of legal separation between the Church and secular power. Therefore, when the Hospitallers and Archbishop Gerald of Apamea (whose position was now almost certainly little more than nominal) fell into dispute over rights to appoint priests in the estate of *Tricharia* in 1174/1175, Patriarch Aimery oversaw the settlement and produced a document confirming its stipulations entirely free of secular involvement.[129] That this occurred at around the same time that Bohemond III issued a re-confirmation of the document which had originally sparked this argument – a gift made to the Hospitallers by Roger of Saone – led Cahen to propose a level tension between ruler and patriarch: the former perhaps expected to play a part in this dispute and his failure to do so was a sign of weakness.[130] It is certainly correct that these documents suggest secular and ecclesiastical justice were recognisably separate, at least in cases when the landlord was not a secular figure. This is further suggested by a document detailing another ecclesiastical settlement, made between the Hospitallers and St Peter's of Antioch by Patriarch Aimery in 1184/1185 (which again carried no secular witnesses), as well as the absence of the Church from the stipulations for Antioch's judicial regulations in the *Assises d'Antioche*.[131] In the case of the latter, this is in direct contrast to the secular landholders, although it is possible that this was a deliberate alteration made to the text by Sempad – who

---

[125] Louis VII, 'Epistolae', *RHGF* XVI, 61–2; MS, III, 326–7.

[126] MS, III, 332–5, 339. See also Hamilton, 'Three Patriarchs', pp. 199–207.

[127] *Codice Diplomatio*, I, pp. 40–1; Le Roulx, *Archives*, 29; *CGOH*, I, 397.

[128] *CGOH*, I, 313; Kohler, 'Saint Lazare', *AOL* 2B, pp. 137–8; Rey, *Recherches*, pp. 22–3; *Codice Diplomatico*, I, pp. 206–7.

[129] *CGOH*, I, 474.

[130] *CGOH*, I, 472; Cahen, *Syrie*, p. 443–4. See also J. Riley-Smith, *The Knights of St. John in Jerusalem and Cyprus, c.1050–1310* (London, 1967), p. 410; Hamilton, *Latin Church*, pp. 107–8.

[131] *CGOH*, I, 665.

would perhaps have wanted to limit the Latin Church's powers over a potentially Armenian ruler. The legal divide between secular and ecclesiastical matters had not always been so clear, as is shown by Prince Roger's intervention in Patriarch Bernard's attempt to interfere in the affairs of the Jacobite Church before 1119, as well as Raymond of Poitiers' involvement in the settlement of the Holy Sepulchre's claim to possessions within Antioch in 1140.[132] However, while notions of tension should not be ruled out, it is probable that Bohemond's charter largely reflects the Hospitallers' desire to safeguard their future rights once the dispute had been settled, rather than the prince's dismay at his powerlessness.

Relations may have softened towards the end of the 1170s, as Aimery is said to have distributed wheat to the citizens of Antioch during a time of great famine in 1178, which again demonstrates the financial superiority of the Church (although this is unlikely to have been a source of tension at this juncture).[133] Likewise, while Pope Alexander III called on the patriarch to excommunicate Bohemond in 1179, perhaps in relation to the ruler's ties with Byzantium (which had been strengthened by his marriage to Theodora Komnena), there are no suggestions that Aimery carried this out as he had done to Renaud in the 1150s.[134] Church appearances in secular governance remained sparing, although in 1180 Aimery made the first of only two charter attestations during his patriarchate. Thus, when Bohemond III confirmed a donation promoting the Spanish Military Order of Santiago to commit to conquests in northern Syria, he did so with the 'advice and good will of the most pious lord, our father Patriarch Aimery'.[135] It is likely that the latter's ties to Iberia, forged while studying at Toledo, acted as a conduit for this, as the rebellion which erupted later that year demonstrates that the prospect of tension retained prominent.[136] Indeed, as already noted, Aimery reacted to Bohemond's marriage to Sybil by excommunicating him and placing Antioch under interdict. The incensed Bohemond then raided ecclesiastical possessions, seizing what he could: an act which again hints at underlying difficulties created by the relative wealth of the Church when compared to the secular authorities. Fleeing the capital for fear of violence, the patriarch and churchmen took refuge at Qusair and Margat, with the scars of these events even prompting certain ecclesiastical institutions to give up their rights at Antioch in the following years.[137] A peace agreement was eventually forged and Church possessions were restored, but there was little Aimery could do to prevent Sybil's long-term status as princess, and the appearance of Bishop John of Tripoli as Bohemond III's chancellor in 1183 could indicate that the principality's

[132] Hamilton, *Latin Church*, pp. 191–2; *CCSSJ*, 76–7.
[133] MS, III, 373–4.
[134] Hiestand, *Papsturkunden*, pp. 278–9. See also Tessera, *Orientalis ecclesia*, pp. 368–9; and pp. 213 of this book.
[135] Mayer, *Varia*, pp. 114–17: consilio et voluntate domni piisimi patris nostri Aimerici patriarche.
[136] Cahen, *Syrie*, p. 509; Hamilton, 'Ecumenist', p. 271.
[137] WT, pp. 1012–16; MS, III, 388–9; Stone, 'Armenian Colophon', pp. 125–9; *CGOH*, I, 108, 397, 651, II, appendix XXII; *Codice Diplomatio*, I, pp. 40–1; Le Roulx, *Archives*, 29. See also Mayer, *Varia*, pp. 162–7.

senior churchmen were unwilling to work with the prince even after the settlement.[138] It is of great interest that the papacy did not seek to punish the prince for his violence against the Antiochene Church, especially as this came so soon after the murder of Thomas Becket in 1170 and Alexander III's earlier attempt to excommunicate Bohemond.[139] The pope possibly overlooked these actions because they damaged Byzantine influence in northern Syria (something he had promoted in 1179), but it is surprising that the prince countenanced provoking Western censure given that, as Miriam Tessera has argued, it could feasibly have affected his chances of securing military aid – and perhaps explains why the Order of Santiago never fulfilled their offer to recover lands.[140] This all serves to demonstrate the divide which had grown between the secular and ecclesiastical authorities of the principality, and even though the nobility appear to have supported the patriarch in the dispute, this, as noted earlier, was more likely to have been driven by their own interests, not those of the Church.

The situation appears only to have altered towards the end of the 1180s, as Aimery of Tripoli witnessed three of the prince's charters between 1186 and 1189 – which was perhaps linked to Bohemond's increased interest in events in the county at this time.[141] Yet it was not only the bishop of Tripoli who found use in Antioch's government, as Archbishop Albert of Tarsus acted as Bohemond's chancellor between 1187 and 1191, issuing at least five documents.[142] While it is unclear how long Albert had been archbishop, or how involved the ruler might have been in his appointment, it can be considered no coincidence that he began to appear, along with Archbishop Bartholomew of Mamistra, at around the same as Frankish interest in Cilicia was recovering and ties with the Armenians were fragmenting.[143] Importantly, Cilicia, and the growing threat of Saladin, may have facilitated a wider thawing in relations between Bohemond and the Church, for the charter confirming the sale of Margat in 1187 included amongst its witnesses Patriarch Aimery (only his second such appearance in office), Archbishops Albert of Tarsus and Bartholomew of Mamistra, Bishops Anterius of Valania and Aimery of Tripoli and Abbot Falco of St Paul's of Antioch.[144] Moreover, the patriarch and the bishops of Jabala and Valania were heavily involved in supporting the prince's request for military aid from the West following the disaster at Hattin later in 1187.[145] Before Bohemond's fateful visit to Baghras in 1193, he also appears to have entrusted control of Antioch to the patriarch: this was almost certainly not Aimery, for he is noted to have died this same year at Qusair (not Antioch) and was replaced by Ralph II, an elderly canon, on

---

138 Buck, 'Noble Rebellion', pp. 102–16; *CGOH*, II, appendix 23.

139 A. Duggan, 'Henry II, the English Church and the Papacy, 1154–76', *Henry II: New Interpretations*, ed. C. Harper-Bill and N. Vincent (Woodbridge, 2007), pp. 154–83.

140 Tessera, *Orientalis ecclesia*, pp. 379–80.

141 *Ibid.*, I, 782–3; *Libri Iurium*, I/2, 342. See also p. 240 of this book.

142 *CGOH*, II, 782–3, 906; *Libri Iurium*, I/2, 342–3. See also Mayer, *Varia*, pp. 93–5.

143 *CGOH*, I, 783. See also pp. 54–5 of this book.

144 *CGOH*, I, 783.

145 Hiestand, 'Antiochia', pp. 115–19; *Patrologiae cursus completus: series Latina*, ed. J.-P. Migne, 221 vols (Paris, 1844–1904), CCI, cols 1403–8; Roger of Howden, *Gesta Regis*, II, 38–9.

Bohemond's orders.[146] Ralph II, along with his successor, Peter of Angoûleme, then formed a key element in a city commune which grew within Antioch in opposition to Armenian attempts to increase their influence after Leon's capture of the prince.[147] With the fragmentation of the principality in the late 1180s, therefore, came a greater need for the princes to work with the Church, perhaps for their importance in courting ties with the West, but also as a source of income to pay for the defences of Antioch. Although beyond the remit of this book, it is significant that this may have prompted a return to demands for ecclesiastical supremacy, for Patriarch Peter of Ivrea demanded that Raymond-Rupen pay homage to him when he became prince in 1215.[148]

For much of the period, however, ecclesiastical authority and influence over secular affairs significantly diminished. While previous historians have often stressed the episodic nature of the disputes which occurred between the princes and the Church, it appears rather to have been a more deep-rooted shift in the balance of relations.[149] One source of this conflict appears to have been money, for successive princes were driven to arrest and even assault the patriarchs, as well as to attempt to seize Church possessions – a fact undoubtedly the product of the severe territorial fluctuations and the increased donation of lands to the military orders which reduced the princely *demesne*. These losses may in fact mark the foundation of the tension. In the early years of Frankish settlement, the creation of the Latin Church helped to cement princely power in difficult frontiers. Yet, the importance of the ecclesiastical hierarchy to the principality's military and political integrity was severely reduced as these areas fell out of Antiochene hands. Thus, while Bernard of Valence's influence may have been propped up by the significance of his suffragan territories, this would have become steadily less important, and simply served to accentuate the jealously over the divergences in income. Consequently, when Ralph of Domfront or Aimery of Limoges sought to exert their power over Antioch's rulers, or during periods of crisis, it made less strategic sense to acquiesce. Meanwhile the archbishops and bishops were no longer key landholders or as useful in governance, at least until the 1180s. There were times when interests converged, particularly when Antioch itself was under threat, but this rarely matched the period of Bernard's patriarchate. It is perhaps also of no coincidence that this change directly correlated to the growing power of Antioch's nobility over key matters of state and during crises, as well as the strengthening of relations with Byzantium, for the emperors frequently sought to impose an Orthodox patriarch over Antioch. Another key outcome of the fluid changes in authority and diplomacy in this period of the principality's history, it is evident that ecclesiastical power had sharply decreased.

---

[146] MS, III, 373–4, 412; *CGT*, pp. 128–32; IS, p. 257.
[147] Prawer, *Crusader Institutions*, pp. 68–76.
[148] Hamilton, *Latin Church*, p. 222.
[149] Cahen, *Syrie*, 501–10; Hamilton, *Latin Church*, pp. 30–50.

Military Service

When looking to understand the nature and extent of princely authority, it is important to assess another key aspect of this: the ability to extract and implement military services owed in return for landholding – long considered as the very heart of 'feudal' landscapes. Debate continues over the use and regulation of knight's service in the medieval West, but it is now largely recognised that the realities varied across the region. Likewise, though it remains questionable whether service and landholding were intrinsically linked, it does appear centralised regulation was attempted by some rulers at the end of the twelfth century through fixed quotas, as well as the English use of 'scutage' (a form of payment which replaced physical service).[150] There were possible exceptions, however, such as on certain military frontiers, where lords were excused services which drew them away from their borderlands, and caution must be used in accepting whether, even at this stage, theoretical claims were ever representative of reality.[151] Edbury has thus argued that, while regulation was present in Jerusalem by the end of the twelfth century, this may have been largely hypothetical, and greater lords would have been able to ignore demands for services, at least to a greater extent than minor vassals.[152] In spite of this, it continues to be assumed that the intense military demands of ruling the principality of Antioch ensured that its rulers could call upon unlimited provisions from their fief-holders.[153] Consequently, while Asbridge has convincingly demonstrated that this was the case before 1130, the changing internal dynamics of power after this year mean a fresh examination of the documentary and narrative evidence must be carried out.

This is made especially pertinent by the fragmentary charter evidence for the exaction of service from Antiochene fief-holders. The first identifiable example comes from Raymond of Poitiers' donation to the Hospitallers in 1149, in which he confirmed all gifts made by the Antiochene *barones*, 'excepting from this those of knightly fiefs which should not be greatly reduced so that the maintenance of its services should be destroyed'.[154] This confirms the existence of knights' fees (or units of land held in return for military dues), yet the absence of any of the great families in the document, as well as the problems in defining a *baro*, makes it difficult to establish if this reflects widespread noble military service. The presence of the household and *familiares* in this document could suggest that these men were provided with princely fiefs – landed or monetary – from which they were expected

---

150 Reynolds, *Fiefs*, pp. 350–68.

151 Lieberman, *March of Wales*, pp. 1–23, 138–72; Power, *Norman Frontier*, pp. 1–23; J. Powers, *A Society Organized for War: The Iberian Municipal Militias in the Central Middle Ages, 1000–1284* (Berkeley, CA, 1987); S. Church, 'The 1210 Campaign in Ireland: Evidence for a Military Revolution?', *Anglo-Norman Studies* 20 (1998), 45–57.

152 Edbury, 'Fiefs', pp. 49–62.

153 Cahen, *Syrie*, pp. 439–52, 527–8; Asbridge, *Creation*, pp. 150–1. See also Martin, 'Structures', pp. 238–42.

154 *CGOH*, I, 183: excepto hoc quod feodum militis non tantum minuatur in his donis ut curia servicium suum perdat.

to provide service (which lends further weight to the notion of their acting as castel-lans), yet it is difficult to expand upon this, or to support notions of a crystallised and vigorous system from which unlimited exactions could be made. Without any foundation charters for the great lordships, it cannot even be adequately accepted that aristocratic fiefs were *feodum militis*.[155] There are suggestions the aristocracy owed service, though, because Renaud II Masoir gave up his rights of 'lordship' and the 'service of one knight' in the estate of *Bearida* in 1178.[156] This document was issued in the presence of Bohemond III, so it is tempting to argue that the knight's service detailed here would have been part of the Masoir contingent should the prince call on him, but this cannot be securely accepted. Neither can it be firmly contended that this reflected a long-established service, or if it was an arbi-trary value set by Bohemond in order to benefit further from the donation. Even when the entire Masoir lordship was sold in 1187, the exact terms of any service owed by the *milites* of Margat – some of whom even witnessed the confirmation charter – were not mentioned, only the vague notion that the prince relinquished his rights to those things 'owed' (*debuerent*) to him as ruler.[157] While it does seem that some form of military service existed, there is no evidence regarding a formu-lated system of precisely calculated provisions, such as those eventually attempted in Anglo-Norman England and the kingdom of Jerusalem.[158] Interestingly, there is one document in which a quota was mentioned. When Bohemond III donated lands to Joscelin III of Edessa in 1179, the charter denoting this stipulated that 'he himself shall owe five knights to serve me, but, should he himself come into my land with three feudal knights who wish to serve for him, I concede to this freely saving my fidelity'.[159] While this confirms the existence of the forms of codified knight service seen elsewhere, Joscelin was not an Antiochene nobleman, and it is of further interest that, whereas personal service could be commuted to financial payments in the West, in Antioch a clause was instead inserted which accepted reduced provision. Finally, and perhaps most tellingly, though the thirteenth-cen-tury jurist, John of Ibelin, included within the law codes of Jerusalem a detailed list of military services (including quotas) owed by each of the kingdom's great fiefs, no such information survives in the *Assises d'Antioche*.[160] Service was alluded to, but at no point was it described as holding a military function, and detailed stipulations existed through which the implementation of even these duties could be circumvented.[161]

---

[155] Conversely, Martin believed the *feodum militis* to be the standard form of fief. See 'Structures', p. 242.

[156] *CGOH*, I, 546: dominii ... servicium unius militis.

[157] *CGOH*, I, 783.

[158] J. Holt, 'The Introduction of Knight-Service in England', *Colonial England, 1066–1215*, ed. J. Holt (London, 1997), pp. 81–101; Edbury, 'Fiefs', pp. 49–50.

[159] *Tabulae Theutonici*, 9: ipse se quintus militum mihi debet servire; sed ipse invenerit tres milites feodatos in terra mea, qui ei servire velint, salva mea fidelitate libenter concedo.

[160] John of Ibelin, *Assises*, pp. 607–16.

[161] *Assises d'Antioche*, pp. 8–43. See also Martin, 'Structures', pp. 246–7.

As a result, the traditional belief in a rigorous 'feudal' regime born from uniquely intense military requirements is not demonstrably sustained by the documentary evidence. The question remains, therefore: who did fight for the prince? In times of need, Antioch's rulers would likely have drawn on support from various sources. Walter the Chancellor mentioned that Prince Roger called upon mercenaries and indigenous forces known as turcopoles before *Ager Sanguinis* in 1119, and while the only further reference to such groups comes from a letter detailing the defeat at Artah in 1164, there is little reason to believe they would not have also played a part elsewhere.[162] Likewise, the military orders could be at times be relied upon for help, as shown by their intervention after Inab in 1149, their involvement at Artah in 1164 and their potential alliance with Bohemond III against Shaizar in 1179.[163] However, as orders subject to papal protection, they would not have owed formalised services for the lands surrendered to them within the principality, and there is little sense that either group became as embroiled in military expansion or defence as they did in the kingdom of Jerusalem: for example, as noted in Chapter 1, neither sought to aid the prince in fighting off Saladin in 1188.[164] In relation to major fief-holder contributions, moreover, it is significant that there is a distinct contrast with the gradual increase in regulation seen elsewhere, as the material for the principality offers only vague suggestions of service. The rate of source survival could impact upon this – it certainly impinges upon a complete understanding of the frameworks of service (for instance, whether the tenants of the great nobles might still have been able to serve even if their lord did not). Nevertheless, the available evidence points towards a far less stringently codified or regulated system. To elucidate further, a discussion is required on the actual practice of warfare, divided into four separate forms of conflict: campaigns of conquest, defensive actions, military alliance and raiding. While this is made somewhat problematic by an over-reliance on William of Tyre, his text, as already noted, should not be discounted, especially when supported by corroborating evidence.[165] Indeed, it remains possible to establish whether the lack of documentary codification was the result of no limitations, as Cahen (and others) seems to have assumed, or if a different perspective can be offered.

Campaigns of Conquest

Albeit not particularly prevalent in this period (undoubtedly a symptom of the inherent dangers in risking open conflict – as witnessed by the disasters at Harran in 1104 and *Ager Sanguinis* in 1119), campaigns of conquest offer an invaluable insight into Antioch's military structures.[166] As the military powers of Muslim

---

[162] WC, pp. 86–8; Louis VII, 'Epistolae', XVI, 60–1. See also Y. Harari, 'The Military Role of the Frankish Turcopoles: A Reassessment', *Mediterranean Historical Review* 12:1 (1997), 75–116.

[163] WT, pp. 772–4; Louis VII, 'Epistolae', *RHGF* XV, 540–1, XVI, 60–1.

[164] Morton, *Military Orders*, pp. 18–35.

[165] See pp. 66–8.

[166] J. France, *Western Warfare in the Age of the Crusades, 1000–1300* (London, 1999), pp. 150–65; R. C. Smail, *Crusading Warfare, 1097–1193*, 2nd edn (Cambridge, 1995), pp. 165–89; C. Marshall, *Warfare in*

Syria and Armenian Cilicia increased, and it proved harder for the Antiochenes to expand or to recover territory, they became increasingly reliant on the support of foreign rulers or Western nobles. In line with traditional historiography, though, it would be assumed that widespread 'feudal' involvement should be discernible, given the significance of such occasions and the fact that they would elicit more time to assemble resources than other forms of warfare. This does appear to be the case before 1130, as Bohemond II was able to 'summon knights from the entire principality' to besiege Kafartab in 1126.[167] The evidence for the years after 1130, however, suggests, that major fief-holder military service was not so extensive, with household forces providing the mainstay of invading Frankish armies.

Excluding Fulk of Anjou's campaign against Zengi in 1133, during which he, like Bohemond II, called upon forces from throughout the principality, the first instance in this period of an Antiochene prince entering enemy territory to expand his borders was Raymond's attempt to recover the Cilician plain from Leon in 1136.[168] The wider composition of his army is unknown, and the only discernible noble involvement came from Baldwin of Marash – who was probably Raymond's brother. As such, he perhaps joined out of familial loyalty, although he may also have been influenced by local concerns: the Marash lordship bordered on Leon's lands, so the Armenian's rise was a direct threat to his own security.[169] Fortunately, more extensive details survive for the campaign launched in conjunction with John Komnenos in 1138. William of Tyre documented that, in preparation for this, Raymond 'gathered forces from all regions', and collected together his 'magnates' to accompany the Greeks into Muslim Syria.[170] This description of the nobility's summons to service mirrored William's formulaic phrasing not only for the majority of similar ventures in the kingdom of Jerusalem, but also those rare instances when he detailed the campaigns of the counts of Tripoli and Edessa.[171] Aristocratic involvement was also attested by non-Latin authors, with Niketas Choniates mentioning a 'count of Antioch', and Ibn al-Qalanisi's remark that the prince had called on 'levies' perhaps alluded to the *arrière-ban*, or the general summons of all forces.[172] The nobles do thus appear to have been heavily involved. Regardless of social contracts, though, the emperor's presence would have made it difficult to abscond, especially in light of their earlier role in opening diplomatic channels over a marriage alliance and the common need to combat Zengi. Sadly, there is no specific information for the composition of Raymond's forces during his only other attempt at conquest, an assault on Buza'a in 1142/1143, beyond a suggestion that Joscelin II of Edessa refused

the Latin East, 1192–1291 (Cambridge, 1992), pp. 145–82. For Harran and *Ager Sanguinis*, see Asbridge, *Creation*, pp. 47–80.

[167] WT, pp. 613–14 (here 614): convocatis ex universo principatu militaribus.

[168] *Ibid.*, pp. 638–9.

[169] Sempad, *RHC Arm.* I, 616; MS, III, 244; *1234*, II, 81–2.

[170] WT, p. 674: convocatis ex universa regione ... copiis ... primores.

[171] *Ibid.*, pp. 608–10, 634–5, 638–9, 661–5, 706–9, 721–2, 734–5, 760–2, 77–7, 789–90, 826–8, 841–2, 872–3, 882–3, 917–19, 927–9, 948–54, 987–8, 996–1004, 1050–2, 1059–60.

[172] Choniates, *Historia*, p. 38 (NC, p. 17): χόμητί ... Αντιοχέων; IQ, p. 243. See also Asbridge, *Creation*, p. 151.

to participate.[173] The picture is, therefore, incomplete, even if there is some support for traditional opinion.

This is less true for Renaud's reign. The presence of the great nobles in his first charter, issued in 1153, could imply their involvement in his first military venture, the apparent capture of three unnamed fortresses from the Muslims that same year, but the evidence is unspecific.[174] It is significant, however, that no mention is made of aristocratic involvement in William of Tyre's report of the Byzantine-sponsored campaign to recover Cilicia in 1154, as the prince is only said to have 'convoked forces'.[175] This is in contrast to the chronicler's usual descriptions of military ventures in the other Latin states, which could either reflect the unusual circumstance of a Frankish ruler acting as an imperial mercenary, or, given Cilicia's strategic value, as well as the nobles' overall prominence in relations with Byzantium, instead signify a limitation to military service. It may also be that Renaud, acting in the return for a sizeable payoff, simply did not wish to share his spoils amongst too wide a force.[176] Importantly, the lack of noble involvement is also seen in 1157, as Renaud brought only his 'household and *familiares*' – not the aristocracy – to besiege Shaizar along with Baldwin III of Jerusalem, Thierry of Flanders and Thoros of Armenia.[177] Shaizar guarded a river crossing and a major route into southern Syria, and was highly important to Antiochene security, hence its inclusion in the 1137 agreement with John Komnenos and Renaud's refusal to allow Thierry to become its lord.[178] As a result, the nobility's apparent absence here is noteworthy. Fear of Nur al-Din's reprisals could have influenced this, as might the concern that a circumvention of the 1137 agreement – by taking Shaizar without imperial support – would elicit a negative response from Byzantium, with whom ties were already fractious after Renaud's assault on Cyprus.[179] The sources for Renaud's tenure thus fail to corroborate notions of unlimited fief-holder military service, with the likely prince-regent perhaps facing greater difficulties than Raymond had.

The opportunities for Bohemond III to launch conquests were limited, as his reign coincided with the zenith of Nur al-Din's authority, the rise of Saladin and the decline of Byzantium. There are some indications that attempts were made at expansion, yet he too struggled to extract service from Antiochene nobles. Bohemond was able to call upon 'the nobles of the region' when he and King Amalric sought to combat the Armenian warlord Mleh in 1171/1172, which offers an interesting comparison with Renaud's campaign into this region in 1154.[180] However, this may have been influenced by the fact that, unlike the earlier venture, this attack was

---

[173] Al-Azimi, p. 151; IQ, p. 264; KD, *RHC Or.* III, 684.
[174] *Urkunden Venedig*, I, 55; Robert of Torigny, IV, 180.
[175] WT, pp. 823–5 (here 824): convocata militia. See also JK, pp. 136–7.
[176] It was the duty of any military leader to distribute spoils to his followers. See Smail, *Crusading Warfare*, p. 103.
[177] WT, pp. 834–40 (here 839): domesticis et familiaribus.
[178] *Ibid.*; Phillips, *Defenders*, p. 280; Asbridge, *Creation*, pp. 47–91.
[179] On this, see also pp. 201–2.
[180] WT, pp. 948–50 (here 949): de regione illius maiores.

carried out for the benefit of the Templars and the wider principality, not simply Byzantium or to fill the prince's coffers. A different picture emerges for the later attempt to recover Harim, launched in conjunction with Raymond III of Tripoli and Philip of Flanders in 1177/1178, as the nobles are absent from all descriptions of the siege.[181] William of Tyre also recorded that the prince failed to call a noble war council when deciding whether to accept a tribute payment from Harim's garrison, which contravened protocol in the kingdom of Jerusalem and even the practices of earlier Antiochene rulers, such as Tancred.[182] The lack of aristocratic involvement is even corroborated by documentary evidence, as a charter issued by Bohemond at the time of the siege included no recognised fief-holders, only officers of state and probable household knights such as Odo of Maire.[183] It appears, therefore, that the nobles had absconded from involvement in a campaign to recapture a possession of singular worth to the principality, just as they had with Shaizar in 1157.

The notion that unlimited military provision could be extracted from landholders cannot thus be substantiated as regards campaigns of conquest. Certain occasions warranted noble involvement, especially when major powers were present, but the most frequent participants appear to have been the ruler's household, which helps to explain why the prince retained such a high control over its composition. The difficulties of the source material means caution must be urged in drawing conclusions over the balance of power, and although it might be argued that limitations to service served to prohibit the pursuit of an expansionist policy, it should also be recognised that the diminished Antiochene ability, or desire, to expand the principality's borders – caused by external factors like the growth of Islamic power – may have made its rulers less prone to summon service. The significance of these findings for challenging existing historical models is nevertheless important, particularly in relation to sieges of strategically vital fortresses like Harim and Shaizar.

Defensive Manoeuvres

It might also be assumed that the inherent danger of an enemy invasion would have elicited widespread military service. Indeed, although such events often left less time to congregate, any direct challenge to the principality's internal security threatened all landholders: it certainly provoked the widespread involvement of Antioch's nobility before 1130 and within Jerusalem for the wider period.[184] Despite this, aristocratic participation again appears far from wholesale.

The first princely move to oppose an invasion in this period was in 1139/1140, when Raymond gathered his forces at the Iron Bridge upon hearing word of a Zengid attack.[185] Muslim accounts do not distinguish between Latin participants,

---

[181] *Ibid.*, pp. 984–7, 994–6; IA, II, 254–60; AS, *RHC Or.* IV, 189–92; MS, III, 375–6; *1234*, II, 142–3.
[182] WT, pp. 681–4, 718–20, 723–6, 775–7, 882–3; Asbridge, *Creation*, pp. 152–3; Martin, 'Structures', pp. 238–9.
[183] *CGOH*, I, 522.
[184] Asbridge, *Creation*, pp. 151–3; Smail, *Warfare*, pp. 140–56.
[185] Al-Azimi, p. 148; KD, *RHC Or.* III, 683.

but charter evidence for the prince's time at this river crossing suggests the nobles were absent, for it was expressly stated that the *optimates* were not at hand to aid Raymond in assessing a suit brought to him by the Holy Sepulchre.[186] This can also be noted in the case of Raymond's last bellicose act: the battle of Inab in 1149. The catalyst for this conflict was Nur al-Din's assault on Harim, which occurred while Raymond raided Muslim territory with his Isma'ili ally, Ali ibn Wafa. William of Tyre recorded that Raymond then 'foolishly hastened to those parts with a small escort without awaiting his knights, who he had ordered to be called forth, because he was a courageous and impetuous man and could not be directed by anyone in these matters'.[187] Arabic and Eastern Christian authors estimated this force to have been between 1500 and 4000 men, which has caused Mallett to argue that this reflected the principality's entire military strength.[188] This is seemingly supported by a letter sent to West by the Templar Seneschal, Andrew of Montbard, who recorded that the prince died alongside 'all his barons and men'.[189] However, as already noted, *baro* remains a difficult term to define, and this missive would undoubtedly have sought to exaggerate the sense of crisis in order to provoke a Western response. Other Latin accounts, moreover, as well as that of Gregory the Priest, support William of Tyre's suggestion of a small force, while Arabic writers likely embellished details in order to boost Nur al-Din's prestige.[190] It should also be remembered that the numbers listed would have included a sizeable contingent of Isma'ilis. As such, the belief that this represented Antioch's full strength appears problematic. There are also prominent doubts over aristocratic involvement, as the only noble participant to be named was Renaud of Marash.[191] Beyond this, the presence of Renaud II Masoir, Tancred Fresnel, Walter of Sourdeval and Garenton of Saone in Renaud of Châtillon's first charter as prince in 1153, demonstrates that, at the very least, these men were not amongst the fallen. The totality of the defeat at Inab, though, makes it far more likely that they had not participated. Importantly, the only disappearances which can be charted after this battle, beyond Renaud of Marash, were members of the princely household, such as Adam of Quorchiya, Ralph of Montibus (the constable) and Peter Armoin (the castellan).[192] Even the marshal, William Tirel, who witnessed Raymond's final charter in 1149, appeared without title in Antioch in the early 1150s, which raises significant doubts over his

---

[186] *CCSSJ*, 77.

[187] WT, p. 771: sicuti homo animosus et impetuosus nec alterius consilio in huiusmodi regebatur, non expectato suorum equitum, quos evocari preceperat, comitatu cum paucis imprudens ad partes illas accelerat.

[188] MS, III, 289–90; *1234*, II, 115–16; IQ, pp. 291–2; AS, *RHC Or.* IV, 61–4; KD, *ROL* 3, 521–2; IA, II, 31; Mallett, 'Inab', pp. 48–60. See also Cahen, *Syrie*, p. 383; Elisséeff, *Nur ad-Din*, II, 430–2; Asbridge, *Crusades*, pp. 239–45.

[189] 'Epistolae A. Dapiferi Militiae Templi', *RHGF* XV, 540: cum suis omnibus baronibus et hominibus.

[190] William of Newburgh, I, p. 68; GP, p. 257.

[191] Although, as seen in Chapter 1 (pp. 38–9), there is confusion over whether he died here or at Kesoun in 1150. Cf. WT, pp. 771–2; MS, III, pp. 293–7.

[192] *Urkunden Venedig*, I, 55.

involvement.[193] It is possible that these were the men who William of Tyre claimed abandoned Raymond on the field of battle, which might explain the marshal's temporary loss of status, but such a widespread act of treachery is unlikely.[194] The more plausible explanation is that most of the aristocracy were absent from Inab. There are potential reasons for this beyond limits to military service, for Raymond is said to have acted impetuously – with the situation of his death (surrounded by a small raiding force) having marked similarities to the demise of his predecessor, Bohemond II.[195] As such, it may be that disaster was caused by his over confidence. Nonetheless, William of Tyre only mentioned the summoning of *milites*, not nobles (two groups he was keen to differentiate between when describing similar instances in the kingdom of Jerusalem), and even stock phrases, such as 'the full strength of the realm' or 'from all over', which might at times imply widespread participation, were omitted.[196] It is likely, therefore, that either through rashness or limitations to military service, Raymond went to Inab without the majority of Antioch's martial strength.

The brevity of Renaud's reign, and perhaps Nur al-Din's focus on Damascene affairs, means there is no evidence that he ever met an invasion force, but Bohemond III was not so fortunate. In 1164, within a year of his accession, the young prince faced a renewed Zengid assault on Harim. Bohemond reacted by hastening to the endangered castle with a force estimated at over 10,000 men, one of the largest ever seen in the Latin East.[197] The size of this assembly raises questions over R. C. Smail's comment that 'Antioch had ceased to count as a military power', although, as this army included various allies such as Raymond III of Tripoli, Hugh of Lusignan, Joscelin III of Edessa, Thoros of Armenia and Coloman, the imperial *dux* of Cilicia, the exact composition of the Antiochene contingent is unknown.[198] William of Tyre did suggest some aristocratic participation, for he stated that 'many other nobles' were taken prisoner alongside the prince and the other Latin leaders after joining battle near Artah.[199] The letters sent to the West in reaction to this defeat are regrettably unspecific: Patriarch Aimery of Antioch detailed simply that Bohemond 'collected his men from all sides', while the Templar preceptor, Geoffrey Fulcher, revealed the involvement of the military orders and

---

[193] *CGOH*, I, 183.

[194] WT, pp. 771–2. Battlefield desertion was not expressly mentioned in the *Assises d'Antioche* (pp. 8–10), but a refusal to do service (if that service was correctly requested and a good reason could not be provided) led to fief confiscation for a year and a day.

[195] Orderic Vitalis, VI, 134–6; WT, pp. 623–5.

[196] This is in contrast to his accounts of the other crusader states, as Joscelin I of Edessa reacted to a Turk invasion in 1131/1132 by calling up 'all the forces of the county' and Baldwin IV of Jerusalem convoked 'all the leading men of the realm' to meet Saladin at Jacob's Ford in 1179. See WT, pp. 634–5, 1003–4.

[197] *Ibid.*, p. 875; MS, III, 324–6; Louis VII, 'Epistolae', *RHGF* XVI, 60–1; KD, *ROL* 3, 538–40; AS, *RHC Or.* IV, 108–9; IA, II, 147–9; *1234*, II, 121–2.

[198] Smail, *Warfare*, p. 35.

[199] WT, p. 875: multi alii nobiles.

also described the participation of the prince's 'brothers and men'.[200] Consequently, although the sources suggest that Bohemond gathered forces more widely than his father had before Inab, it is unclear whether this specifically reflected the presence of Antiochene fief-holders, rather than distinguished allies. Significantly, it is again difficult to identify any noticeable departures of the great families in the aftermath of defeat, with the exception of Tancred Fresnel, the likely lord of Harim.[201] Most disappearances came instead from within Bohemond III's supporters at Latakia in 1163, such as Robert of Verdun, Walter Doella, Arnaud of Lambos, Bernard Cavalarius and Peter of Becar. There were also temporary absences for minor figures like William of Loges, Robert Mansel and the mysterious kinsman of the prince, Sylvester (perhaps indicating that they were captured and later released).[202] William of Tyre also recorded that, when King Amalric arrived at Antioch in late 1164/early 1165, he was met by the 'nobles and people' of the principality.[203] This is in contrast to accounts of the aftermath of *Ager Sanguinis* in 1119, as Baldwin II had been met by churchmen and the general populace rather than nobles.[204] As such, it appears likely that those *nobiles* described as having been taken prisoner in 1164 were not specifically Antiochene.

Like Inab, the evidence for the battle of Artah thus suggests the emergence of a pattern of aristocratic non-activity which undermines notions of unlimited military service. It is possible that the problems arising from Bohemond III's accession continued to cause him difficulties, but a distinct lack of co-ordinated action can also be noted during Saladin's invasion in 1188, as the Ayyubid Sultan swept through the principality without any concerted resistance.[205] Coupled with the doubts over whether services were also rendered for campaigns of conquest, significant questions are raised over the extent of princely authority during this period. Indeed, whereas Asbridge has demonstrated that Antioch's rulers had earlier enjoyed widespread aid in expelling invasions, it is possible that enduring memories of crippling defeats like *Ager Sanguinis* prompted the aristocracy to alter this custom in their favour after 1130. Although this helped to limit the short-term problems caused by disasters, especially while the Islamic world remained disunited, in the long term it may have served to make Saladin's conquests all the more achievable.

---

200 Louis VII, 'Epistolae', *RHGF* XVI, 60–1 (here 60): fratres et homines; 61–2 (here 61): contractis undique viribus.

201 Although he may already have been dead, given that his last charter appearance was in 1160 (*Codice Diplomatico*, I, pp. 206–7) and Harim's defences were reportedly led by a certain *Arugad* in 1164 (*1234*, II, 121–2). See also pp. 144.

202 *Memorie Storico*, I, p. 202; *CGOH*, I, 311. Michael the Syrian (III, 365–6) noted that, in the 1160s and 1170s, money was frequently sent to secure Renaud of Châtillon's release following his capture in 1161, but that he diverted it instead to saving other Latins, likely including those taken in 1164.

203 WT, pp. 877–9 (here 878): nobiles et plebeios.

204 Fulcher of Chartres, pp. 624–31; WC, pp. 96–8; WT, pp. 560–1.

205 R. B. C. Huygens, 'La campagne de Saladin en Syrie du Nord 1188', *Colloque Apamée de Syrie: Bilan de recherches archéologiques* (Brussels, 1974), pp. 273–83.

Military Alliance

Another prominent form of warfare was the assistance provided to the other crusader states. Joint ventures such as these were well known in the Latin East before 1130, for example Bohemond I's aid for the county of Edessa at Harran in 1104 and Roger of Salerno's presence in the kingdom of Jerusalem in 1118 – although reports of these only differentiated between knights and foot-soldiers.[206] William of Tyre's account of Bohemond II's role at the siege of Damascus in 1128 is of greater interest, as he chose to utilise the formulaic phrase that the prince, along with the other Latin leaders, 'gathered knights from all around'.[207] This lack of precision, while unusual for William, demonstrates the difficulties faced when using this source, although it perhaps reflects a desire to emphasise the unity of purpose throughout the army by not delineating the social status of participants. Nevertheless, it could also indicate that geographical limitations to aristocratic service were instituted early on in Antioch's history. This is of great importance because, just as it appears the Antiochene nobles rarely departed the principality during diplomatic missions, the same also seems true for military ventures.

Our first example is Raymond of Poitiers' decision to support Fulk of Jerusalem and Raymond II of Tripoli at Montferrand, where they were besieged by Zengi, in 1137. William of Tyre recorded that, after the prince had 'called together the nobles and major peoples, revealing to them his entire conscience, he invited and easily persuaded them to go to the aid of the king'.[208] In this instance, William possibly hoped to provide an idealised lesson in how the leaders of the crusader states should react to mutual security threats. This certainly helps to explain his comment that Prince Raymond 'judged it better to put up with whatever evils with his brothers than to withdraw so as to abound in prosperity and rejoice in tranquillity in any way'.[209] It remains noteworthy, though, that the nobles were demonstrably involved in the decision to go to battle; especially when equated to William's other accounts of Antiochene military ventures in this period. As already noted, the convocation of a war council was known at Antioch before this date, but there are no other recorded examples afterwards, or in relation to military campaigns launched in support of the other crusader states.[210] Indeed, the only comparisons are with Jerusalem, as Fulk took noble counsel when deciding whether to aid the count of Tripoli in 1137, and then 'summoned' (not invited) 'all the princes of the kingdom' to accompany him.[211] Queen Melisende even 'directed' (*dirigit*) Philip of Nablus and Elinard of

---

[206] Asbridge, *Creation*, pp. 151–3.

[207] WT, pp. 620–2 (here 620): collectis undique militaribus.

[208] *Ibid.*, p. 666: convocat igitur proceres et populi maiores, revelata cunctis propria conscientia invitat omnes ad regis subsidium et facile persuadet.

[209] *Ibid.*, p. 666: satius iudicat cum fratribus quantumlibet adversa sustinere quam eis sic deficientibus habundare prosperis et qualibet tranquillitate gaudere. See also Edbury and Rowe, *William of Tyre*, pp. 151–66.

[210] Asbridge, *Creation*, pp. 151–3.

[211] WT, pp. 663–6 (here 664): convocatis ... universis regni principibus.

Tiberias to march to Edessa's aid in 1145.[212] Significantly, the lack of Antiochene noble involvement also appears true for William's account of Raymond's subsequent decision to aid to Fulk in the capture of Banyas in 1140, as they were not overtly listed among 'the many hoped for forces and strong soldiers'.[213] For William to overlook the aristocracy in a venture to support Jerusalem is important, as he frequently sought to demonstrate the kingdom's central significance to *Outremer*. It would be dangerous to assume too much narrative intent on William's behalf, but Raymond's apparent need to 'invite' and 'persuade' the aristocracy, as well as their absence from Banyas, suggests that the author may have sought to imply the prince's limited authority to exact service outside of the principality.

The support offered to Baldwin III of Jerusalem by Robert II of Sourdeval and the *Antiochenos magnates* during his defensive withdrawal from the county of Edessa in 1151 nevertheless shows that the nobles were prepared to aid their Latin neighbours when a prince was not *in situ*.[214] Yet, it appears Renaud of Châtillon faced similar difficulties to Raymond, as, when he came to help defend Banyas from Nur al-Din in 1157, he is said to have brought only a 'distinguished retinue'.[215] This demonstrates a clear level of continuity in William of Tyre's text, both in relation to alliances outside of the principality and also Renaud's reign as a whole. The more extreme nature of William's portrayal of the limits of support for Renaud possibly represents an attempt to show the internal disdain for a prince he personally disliked, but the wider consistency, the archbishop's general care when utilising social terminology, as well as the fact that this even extended to campaigns in support of Jerusalem, is perhaps indicative of Renaud's reduced status and, more importantly, the geographical limits to military service.

The reign of Bohemond III, who showed a more active interest in the affairs of the other crusader states than his predecessors, provides a valuable case study in this regard. For example, when the prince entered Jerusalemite territory with Raymond III of Tripoli in 1179/1180, perhaps with the aim of enacting a coup to install their favoured candidate as a husband for Baldwin IV's sister (and heir), Sybil, he had with him only *militia*.[216] Likewise, when Bohemond assembled at Sephorie to join the attempt to break Saladin's siege of Kerak in 1183, William of Tyre noted that the prince came only 'with a modest retinue' – seemingly 'so as to not leave his lands devoid of military forces' and thus open to attack from Saladin (who was at this time threatening Aleppo).[217] Usefully, a princely document issued at Acre in 1183 demonstrates that the *comitatu* included Peter of Loges, Richier of Armenaz, Walter of Arzghan, William of Mt Hingron and William of Mt Cornet.[218]

---

[212] *Ibid.*, pp. 718–20 (here 720).
[213] *Ibid.*, p. 687: ingentibus copiis et valida manu optato.
[214] *Ibid.*, pp. 782–3.
[215] *Ibid.*, pp. 832–3 (here 833): honesto comitatu.
[216] *Ibid.*, p. 1007.
[217] *Ibid.*, pp. 1046–8 (here 1047): cum modico comitatu, ne terram suam militaribus copiis relinqueret destitutam.
[218] *Urukunden Venedig*, I, 68.

With the possible exception of Peter of Loges, these figures formed part of the princely *familiares* and so were not aristocratic lords. This demonstrates the accuracy of William's lexicological choice. As such, much like the diplomatic journeys of Antioch's princes, Bohemond brought household retainers, not the principality's landed nobility.

This points towards there being geographical limitations to military service throughout the period. It would be wrong to ascribe this to a lack of interest in the common good of the Latin East, as Montferrand and the withdrawal from Edessa suggest the Frankish nobility was prepared to participate when the need was dire. However, the traditional idea that the rulers of Antioch could (and did) draw upon unlimited martial provisions is unsubstantiated. This could again have been influenced by the changing military aims of the princes, or personal concerns for the principality's safety (as suggested by William of Tyre's comments regarding 1183), but the fact that it appears so consistently implies something different. It indicates instead that the balance of power between the ruler and the landholders was far more dynamic than has been recognised: with the security of lordships potentially placed over the desires of the prince, the nobles accordingly stayed at home.

Raiding

The most frequent form of warfare in northern Syria, as in the West, was raiding. Quick, small-scale attacks with the potential for great material gains, these were theoretically less of a risk than full campaigns, although they were not without danger, as shown by Bohemond II's death alongside the 'two hundred young men' who accompanied him on a raid into Cilicia.[219] It is true that Bohemond had not called upon the nobles, undoubtedly because the very nature of such campaigns relied on speed and small numbers, but it is worth assessing whether any evidence can be found to the contrary after 1130.

Unfortunately, the source material is rather vague, and while princely raids of the 1140s were listed around Sarmin, the Iron Bridge and Kafartab, as well as during Bohemond III's reign, no real insight can be gleaned into how such activities related to military service. Nevertheless, reports of independent ventures by the 'lord' of Barsutah and Princess Alice suggest it was not an activity limited to the ruler.[220] William of Tyre did note, though, that Renaud 'convoked forces' – which included the 'army and all of his men' – to raid Cyprus in 1156.[221] Again the nobles were not mentioned, so William possibly hoped to articulate that this act of violence against fellow Christians was deplored even within Antioch. Yet, aristocratic absence is a

---

[219] France, *Warfare*, pp. 150–65; Marshall, *Warfare*, pp. 183–209; Orderic Vitalis, VI, 134–6 (here 134): cc iuvenibus. WT, pp. 623–5.

[220] KD, *RHC Or.* III, 683–5; al-Azimi, pp. 148–54; IQ, pp. 290–4; AS, *RHC Or.* IV, 61–4; MS, III, 315; Otto of Freising, *Duabus Civitatibus*, pp. 363–64. For Bohemond III's raids, see pp. 53, 56–7, 59 of this book.

[221] WT, pp. 823–5 (here 824): convocata militia … exercitum et universas eorum. See also JK, pp. 136–7; *Eracles*, II, 209; MS, III, 315; Sempad, *RHC Arm.* I, 621.

frequent theme of Antiochene military matters, and so geographical limitations to service, fears of imperial reprisals, or even a princely desire to monopolise spoils, are all plausible factors behind noble non-participation. The same also appears true for the raiding expedition in which Renaud was taken prisoner in 1161, as he was ambushed along with his band of *militaribus*, which Eastern Christian sources suggested amounted to some 650 to 1000 men.[222] While this is not an insubstantial number, it is unlikely to have reflected the size of an army also comprised of aristocratic retinues, and there is again a lack of noble disappearances beyond Tancred Fresnel – who, as lord of Harim, is unlikely to have been associated with this raid. Fragmented as it is, the evidence seems to indicate that raiding was a private affair, both for the prince and the nobles. The small-scale nature of such enterprises likely precluded a need to extract military service from the great fief-holders, although the source material lends further weight to the belief that the prince did not enjoy, or perhaps utilise, the full capacity of the principality's martial might throughout the period 1130–1193.

Conclusion

This chapter set out to explore the powers of the princes of Antioch over the central mechanisms of government, as well as the exaction of 'feudal' service. It challenged the existing historiographical notion, championed by Cahen and others, that the rulers of Antioch exercised almost complete authority over a rigid Norman-esque 'feudal' polity. Despite the holes in the surviving source material, what has emerged instead is a highly fluid and complex state which defies suggestions of deeply engrained autocratic regulation, and resonates with modern research on the nature of medieval feudalism and frontier governance.[223] Indeed, it appears that, after 1130, Antioch's ruling elites had a much greater influence over princely affairs than has been imagined, and were generally less inclined to facilitate unlimited demands for service. While this did not necessarily lead to constant supervision of the central mechanisms of governance, for the ruler did hold a strong level of control over the household and his *demesne*, the aristocracy's influence is observed in matters of great importance, such as the succession, diplomatic ties with Byzantium and the selling of significant possessions. Likewise, the surviving sources do not sustain traditional conceptions of unlimited provisions for princely warfare, as while there were occasions in which wider participation can be seen, this was far from complete. Instead, the lack of demonstrable support in ventures of great importance to the principality, such as Inab, Artah or the attempts to recapture Harim, reveal that the balance of power was not so heavily weighted in the ruler's favour. It may even have served to limit his military capabilities and ambitions. As will also be explored in Chapter 4,

---

222 WT, p. 851; MS, III, 319; GP, pp. 278–9.
223 See e.g. Power, *Norman Frontier*, pp. 1–23; Lieberman, *March of Wales*, pp. 1–23.

it also perhaps led to a growing divide between the ruler and the aristocracy, most obviously indicated by the rebellion of 1180–1182, as the lack of discernible military service or involvement in visits to foreign powers suggests that their interests did not always converge with those of the prince. It has long been believed that the constant martial threat to the crusader states created a rigorous system in which Frankish settlers banded together to defend and expand their lands. However, the internal changes instituted following Bohemond II's death in 1130 point towards an attempt to prevent an overly centralised state subject entirely to the will of one ruler. The most likely catalyst for this was a desire to ensure that the longevity of the polity was not entirely dependent upon the life expectancy of its prince. While this may have served to somewhat diminish the ruler's personal standing and perhaps eventually facilitated Saladin's successes in 1188, the principality's endurance through a series of disasters up to that point attests to the success of this policy.

Appendix 1: The Officers of the Principality, 1127–1201

The Constable of Antioch

Name	Years Active	References
Renaud I Masoir	c.1127–c.1134	Hiestand, 'Ein unbekanntes Privileg', pp. 44–6; *Libri Iurium*, I/2, 337; WT, pp. 636–7; *CCSSJ*, 73
Roger *de Montibus*	c.1140–1149	*CCSSJ*, 76–7; *Urkunden Venedig*, I, 46; *Libri Iurium*, I/2, 338; *CGOH*, I, 183
Archimbaud	1153	*Urkunden Venedig*, I, 55
Geoffrey Jordan	1154	*CGOH*, I, 222; *Documenti Toscane*, 4
Guiscard *de Insula*	c.1170–c.1172	*Documenti Toscane*, 13; *CGOH*, I, 437
Baldwin	c.1175–c.1180	*CGOH*, I, 475; Mayer, *Varia*, p. 117; WT, pp. 1015–17
Ralph *de Montibus*	c.1186–c.1193	*CGOH*, I, 783; *Libri Iurium*, I/2, 343; *CGT*, pp. 165–72
Roger	1194–1201	*CGOH*, I, 966; Rey, *Recherches*, p. 25; *Documenti Toscane*, 50

The Marshal of Antioch

Name	Years Active	References
Garinus Malmut	1140–c.1149; 1160	*CCSSJ*, 76–7; *CGOH*, I, 183; *Codice Diplomatico*, I, pp. 206–7
Raymond	1140	*CCSSJ*, 76–7
William Tirel	c.1149–c.1152; c.1162–1169	*CGOH*, I, 183, 390–1; *Urkunden Venedig*, I, 61; *Libri Iurium*, I/2, 340
William *de Cavea*	c.1175–February 1179; c.1186	*CGOH*, I, 472, 559, 782–3; *Tabulae Theutonici*, 9
Bartholomew Tirel	c.1183–1193	*CGOH*, I, 783, 906; Mayer, *Varia*, pp. 118–21; *Libri Iurium*, I/2, 343; *CGT*, pp. 165–72
Hugh Flauncurt	c.1193–1194	*CGOH*, I, 948, 966
Thomas	1201	*Documenti Toscane*, 50

The Seneschal of Antioch

Name	Years Active	References
Eschivard of Sarmenia	c.1149–c.1169	*CGOH*, I, 182, 231, 367, 390–1; *Codice Diplomatico*, I, pp. 206–7; *Urkunden Venedig*, I, 61; *Libri Iurium*, I/2, 340
Gervaise of Sarmenia	c.1180–1194	*CGOH*, I, 614, 782–783, 906, 948, 966; Mayer, *Varia*, pp. 114–21; *Libri Iurium*, I/2, 342–3

The Butler of Antioch

Name	Years Active	References
Martin of Margat	1140–c.1144	*Urkunden Venedig*, I, 46; *Libri Iurium*, I/2, 338
Peter Salvarici	1149	*Urkunden Venedig*, I, 55; *CGOH*, I, 222
William *de Monci*	1169	*Libri Iurium*, I/2, 340

The Chamberlain of Antioch

Name	Years Active	References
Trigaud	1138	*CGOH*, I, 127
Basil	1140	*CCSSJ*, 76–7
Peter	1153–1172	*Urkunden Venedig*, I, 55, 61; *CGOH*, I, 222, 231, 390–1, 437
Oliver	1179–1181; *c.*1187–1201	*Libri Iurium*, I/2, 343; Le Roulx, *Archives*, pp. 142–4; Mayer, *Varia*, pp. 114–17; *CGOH*, I, 614, 782–3, 906; *WT*, p. 1016; *CGT*, pp. 165–72; Sempad, *Chronique*, p. 81

The Chancellor of Antioch

See also Mayer, *Varia*, pp. 86–109.

Name	Years Active	References
Franconis	1134–1135	*CCSSJ*, 73–4
Odo	1140	*CCSSJ*, 76–7; *Urkunden Venedig*, I, 46
John	1149	*CGOH*, I, 183
Geoffrey	1154	*Documenti Toscane*, 4
Burchard	1155	*CGOH*, I, 231
Bernard	1163–1170	*CGOH*, I, 311, 367, 390–1; *Urkunden Venedig*, I, 61; *Libri Iurium*, I/2, 340, *Documenti Toscane*, 13
William	1172	*CGOH*, I, 437
John, bishop of Tripoli	1177–1183	*CGOH*, I, 522, 648, II, Appendix 22; *Tabulae Theutonici*, 9; Le Roulx, *Archives*, pp. 142–4; Mayer, *Varia*, pp. 114–18
Albert, archbishop of Tarsus	1186–1193	*CGOH*, I, 782–3, 906; *Libri Iurium*, I/2, 342–3
Alexander	1193–1200	*CGOH*, I, 948, 966; Rey, *Recherches*, p. 25

The Castellan of Antioch

Name	Years Active	References
Peter Armoin	1140–1149	*CCSSJ*, 76–7; WT, pp. 699–700; *Libri Iurium*, I/2, 338; *CGOH*, I, 183
Payen *de Castellud*	1160–January 1168	*Codice Diplomatico*, I, pp. 206–7; *CGOH*, I, 391
Ralph *de Rivera*	1191–1193	*CGOH*, I, 906

The Viscount of Antioch

Name	Years Active	References
Thomas	1134–1144	*CCSSJ*, 73–4; *Urkunden Venedig*, I, 46; *Libri Iurium*, I/2, 338
Godfrey, son of Raimbaud	April 1140	*CCSSJ*, 76–7
Peter	1149	*CGOH*, I, 183
Boneth	Before 1154	*CGOH*, I, 222
Vasilius	September 1166–March 1167	*CGOH*, I, 367
Peter of Amalfi	1167–1174	*Urkunden Venedig*, I, 61; *CGOH*, I, 391; Rey, *Recherches*, pp. 22–3

The Duke of Antioch

Name	Years Active	References
Leo Maipoli	c.1134–1154	Al-Azimi, p. 142; *CCSSJ*, 73–4, 76–7; *CGOH*, I, 183, 222; *Urkunden Venedig*, I, 46, 55; *Libri Iurium*, I/2, 338; *Documenti Toscane*, 4
Geoffrey Falsard	1155–c.1160; 1167–1168	*CGOH*, I, 231, 390–1; *Codice Diplomatico*, I, pp. 206–7
William Baufre	1166; 1169 (?)	*CGOH*, I, 367; *Libri Iurium*, I/2, 340

Simon Burgevins	1174–c. February 1179; 1181	Rey, *Recherches*, pp. 22–3; *CGOH*, I, 472, 522, 559, 614
Roger *de Corbelli*	c. September 1180; c.1182	Mayer, *Varia*, pp. 114–17
William of St Paul	1187–1191	*CGOH*, I, 783, 906; *Libri Iurium*, I/2, 343
Ralph *de Riveria*	1193	*CGOH*, I, 948
Nicholas Jalnus	1194	*CGOH*, I, 966

The Duke of Latakia

Name	*Years Active*	*References*
Theobold of Corizo	January 1134	Mayer, *Varia*, p. 112
George	July 1134	Mayer, *Varia*, p. 114
Assetus	1151	*CGOH*, I, 198
William *de Cavea*	1183	*CGOH*, II, 23

The Duke of Jabala

Name	*Years Active*	*References*
William *de Cursibus Altis*	January 1134	Mayer, *Varia*, p. 112

4

Lordship in the Principality

Landholding was an imposing challenge in the principality of Antioch. The fragile military and political world of twelfth-century northern Syria, coupled with the region's unique topographical and religious variances, meant Latin settlers faced multi-faceted threats to their presence and security.[1] For Cahen, and to a large extent Mayer, this allowed the powerful ruling house to keep a strong hold over the nobility through its military and political dominance.[2] Martin has likewise noted Antioch's robust rulership, arguing that effective challenges to supremacy were prevented by the retention of key towns and cities within the princely *demesne*. Despite this, he also accepts that the *Assises d'Antioche*, created as it was through a process of negotiation (a sentiment echoed by Edbury), reflect an aristocracy heavily focused on their own rights, and that direct princely control over Antioch's landholding, as exercised through the office of the *secreta*, eventually became more relaxed than elsewhere, particularly Norman Sicily.[3] Asbridge went further, as in spite of recognising princely influence over charter creation in the principality's lordships, he also argued for the establishment – before 1130 – of a number of independent seigneuries which he classified as holding 'marcher' status: thus echoing the independent lordships seen on the Anglo-Welsh borders during the twelfth and thirteenth centuries. The holders of these fiefs, in the interests of defence, were thus granted a level of hereditary status and freedom from centralised control.[4]

The diversity of opinion here helps to introduce the difficulties inherent to this discussion, yet is not unique to the principality. Indeed, traditional notions of a deeply entrenched and powerful nobility in the kingdom of Jerusalem, such as that proposed by La Monte and Prawer, have since been challenged by Tibble, who instead highlighted the frequency and effectiveness of royal intervention in aristocratic matters.[5] Moreover, modern studies on the interplay between central

---

[1]   Cahen (*Syrie*, pp. 105–8) remarked that northern Syria's geographical composition – mountains, marshes and deserts – made settlement particularly difficult.

[2]   Cahen, *Syrie*, pp. 435–52, 527–43; Mayer, *Varia*, pp. 174–83.

[3]   Martin, 'Structures', pp. 245–7.

[4]   Asbridge, *Creation*, p. 168. See also R. Davies, 'Kings, Lords and Liberties in the March of Wales, 1066–1272', *TRHS* 5th Series 29 (1979), 41–61.

[5]   La Monte, *Feudal Monarchy*, pp. 88–9; Prawer, *Crusader Institutions*, pp. 20–45; Tibble, *Monarchy and Lordships*, pp. 186–8.

authority and frontier lordships on the disputed borderlands of the West have also emphasised the varied nature of relations. In discussing the Norman frontier with France, Daniel Power – mirroring findings for other contemporary borderlands – has suggested that, while 'rulers frequently had to appease the landowners at the fringes of their territories in order to retain and cultivate their loyalties, or to give to their local commanders a freer hand in dealing with the military exigencies that arose ... one of the striking features was the variety of territorial organisation at a local level'.[6] When seen in the context of the previous chapters, this renewed historiographical interest in medieval frontier lordship, as well as the groundwork put in place by Asbridge, demonstrates the need to reassess the nature of devolved aristocratic power in Antioch beyond 1130. The present chapter thus seeks to unpick the complex array of evidence in order to examine the true nature of the principality's internal balance of power. What emerges is the belief that, contrary to those who have offered rigid theories both in favour of, and in opposition to the strength of princely authority, the Antiochenes appear instead to have adopted a reactive fluidity – similar to that identified on other frontiers – which developed to meet the needs of governance and security on a local level.

Key Individuals and Lordships

It is at times difficult to identify the individuals who formed the great nobility in Antioch, with a simple topographic surname, as noted in the previous chapter, not enough to ascribe independent landholding or a place within the aristocratic strata. Further problems are created by the disappearance of certain lordships prominent in the years before 1130, such as those at Tarsus, Mamistra, Sarmin and Kafartab, as well as the frequent military disasters, for it means that the composition of the aristocracy differs to the period examined by Asbridge.[7] Despite this, there are some families or seigneuries which, to varying degrees, can be assigned lordly status.[8]

The most prominent were the Masoirs, who held the powerful fortress of Margat and much of the southern half of principality. Possibly of French origin, the family's earliest representative in northern Syria, Renaud I Masoir, enjoyed great influence in the opening decades of Latin rule as Antioch's constable.[9] The exact dates for Margat's capture and Renaud's receipt of the castle are unclear, as despite a general belief that it was taken by Tancred in 1117/1118 and then handed to the nobleman,

---

6   Power, *Norman Frontier*, pp. 4, 469–70. See also Davies, *The Age of Conquest*, pp. 93–6; Lieberman, *March of Wales*, pp. 5, 246–63; K. Thompson, *Power and Border Lordship in Medieval France: The County of the Perche 1000–1226* (Woodbridge, 2002), pp. 190–4.

7   Asbridge, *Creation*, pp. 158–62.

8   For an overview, see Appendix 2.

9   Asbridge, *Creation*, pp. 161–2; Cahen, *Syrie*, pp. 537–8; F. Chandon de Brialles, 'Lignages d'Outre-Mer, les seignors de Margat', *Syria* 25 (1946), 31–58; Mayer, *Varia*, pp. 162–83; Deschamps, *Châteaux*, pp. 191–202; J. Burgtorf, 'The Hospitaller Lordship of Margat', *East and West II*, pp. 11–50.

the Genoese chronicler Caffaro's report of its seizure by Renaud II Masoir in 1140 suggests either a later date, or that it had fallen out of Latin hands in the intervening period.[10] Due to the gradual sale of their lordship to the Hospitallers in the 1170s and 1180s, this dynasty is better attested than any other in northern Syria, with fourteen seigneurial charters.[11] Cahen has rightly cautioned against overstating the Masoirs' importance given the relative paucity of material for other noble houses, but the reality of their prominence cannot be ignored due to the scale of their holdings – which stretched from Margat and Valania to the south, and to the Ruj valley in the north – as well as their central role in the rebellion of the early 1180s.[12] Their prestige is further attested by their position as first secular witness in almost all of the princely charters they were involved in, as well as William of Tyre's description of Renaud II as a 'noble and powerful man' – a formulaic yet important phrase in the archbishop's chronicle.[13] The Masoirs can therefore provide a significant insight into aristocratic frameworks of power.

Often second to the Masoirs in princely documents were the lords of Saone, a castle which protected the main route leading from Jisr ash-Shughur into the heart of the principality, and one of the most impressive fortresses of northern Syria.[14] It was first held, along with Zardana and Balatanos, by Robert fitz-Fulk the Leper, whose power stretched into the southern and eastern frontiers of Antiochene territory before his death in the aftermath of *Ager Sanguinis* in 1119.[15] His successor, William of Saone, is said to have been powerful enough to take a lead role in the inter-Latin civil war of 1132 – although the reality of this is far from secure.[16] Recent archaeological findings have revealed extensive crusader renovations to Saone, which suggests that its lords were financially influential, although that the works seemingly remained unfinished when Saladin captured the site in 1188, suggests there were limitations to this – probably a result of territorial fluctuations east of the Orontes.[17] Documentary evidence for this family is unfortunately far less prevalent than for the Masoirs, with only one surviving seigneurial charter and a limited number of appearances at court; leading to questions over whether involve-

---

[10]   Asbridge, *Creation*, pp. 161–2; Burgtorf, 'Hospitaller Lordship', p. 14. For 1140, see Caffaro di Caschifellione, 'Annali genovesi di Caffaro e de' suoi continuatori', ed. L. T. Belgrano, *Fonti per la storia d'Italia*, 118 vols (Rome, 1887–1993), XI, 115–16. Although some doubts exist regarding the validity of this, Renaud II's absence from the Holy Sepulchre charters issued by Raymond of Poitiers in 1140 (*CCSSJ*, 76–7), despite the presence of all of the other great families, implies he was detained by other business.

[11]   *CGOH*, I, 201, 341, 457, 546, 613, 623, 763, 783, 787, IV, 595, 624; Le Roulx, *Archives*, pp. 134–5; *Codice Diplomatico*, I, pp. 206–7, 250.

[12]   Cahen, *Syrie*, p. 537; Buck, 'Noble Rebellion', pp. 93–121. Caffaro (XI, 115) also suggests the Masoirs governed the city of Maraclea in the county of Tripoli, but this is not corroborated.

[13]   WT, p. 1014: vir nobilis et potens.

[14]   Cahen, *Syrie*, pp. 538–40; Asbridge, *Creation*, pp. 159–61; Deschamps, *Châteaux*, pp. 217–48; Grandin, 'Introduction', pp. 139–80; Michaudel, 'Saône/Sahyûn', pp. 1–39.

[15]   Asbridge, *Creation*, pp. 176–7.

[16]   WT, pp. 635–6. See also pp. 222–4 of this book.

[17]   Grandin, 'Introduction', pp. 150–7.

ment in 1132, if it occurred, permanently undermined their standing.[18] Nonetheless, when present, the lords of Saone were afforded a privileged position, and the scale of their holdings would have ensured they were a recognised authority.

Next in significance is the lordship of Harim. As a castle of great strategic importance on the frontier between Antioch and Aleppo, it might be imagined that Harim's lord would have been afforded a position of high status.[19] This certainly seems to be the case, as Bohemond III married its heiress, Orgeuillse, in the late 1160s.[20] Having originally been handed to a Norman nobleman, Guy Fresnel, in around 1111, the fortress had a turbulent history – passing in and out of Latin control before its definitive loss in 1164.[21] While there is little reason to believe that it was confiscated from Guy's descendants before its capture by Nur al-Din in 1149, there is evidence that it was held after this date by a Western nobleman, Renaud of Saint Valery, and Joscelin III of Edessa, despite the continued presence of a Fresnel heir, Tancred, until 1160.[22] This ensures that, although knowledge of the lordship's extent is hampered by a lack of seigneurial charter material, the complicated nature of its succession retains distinct importance here.

An aristocratic ever-presence in Antioch during the twelfth century was the Sourdeval family. Of Norman descent, they quickly established their prominence in the immediate aftermath of the crusader conquest and were frequent attesters to princely documents throughout the period.[23] Mystery surrounds their central possession, Laitor, for although Walter the Chancellor suggests it was in the coastal region to the north of Latakia, as does the family's prominence in this area, Asbridge has argued it was on the Jabal as-Summaq.[24] The rest of their holdings are even harder to identify, as only a palace at Latakia, surrendered to the Hospitallers in 1135, as well as a money fief drawn from there, and nearby Jabala, are known.[25] Albeit limited, the surviving knowledge of the Sourdevals suggests their influence was predicated on the proximity of their holdings to the financially important coastline. Their prestige is certainly indicated by a prominence in the charters, as well as William of Tyre's comment that Robert II of Sourdeval was, like Renaud II Masoir, 'a noble and powerful man'.[26] The Sourdevals thus provide a useful comparison to those whose lordships lay in areas more vulnerable to attack.

---

[18] *CGOH*, I, 417. See also Saadé, 'Histoire', pp. 991–6.
[19] Cahen, *Syrie*, p. 540; Asbridge, *Creation*, pp. 163–4; and 'Field of Blood', pp. 301–16; Deschamps, *Châteaux*, pp. 59–60, 341–2; Gelichi, ' Citadel of Harim', pp. 184–200; Buck, 'Castle and Lordship of Harim', pp. 113–31.
[20] *Lignages d'Outremer*, p. 83.
[21] Asbridge, *Creation*, pp. 163–4.
[22] Robert of Torigny, IV, 199–200; R. Nicholson, *Joscelyn III and the Fall of the Crusader States 1134–1199* (Leiden, 1973), pp. 28–9; Cahen, *Syrie*, p. 398; Deschamps, *Châteaux*, p. 350. This is discussed further below. For Tancred Fresnel, see *Urkunden Venedig*, I, 55; *Codice Diplomatico*, I, pp. 206–7.
[23] Asbridge, *Creation*, pp. 165–6, 177; Cahen, *Syrie*, p. 535; Mayer, *Varia*, p. 173.
[24] WC, p. 258; Asbridge and Edgington, *The Antiochene Wars*, p. 141, n. 148. See also Cahen, *Syrie*, pp. 166–7, 535; Deschamps, *Chateaux*, p. 79.
[25] *CGOH*, I, 109; Le Roulx, *Archives*, pp. 142–4.
[26] WT, p. 783: vir nobilis et potens.

One such exposed lordship is that of Marash and Kesoun. Lying far to the north of Antioch, it was the only Cilician seigneurie to survive beyond 1130, and was clearly of significance: certain sources described it as a 'county', while Gregory the Priest stated that its influence stretched 'from the borders of Melitene to the gates of Antioch' itself.[27] Incumbents of the lordship included Richard of Salerno, father to Prince Roger of Antioch, and Geoffrey the Monk, a figure renowned for his military prowess.[28] Confusion remains over the true extent of Marash's independence, with both Amouroux-Mourad and Asbridge suggesting that it began to break away from princely control as early as the 1120s, perhaps even to the extent of owing fealty to the counts of Edessa instead.[29] Nevertheless, the evidence for this is far from secure, and it is significant that the two lords of Marash known in the period of this study, Baldwin and Renaud, were said to have been brothers of Raymond of Poitiers.[30] It thus remains pertinent to a discussion of Antiochene lordship. Fortunately, a seigneurial charter has survived, albeit with problematic dating, from which comparisons can be made to other noble landholdings.[31]

Another useful example is the short-lived lordship of Princess Alice of Antioch. Formed in 1130 after the death of her husband, Bohemond II, and surviving until her demise in c.1150, it was centred on the vital coastal cities of Latakia and Jabala, which had formed her dower. Asbridge has demonstrated that Alice created a dynamic and independent seigneurie, whose administration far exceeded anything identified outside of the princely household.[32] Importantly, it was also temporarily passed to her daughter, Constance, who acted as sole ruler of the principality between 1149 and 1153. As such, the nature of this succession, coupled with the relative wealth of documentary and prosoprographical evidence (at least in comparison to the other lordships), affords Latakia-Jabala a key place in the following discussion, even if Asbridge's work leaves little room for innovation.

Finally, evidence also exists for a county centred on the fortress al-Atharib, which lay only thirty-five kilometres west of Aleppo and was vital to Latin hopes of controlling the Muslim city.[33] Before 1130, al-Atharib was held by a certain Alan, who also controlled nearby Hisn ad-Dair and made his final appearance in the sources leading an attack on Aleppo in 1123.[34] Al-Atharib fell out of Latin hands sometime in the mid-1130s, only to be handed to a 'count of Antioch' following

---

27 GP, p. 243. See also Mayer, *Varia*, pp. 65–9.

28 Asbridge, *Creation*, pp. 162–3; Cahen, *Syrie*, pp. 117–23, 137–8, 357–60; Mayer, *Varia*, p. 65; Beech, 'Marash', pp. 39–45; Deschamps, *Châteaux*, pp. 66–9.

29 Amouroux-Mourad, *Edesse*, pp. 123–4; Asbridge, *Creation*, pp. 162–3. See also Mayer, *Varia*, pp. 65–9; Beech, 'Marash', pp. 35–52.

30 Beech, 'Marash', pp. 45–51.

31 *CGOH*, I, 313. This charter is dated 1163, which is considered impossible given Baldwin's reported demise at Edessa in 1146 (WT, pp. 734–8). Mayer (*Varia*, pp. 69–74) suggests Baldwin may have been captured and later released, although he accepts that the date is more likely to have been the result of a later copy of the charter made to protect Hospitaller rights amid fears of Byzantine intervention.

32 Asbridge, 'Alice', pp. 36–7, 39–44.

33 Asbridge, 'Field of Blood', pp. 301–16. See also Abu'l Fida, *RHC Or.* I, 18–19.

34 Asbridge, *Creation*, pp. 161, 169; Deschamps, *Châteaux*, pp. 136–9; Cahen, *Syrie*, pp. 154–6.

its recapture by John Komnenos in 1138.[35] Reference to a *comitisse de Cereph* – a corruption of *Cerep*, the Latin name for al-Atharib – in a charter of 1163 appears to indicate a county had thus been created here.[36] The site's permanent loss to Zengi in 1138, followed swiftly by its destruction in an earthquake, made such a title little more than ceremonial; but, while the lack of any seigneurial evidence makes further investigation impossible, the lordship's very existence has never before been noted, and it can provide a useful insight into inheritance rights and princely interventions in landholding.[37]

The Administration of Lordships

It was contended earlier that most historians no longer hold to the belief that medieval authority was uniformly absolute, arguing instead for varied expressions of power, as well as that lords on the peripheries were able to create their own spheres of influence, albeit to varying degrees of success.[38] In short, to argue in favour of rigid administrative systems is now seen to reflect a fundamental misunderstanding of governance in the Middle Ages. Ronnie Ellenblum has to some extent recognised similar patterns for the kingdom of Jerusalem, and while Asbridge and Martin have offered some fresh evaluation for Antioch, a rigorous re-examination of seigneurial administration in the principality after 1130 has not yet been undertaken.[39] However, such an approach yields important information on the ways in which lordly power was manifested on a local level, the tactics deployed to maintain control over difficult regions and also the nature of the internal balance of power. Above all, it can be shown that, contrary to a belief in the uniform hardening of either princely or seigneurial rights, matters were altogether less clear.

Issuing Charters

One of the most useful avenues through which to seek indicators of lordly independence is the creation of charters. These documents not only reveal the existence of decentralised administrative frameworks, but their titles and seals can also help to reveal the ways in which nobles viewed themselves and advertised their status. For this timeframe, there are twenty-three surviving charters issued from within Antiochene lordships, although this does not include princely confirmations, which are discussed separately. The vast majority (fifteen) were created by the Masoirs, with the rest emanating from Saone (one), Marash (one), the Sourdevals (one)

---

[35] Choniates, *Historia*, p. 38 (NC, p. 17): χόμητί ... Ἀντιοχέων.
[36] Le Roulx, *Archives*, pp. 97–9.
[37] See pp. 33–4.
[38] Bisson, *Crisis of the Twelfth Century*, pp. 1–12; Power, *Norman Frontier*, pp. 1–22; Lieberman, *March of Wales*, pp. 1–22.
[39] Ellenblum, *Castles*, pp. 105–45; Asbridge, *Creation*, p. 168; Martin, 'Structures', pp. 239–50.

and Alice's lordship at Latakia-Jabala (five).[40] There are also others issued by lesser individuals, such as Robert of Loges and Hugh of Corbeil, which provide useful comparisons.[41] Not all survive as originals, rather as stubs or cartulary entries, so while caution must be utilised when assessing their evidence, they are still of great use for determining the exercise of local governance and weighing the validity of existing historiographical models.

Regarding the use of titles before 1130, Asbridge has urged restraint in concluding too much from ascribed designations within the principality, noting that the available evidence provides 'vague and even inconsistent titles for landholders'.[42] Such caution fits with other recent work on medieval frontier lordship, with Power noting that 'titles are an incomplete guide to the power, authority and dignity of frontier magnates' in Normandy – with the exact status of a count, *dominus* or simply one who was 'of' (*de*) a site often not particularly divergent; a sentiment echoed by Dominique Barthélemy for the Vendôme region of France.[43] This is also discernible in the principality throughout the twelfth century. While *dominus* proved the major form of lordly ascription in seigneurial charters, for instance at Margat, Marash and Saone, there are possible exceptions: the Fresnels and Sourdevals were never called 'lords', while Alice was 'princess' at Latakia-Jabala (although this seemingly grew from her position as Bohemond II's wife, not her lordship).[44] Moreover, as noted earlier, non-nobles can also be seen with this title, while it was not until the early 1180s that Renaud II Masoir actually used the epithet *dominus Margati* himself, despite issuing a number of documents in the 1170s and being afforded this title by Renaud of Châtillon in 1160.[45] Further to this, while historians have traditionally propagated a belief in 'counts' of Marash, and it is true that both Orderic Vitalis and Matthew of Edessa offered this moniker to its lords, this is not altogether supported by other evidence.[46] Of particular significance is that Baldwin of Marash, in his only surviving seigneurial charter, used the designation 'lord', a title which was also carried on his seal and was similarly attributed to him, and his brother Renaud, by William of Tyre – who likewise described an earlier lord, Geoffrey the Monk, as simply one of the 'magnates of the region'.[47] This confusion has been alluded to, with Mayer suggesting that Matthew of Edessa equated count

---

40   *CGOH*, I, 109, 126, 133, 163, 201, 313, 341, 417, 457, 545, 546, 613, 623, 763, 783, IV, 595; Le Roulx, *Archives*, pp. 134–5; Le Roulx, 'Inventaire', 123, 149, 152; *Codice Diplomatico*, I, p. 250; Mayer, *Varia*, pp. 110–14.

41   *CGOH*, I, 133; Marsy, 'Saint Lazare', pp. 137–8.

42   Asbridge, *Creation*, pp. 156–7.

43   Power, *Norman Frontier*, pp. 213–22; Barthélemy, 'Castles, Barons and Vavassors', pp. 58–60.

44   *CGOH*, I, 313, 417, 613, 623, 783; *Codice Diplomatico*, I, p. 250; Mayer, *Varia*, pp. 110–14.

45   *CGOH*, I, 457, 546; Le Roulx, *Archives*, pp. 134–5; *Codice Diplomatico*, I, pp. 206–7. See also p. 93 of this book.

46   Orderic Vitalis, VI, 124–6; ME, pp. 238–9. Interestingly, the Armenian is rendered as 'prince' in the English translation of Matthew of Edessa, but, as noted by Mayer (*Varia*, p. 67), it is 'comte' in the two French translations.

47   *CGOH*, I, 313; WT, p. 634: magnatibus regionis; and pp. 734–8, 770–2. For the seal, see *Codice Diplomatico*, I, Plate II, no. 24.

with *dominus*, whereas Beech argued that the two authors' designations simply lacked precision.[48] Both are possible, and the preference for lord in other non-Latin sources demonstrates that the notion of a 'county' is problematic: Marash certainly cannot be attributed any greater independence merely through its title.[49]

Similar problems arise when assessing the use of *dei gratia* clauses. The notion of authority sanctioned by divine agency was undoubtedly an important one in the Middle Ages. It was utilised by rulers throughout the Latin world, including the princes of Antioch and even Jerusalemite nobles such as Walter, prince of Tiberias, to help legitimise their authority.[50] Within the principality, it is true that Alice used *dei gratia* in the early 1130s, while the lords of Marash and Saone used variants such as 'lord by divine compassion' or 'lord in the name of God'.[51] In contrast, the lords of Margat never laid claim to divine support, which is surprising given their clear prominence. As such, the use of *dei gratia* – or similar phrases – presents problems in assuming the extent of actualised authority, as opposed merely to an attempt at self-fashioned prestige: which also appears to have been the case in areas of France and Normandy during the twelfth century.[52]

The sigillographic evidence is even more problematic. Surviving impressions exist for Marash and Margat, as well as a document suggesting Alice had her own seal.[53] Those of Marash and Margat, like that of the prince and almost all twelfth-century secular lords and rulers, carried a mounted knight with couched lance.[54] There is some debate regarding the extent to which such seals represented elite status in this period, with David Crouch arguing that they were the preserve only of the very powerful, whereas others have posited that any knight might have possessed one.[55] It can nevertheless be advanced that, regardless of the extent of sigillographic proliferation, the existence of Antiochene aristocratic seals outside of the princely chancery reflects a certain degree of noble independence, or at least the attempt to advertise it. The extent of such freedom, however, is harder to discern from this material alone.

In this regard, a discussion on charter production is more significant. For the kingdom of Jerusalem, it seems that certain lordships, such as the county of Jaffa, had their own chancellors; although the widespread use of the formula *factum patriarcho* or *regno* suggests many Jerusalemite lords utilised patriarchal or royal

---

48 Mayer, *Varia*, p. 67; Beech, 'Marash', pp. 44–5.
49 JK, p. 23; MS, III, 270.
50 *CGOH*, I, 398.
51 Mayer, *Varia*, pp. 110–14; *CGOH*, I, 313: miseracione divina … dominus; and 417: in Dei nomine dominus.
52 Power, *Norman Frontier*, pp. 217, 219–20.
53 Mayer, *Varia*, pp. 110–14.
54 *Codice Diplomatico*, I, plate II, nos. 24, 34. Cf. plate II, no. 14. On the West, see A. Ailes, 'The Knight's Alter Ego: From Equestrian to Armorial Seal', *Good Impressions: Image and Authority in Medieval Seals*, ed. N. Adams, J. Cherry and J. Robinson (London, 2008), pp. 8–11.
55 D. Crouch, *The Image of Aristocracy in Britain* (London, 1992), pp. 138–9, 230, 243; P. Harvey and A. McGuinness, *A Guide to British Medieval Seals* (London, 1996), p. 43.

offices to create their documents.[56] Within the principality of Antioch, the evidence is again difficult. There are indications that, until around 1135, Alice had her own chancellor, an office which was also utilised by Walter I of Sourdeval, while notaries and a *magister* are occasionally identified at Margat.[57] For the most part, though, the method of creation is unclear, and the varied style of Alice's acts suggests that, even with the appearance of a chancellor, this office remained fluid.[58] It seems possible, therefore, that the majority of documents were drafted by the beneficiary. The sole charter for Marash, even if it now survives only as a later copy, was created by, or for, Raymond of *Palacio*: a Hospitaller and thus representative of the recipient.[59] Third-party scribes can also be discerned in other documents, such as the act confirming the minor Antiochene landholder, Hugh of Corbeil's gift to the abbey of Josaphat, which was ratified via the notarial auspices of the abbot of Saint George's of Antioch.[60] Importantly, Power has noted that the practice of religious houses drafting their own documents, even when confirming gifts received, was also known on the Norman frontier.[61] Yet, unlike Jerusalem, there are a distinct lack of references to princely notaries within seigneurial charters, with the sole exception of a charter issued by Renaud II Masoir, in which he confirmed a donation in the presence of Bohemond III and utilised the ruler's cleric.[62] From this, it can be argued that the aristocracy either used their own, unnamed notaries, or that beneficiaries produced most documents. Care certainly needs to be exercised in assuming that the scarcity of named seigneurial officials denotes tight princely control over lordly charter production.

While a clear internal lordly hierarchy is not entirely evident, the existence of Antiochene seigneurial charters can still help to reveal insights into internal relationships of power. Indeed, it seems possible that, like the aristocracy of Western Europe, the principality's nobility – albeit far more closed to the rise of new men than in the West (perhaps as a consequence of the lack of territorial growth) – merged into one social class defined not by title, but by lineage or status, in which 'the hierarchy is intangible in its principle'.[63] Furthermore, although the charter evidence does not overtly prove the existence of advanced internal administrative frameworks, it can at least be affirmed that documents were mostly produced away from the princely chancery. This does not quite allow for Asbridge's ascription of

---

[56] See e.g. *RRH*, 113, 115, 139, 147, 243, 274, 278, 297. More generally, see H. E. Mayer, *Die Kanzlei der lateinischen Könige von Jerusalem* (Hannover, 1996).

[57] For Alice, see *CGOH*, I, 109; Mayer, *Varia*, pp. 87–8. For Margat, see *CGOH*, I, 457, 613, 623, 783; Le Roulx, *Archives*, pp. 134–5; *Codice Diplomatico*, I, p. 250.

[58] On Antioch's chancellors, see Mayer, *Varia*, pp. 75–109.

[59] *CGOH*, I, 313; Mayer, *Varia*, pp. 69–74.

[60] Marsy, 'Saint Lazare', pp. 137–8. Hugh was not demonstrably a noble, so the use of a monastic scribe could simply denote lesser prestige.

[61] Power, *Norman Frontier*, pp. 42–3.

[62] *CGOH*, I, 546.

[63] Barthélemy, 'Castles, Barons and Vavassors', pp. 58–68; Power, *Norman Frontier*, pp. 201–2; Reilly, *Medieval Spains*, pp. 146–7.

the same 'marcher identity' claimed by the nobles of the Anglo-Welsh frontier, but some hints of Antiochene aristocratic independence are noticeable.[64]

Households

Levels of devolution can also be discerned through the existence of lordly households, with Power noting that the witness lists to seigneurial charters 'offer insights into magnatial power, for they may reveal the composition of baronial retinues'.[65] Like a ruler's household and *familiares*, seigneurial officials and landholding retainers aided a noble in local governance and military duties, perhaps in return for lands or patronage. In the kingdom of Jerusalem, despite Tibble's belief in a powerful monarchy, it can still be noted that Hugh of Jaffa had two viscounts, a seneschal and a chancellor in the 1130s, while Walter of Galilee boasted a constable, marshal and viscount in 1166.[66] To date, a comprehensive study of similar retinues in the principality has not been carried out for this period, although Asbridge has made useful contributions for the years before 1130, positing that the seneschal (an office which appeared in Tarsus and Marash) was the most likely component of a noble household, as it was in the West.[67] He has also shown that the ambitious Princess Alice created an advanced administrative following, including a constable, two dukes, a chancellor and a number of retainers.[68] Yet, it is possible to expand on this.

Given Asbridge's comments, perhaps the most pertinent issue concerns the prominence of the seneschal, as it might be expected that this office would prove widespread in the more varied documentary evidence after 1130. However, this is not the case. In fact, no seigneurial seneschals can be located outside of Marash after 1130.[69] Some potential explanations exist for this. First, both Marash and Tarsus were former imperial cities, if with a more Armenian character than some others, so it may be that the role grew from an earlier Greek position, like the duke. Direct comparisons between these two offices are, nevertheless, limited by the absence of allusions to the seneschal's actual role, as well as Alice's preference for a duke in the other formerly Byzantine cities of Latakia and Jabala. If they were similar, then the Armenian influence within Marah and Tarsus potentially contributed to the differences in title, but this is unclear. More importantly, it can also be questioned whether the existence of this office actually represented noble independence. While Asbridge has noted the prominence of lordly seneschals in the West, Power has contended that – on the Norman frontier at least – this officer actually acted as a ducal agent.[70] Rather than noble autonomy, the *dapifer* of Marash could thus have

---

[64] Asbridge, *Creation*, p. 159; Davies, 'Kings, Lords and Liberties', pp. 41–61; Lieberman, *March of Wales*, p. 254.

[65] Power, *Norman Frontier*, p. 286.

[66] *Codice Diplomatico*, I, pp. 42, 201.

[67] Asbridge, *Creation*, p. 158; Crouch, *Image of Aristocracy*, pp. 290–2.

[68] Asbridge, 'Alice', pp. 39–44.

[69] *CGOH*, I, 313.

[70] Power, *Norman Frontier*, pp. 23–4.

actually represented theoretical central interference, even if there are suggestions at a growing alienation from the prince. Cilicia's strategic significance, as outlined in the opening chapter, as well as Marash's isolation from the rest of the principality, certainly makes it unsurprising that a ruler may have sought to retain some influence here. Similar tactics were certainly utilised by other twelfth-century rulers, such as the counts of Barcelona.[71] As such, it cannot be assumed that the existence of a seneschal demonstrates that Marash enjoyed complete freedom from princely governance, as also becomes clear when issues of succession are examined.[72]

The seneschal was not the only seigneurial officer to appear in the principality, though; for, while there is no surviving evidence for household officers for Saone, Harim or the Sourdevals, Margat is known to have had notaries, *magisters*, castellans and two *ru'asa*.[73] The presence of notarial figures here, as well as in Alice's seigneurie at Latakia-Jabala, suggests charter-creating facilities and a desire to promote a level of independence. Likewise, the prevalence of castellans reflects the high number of fortresses in the region around Margat, and helps to indicate that, in a similar vein to Western frontiers, local lords were expected to provide for their own defences – although this was seemingly not as regulated as in Iberia.[74] The *ru'asa*, an indigenous official who acted as a headman for non-Latin communities (as seen elsewhere in the Latin East and on other medieval Christian–Muslim frontiers), could also reflect a greater need to court the cooperation of indigenous communities here than in the other lordships.[75] Generalisations cannot be made given the small evidence base, but this is made more likely given that Masoir lands covered the largely rural and mountainous southern areas of the principality, some of which bordered on Isma'ili holdings.[76] Consequently, the lack of urban officials, like the seneschal or duke, as well as a concern for interaction with non-Latins, suggests that lordly frontier administration here, like in the West, evolved to meet the needs of a locality, rather than following distinct patterns.[77]

Also of significance are the retainers attached to the households of the lords of Margat, Saone, Marash and Latakia-Jabala, as the presence of such individuals helps to reveal the extent of lordly influence in the surrounding areas. It can also indicate levels of seigneurial ambition, with the portioning of lands to followers helping to create loyal bases of support which could ensure regional authority and autonomy.[78] Whilst the processes of fief alienation will be discussed in depth below, an analysis of retinue size remains pertinent. If importance is to be ascribed by extent, then it becomes evident that the lordships of Margat, Marash and Latakia-Jabala were

---

[71] T. Barton, 'Lords, Settlers and Shifting Frontiers in Medieval Catalonia', *JMH* 30 (2010), 7–8.
[72] See pp. 142–3.
[73] *CGOH*, I, 457, 613, 623, 783, IV, 595; *Codice Diplomatico*, I, p. 250; Le Roulx, *Archives*, pp. 134–5.
[74] Riis, 'Übernahme', pp. 151–6. See also Lieberman, *March of Wales*, pp. 138–72; Barton, 'Lords', pp. 32–3; Reilly, *Medieval Spains*, p. 120.
[75] MacEvitt, *Rough Tolerance*, pp. 150–3. See also pp. 179–80 of this book.
[76] Riis, 'Medieval Period', pp. 85–115.
[77] Power, *Norman Frontier*, pp. 187–8; Lieberman, *March of Wales*, pp. 215–17.
[78] Power, *Norman Frontier*, p. 300; Lieberman, *March of Wales*, pp. 56–101.

more powerful than Saone. In 1170, its lord could summon only three witnesses, whereas fourteen figures are found in Masoir documents, thirteen in Alice's and eleven at Marash.[79] It is possible that a direct correlation exists between the desire for independence and the numbers of retainers, as the latter three lordships are each believed to have challenged princely authority. Yet, the lords of Saone are also said to have made a bid for power in 1132, and so other factors cannot be discounted, in particular topography. Margat, Marash and Latakia-Jabala all lay in areas conducive to settlement or commerce – although the extent to which Alice attracted new followers, or merely accepted those who were already influential in these cities, is unknown. Conversely, Saone guarded a rocky region near to the Jisr ash-Shughur–Antioch road, and the difficult terrain, coupled with the frequency of Zengid assaults in the surrounding region (if not against the castle itself), perhaps hampered attempts to attract retainers.[80] Evidence for lordly vassals elsewhere nevertheless helps to show that, like their counterparts in the West, Antioch's aristocracy sought to attract followers, almost certainly with the intention of demonstrating and increasing their authority.

The variability of aristocratic households in the principality is evident, however, as is the realisation that local government adapted to meet lordly ambitions and the needs of the area – a trend also seen in other medieval polities, such as Iberia or Norman Italy.[81] Despite this, princely interference might also be detected, for it could be concluded – as Cahen seems to have done – that the lack of seigneurial officers, when compared to Jerusalemite lordships, indicates lower levels of power devolution. Yet, the situations are very different. Whereas most of Jerusalem's baronies were only infrequently subject to attack, and were mostly in close proximity to the Holy City, the principality's lordships were generally more dispersed and vulnerable to assault.[82] Military concerns would thus have been prioritised over those of mundane administration, and it cannot be considered a coincidence that the most demonstrably advanced lordship, Latakia-Jabala, consisted of coastal possessions which, albeit not free from danger, was far less exposed than its counterparts. Furthermore, as already noted, the Antiochene nobles – whether through distance from the capital or a diminishing need to attend the princely court – were far less involved in centralised governance than those in the kingdom of Jerusalem, a trait similar to that identified for Norman Italy and Angevin England.[83] Therefore, the lack of aristocratic household figures may not indicate less devolution; rather, that the static nature of the principality's aristocracy allowed them to take a more personal approach to lordly administration than in Palestine. Asbridge's argument

---

[79] For Saone, see *CGOH*, I, 417. For Margat, see *CGOH*, I, 457, 546, 613, 623, 783, IV, 595; *Codice Diplomatico*, I, p. 250; Le Roulx, *Archives*, pp. 134–5. For Alice, see Mayer, *Varia*, pp. 110–14; *CGOH*, I, 109. For Marash, see *CGOH*, I, 313.

[80] Cahen, *Syrie*, pp. 109–76.

[81] Barton, 'Lords', pp. 3–5; Reilly, *Medieval Spains*, pp. 144–5; J.-M. Martin, 'Settlement and the Agrarian Economy', *The Society of Norman Italy*, ed. G. Loud and A. Metcalfe (Leiden, 2002), pp. 31–3.

[82] Ellenblum, *Castles*, pp. 146–64.

[83] Matthew, *Sicily*, p. 144; Vincent, 'Court', pp. 292–3.

that noble administrative frameworks would have developed to meet the needs of an increasingly independent 'marcher' nobility, while not without support, is consequently not consistently sustained, as the extant evidence suggests a far greater diversity and fluidity than he envisaged.

Rights of Inheritance

Perhaps the most significant indicator of lordly independence is the extent to which nobles claimed inheritance rights. By passing seigneuries along distinct familial lines, as well as alienating lands to loyal followers, nobles could establish deeply entrenched networks of power. This trend has provoked debate for regions across the medieval world. Tibble has suggested that the kings of Jerusalem frequently altered the composition of lordships in order to undermine aristocratic authority.[84] Moreover, recent works on Western frontiers, such as the Anglo-Welsh Marches or the Norman borders with France, have emphasised that the diverse relationships between noble inheritance and centralised interference prevented uniform seigneurial independence, although certain lords were able to claim autonomy and to forge strong centres of influence.[85] For Antioch, Asbridge has challenged Cahen and Mayer by arguing that the principle of hereditary right did emerge before 1130, while Martin has seen in the *Assises d'Antioche*, as well as diminished references to the *secreta*, evidence that central control over lordly succession rights were relaxed so long as military service was not diminished.[86] There nevertheless remains a need for a more systematic re-examination of the principality's lordly inheritance rights after 1130, particularly in relation to wider advances in frontier scholarship and the evidence presented here regarding the principality's internal balance of power. Indeed, as will be argued, the diversity of identifiable custom belies notions of rigid systems or uniform evolution.

Familial Succession

At the heart of this lies the issue of familial succession. By succeeding through various generations, dynasties could be formed that built relationships which permeated the frameworks of authority throughout the surrounding region. It was not only local lords who realised the benefits of a stable, long-standing nobility: rulers could also use established landholding networks to call upon influential allies, provided their loyalties were retained. A delicate balance was thus required

---

[84] Tibble, *Monarchy and Lordships*, pp. 186–8. Cf. La Monte, *Feudal Monarchy*, pp. 88–9; Prawer, *Crusader Institutions*, pp. 20–45.

[85] Lieberman, *March of Wales*, pp. 56–74, 246–3; Power, *Norman Frontier*, pp. 467–7; Thompson, *Power and Border Lordship*, pp. 190–4.

[86] Asbridge, *Creation*, p. 168; Cahen, *Syrie*, pp. 435–52, 527–43; Mayer, *Varia*, pp. 174–83; Martin, 'Structures', pp. 241–7.

between demonstrations of largesse – important for retaining aristocratic goodwill and ensuring lordships were strong enough to administer and defend themselves – and maintaining the paramount prestige of central authority. For Jerusalem, Tibble has argued that royal attempts to strike such an equilibrium led its kings to interfere too frequently in the composition of seigneuries, leaving them too fragmented to repel Saladin's invasions in the 1180s.[87] Similar patterns have been identified in the Shropshire region of the Welsh Marches, especially during the tumultuous decades following the Norman Conquest (although for the most part royal interest was sporadic), whereas the male right to succession seems to have been protected in ducal Normandy until the latter part of the twelfth century.[88] The situation was patently complex throughout Latin Christendom, but the evidence for the principality can offer important insights into the balance of power here and also the wider nature of frontier authority.

It must first be noted that, since no foundation charters survive for Antioch's great lordships, the extent to which Asbridge is correct to argue that dynastic successions were formally enshrined in the creation of these seigneuries, or if they emerged on a more ad hoc basis, is unclear. As Alice's lordship of Latakia-Jabala evolved from her dower lands, and reverted back to the princely *demesne* via Princess Constance in the 1150s, its use to the present discussion is limited.[89] Moreover, given that Alice's charters alluded to princely authority as early as 1140, it appears her freedoms had already diminished.[90] There is more evidence regarding the nature of familial descent for Antioch's other lordships. Margat passed along three generations of the Masoir family before its sale to the Hospitallers in 1187, while the same seems likely for Saone, as the retention of the forename Garenton suggests dynastic continuity even if the lack of a surname prevents categorical definition.[91] In the case of the Masoirs, however, there is a possible example which has been taken to imply princely influence over the composition of the lordship. As already noted, the southern fortress of Bikisrail was sold to the Order of Santiago in 1180 after it had been 'returned' (*reddidit*) to Bohemond III by a certain William Bucellus, who is likely to have been a *familiares* sent to act as castellan.[92] Questions arise, though, due to al-Azimi's comment that Renaud I Masoir was its lord when he intervened to halt a Muslim uprising there in 1131.[93] Renaud II Masoir was likewise present in the 1180 charter, but there are no indications from this document that he held any claim to these lands, or that he had a pre-existing vassalic relationship with William. This did not prevent Cahen and Mayer from commenting that the lord of Margat held Bikisrail as a residence in the 1130s, although both neglected to explain how it then came into

87 Tibble, *Monarchy and Lordships*, pp. 186–8.
88 Lieberman, *March of Wales*, pp. 56–101; Davies, *Age of Conquest*, pp. 93–6; Power, *Norman Frontier*, pp. 224–63.
89 *CGOH*, I, 198.
90 *Ibid.*, I, 133.
91 Appendix 2.
92 Mayer, *Varia*, pp. 114–17 (here p. 116):
93 Al-Azimi, p. 127.

the hands of William Bucellus, beyond an assumption that he was able to secure a theoretical claim between 1131 and 1180 – presumably once it was retaken after its capture by Turcomans c.1136.[94] There are indications fiefs could revert back to the prince following dynastic extinction, or perhaps due to voluntary submission, as the *Assises d'Antioche* list stipulations regarding the terms under which this could happen – albeit the sale of Margat to the Hospitallers in 1187 suggests that this did not mean a ruler could necessarily prevent a fief from being sold.[95] Both Cahen and Mayer appear to have assumed that the prince could seize seigneurial lands lost to the enemy – like Bikisrail – and permanently redistribute them. As will be seen below in the case of Harim, this does not appear to have been the case, nor does it accurately reflect the other material regarding the Masoir lordship. Perhaps more likely is that historians have wrongly trusted the validity of al-Azimi's information. In 1131, Renaud I Masoir was acting-constable of Antioch during the interregnum, and would thus have taken military responsibility for the princely *demesne* (which Bikisrail is likely to have remained part of following its capture by Tancred in 1111).[96] Renaud would thus not have been its *dominus* (a title William Bucellus was never afforded), but its protector. The attempt to install the Order of Santiago in an area of Hospitaller prominence – they had steadily increased their holdings here under the patronage of the Masoirs – could possibly reflect an attempt to challenge the latter Order's power, yet the underlying assumption that Bikisrail was forcibly taken from the Margat lords is difficult to substantiate.

The Sourdevals similarly established a long-standing dynasty, despite members of this family seeking careers elsewhere; although questions remain over the succession of their fief.[97] In a charter of 1179, Bohemond III confirmed Walter II of Sourdeval in possession of a money fief to be drawn from Latakia and Jabala, which had previously been held by the latter's father and grandfather.[98] This suggests that this particular holding had to be renewed upon succession, and may well have depended on the prince's goodwill (albeit seemingly without the sort of 'feudal relief' seen in the West, in which heirs had to pay the king to enter their inheritance, or the interventionism noted by Tibble for Jerusalem).[99] Without evidence for the rest of the Sourdevals' seigneurie, it is impossible to know whether this reflected their entire estate or merely a specific possession held directly from the princely *demesne*. The latter would appear to be more likely given that this is the only Antiochene lordly charter to suggest such practice, as well the use of the term *hominio ligio* to refer to Walter, but caution must be exercised.

Difficulties are also presented by the example of Marash. Before 1136, this lordship was held by Richard of Salerno, father of Prince Roger, and then by Geoffrey

---

94 Cahen, *Syrie*, p. 353, 537–8; Mayer, *Varia*, p. 115. See also pp. 26–7 of this book.
95 *Assises d'Antioche*, pp. 10–12.
96 Asbridge, *Creation*, p. 65.
97 For example, a Robert of Sourdeval was part of the Templar Order in 1184. See F. Abel, 'Lettre d'un templier récemment trouvée à Jérusalem', *Revue biblique* 35 (1926), 288–95.
98 Le Roulx, *Archives*, pp. 142–4.
99 Reynolds, *Fiefs and Vassals*, p. 49; Tibble, *Monarchy and Lordships*, pp. 5–98.

the Monk, although neither established a discernible dynasty. When Raymond of Poitiers arrived in northern Syria, he installed his brother (or half-brother) Baldwin, who was followed in 1146 by another sibling, Renaud.[100] The lack of a direct and independent line of succession may have been a simple matter of circumstance: no sons were born to its lords, meaning it was simply handed to the most able candidate. However, it is of interest that three of Marash's known lords had direct familial links to the princely house. This was unparalleled in Antioch, but may suggest comparable circumstances to the Jerusalemite county of Jaffa, which was successively held by siblings of the king in the second half of the twelfth century.[101] It also has similarities to the practices of the dukes of Normandy, who often established family members in 'counties' to provide them with some personal authority.[102] Although Raymond was of Poitevin descent, he would have gained knowledge of Norman customs as a *iuvenis* at Henry I of England's court, so parallels are plausible. The apparent county of al-Atharib may even have been created in a similar fashion, with possession given to Renaud or another family member, such as Henry, the brother of Raymond who William of Tyre claimed was to be invited to marry Princess Alice.[103] Equally, Raymond may simply have portioned this vulnerable and isolated fief to those he felt he could trust (like a family member), which at least demonstrates that the princes of Antioch, like rulers in Jerusalem and in the West, could redistribute the seigneuries of defunct lordly families.

By far the most complex case study is Harim.[104] Received by the Fresnels in the opening years of Latin rule, the continued presence of William and Tancred Fresnel in princely documents between 1140 and 1160 suggests continued familial succession. Although they were never demonstrably described as its lords, or even other assignations such as 'of Harim', the prominent position afforded them in princely charters indicates they held a fief of suitable importance. Moreover, their link to this fortress is maintained by the fact that their position appears to have waxed and waned in accordance with Latin possession, with a noticeable diminution in status in the witness lists by 1153, at which point it was held by Nur al-Din.[105] Harim's turbulent history, which was outlined in Chapter 1, thus provides a key example of how lordly inheritance rights may have developed in relation to territorial losses. Significantly, there are potential suggestions that two other lords controlled Harim in this period. The first is Renaud of Saint Valery, a Western nobleman who Robert of Torigny states was handed the castle by Renaud of Châtillon following its recapture in 1158, and the second is Joscelin III of Edessa, who is said to have governed

---

[100] Asbridge, *Creation*, pp. 162–3; Cahen, *Syrie*, pp. 357–60; Mayer, *Varia*, pp. 65–6; Beech, 'Marash', pp. 45–51; Deschamps, *Châteaux*, pp. 66–9.
[101] Tibble, *Monarchy and Lordships*, pp. 38–40; H. E. Mayer, 'The Double County of Jaffa and Ascalon: One Fief or Two?', *Crusade and Settlement*, ed. P. Edbury (Cardiff, 1985), pp. 181–90.
[102] Power, *Norman Frontier*, pp. 213–14.
[103] WT, pp. 657–9. This Henry is not known in any Antiochene documents, although it is possible that he is the 'lord Henry' mentioned founding a church within Antioch in the 1150s. See MS, III, 300–4; and pp. 181–2 of this book.
[104] This is also examined in Buck, 'The Castle and Lordship of Harim', pp. 113–31.
[105] Cf. *Urkunden Venedig*, I, 55 with *CCSSJ*, 76–7 and *Codice Diplomatico*, I, pp. 206–7.

the fortress in 1159 whilst he raided the nearby region.[106] Complications arise, though, because Tancred Fresnel appeared in a prominent position as witness to a princely charter of 1160, by which time Joscelin was a prisoner of Nur al-Din and Renaud of Saint Valery was in the kingdom of Jerusalem.[107] Historians have still accepted that Renaud and Joscelin held Harim; advocating a belief that the prince could re-distribute the fief to these two men, despite the continued existence of a male heir.[108]

Yet, great problems arise in accepting either of these figures. For Joscelin, although the *1234 Chronicle* – the only source to mention this – is a useful text, it is far removed from the period in question, and the extent of its anonymous author's knowledge of Antioch's 'feudal' structures is unclear. Meanwhile, all other accounts of Joscelin's capture fail to note his position as lord, chronicling simply that the Edessan count was seized during a raiding expedition.[109] Joscelin's appearance at Harim thus appears more likely to have represented his using it as a base for attacks, rather than his acting as its governor, even if the latter cannot be conclusively ruled out. The evidence for Renaud of Saint Valery is harder to refute, as the *1234 Chronicle*'s description of an *Arugad* – the accepted Syriac transliteration of Renaud – leading Harim's defences against Nur al-Din in 1164 has been considered explicit support for Robert of Torigny's account.[110] Such a view presents difficulties, for Renaud was in the kingdom of Jerusalem in 1159 and 1160, and, perhaps more significantly, was in the West to attest an agreement made between Count Philip of Flanders and Henry II of England at Dover in 1163.[111] Mayer has argued that this was actually Renaud's son, citing as evidence an 1166 charter of Henry II which lists the existence of two Renauds, the elder of which, he posits, had only returned to Europe once Harim had fallen in 1164.[112] However, this relies on an inaccurate nineteenth-century transcription of this document, which instead includes Renaud and his son Bernard.[113] As such, it is difficult, perhaps impossible, to adequately link Renaud and *Arugad*.

Matters may be clarified by the fact that Renaud's first Jerusalemite appearance in 1159 was alongside Bishop Gerard of Latakia who, as already noted, seems to have been displaced from his See during Manuel Komnenos' visit to Antioch in

---

[106] Robert of Torigny, IV, 199–200; *1234*, II, 119. On the Saint Valery family, see I. J. Sanders, *English Baronies: A Study of their Origin and Descent, 1086–1327* (Oxford, 1960), pp. 9–10.

[107] *Codice Diplomatico*, I, pp. 206–7. For Joscelin, see MS, III, 316; *1234*, II, 119; GP, p. 277; KD, *ROL* 3, 533. For Renaud, see *Urkunden Venedig*, I, 196, 251.

[108] Cahen, *Syrie*, p. 398, n. 6; Deschamps, *Châteaux*, pp. 59–60; Nicholson, *Joscelyn*, pp. 28–9.

[109] MS, III, 316; GP, p. 277; KD, *ROL* 3, 533. See also Nicholson, *Joscelyn*, pp. 28–9.

[110] *1234*, II, 121; Cahen, *Syrie*, pp. 408–9.

[111] *De Oorkonden der Graven van Vlaanderen (Juli 1128–September 1191): II. Uitgrave – Band I (Juli 1128–17 January 1168)*, eds. T. de Hemptinne, A. Verhulst and L. de Mey (Brussels, 1988), pp. 321–5.

[112] *Recueil des Actes de Henri II Roi d'Angleterre et Duc de Normandie Concernant les Provinces Françaises et les Affaires de France*, ed. L. Deslisle and É. Berger, 4 vols (Paris, 1909–1927), I, 437: Reginaldo de Sancto Walerico et Reginaldo filio suo; *Urkunden Jerusalem*, I, 196, 251.

[113] It should instead read: Regin[aldo] de Sancto Walerico et Bern[ardo] filio suo. See Arras AD Pas-de-Calais 12H (Fonds Cercamp) Carton 3 piece no.182.

1158.[114] Renaud may have temporarily held Harim, but that he left the principality in the company of an exile suggests changing political circumstances also account for his departure. The most likely cause of this is the return of a Fresnel lord from captivity. Interestingly, Ibn al-Qalanisi recorded that when a party of Franks was captured near to the Jerusalemite city of Sidon in the month of *Rabi' al-awwal* 553 (April–May 1158), amongst them was 'the son of the commander who was in charge of the castle of Harim'.[115] Renaud of Saint Valery does not appear to have taken a son with him to the East, a point further strengthened by the Bernard who appeared in 1166, while an heir to Joscelin III could not yet have reached fighting age.[116] The Muslim chronicler was thus almost certainly referring to a Fresnel, with the description of a son either a simple mistake, or it could reflect Tancred's actual status at this point – it is unknown whether he came into his inheritance before Harim fell to Nur al-Din, so he may still have been its heir and referred to as son of its previous lord. Importantly, if the dating of this event is moved from *Rabi' al-awwal* 553 (1158) to *Rabi' al-awwal* 552 (1157), then the picture becomes clearer, as it was during this month that Renaud of Châtillon brought forces into the kingdom of Jerusalem to aid in the defence of Banyas, which lies near to Sidon.[117] Harim was at this point still in Muslim hands, which explains an Antiochene aristocrat's military presence in the kingdom alongside the prince (an otherwise unknown occurrence). Furthermore, by accepting that Tancred had been captured, it is also possible to explain Renaud of Saint Valery's departure, as, at the time of his and the bishop of Latakia's migration, Manuel Komnenos had secured the release of Latin prisoners held by the Zengid ruler, probably including the Fresnel lord.[118] That Tancred, having gained his freedom, then recovered Harim (or came into his inheritance), explains both Renaud of Saint Valery's presence at Jerusalem and the Fresnel's prominent position in the princely charter of 1160.

The status afforded to Joscelin III can thus be largely dismissed, but it is not implausible that Robert of Torigny's evidence can still be accepted, albeit with the recognition that Renaud of Saint Valery was a temporary castellan, rather than an enfeoffed noble. Ibn al-Athir, although a thirteenth-century source and far removed from events, believed that Harim was actually held by Bohemond III in 1158.[119] Cahen correctly described this as 'impossible', for Bohemond would have been under ten years of age, but it is conceivable that Renaud of Châtillon instead took responsibility for the fortress in the immediate aftermath of Tancred Fresnel's capture, before temporarily handing it to a suitable custodian.[120] This implies rights

---

[114] *Urkunden Jerusalem*, I, 194, 196; Kedar, 'Gerard of Nazareth', pp. 55–77.

[115] IQ, pp. 346–7. See also AS, *RHC Or.* IV, 98.

[116] Joscelin III himself cannot have been born much earlier than 1134, as he was son of Joscelin II and Beatrice, widow of William of Saone (who died in 1133). See pp. 147–8.

[117] WT, pp. 832–3; IQ, pp. 330–2.

[118] WT, p. 849; JK, p. 144; MS, III, 316; *1234*, II, 119; GP, pp. 274–5; Sempad, 'Armenian Chronicle', p. 149. See also p. 205, n. 99 of this book.

[119] IA, III, 79.

[120] Cahen, *Syrie*, p. 395, n. 1.

of wardship similar to the later Western practice of the *escheat*, albeit without either the demonstrable fines or the level of fief confiscation and alteration seen in Anglo-Norman England and Jerusalem.[121] The notion of fief guardianship is listed under the term 'bailliage' in the *Assises d'Antioche*, where it is noted that a liege lord could oversee property until a successor reached their majority, at which time it had to be handed back to them.[122] Yet, this only related to difficulties arising from an heir in their minority, rather than incarceration. The appearance of an *Arugad* was perhaps just an authorial error, although Tancred's disappearance after 1160 means it cannot be ruled out that he was another castellan or an otherwise unknown Fresnel who perished following Nur al-Din's victory in 1164.

With such confusing evidence, secure conclusions are problematic. That the arguments presented here remain the most likely explanation is nevertheless supported by Bohemond III's marriage to Harim's heiress, Orgeuillse, in the 1160s.[123] To be elevated to the status of princess, Orgeuillse would have needed to come from a family deeply entrenched within Antioch's political history. Renaud of Saint Valery could not claim this, and he certainly would not have left a daughter behind in the East. Added to this, it is improbable that the *Lignages d'Outremer*, a thirteenth-century source heavily focused on detailing dynastic prestige and which details Orgeuillse's marriage to Bohemond, would have failed to report a familial connection to Joscelin III. There can be little doubt, therefore, that she was a Fresnel. Bohemond III's various efforts to recover Harim in the 1170s and 1180s, moreover, indicate that he considered the castle his to take – which perhaps explains the underlying motives for the union and shows that the princes of Antioch did take a keen interest in the administration of certain lordships. This also has implications for an understanding of female inheritance rights in the principality. Alongside Orgeuillse, there is evidence of a Hugh *Darenc* (a potential corruption of the Latin name for Harim: *Harenc*) at Antioch in 1166, a John *de Herenc* in a charter of Baldwin IV of Jerusalem in 1179, as well as a Templar called Robert Fresnel in 1183.[124] This could suggest that male heirs existed for Harim, although it should be noted that a *Gunfridus de Freisnel*, who witnessed a charter of Fulk of Jerusalem in 1138, indicates that other branches of this family also migrated to *Outremer*.[125] The opportunity for female succession was included within the *Assises d'Antioche*, though, and that the rights to Harim appear to have passed through the female line demonstrates the

---

[121] Reynolds, *Fiefs and Vassals*, p. 296; Lieberman, *March of Wales*, pp. 56–74; Tibble, *Monarchy and Lordships*, pp. 1–4.

[122] *Assises d'Antioche*, p. 16.

[123] *Lignages d'Outremer*, p. 83.

[124] For Hugh, see *CGOH*, I, 367. For John, see *Tabulae Theutonici*, 9. For Robert, see *Chartes Josaphat*, 42. It has also been suggested that the *Sylvester consanguineus principis* who appeared in a number of Antiochene charters of the 1160s–1180s was a Fresnel relative of Orgeuillse, but there is no real evidence for this. See W.-H. Rudt de Collenberg, 'A Fragmentary Copy of an Unknown Recension of the "Lignages d'Outre-Mer" in the Vatican Library', *EHR* 387 (1983), 311–27.

[125] This is made especially possible given that Guy Fresnel was one of eight brothers. See Asbridge, *Creation*, pp. 163–4.

diverse inheritance customs which evolved.[126] The example of Harim, problematic as it is, therefore portrays a complex notion of lordly succession, in which dynastic rights were protected, while the ruler retained the opportunity to ensure defensive continuity at a time of crisis.

Familial inheritance in the principality of Antioch appears to have created a series of fluid and variable customs. Alongside cases of established dynastic descent, traces are also found of princely interference over certain types of possession, such as money fiefs, or during times of crisis, like the capture or death of a male heir. This was to be further demonstrated in the thirteenth century, as Bohemond IV was able to distribute Saone to the Genoese Embriaco family of Gibelet in 1204 now that the castle had fallen into Muslim hands and its ruling family had disappeared from record.[127] That is not to say that there is evidence for the style of interventionism seen by Jerusalemite monarchs or the financial reliefs of the West, which argues against traditional belief in an overbearing ruler. There is also little to indicate the type of extensive, formalised 'marcher rights' claimed by Anglo-Welsh border lords in the thirteenth century.[128] Asbridge's suggestion that Antiochene marcher-style independence would have increased is consequently not entirely borne out, although neither is Martin's belief in the relaxation of princely interest in the principality's feudality. Instead, a rather more dynamic approach can be identified, which likely ensured that lordships remained both adequately governed and strongly defended.

Noble Marriage

A less tangible, albeit still important, element of noble familial status relates to marriage. Throughout the medieval world, marital unions helped to cement peaceful relations between neighbours and increase the prestige of ambitious aristocratic dynasties, like the Rotrou counts of Perche.[129] The surviving evidence for the matrimonial strategies of Antioch's noble houses is fragmentary, but some useful observations can be made regarding how these families may have sought to augment their status, and, more significantly, how such unions may have been used to preserve inter-Latin unity.

Two particularly important examples relate to involvement with the county of Edessa's ruling family, the Courtenays. First, Count Joscelin II married Beatrice, widowed in 1133 by the death of her first husband, William of Saone; while in the late 1140s, Joscelin's daughter, Agnes, married Renaud of Marash, although she too

---

[126] *Assises d'Antioche*, pp. 18–20, 37–8, 44–56. See also Edbury, 'Assises', pp. 241–8; Hodgson, *Women*, pp. 54–235.

[127] *Codice Diplomatico*, I, pp. 102–4. The exception to this is Paschal of Saone, who witnessed Bohemond III's last charter in 1201 but then did not re-appear until 1209, by which point he had become a priest – an act which had probably prompted Saone's sale in 1204. See Appendix 2.

[128] Davies, 'Kings, Lords and Liberties', pp. 41–61; Lieberman, *March of Wales*, pp. 218–45.

[129] Thompson, *Power and Border Lordship*, pp. 192–4; Power, *Norman Frontier*, pp. 224–46; Hodgson, *Women*, pp. 71–4.

was widowed in 1149.[130] These unions do not appear to have brought with them any particular rights over the central possession of the lordships of Saone or Marash: Beatrice was only part of the former's ruling family through marriage, and Renaud was the incumbent lord.[131] Their likely purpose was rather to aid cohesion between Antioch and Edessa, as both occurred during periods of tense relations between the two polities. William of Saone's death in 1133 came at a time of inter-Latin strife, and Joscelin had seemingly attempted to use the instability caused by the deaths of Bohemond II of Antioch, Baldwin II of Jerusalem and his own father, Joscelin I of Edessa, to further his influence in northern Syria.[132] The marriage to Beatrice might be viewed as part of this strategy, but is more likely to have served to appease his interests, with her dower possessions probably offering a rich reward, even if only for her lifetime.[133] An attempt to mend a fracture almost certainly also accounts for the marriage of Agnes and Renaud. Hodgson has noted that this was an advantageous match for Renaud, but it should not be forgotten that he was also one of the principality's foremost nobles, and reportedly even a relation of Raymond of Poitiers.[134] Coming as it did at a time of deep division between Antioch and Edessa following Zengi's capture of the latter city in 1144, this union thus represented a high-profile alliance for both sides.[135] With Agnes' status and age, the marriage would not have occurred before Renaud became count – that is after his brother, Baldwin's death near Edessa in 1146; while Renaud's presence at Inab discounts notions that this represented an attempt to pull away from the Antiochene sphere of influence.[136] It can be posited, instead, that the marriage of Agnes and Renaud served as an attempt to mend the fracture between Raymond and Joscelin II, bringing the two northern crusader states together just as the Muslim counter-offensive, led by Nur al-Din, threatened to break Latin power in the region.

Another prominent example is Renaud II Masoir's marriage to Agnes, daughter of Count Pons of Tripoli and sister to Count Raymond II, which occurred sometime before 1160.[137] The impetus for this match is unrecorded, although it brought with it Pons' claim to half of the financially important estate of Rugia – while the rest of this estate, as well as the river port of Arzghan (which had belonged to the count through his marriage to Tancred's widow, Cecilia of France), was returned to the princely *demesne*.[138] With Pons' death in 1137, Agnes could have reached

---

[130] WT, p. 635; B. Hamilton, 'The Titular Nobility of the Latin East: the Case of Agnes of Courtenay', *Crusade and Settlement*, ed. P. Edbury (Cardiff, 1985), pp. 197–203.
[131] This follows similar patterns to the Welsh Marches. See E. Cavell, 'Aristocratic Widows and the Medieval Welsh Frontier: the Shropshire Evidence', *TRHS* 6th Series 17 (2007), 57–82.
[132] MS, III, 233. See also pp. 222–4 of this book.
[133] *Assises d'Antioche*, pp. 18–20. In the case of Pons of Tripoli's marriage to Cecilia, widow of Prince Tancred, his control over her dower possessions of Arzghan and *Rugia* clearly altered after her death, with the former, and half of the latter, returning to the princely *demesne*. See WT, pp. 636–7 and below.
[134] Hodgson, *Women*, p. 72.
[135] See pp. 232–3.
[136] WT, p. 737; MS, III, 270–1; *1234*, II, 104–9; GP, pp. 244–5.
[137] *Codice Diplomatico*, I, pp. 206–7.
[138] Cahen, *Syrie*, pp. 537–8.

marriageable age by around 1150, and so this union should be considered in the context of the period of change which followed the disaster at Inab in 1149.[139] Even if it followed Renaud of Châtillon's elevation as prince in 1153, the pursuit of closer ties between Antioch and Tripoli through a high-profile marriage alliance would have been highly beneficial. The Masoir lords, whose lands governed the frontier between the two states, served as the ideal candidates. Whether or not it was done at the prince's behest is unclear, although the chance to bring Arzghan and Rugia back into the Antiochene sphere of influence would have been desirable, and Renaud II Masoir's continued prominence within the principality, as well as the later bond between Bohemond III and Count Raymond III, argues against notions that the nobleman tried to distance himself from princely authority.[140] It is even possible that, following Count Raymond II's assassination in 1152, the Tripolitan nobility sought an enfeoffed eastern Latin husband for Agnes so that she could not create difficulties in the succession.[141]

It should also be noted that Bohemond III twice married Antiochene noblewomen: first, Orgeuillse of Harim in the 1160s, and then, in 1180, a certain Sybil, supposedly a relation of Bourzey's ruling family.[142] The former's elevation, as already demonstrated, should be seen in the context of an attempt to assert a level of control over the vital frontier fortress of Harim following its loss in 1164. Meanwhile, Sybil's exact social status, as well as that of her family, remains decidedly unclear. Even if they controlled Bourzey before this marriage, as opposed to receiving favour as a result of it, they were very unlikely to have been one of the principality's elite families (perhaps instead part of the *familiares*).[143] For any medieval ruler to marry within their own nobility was rare, but Bohemond was evidently willing to do so; especially if – as was the case with Orgeuillse – he could extend his own power in the process.

Marriages between the principality's nobles and other ruling houses in *Outremer* thus acted as an important form of inter-Latin diplomacy. This probably does not represent fully independent dynastic policies commensurate with ambitious Western families like the counts of Perche, as the evidence suggests that these unions occurred either at the ruler's instigation or with their complicity.[144] However, a certain amount of common purpose in strengthening ties with neighbouring states can be discerned, at least until the 1150s. Suggestions that the ruler also used marriage to attempt to further his own internal authority nevertheless demonstrate that the interplay between Antioch's rulers and the established nobility was highly complex.

---

[139] WT, pp. 661–2.
[140] See pp. 237–9.
[141] WT, pp. 786–7. This may have been something of a concern given the instabilities caused in Jerusalem and Antioch by succession disputes involving a female claimant (see pp. 80–4 of this book).
[142] On Orgeuillse, see *Lignages d'Outremer*, p. 83. On Sybil, see ID, p. 139; AS, *RHC Or.* IV, 372–5.
[143] The marriage to Sybil appears to have been one of love, rather than politics. See Buck, 'The Noble Rebellion', pp. 96–102.
[144] Thompson, *Power and Border Lordship*, pp. 192–4.

Alienation of Possessions

Perhaps the clearest indicator of seigneurial independence was the right to alienate portions of a fief. It was established above that retainers can be identified for certain lordships, and that the practice by local lords of patronising loyal followers, who helped to govern a locality and provide military support, was well known in the West.[145] The evidence base for secular donations by Antiochene nobles is regrettably slim, certainly not as extensive as that of Jerusalem or the Latin West. Yet, there are charters relating to seigneurial donations to the military orders and religious foundations which provide important insights into the level of lordly independence.[146] Indeed, twenty-three seigneurial charters survive from within the principality during this time (although three of these date to the interregnum of 1130–1136), as well as five princely confirmations of lordly gifts and a number of others pertaining to noble possessions.[147] Further evidence can also be found in the *Assises d'Antioche*, such as the clauses outlining the punishments for fief abandonment or showing infidelity to a lordship.[148]

There are a few ways in which the extent of independence may be gauged: through charter consent clauses such as 'in the presence of the lord Bohemond, prince of Antioch, of his own goodwill and conceded by my requests', or 'with the assent and goodwill of the lord Bohemond, prince of Antioch'; through the use of dating formulas referring to prince's regnal year; and even instances of princely confirmation.[149] A comprehensive study of this type has not yet been carried out for Antioch, although Asbridge noted that the prince's influence can be identified in the consent clauses and confirmations of aristocratic gifts before 1130, and Martin has suggested that fief-holders, albeit not specifically nobles, were able to alienate possessions so long as the knight's service remained undiminished.[150] Mayer has likewise concluded that, although the prince could not simply eject a fief-holder, he could influence matters to the point of forcing a sale, which he argues was the case with Margat in 1187.[151] Importantly, the available evidence does not fully sustain these opinions, as dynamic administrative practice can again be discerned.

The clearest indication of princely influence over seigneurial land donations is the existence of consent or dating clauses which recognised his authority. Although such practice was not universally established throughout the West – particularly in Norman Italy – it was common in the principality before 1130, such as in Cecilia

---

[145] Power, *Norman Frontier*, pp. 224–300; Lieberman, *March of Wales*, pp. 56–101.

[146] *CGOH*, I, 545.

[147] For references, see below.

[148] *Assises d'Antioche*, pp. 12–16, 30–4. See also Martin, 'Structures', pp. 239–50; Edbury 'Assises', pp. 241–8.

[149] See e.g. *CGOH*, I, 546: in presentia domini Boamundi, principis Antiochie, ipsius voluntate et concessione meis precibus firmatum et concessum; 623: cum assensu et voluntate domini Boamundi, principis Antiochie.

[150] Asbridge, *Creation*, 157–8; Martin, 'Structures', pp. 239–43.

[151] Mayer, *Varia*, pp. 174–83.

of Tarsus' gift made during the reign of Bohemond II in 1126.[152] It was also prominent in the other crusader states. For example, such allusions appear in all of the surviving seigneurial charters for the county of Tripoli, as well as in roughly two-thirds of those issued within Jerusalemite baronies.[153] There are some exceptions: for instance, royal rights were overlooked in seven of the nine lordly documents issued in the kingdom during the difficult first years of King Amalric's reign, in which his relationship with the nobles had been made fractious by his marriage to Agnes of Courtenay.[154] By contrast, in the more settled years 1167–1174, all eight lordly charters alluded to the monarch. The absence of these clauses was not limited to times of crisis, but such patterns can still help to indicate underlying tensions in the balance of power. It is perhaps instructive, therefore, that sixteen of the twenty seigneurial charters issued by Antiochene nobles between 1130 and 1201 (excluding the interregnum of 1130–1136) lack such clauses.[155] This amounts to a 20 per cent recognition rate of princely authority. Those without such allusions comprise Baldwin of Marash's c.1143 donation to the Hospitallers, the lord of Saone's gift to that same order in 1170, and a number of Masoir charters dating between 1151 and the 1180s.[156] It is true that this includes some stubs, for which it cannot be ruled out that their now lost originals contained such clauses, yet the rate of recognition is still limited to 34 per cent even if these are discounted. This is evidently much lower than in Jerusalem and Tripoli, although it may be comparable to document production on the Norman frontier.[157] The lack of such clauses raises pertinent questions regarding certain lordships.

First, the overwhelming evidence for noble alienation without recourse to permission supports Asbridge and Martin's aforementioned belief in growing aristocratic rights, although the complication offered by the four documents which *do* accept the ruler's involvement ensures distinct guidelines are not easily identified. It is possible that personal relations with the prince were important, as the lords of Marash, Saone and Margat each reportedly experienced difficulties with the ruling house.[158] Martin is perhaps also correct to suggest that landholders could act

---

[152]   H. Enzensberger, 'Chanceries, Charters and Administration in Norman Italy', *The Society of Norman Italy*, ed. G. Loud and A. Metcalfe (Leiden, 2002), p. 119; Matthew, *Sicily*, p. 143. For Cecilia, see Kohler, 'Chartes de Josaphat', p. 123. For the Masoir documents, see *CGOH*, I, 546, 623, 783.

[153]   For Tripoli, see *RRH*, 270, 378, 520, 535c, 569b, 595, 642; and J. Richard, 'Le comté de Tripoli dans les chartes du fonds des Porcellet', *Bibliothèque de l'école des chartes* 130:2 (1972), 366–9. For Jerusalem, see *RRH*, 102a, 112–3, 114b, 115, 131, 139, 147, 162b, 200, 243, 255, 257, 266, 274, 278–79, 297, 300, 308, 315, 315b, 324, 330, 356, 360–1, 361a, 417, 423, 426, 433, 447–8, 454, 472, 479, 522, 546, 553, 567, 570, 597, 619, 640b, 657d, 736.

[154]   For those without clauses or references to the king, see *RRH*, 115, 137c, 237, 283, 298a, 303, 332–4, 342, 373, 393c, 395, 401, 410a, 414, 418, 419–20, 425, 433, 488a, 533, 542, 551, 566, 627, 768, 784. On Amalric and Agnes, see Hamilton, 'Titular Nobility', pp. 197–203.

[155]   For the four which do recognise the prince, see *CGOH*, I, 133, 546, 623, 783.

[156]   *CGOH*, I, 126, 163, 201, 313, 341, 417, 457, 613, 763, 786, 787, IV, 495; Le Roulx, *Archives*, pp. 134–5; Le Roulx, 'Inventaire', 149, 152; *Codice Diplomatico*, I, p. 250.

[157]   Power, *Norman Frontier*, pp. 43–4.

[158]   For Marash, see Mayer, *Varia*, pp. 65–9; Beech, 'Marash', pp. 46–7. For Saone, see Saadé, 'Histoire', pp. 991–6. For Margat, see Mayer, *Varia*, pp. 162–83.

freely so long as gifts did not weaken the overall military value of the fief. There is evidence to support this outside of a seigneurial context, as Raymond of Poitiers' charter recognising Hospitaller possessions in 1149 allowed his *barones* to make gifts as long as their service was not diminished.[159] None of those involved in that document held a major lordship, though, and whilst such customs might be implied by Bohemond III's presence in Renaud II Masoir's confirmation of the sale of the estate of Bearida (with provision for the service of one knight lost through its alienation), as well as the same prince's involvement in the sale of Margat, explicit proof is not forthcoming.[160] The picture is further complicated by the sizeable Masoir land donation made, without recourse to princely permission, to the Hospitallers in 1174, as this would likely have diminished the strength – and thus service – of the lordship.[161] It is quite clear, therefore, that the majority of the principality's surviving seigneurial donations reflect a strong level of aristocratic freedom. This offers support for Asbridge, and to some extent Martin, but certain irregularities ensure that full noble independence cannot be adequately accepted. Consequently, the role of princely confirmations must be examined.

This form of princely involvement in seigneurial alienations is clearly demonstrable in Antioch before 1130, with Asbridge interpreting Roger of Salerno's 1114 affirmation of the bequest made to the abbey of Josaphat by Guy of Chevreuil, lord of Mamistra, as evidence that the prince 'exerted a considerable degree of authority' over the nobles. He has even posited that every confirmation reflected the creation of separate seigneurial documents which would have then needed central ratification, a view seemingly shared by Mayer.[162] In short, even though charters existed that did not overtly recognise princely authority, the production of later confirmations could still imply that the balance of power was not entirely weighted against the ruler. Such a practice was enshrined in the *Assises d'Antioche*, as a vassal could not leave their possession without the lord's permission: which, if true, further hampers Martin's belief in the relaxation of princely interest in Antioch's feudality.[163] The source sample for an examination of this is small, amounting to five princely confirmations of seigneurial gifts made after 1130, as well as a number of other charters which either suggest attempts to coerce seigneurial alienation or imply multi-layered 'feudal' relations.[164] However, these documents can significantly help to aid an understanding of the principality's internal balance of power, as they appear to indicate that princely control over the composition of lordships was far from complete.

The first such example is Bohemond III's charter regarding Roger of Saone's aforementioned 1170 donation to the Hospitallers. In this, the prince relinquished

159 *CGOH*, I, 183.
160 *Ibid.*, I, 546, 783.
161 *Ibid.*, I, 457.
162 Asbridge, *Creation*, pp. 157–8; Mayer, *Varia*, pp. 162–83.
163 *Assises d'Antioche*, pp. 12–16.
164 For the reconfirmations, see *CGOH*, I, 472, 783, IV, 624; *Codice Diplomatico*, I, pp. 206–207, 281. For the rest, see *CGOH*, I, 391, 545, 546, 827; Mayer, *Varia*, pp. 114–17.

'whatever rights of lordship ... I possess or ought to possess' in the alienated estate of *Tricharia*.[165] On initial inspection, this maintains the notion that princely authority required that he confirm lordly donations. Nevertheless, there are some indicators that the picture is not so clear. First, the lord of Saone did not demonstrably offer his support to Bohemond – which could mirror the reality of Roger of Salerno's 1114 document, for no witness list was preserved to demonstrate that Guy contributed to its creation.[166] While there are a number of comparative examples of royal confirmations at Jerusalem, in these the original donating fief-holder was either present as witness or they (or their heirs) had requested that the charter be made.[167] The notion of an heir requesting confirmation of earlier acts – perhaps to settle a dispute – is also seen at Antioch, but exclusively for burgesses or lesser figures, and not in the context of the great seigneuries.[168] Therefore, although a confirmation might suggest Bohemond theoretically held enough authority to convince the Hospitallers to seek his endorsement (and thus protection from later legal challenges), doubts are raised whether this right to involvement was recognised by the nobility. Answers might be sought not in the actual balance of power, but in the needs of the beneficiary. The 1160s and 1170s marked a significant era for the Hospitallers, as a financial crisis halted the expansion instigated by Grandmaster Gilbert d'Assaily.[169] It was in the context of this instability that a dispute arose between the Order and the archbishop of Apamea over church rights at *Tricharia*. Patriarch Aimery then secured a settlement for this in March 1174 (which Cahen has argued demonstrates a lack of princely authority over church affairs), with Bohemond III issuing his confirmation a year later.[170] The timing of this is certainly strange. It could be that the prince had merely been angered by a lack of involvement in the original donation and subsequent settlement, but this would not explain the delay. For the Hospitallers to have preserved the document, moreover, suggests they had requested it. As such, it seems likely that, having secured a ruling in their favour, the beneficiary had the charter produced so that no further challenge could be made to their rights over the estate. Although this implies an understanding by the Hospitallers that Bohemond could *theoretically* cause problems, it stretches the evidence to argue that it reflects the level of actualised influence over lordly landholding suggested by Asbridge.

---

[165] *CGOH*, I, 472: iuris quicquidque dominii ... possideo, et possidere debeo.
[166] *Ibid.*, I, 472. For the dating of this charter to 1175, see Mayer, *Varia*, p. 43. For the 1114 document, see *Chartes Josaphat*, 4.
[167] *RRH* 79, 80, 130, 299, 525, 601. There are some exceptions, such as later confirmations of gifts made by those now dead (*RRH*, 293, 309), when a donor was of low status (*RRH* 368, 369, 450, 465, 514, 603), or Humphrey of Toron's sale of Banyas to the Hospitallers in 1157 (*RRH* 325). The latter was likely because he would have been unable to absent himself from his fief due to the threat of Nur al-Din.
[168] *CGOH*, I, 198, 367, 522.
[169] Riley-Smith, *The Knights of St. John*, pp. 60–84.
[170] *CGOH*, I, 472, 474; Cahen, *Syrie*, p. 444; Riley-Smith, *Knights of St. John*, p. 410. See also pp. 106 of this book.

Crucially, these same issues arise in relation to Margat. The relative wealth of documentary evidence for this seigneurie makes it an ideal case study into the principality's balance of power, despite Cahen's warning against allowing this to overly influence conclusions.[171] On the interplay between Bohemond III and the lords of Margat in the second half of the twelfth century, Mayer has produced a detailed survey in which he argues that the prince steadily increased his influence over the southern lordship in the hope of creating a military order buffer zone, similar to those seen to the north and east of the principality – a process which he accelerated after the 1180–1182 rebellion, to the point of coercing the Masoir family to sell their entire estate.[172] Mayer does not go so far as to credit the prince with powers of interference similar to those suggested by Tibble for Jerusalem, but he nevertheless attributes Bohemond with enough to enforce his will over others. Although the documents confirming the eventual sale of Margat did see Bertrand Masoir recognise Bohemond III's position as overlord, as well as his right to provide consent, the evidence which underpins the rest of Mayer's hypothesis requires further scrutiny.[173]

The material pertinent to this debate may start as early as the 1130s, if traditional assumptions on the aforementioned sale of Bikisrail in 1180 are to be accepted. However, this has been challenged above, and so Renaud of Châtillon's 1160 confirmation of a gift made by Renaud II of Margat to the Templars at Valania is a more pertinent example.[174] As in the case of the Saone charter, the Masoir lord was not involved in the production of this deed, either as witness or through his assent in the main body of the text. The potential motivating influence of legal difficulties can also again be identified. In 1163, three years after the gift, the bishop of Valania – whose successors were also to prove their willingness to oppose military order independence – issued a document noting he had come to an agreement with the Templars over their possessions in the city, which suggests they had earlier been in dispute.[175] Doubts thus again emerge regarding whether such confirmations reflect the actual exercise of princely authority over seigneurial actions. Indeed, these charters could instead represent a ruler vainly hoping to assert his authority, or, as is more likely, emanate from the concerns of a beneficiary seeking to eliminate the possibility of future legal challenges. For the balance of power, such differentiations are crucial, as they not only suggest a greater level of antagonism between the prince and the aristocracy than has been envisaged, but also a higher degree of seigneurial independence.

In this regard, the sale of the estate of Rugia proves significant. This almost certainly referred to the Ruj Valley, a fertile region – probably centred on the castle of the same name (otherwise known as *Chastel Rouge*) – which cut across the strategically significant central zone of the principality. As we examined in Chapter 1,

---

[171] Cahen, *Syrie*, p. 537.
[172] Mayer, *Varia*, pp. 162–83. See also Burgtorf, 'Hospitaller Lordship', pp. 11–50; Riis, 'Übernahme', pp. 151–6.
[173] *CGOH*, I, 783.
[174] *Codice Diplomatico*, I, pp. 206–7.
[175] *Ibid.*, I, pp. 40–1. See also Riley-Smith, *Knights of St. John*, pp. 411–13.

this area's alienation to the Hospitallers, along with nearby sites such as Arzghan, reflected an apparent desire to strengthen Antioch's eastern borders. Charter evidence suggests that before the donation it was divided between the princely *demesne* and the Masoirs, thanks to Renaud II's marriage to Agnes of Tripoli.[176] Yet, in 1168, Bohemond III made a sizeable donation to the Hospitallers, including his 'half of Rugia with its appurtenances, and the other half with its appurtenances, which I have encouraged them [to gain], [and] that it shall have to be liberated and acquired from Renaud Masoir and his heirs'.[177] Mayer has described this as a blatant and 'rash' attempt to oust the Masoirs from Rugia, and while the clause may simply reflect proposals under consideration, it certainly confirms the prince's vigour for creating a central Hospitaller buffer zone following the losses of Harim and Arzghan.[178] In spite of Bohemond's designs, Renaud – who also appeared as witness to the princely charter – took a full six years to agree to relinquish his half, and a further eight to actually do it.[179] It was stipulated in the *Assises d'Antioche* that a husband had to relinquish half of his wife's estates should she die before him, but Agnes survived until at least 1183, and no regulations allowed a lord to oust a fief-holder without due cause or proper ceremony.[180] The implication this has for an understanding of the internal balance of power is largely overlooked by Mayer, although he does note the fourteen-year delay.[181] Significantly, contrary to the belief that the prince could instigate enough pressure to force lords into relinquishing their estates, the example of Rugia actually suggests the opposite: that the Antiochene nobles could not be coerced into surrendering a possession, regardless of interference or princely will.[182]

Another complex but potentially revealing case study is Thomas of Jabala's sale of *Beauda* to a Hospitaller brother, Nicholas, in return for 1500 besants and an annual pension of a further 200 besants, in 1178.[183] In what almost certainly reflects the granting of a *corrodie* – a pension for the recipient's life time – to Thomas, it was not only revealed that he held the fief from Renaud II Masoir, but also that Bohemond III's consent was required to ratify the agreement. The lord of Margat issued a further confirmation of this a few days later, again in the presence of the prince, in which he relinquished his lordship rights.[184] Thomas' exact standing is unclear, but it is known that he was the son of Robert Mansel of Bethlehem (who supported Bohemond III's bid for power in 1163 and led a contingent of French pilgrim forces

---

[176] Cahen, *Syrie*, pp. 537–8.
[177] *CGOH*, I, 391: et medietatem Rogie cum pertinentiis suis, et aliam medietatem cum pertinentiis suis eidem Hospitali concedo, quam cito liberaverit et aquitaverit eam a Reinaldo Masoerio et ab heredibus eius.
[178] Mayer, *Varia*, p. 180.
[179] *Ibid.*; *CGOH*, I, 457, 623.
[180] *Assises d'Antioche*, pp. 18–20; Le Roulx, 'Inventaire', 152.
[181] Mayer, *Varia*, pp. 180–2.
[182] It is possible that attempts such as this influenced their composition.
[183] *CGOH*, I, 545.
[184] *Ibid.*, I, 546.

at the battle of Buqay'a Gap that same year).[185] Mayer has pointed to the great embarrassment this deal would have caused the Hospitallers, as it was stipulated that Nicholas was to hold the estate personally until his death (which contravened the Order's Rule), and only then would it pass to his brethren.[186] This implies that any attempt by the Order's hierarchy to intervene would have allowed possession to revert back to either Renaud II Masoir or the prince. Of greater significance to the present discussion is the suggestion of a multi-layered social contract – albeit not one described as liege homage – through which the prince retained a stake in the alienation of this estate. Matters are further complicated by a stub of January 1187, in which Thomas sold his annual rent of 200 bezants, with only Bohemond and Princess Sybil listed as attesters: implying that the prince was now considered Thomas' direct overlord. It must be remembered that by this point Bertrand Masoir had agreed to sell Margat, which limited the long-term benefit of his confirmation, but Bohemond's influence is clear.[187] This demonstrates that there were occasions in which princely involvement was required, even if he did not make any explicit claim to dominion. The scandalous nature of this agreement again points towards the influence of a beneficiary's desire to prevent any future legal dispute by receiving multi-layered affirmation. Given that Thomas' possessions were exclusively limited to the region around the now princely held Latakia and Jabala, it is also possible that he was a vassal of both parties, and so each was required to accept an alienation which would have affected the fief's service. Both explanations remain plausible, which further confirms the complex nature of the available evidence and suggests that, although strong levels of independence can be identified, there remained occasions when co-operation – or at least a unity of purpose – was possible.

In many ways, Mayer's central thesis on the interplay between Bohemond III and the Masoirs relies on the assumption that the noble rebellion of the early 1180s intrinsically altered the balance of power in favour of the prince, who used the indignation of a civil war to oust those he disliked. It was argued in Chapter 3 that this was not the case, that those of Bohemond's household who were exiled to Cilicia received this punishment at the behest of the rebels, not the ruler. Moreover, the surviving evidence for noble independence argues against the ruler being able to wield such a strong influence over them. The charters issued by Renaud II Masoir between 1181 and 1182 regarding the sale to the Hospitallers of the estates of *Astanor* and *Astalorin* clarify this.[188] Mayer argued that the princely confirmations for these two gifts represented a thawing of relations at the end of the rebellion, implying that their production required a certain level of co-operation between Bohemond III and Renaud II Masoir.[189] Yet, consistent trends can again be identified, such as the donor's lack of involvement, as well as the overarching influence of a dispute. Given the instability caused by the rebellion, it thus seems more

185   *Ibid.*, I, 311; WT, pp. 873–4.
186   Mayer, *Varia*, pp. 179–80.
187   *CGOH*, I, 827.
188   *CGOH*, I, 613, IV, 595, 624.
189   Mayer, *Varia*, pp. 167–70.

likely that the Hospitallers – having previously shown a desire to cover all legal possibilities – sought confirmation from both parties to ensure that their possession rights would remain uncontested whatever the conflict's outcome. This also hints at theoretical princely prerogatives, but does not go so far as to prove actualised power over seigneurial actions. It also intimates that, in a similar vein to other medieval polities, Bohemond could have confiscated the Masoir fief had he met and defeated the rebels in battle, even if this does not appear to have been the favoured option.[190] That the prince's failure to achieve victory precluded his confiscation of the Masoir lordship offers implicit support for the limitations listed in the *Assises d'Antioche*, which noted that a meeting of the *haute cour* had to be convened before a recalcitrant vassal's lands could be seized.[191] Nonetheless, it does not appear that these regulations were followed to their fullest extent, for sources note efforts at reconciliation but no process of trying the rebels. Returning to the charters, it is unsurprising that the prince would have approved a Hospitaller request for a confirmation of their rights, as the Order's close ties to Margat, as well as their growing influence in the southern and eastern regions of the principality (which the prince perhaps sought to offset by promoting the settlement there of the Spanish Order of Santiago in 1180), might have allowed them to block Bohemond's attempt to combat the Masoir.[192] By showing support for the Hospitallers, the prince perhaps sought to ensure their non-involvement in the dispute. Therefore, these documents may represent neither co-operation between the ruler and the aristocracy nor recognised influence. In this context, Mayer's arguments go too far, with the existence of princely confirmations not irrefutable proof of real power.

It cannot be denied, though, that Bohemond III was afforded a prominent position in the documents relating to the sale of Margat in 1187, as Bertrand Masoir's charter of donation – which was also confirmed by the ruler – described the prince as 'my lord Bohemond, magnificent prince of Antioch'.[193] This was on a grander scale to earlier gifts, and the alienation of an entire fief was important enough to warrant inclusion in the *Assises d'Antioche*, with clear regulations to prevent its occurrence without proper assent.[194] The ruler's involvement in the relinquishing of a seigneurie, caused either by the holder's death or voluntary submission, is also confirmed by the examples of Marash, and potentially those of al-Atharib and Harim. This places a certain level of authority in the prince's hands, albeit not enough to rival that of the Anglo-Norman kings or, if Tibble is to be believed, the monarchs of Jerusalem (both of which frequently appear to have been able to assert strong influence over seigneurial domains). Nevertheless, it should not be forgotten that this confirmation followed a decision made explicitly by Bertrand – albeit apparently with the consent of the prince, the patriarch and Raymond III of Tripoli

---

[190] Lieberman, *March of Wales*, pp. 55–74; K. Thompson, 'Robert of Bellême Reconsidered', *Anglo-Norman Studies* 13 (1991), 263–86.

[191] *Assises d'Antioche*, pp. 12–14

[192] Mayer, *Varia*, pp. 114–17.

[193] *CGOH*, I, 783: domini mei Boamundi, magnifici principis Antiochie.

[194] *Assises d'Antioche*, pp. 12–16.

– who had decided he could no longer afford to maintain Margat's defence.[195] Mayer has posited that Bohemond gave his assent because of his long-held aim to create a southern military order buffer zone similar to those to the north and east of the principality, but Margat's sale still marked the alienation of Antioch's largest lordship and the biggest loss of land to an external power since Nur al-Din's campaign of 1149. Furthermore, whereas sales in the Amanus Mountains or the Orontes Valley relinquished castles overlooking key roads or river crossings, with some success in the case of the Templars, earlier donations remained close to Antiochene centres of power, such as Antioch in the case of Baghras, and Saone or Jisr ash-Shughur to the east. This ensured military order holdings were incorporated into the fabric of the principality's internal frameworks. The loss of the Masoir lands altered this by surrendering the southern frontier's main hub of authority to a group far less invested in the long-term survival of the principality and not in any way answerable to the ruler. Consequently, whereas the Hospitallers ably defended Margat against Saladin in 1188, they lacked the same impulse to act in support of surrounding non-military order fortresses which the Masoirs would probably have shown. This perhaps contributed to the near-total lack of concerted action in the face of the Ayyubid invasion, with the principality's southern half swept away with no indication that the Hospitallers offered aid to their beleaguered neighbours or worked in conjunction with Antiochene forces. Despite the financial reparations Bohemond received, the acceptance of this sale was thus either an error of judgement or an implicit confirmation that he had neither the power to defend the whole polity (a reality made harder to the south by deteriorating relations with the Isma'ilis), nor the ability to prevent the Masoirs from departing. Though still the biggest landholder, the losses suffered along the eastern frontier may have ensured that, even had he wished to, the prince was simply not in a position to outbid the Hospitallers. It is perhaps also significant that, whereas the aforementioned William Bucellus – if he was a fief-holder and not a *familiares* – followed the protocol for the relinquishing of entire fiefs listed in the *Assises d'Antioche* by coming before the prince to surrender the possessions, the Masoirs did not: although they nevertheless followed thirteenth-century custom by seeking permission.[196] This adds to the abovementioned conclusions that the holder of Bikisrail was of a lesser status than the lords of Margat, while the evidence for the Masoir lordship refutes suggestions that lands could simply be taken from an established *dominus*. It is undeniable that the prince's position of authority was recognised in this instance, yet it pushes the evidence too far to agree with Mayer that it reflected the culmination of a long-standing policy aimed at ousting the Masoirs. It cannot be assumed that Bohemond had the power to oppose the sale once Bertrand had decided to relinquish his fief, and although thirteenth-century practice appears to have been followed, it remains possible that the prince's assent was courted (in particular by the Hospitallers) out of little else but a desire to retain good relations.

---

[195] *CGOH*, I, 783.
[196] *Assises d'Antioche*, pp. 10–16.

Seigneurial inheritance rights in the principality of Antioch were thus evidently far more complex than historians have hitherto appreciated.[197] The traditional view that a powerful prince was able to keep the nobility in line is not sustained by an examination of the charter evidence. Nor is Asbridge's suggestion that 'marcher style' independent lordships continued to formalise, having emerged before 1130. His theory is undoubtedly attractive, but it represents an over-simplification of the realities (both in relation to Antioch and the Anglo-Welsh borders), with a widespread fluidity and dynamism found which belies uniform concepts. Martin perhaps came closest to reality, as there are indications that the nobility expanded their right to disseminate lands, and certain of the *Assises'* customs can be discerned in practice; but his belief in the relaxation of centralised interest in Antioch's 'feudality' provided that military service was maintained also has its shortcomings, for it overlooks important evidence to the contrary at Marash and Harim, as well as the issue of princely confirmations. In reality, while strong signs can be found which indicate that land alienation could be – and was – carried out without recourse to princely interference, there remained occasions when this was not so. Quite what dictated this is hard to discern, and doubts can even be raised in regard to the sale of an entire fief. The existence of princely confirmations at least demonstrates that theoretical checks existed, even if in practice they were hard to implement. Like much of the principality's administrative practices, rigid uniformity was overlooked in favour of dynamic custom.

Conclusion

Studies on the crusader states typically attempt to locate rigid formalisation of administrative frameworks, perhaps as a result of the belief that endemic warfare forced settlers into strict regulation. For Jerusalem, despite Tibble's challenge to established opinion on royal power, both he and his detractors still argue for a polarised state firmly divided between the authority of the nobles and that of the king.[198] This same pattern can be seen in the historiography of Antioch with the belief of Cahen and Mayer in a centralised state under the sway of the prince. Moreover, while Asbridge and Martin have questioned elements of the ruling house's influence, both still argue for a greater formalisation of custom over time. The requirements of the kingdom of Jerusalem might well have allowed for such firmness to exist, yet the principality of Antioch operated in a political climate far removed from this, having been forced to adapt to myriad disasters without succumbing to total fragmentation. Caution must be urged in making steadfast conclusions, but the surviving material points towards an emergent fluidity and

---

[197] See especially Cahen, *Syrie*, pp. 435–52, 527–43; Mayer, *Varia*, pp. 174–83; Asbridge, *Creation*, pp. 155–68; Martin, 'Structures', pp. 239–50.
[198] Tibble, *Monarchy and Lordships*, pp. 1–4, 186–8.

flexibility – a characteristic which has hitherto been overlooked – similar to that now identified for contemporary Western frontiers like Wales and Normandy.[199] This largely allowed the nobility to administer their lands freely, establishing households and retinues suited to the needs of their localities. Still, changes to the ownership of the great seigneuries were not carried out without at least the assent or involvement of the prince, while there are indications that the ruler interceded to ensure security was maintained in times of crisis and was involved in aristocratic marriages. The dynamism of the principality may well have caused tension and, like the Welsh Marches and the Norman frontier, sporadic bouts of discontent emerged between the ruler and the aristocracy, even resulting in open rebellion in the early 1180s. On the whole, however, the principality's administrative organisation appears to have been successful, as Antioch endured a number of disastrous reverses which would have destroyed many other states. This could not prevent Saladin's conquests of 1188, which demonstrates that that the danger of Islamic unity could be only be deflected for so long, especially once the military orders began to alter internal dynamics. Nevertheless, the diverse and fluid balance of power seen here, and outlined in Chapters 2 and 3, proved central to the principality's survival for much of this period.

Appendix 2: The Noble Families

The Masoir

Name	Years Active	References
Renaud I Masoir	1109–c.1135	WC, pp. 84–91; *Libri Iurium*, I/2, 337; Hiestand, 'Ein unbekanntes Privileg', pp. 44–6; al–Azimi, p. 127; WT, p. 637; *CCSSJ*, 73–4
Renaud II Masoir	1140–c.1185	Caffaro, XI, 115–16; *Urkunden Venedig*, I, 55, 61; *Codice Diplomatico*, I, 206–7, 250, 281; *CGOH*, I, 341, 391, 457, 546, 559, 613, 623, 763, IV, 595, 624; Le Roulx, 'Inventaire', pp. 62, 67–8; Le Roulx, *Archives*, pp. 134–5, 142–4; *Tabulae Theutonici*, 9; Mayer, *Varia*, pp. 114–17; WT, pp. 1013–15

---

[199] Power, *Norman Frontier*, pp. 1–22; Lieberman, *March of Wales*, pp. 1–22.

Thomas Masoir, son of Renaud II	1160	*Codice Diplomatico*, I, 206–207
Amalric Masoir, son of Renaud II	1165–1183	*CGOH*, I, 341; Le Roulx, 'Inventaire', pp. 62, 68
Bertrand Masoir	1165–c.1217	*CGOH*, I, 341, 546, 613, 763, 782–3, IV, 595; Le Roulx, 'Inventaire', pp. 62, 68; Le Roulx, *Archives*, pp. 134–5; *Codice Diplomatico*, I, p. 250

The Sourdevals

Name	*Years Active*	*References*
Walter I	Before 1134–1154	Mayer, *Varia*, pp. 113–14; *CGOH*, I, 109, 222; *CCSSJ*, 76–7; *Urkunden Venedig*, I, 55; *Documenti Toscane*, 4
Robert II	1134–1163	Mayer, *Varia*, pp. 113–14; *CGOH*, I, 109, 231, 311; WT, pp. 782–5; *Urkunden Venedig*, I, 55; *Documenti Toscane*, 4; *Memorie Storico*, I, p. 202
William (?)	1151	*CGOH*, I, 198
Roger	1167–1183	*Urkunden Venedig*, I, 61; *CGOH*, I, 391, 475, 522, 546, 614, II, 23; *Libri Iurium*, I/2, 340; *Documenti Toscane*, 13; Rey, *Recherches*, pp. 22–3; Le Roulx, *Archives*, pp. 142–4; Mayer, *Varia*, pp. 114–21; *Codice Diplomatico*, I, p. 281
Walter II	1179–1187	Le Roulx, *Archives*, pp. 142–4; *CGOH*, I, 782–3

The Fresnel

Name	*Years Active*	*References*
William Fresnel	1140	*CCSSJ*, 76–7

Tancred Fresnel	1153–1160	*Urkunden Venedig*, I, 55; *Codice Diplomatico*, I, 206–7
Orgeuillse of Harim	1171–1176	*Documenti Toscane*, 13; *CGOH*, I, 437, 472, 475; Rey, *Recherches*, pp. 22–3; *Lignages d'Outremer*, p. 83
Hugh *Darene (de Harenc?)*	1166	*CGOH*, I, 367
John *de Herenc* (?)	1179	*Tabulae Theutonici*, 10
Robert Fresnel, Templar	1183	*Chartes Josaphat*, 42

Marash

Name	Years Active	References
Baldwin	c.1136–1146	*CGOH*, I, 313; WT, pp. 734–8; JK, p. 23; GP, pp. 243–57; MS, III, 244, 269–71; *1234*, II, 81–2, 104; Sempad, *RHC Arm.* I, 616
Renaud	c.1146–1149/1150	WT, 771–2; *MS*, III, 293–7

Saone

Name	Years Active	References
William	c.1121–1133	KD, *RHC Or.* III, pp. 629–33; WT, pp. 634–6; IQ, p. 215
Garenton	c.1133–c.1155	WT, pp. 634–6; *CCSSJ*, 76–7; *Urkunden Venedig*, I, 55; *Documenti Toscane*, 4; *CGOH*, I, 231
Roger	1170–1175	*CGOH*, I, 417, 474
Garenton II	1170	*CGOH*, I, 417
Joscelin	1170	*CGOH*, I, 417
Matthew	1183	*CGOH*, II, 23

| Paschal | 1193–1209 | CGOH, I, 948, II, 1336; *Documenti Toscane*, 50; Rey, *Recherches*, p. 25 |
| Roger II | 1194 | CGOH, I, 966 |

Al-Atharib

Name	Years Active	References
Χόμητί ... Ἀντιοχέων	1138	NC, p. 17
Comitisse de Cereph	1163	Le Roulx, *Archives*, pp. 97–9

Loges

Name	Years Active	References
Robert	1140	CGOH, I, 133
Roger	1151	CGOH, I, 198
William	1163–1170/1171	CGOH, I, 311; *Memorie Storico*, I, p. 202; *Documenti Toscane*, 13
Henry	1170/1171	*Documenti Toscane*, 13
Hugh	1176–1190	CGOH, I, 475, 546, 648, II, 23; Le Roulx, *Archives*, pp. 142–4; Mayer, *Varia*, pp. 114–22; *Libri Iurium*, I/2, 343
Philip	1179–1186	*Tabulae Theutonici*, 9; CGOH, I, 614, 648; Mayer, *Varia*, pp. 118–22
Peter	1183–1191	*Urkunden Venedig*, I, 68; *Libri Iurium*, I/2, 343; CGOH, I, 906

5

A Frontier Society? The Nature of Intercultural Relations

The study of intercultural relations in the Latin East remains one of the most controversial and contested fields in modern crusader studies. Subjected to frequent reinterpretation – from nineteenth- and early twentieth-century historians who viewed the Frankish polities as idylls of *convivencia* (or living together), to mid- to late twentieth-century scholars who proposed an entirely negative form of exploit-ative colonialism characterized by social exclusion and fear of the other – the crusader states have often come to reflect contemporary attitudes towards war and inter-faith contact.[1] More recently, attempts have been made to bridge the gap between these polarised models. Benjamin Kedar has sought to show that socio-re-ligious interaction occurred at many levels of Frankish society, and Ronnie Ellen-blum has demonstrated that, rather than hiding in their walled cities, the Franks settled in rural areas of the kingdom of Jerusalem, albeit only in regions populated by Eastern Christians.[2] Andrew Jotischky, meanwhile, has argued that Latin inter-action with indigenous communities was not defined only by religion, but also by language and social custom. Furthermore, that due to the great divergences – over space and time – within the different polities, it is difficult to find distinct rules of intercultural contact over the entire 'crusader' period.[3] Christopher MacEvitt has nevertheless proposed such an overarching model for interaction: 'rough toler-ance'. In this, Frankish overlords granted freedoms to non-Latins, yet also used targeted bouts of violence to keep them in line.[4] Likewise, Alan Murray has offered a hierarchical model for social interaction across the Latin East, in which a group's military capabilities, as well as their suitability for intermarriage, are viewed as the most valuable impetus for their interaction with the Franks. As such, the Armenian Christians, with whom such unions were prominent, sit at the top, followed by

---

[1]   The best modern overview of these historiographical trends is Ellenblum, *Crusader Castles*, pp. 43–102.

[2]   B. Z. Kedar, 'The Subjected Muslims of the Frankish Levant', *Muslims under Latin Rule, 1100–1300*, ed. J. M. Powell (Princeton, NJ, 1990), pp. 135–74; R. Ellenblum, *Frankish Rural Settlement in the Latin Kingdom of Jerusalem* (Cambridge, 1998).

[3]   A. Jotischky, 'Ethnographic Attitudes in the Crusader States: The Franks and the Indigenous Orthodox People', *East and West in the Crusader States III*, ed. K. Ciggaar and H. Teule (Leuven, 2003), pp. 1–19.

[4]   MacEvitt, *Rough Tolerance*, pp. 21–6.

the Greeks and other Christians (predominantly the Jacobites and Melkites), while Jews, Samaritans and Muslims are at the bottom.[5]

Despite this interest, because the preponderance of academic output has either focused primarily on Jerusalem or offered general overviews, and whereas some important work has been carried out for the counties of Edessa and Tripoli, Antioch has not yet been the subject of a modern systematic study.[6] In fact, the most thorough examination remains that of Cahen, who was a proponent of the anti-colonial model. Therefore, while he recognised the Frankish adoption of Eastern customs, some fraternity with Eastern Christians and that non-Latin groups were allowed to manage their own community and judicial affairs, he nevertheless noted that these rights were not extended to the Greeks, and that Western settlers withdrew into their cities and castles rather than live amongst the locals. The relationship between the Franks and their subjected populations, due in part also to the violence of the crusader conquest, was thus largely negative.[7] Asbridge has challenged this somewhat, arguing that although holy war rhetoric and religious divisions endured into the early years of Frankish settlement, these were not strong enough to prevent the adoption of Eastern-style administrative frameworks or the use of indigenous peoples in governance.[8] Additionally, Hamilton, Weltecke and Jotischky have all demonstrated the relative religious freedoms afforded to Eastern Christians, including the Greeks (who were subsumed into the Latin ecclesiastical hierarchy) – even if Patriarch Aimery sought to promote Eastern Orthodox communion with Rome.[9] Archaeological findings have also shown that the Franks adopted Eastern material cultures, customs and methods of agriculture, while there is some evidence for a Latin rural presence similar to that proposed by Ellenblum for the kingdom of Jerusalem, particularly around the small towers found in the Syrian country-

---

5   A. V. Murray, 'Franks and Indigenous Communities in Palestine and Syria (1099–1187): A Hierarchical Model of Social Interaction in the Principalities of Outremer', *East and West in the Middle Ages and Early Modern Times: Transcultural Experiences in the Premodern World*, ed. A. Classen (Berlin, 2013), pp. 289–307.

6   Amouroux-Mourad, *Edesse*, pp. 93–108; S. Redford, *The Archaeology of the Frontier in the Medieval Near East: Excavations at Gritille, Turkey* (Boston, MA, 1998); MacEvitt, *Rough Tolerance*, pp. 74–99; Richard, *Tripoli*, pp. 86–8; and 'Affrontement ou confrontation? Les contacts entre deux mondes au pays de Tripoli au temps des Croisades', *Chronos: Revue d'Histoire de l'Université de Balamand* 2 (1999), 7–28; G. Dédéyan and K. Rizk (ed.), *Le comté de Tripoli: état multiculturel et multiconfessionnel (1102–1289)* (Paris, 2010), pp. 31–99, 157–68; Lewis, *Rule and Identity*, pp. 263–322; and 'Medieval Diglossia: The Diversity of the Latin Christian Encounter with Written and Spoken Arabic in the "Crusader" County of Tripoli, with a Hitherto Unpublished Arabic Note from the Principality of Antioch (MS, AOM 3, Valletta: National Library of Malta, no. 51v)', *Al-Masaq* 27:2 (2015), 119–52.

7   Cahen, *Syrie*, pp. 326–45, 461–2, 561–8.

8   Asbridge, 'Crusader Community', pp. 305–25; Asbridge and Edgington, *The Antiochene Wars*, pp. 59–68.

9   Hamilton, *Latin Church*, pp. 159–87; 'Ecumenist', pp. 269–90; and 'Aimery of Limoges, Patriarch of Antioch (c.1142–c.1196), and the Unity of the Churches', *East and West in the Crusader States II*, ed. K. Ciggaar and H. Teule (Leuven, 1999), pp. 1–12; D. Weltecke, 'On the Syriac Orthodox in the Principality of Antioch during the Crusader Period', *East and West I*, pp. 95–124; A. Jotischky, *The Perfection of Solitude: Hermits and Monks in the Crusader States* (University Park, PA, 1995).

side.[10] Numerous studies have even pointed to Antioch as a place of intellectual exchange, particularly the translation of Arabic medical treatises – a sentiment challenged by Susan Edgington, who views this as a largely early-twelfth-century phenomena.[11] Finally, in an article on 'interculturality' in the principality, Kristin Skottki has recently argued against so-called 'positivist' notions of interaction (that is those who see positive contacts in the medieval texts), stating that Frankish chroniclers described cross-cultural contact in ways that suited Western audiences, not to demonstrate tolerance. As such, their works are more useful for gauging Western attitudes towards the other than they are for the realities of intercultural contact in the Latin East.[12]

This chapter will aim to pull together these various strands of existing research, and to more comprehensively assess the nature of society in the principality. It is argued that, whereas some historians have proposed clear models of behaviour and social structure, the surviving evidence suggests that, in a polity so strongly characterised by diversity and fluidity, intercultural relations, while distinctly possible, were difficult to uniformly govern and were also subject to limitations which hint at a certain level of distrust.

The Non-Latin Communities of the Principality of Antioch

In order to better understand the various interactions between Frankish settlers and non-Latins, however, it is first important to establish the groups who populated the principality and where they were situated. One of the most significant Christian communities was the Armenians. With Armenian as their liturgical language, they were especially known in Cilicia, northern Syria and the would-be county of Edessa even before the First Crusade.[13] Cahen nevertheless believed them to be the principality's least numerous Eastern Christian community, although MacEvitt has gone so far as to suggest that they actually 'dominated the cities and coun-

10 Major, *Rural Settlements*, pp. 68–90; and 'The Medieval Mill of Banyas and some Notes on the Topography of the Town of Valania', *East and West II*, pp. 367–90; Riis, 'Medieval Period', pp. 85–115; Vorderstrasse, *Al-Mina*, pp. 102–11; K. Ciggaar, 'Adaptation to Oriental Life by Rulers in and around Antioch: Examples and Exempla', *East and West I*, pp. 261–82; Kaniewski *et al.*, 'Vegetation Patterns', pp. 251–62.

11 C. Burnett, 'Antioch as a Link between Arabic and Latin Culture in the Twelfth and Thirteenth Centuries', *Occident et Proche-Orient: contacts scientifiques au temps des croisades*, ed. A. Tihon, I. Draelants and B. van den Abeele (Louvain-la-Neuve, 2000), pp. 1–78; 'Stephen, the Disciple of Philosophy, and the Exchange of Medical Learning in Antioch', *Crusades* 5 (2006), 113–29; Hiestand, 'Centre intellectual', pp. 7–36; B. Kedar and E. Kohlberg, 'The Intercultural Career of Theodore of Antioch', *Intercultural Contacts in the Medieval Mediterranean*, ed. B. Arbel (London, 1996), pp. 164–76; S. Edgington, 'Medieval Antioch: City of Culture', *East and West I*, pp. 247–59. See also Lewis, 'Diglossia', pp. 133–8.

12 Skottki, 'Pious Traitors', pp. 75–115.

13 MacEvitt, *Rough Tolerance*, pp. 7–9; Major, *Rural Settlements*, pp. 152–3.

tryside'.[14] When the crusaders arrived in 1097, Armenians therefore aided them in the surrender of Tarsus, Mamistra and Adana, while they also experienced and supported the capture of Antioch, as well as its defence, in 1098.[15] Importantly, it is clear that even at this early stage they were seen as a distinct religious community by the chroniclers and the crusaders themselves, as shown by the letter of the leaders to Pope Urban II in 1098 and that of Stephen of Blois to his wife Adela.[16] An Armenian presence continued after the crusader conquest. Albert of Aachen noted them around Apamea and in Cilicia (particularly Mamistra), and Walter the Chancellor, although critical of this group, mentioned Armenians at Antioch during the 1110s.[17] The growth of the Frankish principality thus does not seem to have entirely displaced this community. William of Tyre's comment that King Baldwin II of Jerusalem sent to Antioch to ask for an Armenian technician skilled in the art of siege warfare during an attack on Tyre in 1124 suggests they even retained a degree of socio-political value.[18] This is in spite of the fact that Cilician Armenians rebelled against Frankish rule in support of the Byzantines in the early 1100s – an event that perhaps explains Walter the Chancellor's antagonism, as well as the lack of evidence for their intermarriage with the Antiochene Franks.[19] Some of the principality's administrative documents also refer to this community. A charter of 1183 listed numerous Armenian families at Latakia, a presence also supported by evidence of its Armenian bishop (alongside one of Apamea) in 1179, and Muslim chroniclers' descriptions of their role in its fall to Saladin in 1188.[20] Likewise, a document of 1193 referred to the 'Armenians of the suburb' of Margat, and a letter of Pope Honorius III in 1225 recorded 'churches of the Armenians' built in the nearby diocese of Valania.[21]

Significantly, the existence of Armenian communities is not limited to Latin chronicles or documents. Gregory the Priest noted his co-religionists at Marash and Kesoun, while another Armenian, Guiragos of Kantzag, as well as Michael the Syrian and Niketas Choniates, all attest to Armenians at Antioch.[22] Ibn al-Qalanisi mentioned Armenians helping the Franks to defend the fortress of Afis near

---

[14] Cahen, *Syrie*, p. 337; MacEvitt, *Rough Tolerance*, p. 9.

[15] Asbridge, *Creation*, pp. 16–24; *Gesta Francorum et aliorum Hierosolymitanorum*, ed. and trans. R. Hill (Oxford, 1962), pp. 29, 33, 37, 41, 43–4, 47–8, 70; Fulcher of Chartres, pp. 221, 230, 235, 264; Ralph of Caen, *RHC Occ.* III, 629; Albert of Aachen, pp. 182–4, 266; Raymond d'Aguilers, *Historia Francorum qui ceperunt Iherusalem*, ed. J. H. Hill and L. L. Hill (Paris, 1969), p. 64.

[16] H. Hagenmeyer, *Epistulae et chartae ad historiam primi belli sacri spectantes. Die Kreuzzugsbriefe aus den Jahren 1088–1100* (Innsbruck, 1901), 10, 16.

[17] Albert of Aachen, pp. 736–8; WC, p. 63.

[18] WT, pp. 597–8.

[19] Asbridge, *Creation*, p. 56. See also, Asbridge and Edgington, *The Antiochene Wars*, pp. 67–8; Skottki, 'Pious Traitors', pp. 94–104.

[20] *CGOH*, I, 648; A. Sanjian, 'The Armenians in Bilad al-Sham', *Proceedings of the First International Conference on Bilad al-Sham* (Amman, Jordan, 1974), pp. 195–221; AS, *RHC Or.* IV, 362.

[21] *CGOH*, I, 941: Armeni suburbii; P.-V. Claverie, *Honorius III et l'Orient (1216–1227)* (Leiden, 2013), pp. 406–7: ecclesias ... Armeniorum.

[22] GP, pp. 243–5; Guiragos of Kantzag, 'L'histoire d'Armenie', *RHC Arm.* I, 417–18; MS, III, 304; Choniates, *Historia*, pp. 39, 108 (NC, pp. 22, 62).

to Ma'arrat an-Nu'uman from Nur al-Din in 1153, Abu Shama commented that they protected Kafar Dubbin from Saladin in 1188, while Izz al-Din ibn Shaddad noted that the Orontes Valley remained home to a strong Armenian community in the thirteenth century.[23] That excavations in and around the castle of Saone have unearthed evidence of Armenian chapels and perhaps even a guard tower which pre-date the Frankish conquest also suggests that they were well known in the area.[24] Thus, while the evidence is not strong enough to overtly support MacEvitt's belief that the Armenians were the dominant population, there is a clear sense that they were found in a number of the urban and rural areas of the principality, including its capital.

A harder group to adequately identify, at least in terms of their liturgical allegiance, are the *Suriani*. This term, which equates to 'Syrian', appears with some frequency in Latin narratives and documents pertaining to *Outremer*, yet it is not always clear who it signified, or if it was deployed with total consistency. What exactly constituted a *Suriani* has engendered a great deal of historiographical debate. In terms of the principality – differentiated here from the rest of the Latin East – the two groups most likely to be designated by this term were the Syriac Jacobites and the Greek Orthodox Melkites. The former used Syriac as their liturgical language and had a patriarch of Antioch during the twelfth century, while the latter were predominantly Arabic speaking, despite their Greek liturgy.[25] Cahen believed *Suriani* referred only to Jacobites, but MacEvitt has noted – in line with others including Joseph Nasrallah, Johannes Pahlitzsch, Weltecke, Jotischky and Murray – that the term is 'particularly fuzzy', and perhaps demonstrates Latin difficulties when differentiating between these groups.[26] Nonetheless, most historians now generally agree that, for the Latin East as a whole, *Suriani* referred primarily to linguistic Arabic identity rather than liturgical allegiance, and that those who appear in the Latin sources were Melkites. For the principality in particular, MacEvitt bases this assumption on the belief that the Melkites were far more numerous than the Jacobites (a statement which itself requires, and will receive, further enquiry).[27] This stance is perhaps influenced by a late twelfth-century text, known as the *Tractatus de locis et statu sancte terre ierosolimitane*, which was later used and expanded upon by the thirteenth-century bishop of Acre, Jacques de Vitry, and clearly distinguished the *Suriani* from the Jacobites in the wider Near East.[28] As Jotischky has noted, however,

---

23 IQ, p. 315; AS, *RHC Or.* IV, 370; IS, p. 45.
24 Major, *Rural Settlements*, p. 153.
25 MacEvitt, *Rough Tolerance*, pp. 8–9.
26 Cahen, *Syrie*, pp. 191, 338; MacEvitt, *Rough Tolerance*, pp. 102–6; J. Nasrallah, 'Syriens et Suriens', *Symposium Syriacum 1972:célebré dans les jours 26–31 octobre 1972 à l'Institut Ponitifical Oriental de Rome: Rapports et Communications* (Rome, 1974), pp. 487–503; J. Pahlitzsch, *Graeci und Suriani im Palästina der Kreuzfahrerzeit* (Berlin, 2001), pp. 14–15, 181–8; Weltecke, 'Syriac Orthodox', pp. 107–11; Jotischky, 'Ethnographic Attitudes', pp. 1–19; Murray, 'Franks and Indigenous', pp. 297–8.
27 MacEvitt, *Rough Tolerance*, pp. 103–5.
28 B. Z. Kedar, 'The *Tractatus de locis et statu sancte terre ierosolimitane*', *The Crusades and Their Sources: Essays Presented to Bernard Hamilton*, ed. J. France and W. G. Zajac (Aldershot, 1998), pp. 111–33; Jacques de Vitry, *Historia Orientalis*, ed. and trans. J. Donnadieu (Turnhout, 2008), pp. 294–312.

works like those of Jacques de Vitry, and perhaps also the *Tractatus*, reflect a period in which there was much greater interest in understanding Eastern Christian religious practices, particularly in the West, and that it cannot be presumed this differentiation was always made.[29] Indeed, Pahlitzsch has recognised the greater difficulties in distinguishing between these communities in northern Syria when compared to the kingdom of Jerusalem, while it should also be remembered that Arabic sources used 'Syrian' solely in reference to Jacobites.[30] Caution must therefore be exercised when making such clear demarcations.

Outside of texts such as the *Tractatus* and Jacques de Vitry, there is in fact evidence that *Suriani* acted as a cover-all term. Whereas the crusade leaders mentioned 'Armenians, Syrians and Jacobites' at Antioch in their letter to Urban II, a differentiation also made by Ralph of Caen when describing the 'Antiochene Syrian' as distinct from them the 'Jacobite of Artah', most First Crusade sources simply described Syrians during the siege of the city in 1098.[31] Perhaps significantly, Walter the Chancellor did not utilise the term *Iacobi*, differentiating instead between 'Greeks, Syrians and Armenians' when listing those affected by an earthquake at Antioch in 1115.[32] William of Tyre was similarly silent on the Jacobites, only ever utilising the term *Suriani* when discussing those who were not Armenian or Greek – a trait which continued for some thirteenth-century writers, such as Wilbrand of Oldenburg's account of Syrians and Greeks at Antioch in 1211–1212.[33] This failure to differentiate is not limited to Latin sources, as Choniates mentioned 'Syrians' at Antioch in 1143 and 1158.[34] While it may be unsurprising that some Latin authors would fail to show due care when noting the ecclesiastical affiliations of Eastern Christians; that a Greek would neglect to differentiate Jacobites from Melkites is of interest. It is possible that Choniates, who had a keen interest in theology, saw the Arabised Melkites as so distinct (or – perhaps – inferior) from the Hellenophonic Orthodox Church that he simply placed them in the same bracket as the other 'Syrians'.[35] Nonetheless, this evidence demonstrates the need to show caution when assuming the demographical composition of Antioch, for it could be read that this represents the Jacobites as the more significant community.

The corpus of surviving charters offer further insights into, and also problems for, the issue of the *Suriani*. In a document issued by Raymond of Poitiers in favour

---

29 Jotischky, 'Ethnographic Attitudes', pp. 4–6.

30 Pahlitzsch, *Graeci und Suriani*, p. 181 n. 348; Nasrallah, 'Syriens', pp. 494–503.

31 Hagenmeyer, *Kreuzzugsbriefe*, 16: Armenos, Syros Iacobitasque; Ralph of Caen, *RHC Occ.* III, 629: Antiochena Syrus ... Artasium Iacobi; *Gesta Francorum*, pp. 29, 33, 37, 41, 43–4, 47–8, 70, 73–4; Fulcher of Chartres, pp. 221, 264; Albert of Aachen, 266, 282, 286.

32 WC, p. 63: Graeci, Syri, Armeni.

33 MacEvitt, *Rough Tolerance*, p. 102; R. C. Schwinges, *Kreuzzugsideologie und Toleranz: Studien zu Wilhelm von Tyrus* (Stuttgart, 1977), pp. 295–9; D. Pringle, 'Wilbrand of Oldenburg's Journey to Syria, Lesser Armenia, Cyprus, and the Holy Land (1211–1212): A New Edition', *Crusades* 11 (2012), 123.

34 Choniates, *Historia*, pp. 39, 108 (NC, pp. 22, 68): Σύροι.

35 L. Bossina, 'Niketas Choniates as a Theologian', *Niketas Choniates: A Historian and a Writer*, ed. A. Simpson and S. Efthymiadis (Geneva, 2009), pp. 165–84.

of the Church of the Holy Sepulchre in 1140, mention is made of three *Suriani*, Nicephorus, Michael and Nicholas, whose knowledge of Antioch helped to verify the church's claim to certain possessions there.[36] The name Nicephorus hints at Greek ethnicity, but the others could easily also be Jacobite. Added to this, an 1163 charter of Bohemond III mentions a house at Latakia owned by 'a Syrian called Asset', a name which lacks any clear Greek overtones.[37] Likewise, the *Surianum* of Jabala called Bon Mossor, who was handed to the Hospitallers by Bohemond III in 1175, as well as the Dabot the Syrian who owned a house at Latakia until 1190, carry names that partly suggest Arabised identity, albeit certainly not Greek.[38] More difficult is one Abd al-Massie, the *rayyis* of Margat before 1174 whose name, while undoubtedly Arabic, is translated literally as 'servant of the messiah'.[39] Coupled with the fact that his son-in-law was called George, it is highly likely that he was a Melkite.[40] The adoption of Arabised names was certainly not unknown amongst Melkites, as is demonstrated by the fact that Symeon II, the patriarch of Antioch appointed by Bohemond IV in 1208 and described by Pope Innocent III as a Greek, was also called Ibn Abu Shaiba ('the white haired one').[41] Additionally, a Melkite priest named al-Mawwad li-Ilah ('the Friend of God') leased a church within Antioch from the monastery of Josaphat in 1213.[42] Importantly, though, neither Abd al-Massie nor George is described as a *Suriani*, even though the mention of the 'Syrians of the suburb' of Margat in 1193 demonstrates that such a community existed there.[43] Antioch's charter material thus paints a rather cloudy picture. While the use of forenames to denote religious affiliation is fraught with difficulties, it is plausible to argue that MacEvitt's belief in the near total absence of Jacobites in the Latin material, and that the Melkites were the predominant group, is unsustainable.[44] This is made all the more pertinent by the fact that, whereas there are surviving Syriac texts – such as Michael the Syrian and the *1234 Chronicle* – which list Jacobite communities, churches and monasteries throughout the principality, including at Antioch, Tarsus, Jabala, Latakia and near to Harim, there are no such Melkite narratives.[45] Greeks are mentioned by Syriac authors, particularly Michael the Syrian who, as head of the Jacobite Church, frequently led the way in demonstrating his disdain for them. Yet, while differentiations are not made between

---

36   *CCSSJ*, 77.
37   *Memorie Storico*, p. 202: Suriani nomine Asset.
38   *CGOH*, I, 472, 891.
39   *Ibid.*, I, 457.
40   *Ibid.*, I, 457, 613, 783.
41   Prawer, *Crusader Institutions*, pp. 71–2; Hamilton, *Latin Church*, pp. 313–14; *Die Register Innocenz' III*, ed. O. Hageneder and A. Haidacher, 12 vols (Graz, 1964–2012), XI, 8.
42   N. Jamil and J. Johns, 'An Original Arabic Document from Crusader Antioch (1213 AD)', *Texts, Documents and Artefacts: Islamic Studies in Honour of D.S. Richards*, ed. Chase F. Robinson (Leiden: Brill, 2003), pp. 157–90.
43   *CGOH*, I, 941: Suriani ... suburbii.
44   On the issue of naming, see Lewis, 'Diglossia', pp. 128–9.
45   MS, III, 231, 255–6, 300–4, 332–5, 339, 360; *1234*, II, 143.

Greek and Arabic speakers, from Michael's perspective they were distinct from the Jacobites, and the Franks understood this.

A full understanding of the term *Suriani* – at least as it was used in the principality – perhaps remains elusive. Its appearance in Latin chronicles (which often prove the source type most likely to generalise) could tell us more about the authors and their audiences than it does about these Eastern Christian communities.[46] The suggestion that *Suriani* denoted language identity, predominantly Arabic, rather than religion, is tempting, especially given the somewhat frequent mentioning of *Armeni* and *Graeci* as distinct groups. However, this is troubled by charter evidence that only infrequently contains Arabised forenames, and very rarely in conjunction with the term *Suriani*. It is likely that, given the unfortunate gaps in our source material, the enduring assumption that Antioch was a Greek city, to be discussed below, has contributed to a belief that the Melkites formed the mainstay of the principality's 'Syrian' population. The evidence put forth here challenges this, and demands historians take greater care when assuming the limited nature of the Jacobites' demographic spread.

The difficulties presented by the term *Suriani* also present a need to discuss the community classed within the Latin narratives as *Graeci*. As already noted, some have assumed that Antioch, and much of what came to be known as the principality, was predominantly ethnically Greek, even if not linguistically so.[47] This is perhaps unsurprising given that Byzantine authority had lasted in northern Syria and Cilicia until the late eleventh century, and there are indications of pre-crusade Greek churches as far east as 'Imm and Yaghra.[48] However, Cahen argued that those who remained Hellenophones, as opposed to the Arabic speaking Melkites, were a small, urban elite even before the First Crusade, and that a general dislike of Byzantium amongst the Franks and the other Christians further isolated them during the twelfth century.[49] Despite this, there is more to be said about this community, as well as the strength of the principality's Greek identity.

First Crusade narratives, as well as the leaders' letter to Urban II, do mention the *Graeci* as a specific community, albeit only within Antioch itself – a sentiment echoed by Walter the Chancellor for the 1110s.[50] Ralph of Caen also noted their presence at Tarsus in the early 1100s, while William of Tyre detailed a similar community at Latakia.[51] The continued issuing of Greek coins at Antioch, as well as the adaption of imperial administrative positions such as the *dux*, likewise implies the influence of a Greek linguistic identity, and thus also its population.[52]

---

[46] This to some extent supports the arguments laid out in Skottki, 'Pious Traitors', pp. 75–115.

[47] MacEvitt, *Rough Tolerance*, pp. 102–5; S. Runciman, 'The Greeks in Antioch at the Time of the Crusades', *Actes du 9e congrès d'études Byzantines (Thessaloniki, 1953)*, 3 vols (Athens, 1955–8), II, 583–91.

[48] Major, *Rural Settlements*, p. 152.

[49] Cahen, *Syrie*, pp. 187, 333–5.

[50] Fulcher of Chartres, pp. 221, 264; Albert of Aachen, 282; Raymond d'Aguilers, p. 64; Hagenmeyer, *Kreuzzugsbriefe*, pp. 161–5; WC, p. 63.

[51] Ralph of Caen, *RHC Occ.* III, 712; WT, pp. 481–2.

[52] Asbridge, *Creation*, pp. 181–94.

Usefully, Michael the Syrian frequently mentions the Greeks of Antioch (albeit without overtly noting their linguistic affiliations), while the continued Byzantine hopes of reinstalling a Greek patriarch at Antioch implies that there was a religious community there to service.[53] This is further suggested by Innocent III's complaints regarding the influence 'of the Greeks' (*Graecorum*) within a commune that emerged in response to Leon's attempted coup to seize Antioch following Bohemond III's capture at Baghras in 1193; Wilbrand of Oldenburg's report of their continued presence and religious independence in 1211–1212; and Pope Honorius III's description of 'churches of the Greeks' at Valania in 1225.[54] Despite this, the term *Graeci* appears only once in Antiochene documents. In 1183, Bohemond III confirmed the transfer of a number of Eastern Christians to the Hospitallers at Latakia and Jabala, and included amongst this were named *Graeci*, including Afanas, Sergius the mason and his family, Leo the barrel-maker, Mambarac and his family, another Mambarac, who was a shoemaker, and a second Leo.[55] No mention was made of *Suriani*, although Armenians were also transferred, and none carry forenames easily associable with Greek origins. It is thus possible that these *Graeci* represent both Hellenophonic Christians and Arabised Melkites – which implies that they formed the same social group and were of a commensurate legal standing. This adds further complications to the earlier discussion on Melkites and Jacobites, but it again demonstrates the need to pay closer attention to the terminology employed within Antiochene charters, for differentiations were being made. There are also a number of Hellenic sounding figures who appear in governance, such as Leo Maiopoli, the duke of Antioch, or Basil the chamberlain, which suggests that at least some of the principality's urban and military centres housed educated Greek elites.[56] However, at no point were any of these expressly described as *Graeci*, unlike those at Latakia and Jabala in 1183, while the fact that Basil had a brother called Oliver, a distinctly Frankish name, shows the need for caution.[57]

A Greek population evidently existed within the principality; yet, whereas in certain areas, and on certain occasions, they were differentiated from the Melkites, in others this was not necessarily the case. Coupled with the problems in differentiating who fell under the term *Suriani*, as well as the proliferation of Armenians, the presupposition that Antioch and its surrounding area was distinctly Greek can be challenged. The apparent influence of the Greeks during the commune – built though it is on somewhat fragile source foundations – suggests that they were not

---

53 MS, III, pp. 255–6, 332–5, 339. See also pp. 196, 203, 212–13 of this book.
54 *Register Innocenz' III*, I, 512, XI, 8; Pringle, 'Wilbrand', p. 123; Claverie, *Honorius III*, pp. 406–7: ecclesias Graecorum.
55 *CGOH*, I, 648.
56 For references, see below.
57 *CCSSJ*, 76–7. Oliver possibly adopted a Frankish name to facilitate a career in administration, a practice seen elsewhere. See MacEvitt, *Rough Tolerance*, pp. 153–5; A. Metcalfe, 'The Muslims of Sicily under Christian Rule', *The Society of Norman Italy*, ed. G. Loud and A. Metcalfe (Leiden, 2002), pp. 294–304.

an insubstantial community.[58] Nevertheless, there are suggestions that the principality was a region of much greater Christian diversity, which could certainly account for the often imprecise nature of the sources.

Much less is known of the non-Christian communities. It is clear that the principality's southern areas were home to Muslims, such as at Bikisrail and Balatanos during the 1130s, and the Isma'ilis who inhabited the Ansarriyah Mountains, while the Muslims of Jabala are said to have helped the city to surrender to Saladin in 1188.[59] Likewise, Wilbrand of Oldenburg mentioned nomadic Muslims living between Latakia and Antioch, as well as those who lived within the capital and observed their own laws.[60] As Islamic communities rarely appear in charters, however, their numeric extent, as well as the denomination, is decidedly unclear, although they were likely to have been strongest in regions closest to centres of power, like Aleppo.[61] Even less was recorded about the principality's Jewish population. Indeed, the evidence is limited to the travel account of Benjamin of Tudela, an Iberian Jew who visited northern Syria in the late 1160s and mentioned – perhaps in reference to heads of families – that there were ten Jews at Antioch and a further one hundred at Latakia, a statement which is supported, at least in terms of geographical spread, by charters of 1173 and 1183, as well as by Wilbrand of Oldenburg.[62]

The nature of the sources, and the extent of their survival, means only an incomplete picture of the principality's socio-religious composition can be gleaned. Nonetheless, the clues available point towards a polity home to a rich blend of faiths, spread throughout its geographical extent. It is even possible that there would have been instances of migration which altered the composition and size of internal groups: for example, the presence of the Jacobite bishop of Edessa, Basil, in Antioch in the 1150s suggests that at least some of the Eastern Christians of Edessa who rebelled against the Zengids in 1146 subsequently fled violent persecution and found a home in the principality.[63] Such complications would have ensured that approaches to indigenous communities would have varied throughout the princi-

---

[58]   On the commune, the *Eracles* continuation of William of Tyre (*RHC Occ.* II, 213–15 (here 214)) simply described the involvement of 'all the people of the city' (*toutes les genz de la vile*). Prawer (*Crusader Institutions*, pp. 68–76) and Burgtorf ('War of Succession', p. 199) argued that it must have been Greeks, for they had the most to lose from an Armenian ruler; a sentiment perhaps supported by Pope Innocent III's letter of January 1199 (*Register Innocenz' III*, I, 512) in which he complained that Latin priests were acting according to the 'judgements and customs of the Greeks' (*iudicium et consuetudines Graecorum*). Yet, this might not indicate a sizeable population; rather that the Greek Church had increased its influence following the death of the long-standing patriarch, Aimery of Limoges, and in response to fears of increased Armenian power.

[59]   Ibn al-Furat, II, 134–5; al-Azimi, pp. 121, 127; KD, *RHC Or.* III, 665; MS, III, 282, 288–94; *1234*, pp. 115–16; Mayer, *Varia*, pp. 114–17; ID, pp. 122, 127; BD, p. 83; KD, *ROL* 4, 186–7; AS, *RHC Or.* IV, 351–63; IA, II, 345–6.

[60]   Pringle, 'Wilbrand', pp. 122–3.

[61]   This is suggested by the local Muslim rebellion against the Franks when Il-Ghazi invaded the easternmost areas of the principality in 1119. See WC, p. 90.

[62]   Benjamin of Tudela, *The Itinerary of Benjamin of Tudela*, ed. and trans. M. N. Adler (London, 1907), pp. 15–16; Pringle, 'Wilbrand', p. 123; CGOH, I, 472, 648.

[63]   MS, III, 300–4. See also MacEvitt, *Rough Tolerance*, pp. 96–7; El-Azhari, *Zengi*, pp. 107–8.

pality, as it was neither a homogenous region, nor was any community limited to an urban or a rural setting.

Government, Security and the Indigenous

With this established, the nature of these groups' interactions with their new overlords must be examined. In addition to discussing whether they posed a threat to security, a potentially productive, albeit enigmatic signifier of intercultural contact regards how the Franks governed these peoples and the extent of their involvement in Latin administration. As Peter Edbury has noted:

> how the Christians ... as an alien elite ... were able to control and exploit the indigenous population [is an] important question ... Historians can call upon a wide variety of sources ... but the social structures and *mentalités* of the Latin East are difficult to unravel. The evidence is uneven and often intractable, and, although there has been much excellent research, it is all too easy for historians to hide behind broad generalisations or build elaborate hypotheses on the slenderest of evidence.[64]

In line with these remarks, it must be noted that a discussion of indigenous interaction with Antioch's governmental frameworks is to some extent limited by the lack of an internal Latin narrative for the principality after the 1120s. Likewise, the silence of the *Assises d'Antioche* on a *cour des Syriens* (the 'court of the Syrians') – which provided justice to non-Latins in the kingdom of Jerusalem – limits conclusions on these communities' recourse to legal action. It even offers the suggestion that such an institution did not exist in the northern crusader states: a reality recently echoed by Lewis for the county of Tripoli and more widely by MacEvitt.[65] A number of other case studies can nevertheless provide useful insights.

Before examining this, though, it is important to establish the extent to which the Franks were ever subject to security issues from within the principality itself. Indeed, the wealth of external threats would almost certainly have made the Antiochenes mindful of the potential danger of internal communities allying with their external co-religionists or allies. This was the case with the Armenians, who supported Byzantine forces against the Latins in the early 1100s, while Alex Mallett has suggested that local Muslim forces supported Mawdud of Mosul and Tughtegin of Damascus during ventures into northern Syria in 1109/1110, as well as Il-Ghazi of Mardin in his *Ager Sanguinis* campaign of 1119.[66] Moreover, it was noted in

---

[64] P. Edbury, *John of Ibelin and the Kingdom of Jerusalem* (Woodbridge, 1997), p. 105.

[65] John of Ibelin, *Le Livre des Assises*, p. 55; Riley-Smith, 'Lesser Officials', 2–15; Lewis, 'Diglossia', p. 127; MacEvitt, *Rough Tolerance*, pp. 151–2.

[66] Asbridge, *Creation*, p. 56; A. Mallett, *Popular Muslim Reactions to the Franks in the Levant, 1097–1291* (Farnham, 2014), p. 51. For Mawdud and Tughtegin, see also IQ, pp. 101–35. Whether he is correct for Il-Ghazi is unclear, as his argument is based upon Walter the Chancellor's (WC, p. 90) comment that the ruler of Mardin had been aided by Muslims 'from the four corners of the world, in addition to

Chapter 1 that there were internal problems in the southern parts of the principality after 1130, as the Isma'ilis were able to forge a power base for themselves in the Ansarriyah Mountains, with Muslim uprisings at Bikisrail and Balatanos around this time seemingly linked to this and also Turcoman raiding incursions.[67] The *qadi* of Jabala – to be examined below – is even said to have aided Saladin in his conquest of that city in 1188.[68] Yet, these are isolated examples, and although Cahen has suggested that Michael the Syrian's report of a divide within Antioch over whether to surrender to Nur al-Din after Inab in 1149 was formed along religious lines (with the Franks favouring Jerusalem and the non-Franks arguing for Muslim rule), this represents a certain degree of supposition.[69] For the most part, therefore, whether due to Frankish military dominance (as MacEvitt's 'rough tolerance' would imply), the lack of surviving source material or another unknown reason, the indigenous communities of the principality were not a demonstrably frequent danger to Antiochene power. An investigation into Latin governance could help to reveal more about why, or whether, this was so.

In his work on Frankish governance in the Latin East, Jonathan Riley-Smith identified a number of lesser administrative offices with links to indigenous populations; however, perhaps tellingly, few of these are known in an Antiochene context.[70] For example, the appearance of *Bernardus interpres*, a role commensurate to the *dragomans* (interpreters) found in the kingdom of Jerusalem, in a charter confirming an agreement made between the Templars and the bishop of Valania in 1163 does not prove this role existed in the principality. Indeed, he may instead have been connected to the other groups represented in this document, the Templars and the counts of Tripoli.[71] The position of *scribae* (scribe) was perhaps more widespread, although this term was never directly used in Antioch's charters. It is also unclear whether all who appeared in such a role equate, as Riley-Smith suggests, to the landholding office of the *secreta*.[72] While Master George of the *secreta* appears in Raymond of Poitiers' charters for the Holy Sepulchre in 1140, this is the only explicit mention of this title.[73] Mention is nonetheless made in other Antiochene documents to Theodore the notary, Constantine the cleric and George the notary of Margat, which at least demonstrates that Eastern Christians were employed on a clerical basis, albeit not overwhelmingly so.[74]

Non-Latins are also seen taking up more important roles. From 1127 to 1154, Leo Maiopoli witnessed a number of documents, almost always as duke of Antioch. His elevation had potentially initially been unpopular, for al-Azimi noted that a

---

those from within the region' (*a IV mundi partibus deforinsecis praeter illos qui intus*). This could either mean those living under Frankish rule, or local allies from places not under Il-Ghazi's direct control.

[67] See pp. 26–7.
[68] See pp. 176–9.
[69] MS, III, 290; Cahen, *Syrie*, p. 384.
[70] Riley-Smith, 'Lesser Officials', pp. 15–26.
[71] *Codice diplomatico*, I, pp. 40–1.
[72] Riley-Smith, 'Lesser Officials', pp. 19–26.
[73] CCSSJ, 76–7.
[74] *Ibid.*; CGOH, I, 472, 475, 546; *Codice diplomatico*, I, p. 250.

new duke (almost certainly Leo) was appointed at Antioch by Fulk of Anjou in 1134, much to the annoyance of the Antiochenes.[75] The longevity of Leo's position at court suggests this antagonism did not last, or that it may have been directed at Fulk instead.[76] The examples of Basil, the chamberlain in 1140, and Vasilius, the viscount of Antioch in 1166–1167, similarly show the possibility for governmental involvement.[77] Yet, the latter example could have been prompted by external forces, as Vasilius' career appears to have begun in the immediate aftermath of Emperor Manuel Komnenos' successful imposition of a Greek Patriarch at Antioch in 1165. As such, his short-lived elevation may also have been related to the deal to pay for Bohemond III's ransom following Artah. Even so, that a certain Angelos later delivered a message from Antioch detailing the disaster at Hattin in 1187 to King William II of Sicily, denotes that princely governance made use of educated Eastern Christians.[78] Despite this, it is of interest that, in a similar vein to the general silence on the *secreta*, a number of other governmental positions which grew from Byzantine precedents, with the exception of the *dux*, seemingly declined or fell into disuse as the twelfth century progressed. So, while there is evidence for a *praetor*, *praecones* and *iudex* before 1130, they are not witnessed after this point.[79] Although this may simply be a quirk of the sources, when coupled with the disappearance of Greek-inscribed coinage, it could also indicate the decreasing status of pre-Latin administrative positions, as well as Greek identity. That this appears to have come with the passing of the principality out of the hands of its Norman founders – which led to a more pronounced affinity with Raymond's Poitevin roots – is unlikely to be a coincidence.[80]

Another indigenous role known in the principality is that of the *qadi*. In Islamic lands, the *qadi* was 'a notable scholar, pious and energetic, who judged on civil and criminal matters, and had authority over the judicial administration'.[81] It must be questioned what position such a figure could enjoy in areas under Latin rule. Alex Metcalfe has highlighted that the Muslims of Norman Sicily had recourse to their own justice, and so the *qadi*s remained.[82] A number of historians have likewise argued that the *qadi* played a useful role in *Outremer* by administering to Muslim cases in the *cour des Syriens*, despite the silence in the sources on both this court

75 Al-Azimi, p. 142.
76 Hiestand, 'Ein unbekanntes Privileg', pp. 44–6; *CCSSJ*, 73–4, 76–7; *CGOH*, I, 183, 222; *Urkunden Venedig*, I, 46, 55; *Libri Iurium*, I/2, 338; *Documenti Toscane*, 4.
77 *CCSSJ*, 76–7; *CGOH*, I, 367.
78 Hiestand, 'Antiochia', pp. 115–17.
79 Asbridge, *Creation*, pp. 192–4.
80 This should not be read as an aversion to ties to Byzantium, rather that Raymond was unlikely to have had the same exposure to Greek administrative practice as his southern Italian predecessors. See pp. 69–77.
81 Elisséeff, *Nur ad-Din*, III, 825–6.
82 Metcalfe, 'Muslims of Sicily', p. 296. See also J. Johns, *Arabic Administration in Norman Sicily: The Royal Diwan* (Cambridge, 2002), pp. 292–7; Matthew, *Sicily*, pp. 90–1.

(outside of Jerusalem) and the *qadis*.[83] In fact, the sole example of this office in the Latin East is Mansur ibn Nabil, the *qadi* of Jabala who reportedly helped to secure its surrender, along with much of the surrounding area, to Saladin in 1188. However, the evidence is limited to, at times, conflicting Arabic narratives, while the extent of ibn Nabil's political influence, particularly regarding the nature of his ties to the Latins, is questionable.

It is at least clear that this *qadi* administered to the Muslim population of Jabala and the surrounding area, with Baha al-Din ibn Shaddad noting that he was appointed to settle local disputes.[84] Later writers extended upon this, with Ibn al-Athir suggesting that ibn Nabil was 'influential and trusted in his dealings with Bohemond [III]', and that 'he enjoyed much respect and high status, wielding authority over all the Muslims in Jabala and its districts in whatever concerned Bohemond'.[85] Abu Shama even went so far as to record that Bohemond had handed over control of Jabala itself to the *qadi*.[86] The suggestion of ibn Nabil's close relationship with the Latins appears to be borne out by Imad al-Din al-Isfahani, who detailed his role in securing favourable terms for the Frankish garrisons of Jabala and nearby Bikisrail at their request.[87] Despite this, al-Isfahani also admits that the defenders of Latakia only accepted ibn Nabil's intervention once all hope of survival was lost; a sentiment echoed by Baha al-Din, and later Kemal al-Din and Ibn al-Athir, who believed that the Latins of Jabala had similarly rejected the *qadi's* offer of mediation.[88] Abu Shama also hinted at potential tensions by suggesting that Jabala's Muslim populace had forcibly prevented Latin resistance to Saladin.[89] Thus, while ibn Nabil appears to have had influence amongst the Muslims of Jabala and the surrounding area, it cannot be assumed that his relationship with the Franks was cordial. This would explain why Ibn al-Athir, alongside noting ibn Nabil's standing, also detailed that Bohemond III had earlier taken hostages from him, an act almost certainly done to ensure good behaviour.[90]

One of the key questions to emerge from this regards the extent to which Jabala's *qadi* reflects wider practice. Ibn Nabil's status within the Muslim community would undoubtedly have pre-dated 1188, but as no evidence survives for his existence – or that of his position – outside of this isolated example, it cannot be accepted that Jabala had always possessed a Latin-sponsored *qadi*. This has been

---

[83]   MacEvitt (*Rough Tolerance*, pp. 151–2) has recently argued that John of Ibelin created a fictional account of this court which, though in Latin lands, acted entirely independently of Latin jurisdiction. See also Kedar, 'Subjected Muslims', pp. 135–74; J. Riley-Smith, 'Government and the Indigenous in the Latin Kingdom of Jerusalem', *Medieval Frontiers: Concepts and Practices*, ed. D. Abulafia and N. Berend (Aldershot, 2002), p. 128. Cf. H. E. Mayer, 'Latins, Muslims and Greeks in the Latin Kingdom of Jerusalem', *History* 63 (1978), 185.

[84]   BD, p. 83.

[85]   IA, III, 345–6

[86]   AS, *RHC Or.* IV, 351–63.

[87]   ID, pp. 122–3, 127–31.

[88]   *Ibid.*, pp. 128–31; BD, pp. 83–4; KD, *ROL* 4, 186–7; IA, II, 345–6.

[89]   AS, *RHC Or.* IV, 351–63.

[90]   IA, II, pp. 345–6.

recognised by Asbridge and Mayer, who believed it to be a later concession, while Cahen remained on the fence and Kedar suggested longer-term practice.[91] Before accepting either side, it is worth assessing what may have driven such a concession. A potential stimulus was the sale of the Masoir lordship to the Hospitallers in 1187. While this may have made the castle of Margat more secure, as noted earlier it also withdrew a sizeable portion of the principality from the prince's sphere of influence. Importantly, included within Bohemond III's confirmation of this sale is the stipulation that:

> if, God forbid, we should make a treaty with the Saracens without consulting them [meaning the Hospitallers], they can hold to the treaty if they should wish, or they can make war with them. If, however, they should make a treaty with the enemies of the cross of Christ who are in the fief of Bokebais and also at Jabala in the past, they shall notify us, and we shall hold to it, and we shall cause our men to hold to it as well.[92]

This implies that the Hospitallers could adopt an independent approach to relations with indigenous populations, potentially undermining Bohemond's ability to keep non-Latin communities, such as the Muslims of Jabala and the nearby area, in check. This had precedence, for a document issued by Bohemond to that same Order in 1168 noted that neither he nor any of his men would make a truce with Muslims without the Hospitallers' advice.[93] Before the sale of Margat, such a stipulation perhaps had minimal consequences; but, with the diminishing of Antiochene authority created by the Masoir withdrawal, Bohemond perhaps needed to adapt by recognising a *qadi* at Jabala.

What may have helped to contribute to this was the Spanish Order of Santiago's decision not to take up the offer of conquest and lordship around Bikisrail and Bokebais, made to them in 1180.[94] This came at a time when the southern reaches of the principality were subject to tension due to the growing antagonism of the Isma'ilis, and the gradual decline of Masoir authority would only have accentuated fears.[95] Thus, while ibn Nabil must have been a figure of some stature to be considered worthy of an alliance by Bohemond III, there are some important reasons why the use of the title of *qadi* could have been an ad hoc situation predicated on a need to ensure the goodwill of the Muslim community. That Bohemond appears to have taken hostages suggests he did not entirely trust ibn Nabil; it also adds further to the belief in the novel nature of his position, for such a stipulation would have been

---

91   Asbridge, 'Crusader Community', p. 324; Mayer, 'Muslims and Greeks', p. 185; Cahen, *Syrie*, p. 462; Kedar, 'Subjected Muslims', pp. 141–2.
92   *CGOH*, I, 783: Si vero, quod absit, eis inconsultis treviam faciemus cum Saracenis, treviam tenebunt si voluerint, vel guerram facient cum eis. Si vero ipsi facient treviam cum inimicis crucis Christi, qui sunt in fedo Bokebeis et a Gabulo in antea, treviam nobis notificabunt, et nos eam tenebimus, et homines nostros tenere faciemus.
93   *Ibid.*, 391: dono et concedo eidem Hospitali quod nec ego, nec homo de terra mea faciemus treugas cum Sarrcenis, sine consilio fratrum eiusdem Hospitalis.
94   Mayer, *Varia*, pp. 114–17.
95   Daftary, *Isma'ilis*, pp. 369–70. See also pp. 52–3 of this book.

unlikely had the use of a *qadi* been a widely performed practice. The apparent Latin reluctance to use him as an intermediary with Saladin, moreover, argues against a long-standing and trusting relationship. It also challenges MacEvitt's argument for 'rough tolerance', whereby Frankish rulers could, in the interests of stability, direct small bursts of violence against elements of indigenous groups while ensuring that the community as a whole felt unthreatened.[96] Perhaps Bohemond realised that he could not simply eliminate such a figure without antagonising the locals, and so instead tied ibn Nabil to him through the bestowal of a title and the taking of hostages. Though an isolated example, it could indicate a certain degree of fear for the implications which internal groups posed to security.

A wider understanding of the interaction between Latin governance and indigenous communities can perhaps be found in the position of *ru'asa* or, in the singular, *rayyis*. Acting as the headmen of a locality, either urban or rural, the *ru'asa* were intermediaries between local communities and their overlords, and are well known in Norman Sicily, Iberia and the Latin East.[97] Interestingly, following on from Cahen's earlier work for Antioch, Lewis has recently argued that the urban *ru'asa* of the county of Tripoli (albeit only those who were Muslim) could have adopted the *qadi's* judicial role.[98] MacEvitt has gone further, noting that the *ru'asa*, whether urban or rural, were a homogenous group of freemen commensurate to the *qadi*.[99] In the context of Latin–Muslim relations, it is therefore significant that all four examples of Antiochene *ru'asa* are almost certainly Eastern Christians.

The earliest is Tadrus ibn al-Saffi: a *rayyis* resident in Antioch, probably in the opening decades of Latin rule, whose status and influence was noted by Usamah ibn Munqidh.[100] The historiographical opinion that his name is an Arabic transliteration of Theodoros Sophianos has now been discredited by Paul Cobb, but the reality that Tadrus equates to Theodoros has not.[101] He was thus clearly an Eastern Christian, albeit one who could converse in Arabic. This likely indicates that he was a Melkite, or perhaps a Jacobite. Riley-Smith argued that this may be the same person as the Theodore, notary of the duke, who appeared in Raymond of Poitiers' 1140 charters, although this is difficult to substantiate.[102] Moreover, that a *rayyis* may also have been the notary of the duke of Antioch – an urban position of some standing but only within the city itself – implies Tadrus was not overly powerful. The next example is one George the *rayyis*, who is mentioned in a charter issued by Bohemond III at Antioch in 1166.[103] This document shows George to have been

---

96   MacEvitt, *Rough Tolerance*, p. 1.
97   Metcalfe, 'Muslims of Sicily', p. 309; Reilly, *Medieval Spains*, p. 110; Barton, 'Lords', pp. 4, 22–3; Riley-Smith, 'Lesser Officials', p. 1; MacEvitt, *Rough Tolerance*, pp. 137, 149–53.
98   Cahen, *Syrie*, pp. 455–6, 462; Lewis, 'Diglossia', p. 130.
99   MacEvitt, *Rough Tolerance*, pp. 149–52.
100 Usamah ibn Munqidh, pp. 153–4.
101 P. Hitti, *An Arab-Syrian Gentleman and Warrior in the period of the Crusades* (New York, 1929), p. 169; Usamah ibn Munqidh, p. 153, n. 252.
102 Riley-Smith, 'Lesser Officials', p. 5; Usamah ibn Munqidh, pp. 153–4, n. 252; *CCSSJ*, 76–7: Theodoro notarii ducis.
103 *CGOH*, I, 367.

a landholder within Antioch, as it protected the rights of his heirs – alongside those of two other Eastern Christians: Michael Magni and the aforementioned Theodore notary of the duke – to revenues extracted from lands now donated to the Hospitallers. The mention of Theodore, who Riley-Smith posits was George's brother, makes it tempting to link this *rayyis* to the *Georgius magister secreta* who likewise appeared in the 1140 documents.[104] Caution must be shown, but if these connections are correct, it suggests that the urban *ru'asa* may indeed have taken on multiple administrative roles, which increases the likelihood of the aforementioned suggestion that they would also have held a judicial function. The final two examples are not from the city of Antioch; rather, they appear in a charter issued by Renaud II Masoir, lord of Margat, in 1174. They are George, *rayyis* of Margat, who is described as *genero* (son-in-law) of Abd al-Messie, who was likewise a *rayyis*.[105] While this appears to indicate two *ru'asa* at Margat, it should be noted that this was Abd al-Messie's only appearance. Moreover, unlike George – who may be synonymous with the *magister Georgius* who witnessed a charter of Renaud II in 1181 (again indicating the propensity for multiple roles) – Abd al-Messie was not among the witnesses in 1174, and so was perhaps dead.[106] What is clear, however, is that Abd al-Massie was both a Christian and a figure of some wealth, for he had been able to make a private donation to the Hospitallers from his own possessions.[107]

While these examples demonstrate very little in terms of the exact nature of the roles played by the *ru'asa*, or whether they were a homogenous group regardless of locality, there are some interesting trends. First, they are all Eastern Christians, meaning they either represented both Muslim and Christian communities (which would have made Arabic-speaking Christians all the more valuable), or that a further layer of administration existed which has left no traces in the extant sources. Second, there are suggestions that these figures performed multiple roles within Frankish governance, which argues against the extensive involvement of non-Latins and in favour of a very selective policy. Finally, in support of this last point, it would appear that these roles were the preserve of certain Christian families, who were perhaps granted lands and patronage by the Franks, or even used existing possessions to purchase favour and influence. Therefore, while Frankish governance interacted with, and included, indigenous peoples, there are reasons to believe there were limitations. This suggests that a certain level of distrust may have influenced Latin policy, which, in turn, could indicate some fears about the threat to security caused by internal communities.

---

[104] Riley-Smith, 'Lesser Officials', p. 5; *CCSSJ*, 76–7.
[105] *CGOH*, I, 457.
[106] *CGOH*, I, 613.
[107] Murray, 'Indigenous Communities', p. 303; MacEvitt, *Rough Tolerance*, p. 150; Lewis, 'Diglossia', p. 129.

Social and Religious Freedoms

To gain a better understanding of the nature of intercultural relations in the principality, though, it is also important to look deeper, and to assess the extent to which the social and religious freedoms of indigenous groups were tolerated. Given this region's numerous faiths and denominations, it might be assumed that all had at least some right to pray. It is certainly true that Jacobites and Armenians maintained their own independent Church hierarchies, with suggestions that both the Jacobite patriarch and Armenian *catholicos* visited Antioch and the cathedral of St Peter during the twelfth century.[108] There is also evidence for Eastern-rite churches at Antioch, Latakia and Jabala, with Major arguing that it is highly likely they would have been present in other areas which housed Christian communities; as well as a number of Orthodox monasteries operating throughout the principality, particularly on the Black Mountain.[109] Even the Greeks and Melkites, subsumed as they were into the Latin hierarchy, were allowed to maintain their own churches and priests.[110] There are also hints at a certain level of inter-Christian devotional contact, as Michael the Syrian related an often overlooked story regarding the foundation of a church at Antioch dedicated to a Syriac Saint, Mar Bar Sauma, in the 1150s. According to Michael, a young Latin boy at Antioch fell into a coma after falling from a tree. Having prayed to God to no avail, the boy's parents, Henry and Elizabeth, turned their devotions to Mar Bar Sauma after meeting with a Jacobite monk. This monk, accompanied by Basil, the Jacobite bishop of Edessa, then came to their home to perform a religious service, at which point Mar Bar Sauma appeared to the boy in a vision, telling him to stand and walk; which he did. So delighted were they at their son's recovery, the parents built a church in Antioch and dedicated it to Mar Bar Sauma. The miraculous elements here should of course not be taken at face value; yet, it is significant that present at the church's consecration in 1157 were not only the Jacobites, but also the Armenians and the Latins, including Princess Constance, Thoros of Armenia, various nobles, as well as the clergy, deacons and monks.[111] Albeit very rare for sources relating to the principality, this story demonstrates the capacity for the sort of religious cross-fertilisation seen elsewhere in *Outremer* at sites like the Holy Sepulchre and the Marian shrine at Saydnaya.[112] However, the noted absences of the prince and patriarch of Antioch, as well as the Greeks (who seemingly abstained out of hatred for the Jacobites),

---

[108] Hamilton, *Latin Church*, pp. 159–87; MacEvitt, *Rough Tolerance*, pp. 106–35; Guiragos of Kantzag, *RHC Arm.* I, 417–18; MS, III, 207–10, 332–5, 360, 377–82.

[109] MS, III, 231, 337–40; Pringle, 'Wilbrand', pp. 122–3; Hamilton, *Latin Church*, p. 168; Major, *Rural Settlements*, pp. 97–103; Jotischky, *Perfection of Solitude*, pp. 61, 81 n.39, 95; Stone, 'Armenian Colophon', pp. 125–9; Hamilton, 'Ecumenist', pp. 269–90.

[110] Hamilton, *Latin Church*, pp. 172–9.

[111] MS, III, 300–4; Weltecke, 'Syriac Orthodox', pp. 113–17.

[112] MacEvitt, *Rough Tolerance*, pp. 115–20, 132–4; B. Kedar, 'Convergences of Oriental Christian, Muslim, and Frankish Worshippers: The Case of Saydnaya', *De Sion exibit lex et verbum domini de Hierusalem: Essays on Medieval Law, Liturgy and Literature in Honour of Amnon Linder*, ed. Y. Hen (Turnhout, 2001), pp. 59–69.

reveals that limits existed. To this can also be added the near-total lack of evidence for mosques or synagogues in areas of the principality while under Latin rule. Despite Wilbrand of Oldenburg's comment that Muslims and Jews observed their own laws within Antioch, the possibility remains that only private demonstrations of faith were allowed.[113]

Another worthwhile aspect to consider is intermarriage. Fulcher of Chartres famously noted that certain Franks 'took as a wife not only compatriots, but also Syrians or Armenians and sometimes Saracens having gained the grace of baptism'.[114] However, while unions between Franks and Eastern Christians, particularly Armenians, are well documented for the other crusader states, there is a distinct absence of evidence for their intermarriage with Antiochene Franks, even amongst the higher echelons of society (where it can be discerned elsewhere). In fact, the sole example is that of Raymond II of Antioch, the son of Bohemond III who married Alice of Armenia in 1195 as part of the settlement forced upon the Antiochene ruler by Leon of Armenia after capturing and imprisoning him in 1193.[115] This could again be a discrepancy born from the difficulty of the sources, although it is possible that the principality's ties to Byzantium – with whom the Armenians had a fractious relationship – could have influenced this. Of interest, though, is that in a charter issued by Raymond of Poitiers in 1149, mention is made of a house being donated to the Hospitallers which 'Barutellus and his wife, *Sarracena*, originally created and constructed in Antioch'.[116] Whether *Sarracena* should be translated as 'a Sarracen', or if *Sarracena* was her name, is unclear; in either case this is an oddity, for the marriage of a Frank to a Muslim was strictly prohibited by the council of Nablus in 1120, and should she have been a Christian convert, then usually a Latin name was adopted, or the epithet *baptizatus*.[117] There is limited evidence for the name *Sarracena* in the region around the French Abbey of Clairvaux in the mid-twelfth century, so she may have been a Frank, but this remains an exceptionally rare name and evokes obvious connotations.[118] It is possible that, like the Western male forename *Paganus*, it denoted one who only received baptism in adulthood.[119] Perhaps the most plausible explanation is that she was a converted Muslim or an Eastern Christian, although a separate piece of evidence could offer a further perspective.

[113] Pringle, 'Wilbrand', pp. 122–3.

[114] Fulcher of Chartres, p. 748: duxit uxorem non tantum compatriotam, sed et Syrum aut Armenam et interdum Saracenam, baptismi autem gratiam adeptam. See also MacEvitt, *Rough Tolerance*, pp. 76–8; N. Hodgson, 'Conflict and Cohabitation: Marriage and Diplomacy between Latins and Cilician Armenians, c.1097–1253', *The Crusades and the Near East: Cultural Histories*, ed. C. Kostick (Abingdon, 2011), pp. 83–106.

[115] Cahen, *Syrie*, pp. 583–90.

[116] *CGOH*, I, 183: Barutellus et uxor sua Sarracena primitus fecerunt in Antiochia et composuerunt.

[117] B. Z. Kedar, 'On the Origins of the Earliest Laws of Frankish Jerusalem: The Canons of the Council of Nablus, 1120', *Speculum* 74:2 (1999), 310–35; and *Crusade and Mission: European Approaches towards the Muslims* (Princeton, 1984), pp. 79–83; MacEvitt, *Rough Tolerance*, pp. 153–5.

[118] *Recueil des chartes de l'abbaye de Clairvaux au XIIe Siècle*, ed. J. Waquet, J.-M. Roger and L. Veyssière (Paris, 2004), 97, 108, 120–1, 178, 330, 332.

[119] P.-H. Billy, 'A Sociology of First Names in the Late Middle Ages', *Name and Naming: Synchronic and Diachronic Perspectives*, ed. O. Felecan (Cambridge, 2012), pp. 56–7.

Usamah ibn Munqidh detailed the story of Ralph, a captured Frank who was taken to Shaizar, was converted to Islam and took a Muslim wife (who bore him two sons). Seven years later, Ralph fled back to Frankish Apamea with his sons (whom he had converted to Christianity) and his wife (whose denominational fate went unmentioned).[120] Albeit unlikely, the possibility therefore remains that there were instances of Latin–Muslim marriage in the principality.[121] The divergences seen here from the evidence found elsewhere in *Outremer* clearly demonstrate the need to be more alive to different situations throughout the Frankish East, and to not uncritically apply general models of behaviour.

Turning to conversion, beyond the examples just examined, there is little evidence that it was a widespread practice. Some First Crusade sources noted that Muslims were converted at Antioch when the city was captured in 1098, although the extent and nature of this is unclear.[122] Ibn al-Athir also mentioned that the *qadi* of Buza'a became Christian, along with 400 others, when John Komnenos helped the Antiochenes to capture the city in 1138, but this is not supported by any other author.[123] The only firm example in fact comes from a charter issued in 1137 by Riso, formerly chaplain of Princes Bohemond I and Bohemond II. In this, Riso retained a room in a house bequeathed to the Holy Sepulchre 'for a certain of my slaves, who I called forth from infidelity to the grace of baptism, for as long as he shall live and serves me faithfully'.[124] The conversion of Muslim slaves was not unknown elsewhere, but that he remained in Riso's service does not appear to follow contemporary practice in the West or the wider Latin East, for conversion usually elevated the person to the status of a freeman and thus ineligible for slavery. It was for this reason that, according to Jacques de Vitry, some slave masters actively prevented their Muslim charges from accepting Christianity, because it meant they could no longer be exploited.[125] It is unclear whether this reflected a particularly close bond between Riso and his slave or if Antiochene customs were different. What Riso's charter does demonstrate, however, is that there were limitations to social freedoms. Despite this, although slavery clearly existed at Antioch around the time of the First Crusade and remained prominent in the kingdom of Jerusalem,

---

[120] Usamah ibn Munqidh, p. 143. Kedar (*Crusade and Mission*, pp. 79–83) also mentions this discrepancy and that such a case was brought by the bishop of Acre to Pope Celestine III in the 1190s, who ruled that should a man convert to Islam and have children with a Muslim, he would be able to convert back to Christianity along with his family. This would seem to suggest that the example identified by Usamah was not a peculiarity, although this does not account for Usamah's failure to mention the wife's reaction to Ralph's actions. Cf. Mallett (*Popular Muslim Reactions*, p. 112), who argues that the wife and children were all converted.

[121] Given the nature of Usamah's text, it is impossible to know when Ralph's actions occurred, and the possibility remains that it was before the council of Nablus.

[122] *Gesta Francorum*, p. 71; Fulcher of Chartres, p. 263. See also J. Birk, 'The Betrayal of Antioch: Narratives of Conversion and Conquest during the First Crusade', *Journal of Medieval and Early Modern Studies* 41:3 (2011), pp. 463–85.

[123] IA, I, 340.

[124] *CCSSJ*, 75: cuidam servo meo quem de infidelitate ad baptismi gratiam evocavi … quamdiu vixerit mihique fideliter servierit.

[125] Kedar, *Crusade and Mission*, pp. 52–6, 74–8; MacEvitt, *Rough Tolerance*, pp. 153–5.

there are few references to suggest it was a prominent practice in the principality.[126] Indeed, while Usamah ibn Munqidh mentioned a former crusade veteran, then resident of Antioch, who had an Egyptian cook, and both Walter the Chancellor and Bar Ebroyo noted that slaves and prisoners flowed into Antioch after victory at Tall Danith in 1115, there was seemingly little existing infrastructure in place to aid John Komnenos and the Franks in transporting captured Muslim prisoners back to Antioch for sale during the joint campaign of 1138 (meaning they were all able to escape).[127] Furthermore, although it is possible that other Latin victories garnered prisoners and would have facilitated the creation of slaves, this is not overtly described in the sources; with the economic benefits of ransom perhaps more favourable.[128] The suggestion can be offered, therefore, that slavery (at least on a grand scale) had fallen into abeyance – perhaps due also, at least in part, to the changing extent of Frankish military success. It is certainly telling that slavery was not considered important enough to mention in the *Assises d'Antioche*, whereas it does appear in the law codes of Jerusalem.[129]

That there were restrictions to liberty is nevertheless indicated by charters issued by Bohemond III in the 1170s and 1180s. In 1175, an unnamed Jew of Latakia and a Jabalan Syrian called Bon Mossor were sold to the Hospitallers, and a similar sale of 1183 included Greeks and Armenians of various professions, seven Jews and even a Latin called Hugh Straigot.[130] Prawer and MacEvitt have noted the difficulties in interpreting these documents, and that while the Hospitallers evidently now owned these individuals, the inclusion of a Latin, as well as the absence of the term *servus*, rules out slavery.[131] Prawer has offered the plausible suggestion that they were former serfs who moved to the city and brought their previous social status with them, although MacEvitt argues that the presence of a Latin again somewhat undermines this.[132] Given the aforementioned example of Riso's slave, it would perhaps be wrong to entirely rule out either slavery or serfdom, for Hugh Straigot was not designated as a Frank, rather a Latin, and may well have been a Christian convert. The exact implications of these donations nonetheless remain a mystery, albeit they show that there were limits to social freedoms, even if slavery was not demonstrably widespread. Moreover, that they are seemingly unique to the principality of Antioch, at least in terms of their urban setting, again shows the need to remain open to divergences in social contracts throughout the Latin East, as well as the pitfalls of relying on overarching theories.

[126] Y. Friedman, *Encounter between Enemies: Captivity and Ransom in the Latin Kingdom of Jerusalem* (Leiden, 2002), pp. 13–54; MacEvitt, *Rough Tolerance*, p. 145, n. 26.
[127] Usamah ibn Munqidh, pp. 153–4; WC, pp. 91–4; GBE, II, 247–8; al-Azimi, pp. 142–3.
[128] KD, *RHC Or.* III, 680, 683; AS, *RHC Or.* IV, 48–9; GBE, II, 272–3; *1234*, II, 119. More generally, see Friedman, *Encounter between Enemies*.
[129] John of Ibelin, *Le Livre des Assises*, pp. 296–7, 796–9.
[130] *CGOH*, I, 472, 648.
[131] MacEvitt, *Rough Tolerance*, pp. 144–9; Prawer, *Crusader Institutions*, pp. 212–14.
[132] MacEvitt, *Rough Tolerance*, pp. 144–9; Prawer, *Crusader Institutions*, p. 213.

A further form of social freedom is that of landholding. This was somewhat prominent during the early decades of Latin rule, as Antioch's princes made deals which allowed local Muslim potentates to retain lands in the regions around Apamea, Jabala, Latakia, Balatanos, Margat and Sarmin.[133] Perhaps the best early example is that of Hamdan bin 'Abd al-Rahim al-Atharibi, a Muslim scholar who travelled throughout the principality in the 1120s and was even given a village (which he rebuilt) by Alan of al-Atharib after helping to cure him of disease in 1127.[134] There are fewer examples after this point, though. One such is the independently wealthy Abd al-Massie, as well as the lands and possessions in the vicinity of Antioch owned by Michael Magni, George the *rayyis* and Theodore notary of the duke, and, as listed in that same charter of 1166, a vineyard owned by a certain *Boordiz*, who may well be Muslim, or at least an Arabised Christian.[135] Likewise, a charter of 1180 suggests that certain of the lands of the Isma'ilis near to Bikisrail might have been held fief from the prince of Antioch, for the sale of possessions in this area to the Order of Santiago was made 'excepting those estates which we have already conceded to the Assassins'.[136] It might even be contended that the indigenous soldiers known as turcopoles would have received some form of fief in return for their service, although their extent within the principality is unknown.[137] A potential addition to this are two figures who witnessed Bohemond III's confirmation charter of the sale of Margat in 1187. In this, there appears after the heading 'knights of Margat' a *dominus Georgius* and a *dominus Theodorus*.[138] The appearance of *dominus* has caused Murray to argue that these, almost certainly Eastern Christian, men possessed lordships.[139] Yet, while this title does often signify such status, for Bertrand Masoir was *dominus Margati*, a number of Margat's knights, even the castle's castellan, were also called *dominus* in these documents.[140] Therefore, although *dominus* might denote elevated status and knighthood – or perhaps an odd quirk of the Masoir seigneurie – it cannot be accepted that it demonstrates Eastern Christian lordship. It was nevertheless clearly possible for non-Latins to own lands, both in an urban and a rural setting, even if it is likely that ties to Frankish lords would have been clearly defined, much like those who were sold to the Hospitallers in the 1170s and 1180s.

Another signifier of cultural freedom, and one frequently used to denote a level of tolerance, is that of trade. Throughout the Mediterranean, trade and commerce

[133] Major, *Rural Settlements*, p. 155; Ibn al-Furat, II, p. 134.
[134] D. Talmon-Heller, 'Arabic Sources on Muslim Villagers under Frankish Rule', *From Clermont to Jerusalem: The Crusades and Crusader Societies 1095–1500*, ed. A. V. Murray (Turnhout, 1998), pp. 113–14.
[135] *CGOH*, I, 367.
[136] Mayer, *Varia*, pp. 115–17 (here 117): excepto illis casalibus, quos concessimus habendos Vetulo Assideorum.
[137] Harari, 'Frankish Turcopoles', pp. 75–116. See also p. 112 of this book.
[138] *CGOH*, I, 783.
[139] Murray, 'Indigenous Communities', p. 304.
[140] *CGOH*, I, 783. See also pp. 134–5 of this book.

brought various faiths into contact.[141] This was no different in the Latin East, with the Frankish rulers of Jerusalem going to great lengths to preserve and facilitate economic agreements with their Muslim neighbours, even during times of war: no doubt due to the importance it had for long-term stability.[142] It is undeniable that trade went on in the principality, for the Italian states of Venice, Genoa and Pisa were all given privileges within the Syrian coastal ports of Latakia, Jabala and St Simeon, while Choniates' description of 'Syrian foodsellers' at Antioch in 1158 suggests indigenous communities also took part.[143] Moreover, archaeological finds such as those made at the port of Al-Mina and near to Harim, show that material production and exchange occurred even outside of the major naval centres.[144] Cahen thus noted that, while mercantile activity was more prominent further south along the Levantine coast, Antiochene trade was not 'insignificant'.[145] There are clues, though, that the principality's Frankish rulers ascribed less overriding value to trade than the other Latin states. For example, during preparations for the joint campaign with John II Komnenos over the winter of 1137 and 1138, Muslim merchants within Antioch were arrested in order to prevent them spreading news of the forthcoming attack.[146] Likewise, Usamah ibn Munqidh described the suspicion and anger with which a friend of his was treated during a visit to one of Antioch's markets.[147] In 1171/1172, and again in 1178, Bohemond III also took advantage of stranded Muslim ships near to Latakia to extract booty, even though the earlier of these contravened a treaty agreed with Nur al-Din.[148] Crucially, violence towards traders was not limited to the Franks, for an Antiochene caravan was attacked and destroyed by Muslim forces in 1143/1144.[149] This would seem to suggest that the sort of mercantile safe-passage agreements made between Jerusalem and its Muslim neighbours were not so prevalent in the principality, if they even existed. In this regard, it is significant that no Latin-made copies of Arabic dinars – produced by the other crusader states, almost certainly to better facilitate the trust of Muslim traders in their dealings with the Franks – have survived for Antioch.[150] Therefore, while there are some conceptual problems for Redford's belief that the polity itself

---

[141] For important introductions to trade in the Mediterranean, including the Latin East, see J. Pryor, *Commerce, Shipping and Naval Warfare in the Medieval Mediterranean* (London, 1987); D. Jacoby, *Commercial Exchange Across the Mediterranean* (Aldershot, 2005).

[142] Asbridge, *Crusades*, pp. 182–3; H. E. Mayer, 'Une lettre de sauf conduit d'un roi croisé de Jérusalem à un marchand musulman (1156/1163)', *La présence Latine en Orient au Moyen Âge*, ed. G. Brunel *et al.* (Paris, 2000), pp. 27–35.

[143] Choniates, *Historia*, p. 108 (NC, p. 68): Σύρον ὀψοφάγον.

[144] Vorderstrasse, *Al-Mina*, 102–132; S. Gelichi, 'Pottery from Ḥārim Castle (Northern Syria): Crusader and Muslim Period', *Çanak: Late Antique and Medieval Pottery and Tiles in Mediterranean and Archaeological Contexts*, ed. B. Böhlendorf-Arslan, A. O. Uysal and J. Witte-Orr (Istanbul, 2007), pp. 457–68.

[145] Cahen, *Syrie*, pp. 472–500. For another useful survey of Antiochene trade see Redford, 'Trade and Economy in Antioch', pp. 297–309.

[146] KD, *RHC Or.* III, p. 675; IQ, p. 246.

[147] Usamah ibn Munqidh, pp. 153–4.

[148] IA, II, p. 200; *1234*, II, 141.

[149] KD, *RHC Or.* III, p. 685; IQ, p. 265.

[150] Metcalf, 'Six Unresolved Problems', pp. 313–18.

was fundamentally flawed from its very inception due to the favouring of Syrian ports over those on the Cilician coast, clues do remain that trade did not play as big a part in promoting intercultural contact as it did further south along the Levant.[151]

The extent of social and religious freedoms in the principality thus provides an incomplete and often obfuscated picture. There is little to suggest outright persecution, and even some examples of active and positive interplay, yet it would be naive to assume that the fragmentary evidence available points towards an extensive level of tolerance and interaction, as the Franks clearly imposed limits on non-Latin rights. In the examples of intermarriage, slavery and trade, there are even telling suggestions of divergences with the practices of the other crusader states, which further indicates the fluidity that could emerge in reaction to the complexities of medieval frontiers.

Conclusion

This chapter has sought to demonstrate the great difficulties in providing a distinct picture of intercultural relations in the principality of Antioch. It is possible to chart the existence of various religious communities, although the imprecise nature of certain terminology ensures that membership of specific denominations cannot always be identified – a difficulty the Franks may also have faced. Likewise, it is evident that Eastern Christians and Muslims were involved in administration, although the extent of this, and the methods by which positions were received, remains open to conjecture. Some may have been provided with long-term status, perhaps at a price, while others, for example Mansur ibn Nabil, may have risen to prominence due to changing political circumstances. This could indicate that fears over security were influential, and even if instances of internal threats are hard to chart with any frequency, it would certainly be dangerous to presume that indigenous participation in governance was widespread. Moreover, while there is evidence of certain religious liberties, at least for Eastern Christians, as well as opportunities for landholding and military contributions, there are also suggestions of slavery, conversion and limitations to social freedoms. Even trade and intermarriage, so often facilitators and signifiers of cross-cultural contact in the Latin East and elsewhere, lack extensive evidential coverage. This all serves to demonstrate the pitfalls of superimposing onto the principality general models for intercultural contacts proposed for the Latin East as a whole. A polity of diverse and dispersed communities, and subject to severe political and geographical fluctuations, it would have been highly difficult, perhaps even impossible, for Antioch's ruling elites to ever impose uniform regulations on its indigenous populations. It may even have been politically inexpedient. This would certainly help to explain the silence of the *Assises d'Antioche* on these groups. Although the negative colonial

---

[151] Redford, 'Trade and Economy in Antioch', pp. 297–309.

model proposed by Cahen and Prawer proves too fixed to match the reality of so fluid a region, the socio-political uncertainty of the principality may indeed have fostered a level of distrust towards non-Latins: which belies suggestions of cultural harmony. In reality, relations between the Franks and non-Franks, such as they can be proven, were messy, complicated and subject not to finite rules, but to variations based on time and place. Only by accepting this can historians truly come close to understanding what it meant to live in the principality of Antioch during the twelfth century.

6

Relations with Byzantium

When the leaders of the First Crusade reneged on an agreement to return Antioch and other former imperial possessions to Emperor Alexios I Komnenos in 1098, they set the soon-to-be-formed principality of Antioch on a collision course with Byzantium – a power which had held much of this region until the second half of the eleventh century.[1] The relationship which developed from this is one of the most important for an understanding of the complicated diplomatic challenges faced by Antioch's ruling elites. Before 1130, it was characterised by frequent bouts of armed conflict which even threatened to fragment the crusader states.[2] Imperial hopes of recovering Antioch were continually thwarted, however, despite Alexios forcing Bohemond I, in 1108, to agree to the Treaty of Devol – which reportedly recognised Greek authority and relegated the prince to satellite status. Indeed, Tancred, now *de facto* prince, refused to recognise the terms whenever Alexios pushed for his rights, including after Bohemond's death in 1111.[3] A brief period of silence followed the emperor's demise in 1118, but imperial interest was renewed with Bohemond II's death. Over the next five decades, Byzantine rulers thrice visited Antioch, frequently offered direct or indirect military support and even forged a number of marriage alliances with the Latins. More significantly, the notion of imperial overlordship – so fervently opposed by the early princes – was now openly discussed, and, during a visit to Antioch by Manuel Komnenos in 1158, finally implemented.

The connection between Antioch and Byzantium has attracted considerable scholarly interest. For the most part, this has focused on the imperial perspective – most prominently the notion that the emperors preferred recognition over possession – or propagated a narrative of conflict emphasising instances of tension.[4] On

---

[1] Asbridge, *Creation*, pp. 92–4; J. Pryor and M. Jeffreys, 'Alexios, Bohemond, and Byzantium's Euphrates Frontier: A Tale of Two Cretans', *Crusades* 11 (2012), 31–86.
[2] Asbridge, *Creation*, pp. 52–3, 56, 62–6; I. Augé, 'Les Comnènes et le comté de Tripoli: une collaboration efficace?', *Le comté de Tripoli: état multiculturel et multiconfessionnel (1102–1289)*, ed. G. Dédéyan and K. Rizak (Paris, 2010), pp. 141–55.
[3] Asbridge, *Creation*, pp. 92–103; Pryor and Jeffreys, 'Alexios', pp. 57–64. Some debate remains over the authenticity of its stipulations (see below).
[4] J. Harris, *Byzantium and the Crusades*, 2nd edn (London, 2014), pp. 1–5; Magdalino, *Manuel*, pp. 27–108.

those occasions when the Antiochene perspective is assessed, two distinct themes emerge: first, that the actions of Frankish rulers and nobles were permanently influenced by an inherent dislike of the Greeks; and, second, that the political changes which occurred in northern Syria during this period left the principality a mere passenger to the desires of both Byzantium and the kingdom of Jerusalem.[5] This chapter re-assesses and challenges these assumptions. It examines closely the actions of the Frankish princes and nobles who played such a key part in this relationship during the four distinct time periods considered significant by historians: John II Komnenos' interventions from 1130 to 1143 (which have been classified as 'the height of confrontation'), the years following the fall of Edessa in 1144 and leading up to Manuel Komnenos' visit in 1158 (a time in which Antioch is viewed as a passive witness to northern Syria's politics), the subsequent phase of imperial overlordship between 1159 and 1182 (when a *condominium* is said to have been implemented over Antioch by Jerusalem and Byzantium) and finally the breakdown in contact after the anti-Latin Andronikos Komnenos became emperor in 1182. Through this, it is argued, the identifiable actions and implicit motives, of the Antiochenes suggest that, although relations were far from always cordial, the Latins were not only more favourable towards a *détente* with Byzantium than has hitherto been acknowledged, but also that a discernible trend of astute diplomatic endeavour can be identified. Importantly, this undermines notions of Antioch's non-participation and argues rather that the Franks often played a key role in determining their fate.

John Komnenos and Antioch, 1130–1143

The thirteen-year period of John II Komnenos' interest in Antioch heralded a number of contacts, including marriage negotiations, two imperial visits to northern Syria and a treaty recognising Greek claims to Antioch. Despite this, David Parnell, advancing from a confrontationist narrative earlier proposed by Lilie, has commented that 'at no other time was the possibility of [Antiochene] cooperation with Byzantium more unlikely'.[6] The presence of an emperor in *Outremer* was certainly unheralded, and relations proved fractious, but to consider this the 'height of confrontation' suggests it was more violent than the preceding period, a time in which imperial armies seized Antiochene possessions and engaged in open warfare with the Franks. This is not the case. Instead, John's reign should be viewed as one in which there occurred a complex, yet clear, paradigm shift; whereby Antioch's previous reliance on Jerusalemite protection was replaced with a desire, perhaps

5   Lilie, *Byzantium*, pp. 96, 175; D. Parnell, 'John II Comnenus and Crusader Antioch', *Crusades – Medieval Worlds in Conflict*, ed. T. Madden, J. Naus and V. Ryan (Aldershot, 2010), pp. 149–57, p. 150; Cahen, *Syrie*, pp. 359, 400–3; Phillips, *Defenders*, pp. 61–71; Harris, *Byzantium*, p. 81; Magalino, *Manuel*, pp. 67–71; Mayer, *Varia*, pp. 48–54; Augé, *Byzantins*, pp. 269–77; F. Chalandon, *Jean II Comnène (1118–1143) et Manuel I Comnène (1143–1180)*, 2 vols (Paris, 1912), II, 438–55.
6   Parnell, 'John', pp. 149–57; Lilie, *Byzantium*, p. 96.

most fervently apparent amongst the nobility, to test the conditions under which the principality could accept the suzerainty of a more powerful patron: Byzantium.[7] There was undoubtedly tension, but to singularly focus on instances of conflict, overlooks important indications for the emergence of a new Latin policy towards the Greeks.

Marriage Negotiations

Contacts began in the wake of Bohemond II's death in 1130 with the diplomatic exchange, introduced earlier, during which discussions had between Byzantium and 'the nobles' (προύχοντες) of Antioch regarding the potential marriage of John's son, Manuel, and the heiress to the principality, Constance.[8] John Kinnamos is the only direct source for this, although William of Tyre's cryptic suggestion that the emperor was angered that Constance had subsequently married Raymond of Poitiers 'without his knowledge or command' has been viewed as corroboration.[9] As has already been established, this has traditionally been placed in 1135, and explained as an attempt by Princess Alice to maintain influence by negotiating a union which recognised her authority – a belief which relies on the assumption that the wider Antiochene elite fostered such a strong anti-Greek stance that they would not have countenanced such an act.[10] Alice's isolation is no longer sustainable, however, especially given that the evidence points only towards the dominant influence of the principality's aristocracy, in this and the wider succession process. This is made all the more significant when the dating of the envoy is considered further.

With the increased likelihood of the general aristocratic predominance over proceedings, as demonstrated in Chapter 2, it is almost certain that the embassy occurred earlier than 1135, as by this year it had already been decided to approach Raymond of Poitiers – with no suggestions that opinion was divided on the matter.[11] Therefore, while the envoy could date to any time between 1130 and 1134, it seems most probable that it was in the immediate aftermath of Bohemond II's death, or at least before 1132. More importantly, it can now be seen to represent an embryonic attempt to broach closer ties to Byzantium just as Jerusalemite influence was waning. Indeed, as will become clear in the following chapter, it was during this period that royal power was challenged by the Antiochenes, while the Armenians also threatened to supplant Latin authority in Cilicia and provoke imperial interest.[12] This shift in the political dynamic of the region provides a far more suitable context for an approach to Byzantium, as when a similar situation had occurred in 1104, Byzantine forces had been able to temporarily reassert their dominance in Cilicia

---

7 For a detailed analysis of Antioch's relations with Jerusalem, see Chapter 7.
8 Kinnamos, *Epitome*, p. 16 (JK, p. 22). See also pp. 70–1 of this book.
9 WT, p. 662; *absque eius conscientia et mandato*. For historiography, see below.
10 Cahen, *Syrie*, pp. 356–7; Chalandon, *Jean et Manuel*, I, 121–2; Lilie, *Byzantium*, pp. 103–4; Phillips, *Defenders*, p. 64; Asbridge, 'Alice', pp. 45–6; Harris, *Byzantium*, p. 88.
11 The exception is Harris, *Byzantium*, p. 88.
12 See pp. 22–3, 221–4.

until Tancred expelled them.[13] Without leadership comparable to Tancred's, any Greek intervention could have had disastrous and lasting consequences, especially as Baldwin II of Jerusalem's failure to assert martial dominance over Muslim Syria in the 1120s, as well as the overbearing style of his regency of Antioch following *Ager Sanguinis* (1119–1126), seems to have made the prospect of Jerusalemite suzerainty less appealing.[14] The new king of Jerusalem, Fulk of Anjou, was likewise unable to recover influence in northern Syria until his defeat of Zengi at Qinnasrin in 1133, so there was an incentive during the early 1130s for Antioch to foster peaceful contacts with the Greeks. Not only could a pro-active diplomatic policy towards Byzantium potentially bring the aid of imperial resources (a significant boon against both the Armenians and Zengi), it was perhaps also considered the only way of preventing John from using this instability to implement an aggressive occupation.

Whether Antioch was actually prepared to accept a Byzantine prince is unknown, although Cahen's argument that 'the barons of Antioch were still too close to the crusade to accept the eventuality of Greek domination' can be challenged.[15] The decision to turn to Raymond of Poitiers does suggest a preference for a Western candidate who would not upset internal power structures, but it is misleading to focus only on the failure of the proposed marriage alliance. Such an approach over-looks the significant fact that the notion of strong ties with Byzantium was, for the first time, a valid part of Antioch's diplomatic policy.

John Komnenos at Antioch, 1137–1138 and 1142–1143

Of greater importance to our understanding of the changing dynamic are the two visits that John Komnenos subsequently made to Antioch in 1137–1138 and 1142–1143. That both of these ventures began, and ended, in Latin–Greek conflict, is undoubtedly the cause of the 'height of confrontation' label. Yet, while a prickly atmosphere permeated relations, historians have placed too great an emphasis on the inevitability of this, and in blaming Antioch for a rupture. Thus, Phillips has argued that Byzantine overlordship was 'clearly not to the taste of the Franks' and Isabelle Augé has suggested 'the Latins were wary of the emperor, who had not hidden his pretentions to their territories, and due to this the idea of a pan-Christian alliance could not be followed to its completion'.[16] A more nuanced inter-pretation is possible, however; one which takes a more careful approach towards Antiochene actions and recognises that the Franks, rather than demonstrating an inevitable opposition to Byzantium, were now willing to approach and engage the emperor.

---

[13]   Asbridge, *Creation*, pp. 56, 62–3.
[14]   Asbridge, 'How the Crusades Could Have Been Won', 73–94.
[15]   Cahen, *Syrie*, pp. 356–7. This is especially so in light of recent scholarship which has demonstrated the complex relationship of conflict and cooperation between Alexios and Bohemond during, and after, the First Crusade. See Pryor and Jeffreys, 'Alexios', pp. 31–79.
[16]   Phillips, *Defenders*, p. 71; Augé, *Byzantins*, pp. 275–6.

It has long been accepted that the first contact between John and Raymond occurred during the emperor's siege of Antioch in 1136 – a reality almost certainly influenced by William of Tyre's account.[17] Despite this, there are suggestions within the non-Latin sources that an earlier meeting occurred in Cilicia, as al-Azimi noted a princely 'outing' towards the emperor, which the *1234 Chronicle* expanded to a summit at Tarsus during which Raymond paid homage to John.[18] If this meeting did happen, then it was perhaps in the context of securing an imperial promise to not attack Antioch immediately, with Raymond at this time seeking to launch a relief effort to save Latin forces besieged by Zengi at Montferrand: an expedition about which Greek authors were surprisingly well informed.[19] The imprecision and chronological distance of these accounts prevents secure conclusions, while John's subsequent encirclement of Antioch – because of which Raymond was perhaps forced to fight his way back into the city – certainly suggests that the emperor did not feel constrained by any deal.[20] Nevertheless, although the speed with which violence erupted demonstrates the fragility of relations, the possibility of this earlier meeting, as well as the rapidity of a settlement to end the siege, indicates a mutual desire to negotiate and avoid extensive conflict.[21] The underlying motives and processes of the subsequent treaty agreed between the two powers are thus worth examining.

The situation facing both rulers was certainly difficult. As many historians have argued, John's sensitivities to potential repercussions in the West, particularly from the papacy, may have forced him to show more restraint than he would have preferred.[22] Instances of aggression undermine this, while a papal reproach issued against him in around 1138 clearly did little to alter John's activities.[23] Conversely, an examination of Antioch's motives has been limited to the assumption that the Franks needed to prevent John from seizing the city.[24] The fall of Antioch was an undeniable concern, yet other matters can also be identified, such as the need to secure help in combating the ever-growing threat of Zengi, and to adjust to the recent return of imperial control over Cilicia – which had seen the Latins expelled from Tarsus, Adana, Mamistra and Anazarba.[25] The Antiochenes may also have sought to prevent a reaction in Europe, as, although Norman Sicily was at this point distracted by a papal schism, the loss of one of the First Crusade's most

---

[17]   WT, pp. 670–1.
[18]   Al-Azimi, p. 138; *1234*, II, 81–2.
[19]   JK, pp. 22–4; NC, pp. 14–16.
[20]   WT, pp. 670–1; Orderic Vitalis, VI, 505; JK, pp. 22–4; NC, pp. 14–16; Michael Italikos, pp. 239–40; MS, III, 245; *1234*, II, 82; ME, p. 239; GP, p. 241.
[21]   WT, pp. 670–1; JK, pp. 22–4.
[22]   Cahen, *Syrie*, pp. 358–63; Magdalino, *Manuel*, pp. 35–41; Harris, *Byzantium*, pp. 79–91; Lilie, *Byzantium*, pp. 121–3; Phillips, *Defenders*, p. 71.
[23]   There is some debate over the timing of this missive, but the most likely date remains 1137/1138. See Hiestand, *Papsturkunden*, pp. 168–9.
[24]   Cahen, *Syrie*, pp. 358–63; Magdalino, *Manuel*, pp. 35–41; Harris, *Byzantium*, pp. 79–91; Lilie, *Byzantium*, pp. 120–3; Phillips, *Defenders*, p. 71.
[25]   See pp. 27–9.

famous conquests may well have restored unity.[26] At the head of any response would have been the anti-Greek southern Italians, whose claims to the principality had only recently been overlooked in favour of Raymond of Poitiers. The Sicilians may have used this opportunity to interfere in northern Syria and in the principality's political structure – seemingly a pressing concern for Antioch's ruling elites.[27] With the situation delicately poised, William of Tyre's belief that 'wise men' (*prudentioribus*) from both camps intervened to elicit a peaceful settlement, even if representative of a literary *topos*, probably reflects the reality that this was the best course of action for both sides.[28] Crucially, the subsequent treaty, which saw Raymond and the nobles do homage to the emperor outside Antioch's walls, and recognise the terms under which Byzantium could recover the city, confirms the willingness to negotiate.

The stipulations of this agreement are recorded in both the Latin and Syriac accounts, although Greek authors largely remained silent, perhaps as a result of John's eventual failure to fulfil its terms. William of Tyre's version remains the most extensive:

> In the presence of the illustrious and famous men of the imperial palace, he [Raymond], along with his nobles, would exhibit liege fealty and obedience to him [John] with due solemnity, tendering a sacred oath that if the lord emperor wished to enter Antioch or its citadel, either in anger or in peace, he would allow him entrance freely and peacefully. Also, if the lord emperor, just as it was inserted into the treaty, should peacefully restore Aleppo, Shaizar, Hama and Homs to the prince, because he [Raymond] was to be satisfied with this and the other surrounding cities, he would restore Antioch to the empire without difficulty to have by right of ownership.[29]

Unsurprisingly, these terms have not gone unnoticed, with historians drawing a number of different conclusions. Indeed, the treaty has been concomitantly viewed as successfully following the traditional Byzantine diplomatic aim of securing recognition of imperial sovereignty, as generally less favourable than the earlier Treaty of Devol (upon which it was supposedly styled) and even explained as an astute piece of Latin negotiation – with John tricked into accepting terms that were all but unenforceable, allowing the Antiochenes to await the first available chance to

---

[26] Lilie, *Byzantium*, pp. 100–3, 112–17.

[27] See pp. 68–80.

[28] WT, p. 671. See also Tessera, '*Prudentes*', pp. 63–71. More generally, see F. Cheyette, 'Suum cuique tribuere', *French Historical Studies* 6 (1970), 287–99; J. Benham, *Peacemaking in the Middle Ages: Principles and Practice* (Manchester, 2011).

[29] WT, p. 671: in presentia illustrium et inclitorum imperialis palatii cum universorum cetu procerum suorum cum debita sollempnitate ei ligiam exhibeat fidelitatem iuretque, prestito corporaliter sacramento, quod domino imperatori, Antiochiam ingredi volenti vel eius presidium, sive irato sive pacato liberum et tranquillum non neget introitum, et si dominus imperator ei Halapiam, Cesarem, Hamam, Emissam, sicut pactis erat insertum, principi restituerat iure proprietatis habendam. See also MS, III, 245; *1234*, II, 82.

break from the alliance.[30] The first of these themes is prominent amongst those who argue that recognition was more important than possession (particularly Harris and Magdalino), and others, like Lilie, who believe in John's sensitivity to the West. However, although the 1137 treaty was a significant achievement for the emperor, at least theoretically, John's actions later on in 1138, and again in 1142 (see below), belie the notion that possession was not a genuine goal.[31] Opinion is perhaps influenced by the fact that Manuel Komnenos did eventually agree to overlordship, and the Greek texts certainly downplayed John's subsequent failure to fulfil the treaty, but it would be wrong to overlook the reality that imperial actions denote a desire for physical control. Moreover, Chalandon and Asbridge have convincingly demonstrated that Devol was a 'dead letter' by 1137, and thus no longer an influence; while the possibility remains that our only source for the 1108 agreement, Anna Komnene's *Alexiad*, exaggerates matters to boost the prestige of her father, and the source's chief protagonist, Alexios Komnenos.[32] In this regard, it is perhaps significant that the form of homage Anna described in 1108, *lizio*, matches William of Tyre's statement that Raymond had exhibited *fidelitatem ligiam* to John, for it is possible that she superimposed the events of 1137 onto those at Devol.[33] The traditional stance also overlooks the fact that, unlike his father, John had finally secured a treaty which promised recognition of imperial suzerainty, the eventual return of Antioch and, most importantly, was accepted by the Antiochenes, not their absent ruler. John did not achieve the treaty's fulfilment, but the securing of the agreement was nevertheless a great success.

It was also an astute piece of business for Antioch, even if it came at the expense of an agreement to surrender the city and forego claims to Cilicia. Raymond and the nobility had diverted the threat of a large imperial army and had even secured extensive support against Zengi. The elimination of the Armenian problem likewise allowed for greater focus on the eastern frontier, which was made pertinent by the Muslim attacks of 1135 and 1136.[34] It has nonetheless been assumed that the surrender of Antioch would have been unthinkable. The city's significance in the history of Christianity and the First Crusade would certainly have made its loss unpalatable, especially in the West; yet, it cannot, perhaps, be assumed that there was not a recognition, at least within Antioch itself, that this was outweighed by the benefits of the promised polity to be carved from Muslim Syria. That there

---

[30] For diplomatic success, see Chalandon, *Jean et Manuel*, I, 122–33; Cahen, *Syrie*, pp. 358–63; Magdalino, *Manuel*, pp. 35–41; Harris, *Byzantium*, pp. 79–91; Augé, *Byzantins*, pp. 269–77. For negative comparisons with Devol, see Lilie, *Byzantium*, pp. 121–3. For the skill of Latin negotiation and duplicity, see Elisséeff, *Nur ad-Din*, II, 362–7; Lilie, *Byzantium*, pp. 121–3; Phillips, *Defenders*, pp. 61–71; Köhler, *Alliances and Treaties*, pp. 138–42.

[31] This is recognised in Parnell, 'John', pp. 149–57.

[32] Anna Komnene, pp. 385–96; Chalandon, I, 122–33; Asbridge, *Creation*, pp. 99–103; P. Buckley, *The Alexiad of Anna Komnene: Artistic Strategy in the Making of a Myth* (Cambridge, 2014), pp. 236–44; P. Magdalino, 'The Pen of the Aunt: Echoes of the Mid-Twelfth Century in the *Alexiad*', *Anna Komnene and Her Times*, ed. T. Gouma-Peterson (New York, 2000), pp. 15–43.

[33] Anna Komnene, pp. 385–96.

[34] See pp. 25–6.

are no suggestions aristocratic fiefs were included in the treaty, although John potentially laid claim to them in 1142, coupled with the fact that John handed sites like as al-Atharib to Latin lords upon their recapture, demonstrates that the agreement had minimal impact on the nobility.[35] Moreover, Raymond's emotional ties to Antioch are unlikely to have been particularly strong: he had only recently arrived in northern Syria; and there is no doubting that his authority, and the security of the wider Latin East, would have been exponentially increased by the creation of a new principality including Aleppo, Shaizar, Hama and Homs. If Ibn al-Qalanisi's – often overlooked – statement that Raymond then arrested the Latin patriarch, Ralph of Domfront, in order to fulfil John's request to install a Greek prelate, then Lilie's argument that 'the majority of the Franks rejected an alliance with Byzantium ... on religious grounds because they were against association with the schismatic Greeks' might even be questioned.[36]

Despite this, Phillips' suggestion that the Latins duplicitously forged the agreement in order to 'maintain the options of co-operation or resistance to the emperor' is not entirely without evidence, for both Gregory the Priest and the *1234 Chronicle* detailed that the decision to attack the inaccessible fortress of Shaizar was such folly as to imply deception.[37] Shaizar was certainly a difficult target, but it was also included amongst the imperial domains linked to Antioch in Devol, and was of great strategic importance to the principality because it guarded a major crossing of the Orontes.[38] It also stood in close proximity to the power base of the Isma'ilis, who created difficulties for the Latins throughout the 1130s. Added to the long-coveted Aleppo, as well as Hama and Homs, this campaign's successful completion would have broken Muslim power in the region and all but ended Zengi's apparent hope of uniting his lands to Damascus.[39] Eastern Christian authors may have considered it deceitful to attempt to capture Shaizar, and the campaign was highly ambitious, yet these conquests were paramount to the creation of a lasting Latin polity. Moreover, while the treaty may well reflect an astute level of negotiation by Raymond and the nobles, it should not be overlooked that it was agreed upon by an emperor whose martial dominance provided him, at least in theory, with the military upper hand. Another aspect of belief in Latin duplicity stems from William of Tyre's account of Raymond's idleness during the subsequent siege of Shaizar – characterised, it was said, by dicing and gambling.[40] This has been readily accepted by many historians and classed by Phillips as 'Frankish recalcitrance'.[41] Nevertheless, a strong level of co-operation is evident throughout the rest of the campaign, with even

35 NC, pp. 16–18.
36 IQ, p. 245; Lilie, *Byzantium*, p. 141; Phillips, *Defenders*, p. 65. See also Hamilton, *Latin Church*, pp. 173–4; Cahen, *Syrie*, p. 502; Augé, *Byzantins*, p. 105. The failure to appoint an Orthodox prelate could still indicate joint concerns over papal reactions.
37 Phillips, *Defenders*, p. 70; GP, p. 241; *1234*, II, 84–6.
38 Anna Komnene, pp. 385–96.
39 On Zengi and Damascus, see Köhler, *Alliances and Treaties*, pp. 127–75.
40 WT, pp. 674–6.
41 Phillips, *Defenders*, pp. 70–1; Augé, *Byzantins*, pp. 274–5.

the Antiochene nobles participating.[42] Likewise, the Greek texts, usually so keen to point out Latin treachery, explained the failure at Shaizar by pointing instead to the strength of its defences and the threat of relief forces – also mentioned by Arabic accounts – under Zengi and the caliph of Baghdad.[43] William's text may thus have been influenced by his own prejudices, such as his dislike of Joscelin II of Edessa (who he blamed for leading Raymond astray) or a desire to promote the notion of imperial military support for *Outremer* by praising John's skill and fervour for the attack.[44] As such, he deployed a well-known literary trope – gambling – to discredit the Latins, while admiring the emperor's actions.[45] Although notions of 'Frankish recalcitrance' cannot be entirely ruled out, there are significant questions regarding the impulses which lay behind William's text, and so the growing unity of the Muslim world, which engendered a greater response to the Christian coalition than may have been expected, remains the most likely explanation for the failure at Shaizar.[46]

Another element which has been seen to validate belief in the underlying Latin opposition to close relations with Byzantium, is the reaction to events which occurred upon John's return to Antioch in 1138, and during his second visit to the city in 1142. On each occasion, Raymond and the nobles reportedly adopted an aggressive stance towards the emperor, who now demanded that certain of his rights be recognised and fulfilled. Indeed, following the failure at Shaizar, the Christians returned to Antioch where, according to William of Tyre, John summoned the Frankish leaders to him and declared his desire to launch future campaigns. To accomplish this, he

> ordered, therefore, that the citadel of the city should be assigned to our protection, just as you hold to by treaty, so that we may safely store our treasury in it, and the city should be made open to our armies so that they shall have complete licence to enter and exit freely without difficulty.[47]

In response, Joscelin II of Edessa is said to have asked for a delay on Raymond's behalf, for 'new things require new counsel'.[48] Parnell has argued that John's demands were entirely in keeping with the treaty of 1137, and that the Antiochenes' subsequent disbelief reveals both their underlying hatred of the Greeks and their desire

---

[42] On this, see p. 113.

[43] JK, pp. 24–5; Michael Italikos, pp. 240–3; NC, pp. 14–16; IA, I, 339–42; al-Azimi, pp. 141–3; KD, *RHC Or.* III, 673–8; IQ, pp. 244–52; MS, III, 245. El-Azhari (*Zengi*, pp. 79–81) suggests the Zengi probably did not want the reinforcements to arrive, as they could have altered the balance of power against him, but it is unlikely that the Christians knew of this.

[44] Edbury and Rowe, *William of Tyre*, pp. 61–84, 130–50.

[45] E. Lapina, 'Gambling and Gaming in the Holy Land: Chess, Dice and Other Games in the Sources of the Crusades', *Crusades* 12 (2013), 121–32.

[46] Phillips, *Defenders*, pp. 70–1. The complicated array of potential factors for the retreat is discussed in Augé, *Byzantins*, pp. 273–5.

[47] WT, p. 677: oportet igitur ut civitatis huius presidium, sicut ex compacto teneris, nostre deputes custodie, ut in eo nostri tutius reponantur thesauri, urbem quoque nostris exercitibus perviam facias, ut liberam omnino intrandi egrediendique habeant sine difficultate licentiam.

[48] *Ibid.*, pp. 676–8 (here 678); res nova novo indigent consilio.

to ignore the treaty.[49] However, this not only overlooks William's comment on the novelty of such a demand, but also his remark that Raymond and the nobles then offered to fulfil John's request to 'transfer the city with the citadel into the hands of the empire'.[50] This latter claim was even repeated and extended in 1142, with John commanding that Raymond 'resign to him the city with the citadel and all the fortifications of the city'.[51] The surrender of Antioch was part of the agreement in 1137, albeit only once the Muslim cities had been taken, yet no other Antiochene fortifications had been mentioned. Certain historians have acknowledged, therefore, that John attempted to subvert the agreement on both occasions, perhaps with the intention of ousting the prince.[52] Accordingly, the Latin reaction was aggressive. In 1138, a riot broke out which forced John from Antioch – with peace only restored at the instigation of the nobles, who calmed the people and dispatched an envoy to secure the emperor's forgiveness and to offer to agree to his demands. He refused, but retired nonetheless.[53] The aristocracy sent another embassy to John in 1142, potentially influenced by the threat to their holdings, decrying his actions and threatening to depose Raymond and Constance if they were coerced into compliance.[54] Then, in 1143, perhaps emboldened by John's subsequent death in a hunting accident in Cilicia, Raymond – according to Kinnamos – sent a further message, this time demanding that the new emperor, Manuel, forego his father's illegal attempt at occupation.[55]

While the corroboration of independent sources for both 1138 and 1142 confirms William of Tyre's portrayal of tension, it should be remembered that his account was also influenced by an apparent desire to both promote imperial interest in *Outremer* and criticise the notion of their actual possession of its lands.[56] In this regard, William may have deliberately portrayed the Antiochenes as more proactively antagonistic so as to show the unity of Latin opposition. Questions thus remain over the extent to which they instigated the fracture. Historians have nevertheless identified Antioch's duplicity on both occasions, noting that the Franks had simply awaited the chance to break from a ratified treaty; with Cahen and Chalandon describing their actions in 1142 as 'illegal'.[57] On the other hand, Magdalino has argued that the Antiochenes 'had done no more than to call [John's] rather

49 Parnell, 'John', pp. 153–4. See also Cahen, *Syrie*, pp. 358–63; Chalandon, *Jean et Manuel*, I, 148.
50 WT, pp. 680–1 (here 681): urbem cum presidio in manus imperii transferre.
51 *Ibid.*, pp. 700–1 (here 701): urbem ei cum urbis presidio et omnibus indifferenter civitatis munitionibus.
52 Lilie, *Byzantium*, pp. 126–33; Phillips, *Defenders*, pp. 61–71; Magdalino, *Manuel*, p. 41; Harris, *Byzantium*, pp. 88–93.
53 WT, pp. 680–1; MS, III, p. 245; *1234*, II, 82. A thirteenth-century depiction of these events can be found on the cover of this book.
54 WT, pp. 700–6. On this, see also pp. 97–9 of this book.
55 WT, pp. 700–6; Otto of Freising, *Duabas Civitatibus*, p. 354; JK, pp. 26–33; NC, pp. 22–27. For a conspiratorial account of this death, see R. Browning, 'The Death of John II Komnenos', *Byzantion* 31 (1961), 229–35.
56 MS, III, p. 245; *1234*, II, 82. See also Edbury and Rowe, *William of Tyre*, pp. 130–50.
57 Cahen, *Syrie*, pp. 366–8; Chalandon, *Jean et Manuel*, I, pp. 183–98.

foolhardy bluff'.⁵⁸ In certain respects both perhaps go beyond the available evidence, yet the predominant belief that the conflict occurred solely because of Antioch can be challenged. Rather, John's role in prompting tension must be recognised. The suggestion that this period clearly reflects the complete Frankish rejection of the idea of imperial overlordship must therefore be doubted, especially as the Latins otherwise appear to have demonstrated a willingness to work with Byzantium. This is similarly suggested by an apparent request for military support sent by Raymond to Constantinople in the early 1140s.⁵⁹

Although the period 1130–1143 has been classified as a time in which the Latins were utterly unwilling to co-operate with the Greeks, greater care is required when assuming Antioch's opposition to Byzantium. Indeed, the fault for the eventual tension does not appear to have been so entirely Antiochene. Raymond and the nobles were hard negotiators, and they opposed abuses of agreements, but the very fact that they willingly approached discussions, as opposed to simply descending into warfare, was a significant development. This has often been understated or overlooked. These developments were undoubtedly influenced by growing issues in Cilicia and Muslim Syria, but to characterise the period as the 'height of confrontation' ignores the conflict of earlier decades. Crucially, for the first time in the principality's history, the door had been opened to Byzantine overlordship. While it would be wrong to suggest that this was not a difficult process, especially with imperial armies in close proximity to the Latins, coupled with an emperor keen to secure prestige, this nonetheless represents a significant phase in Antioch's history: one that laid the groundwork for what was to come under Manuel.

The Path to Overlordship, 1144–1158

In the summer of 1158, Emperor Manuel Komnenos came to Mamistra, where he accepted the submission and homage of Renaud of Châtillon, thus securing imperial overlordship of the principality. The events of the preceding fourteen years, in which Zengid attacks caused the disintegration of the county of Edessa and the principality's northern and eastern frontiers, have been outlined in Chapter 1, but it is important to note here that they have been historically characterised as reducing Antioch's status to that of a mere passenger in Near Eastern politics. Indeed, Cahen saw Manuel's visit as the creation of a new political world, arguing that 'Antioch thus formed the transition between the two political systems [of Byzantium and Jerusalem] ... [as] the alliance of Manuel and Baldwin [III of Jerusalem] ... allowed the Antiochenes to admit, through the protection of Baldwin, to a suzerainty

---

⁵⁸ Magdalino, *Manuel*, p. 41. See also Lilie, *Byzantium*, pp. 134–40.

⁵⁹ WT, pp. 700–1. Chalandon (*Jean et Manuel*, I, 183–4) dismissed this as an empty oath, but this ignores the fact that it represents an attempt *by* the Antiochenes to promote imperial involvement in northern Syria, which they are unlikely to have done had they utterly opposed the notion.

which otherwise they had considered intolerable ... [Now] there was exercised over Antioch a sort of condominium of the two princes.'[60] Although not all have gone quite so far, the assumption that the staunchly anti-Greek Antiochenes were simply too powerless to stop the coercion of Jerusalem and Byzantium remains largely unchallenged.[61] However, it has become evident here that the principality's ruling elites were far more active diplomats, and also more open to close contacts with the Greeks, than this suggests.[62] In this context, there is a need to re-examine the Antiochene perspective for these years, and to discuss their actions both leading up to, and during, Manuel's visit. A more variegated picture can therefore be presented, in which it is argued that, through their astute and careful diplomacy, the Antiochenes placed themselves at the very centre of the changing relationship with Byzantium.

Shifting Allegiances

The years following Edessa's fall in 1144 were disastrous for Antioch. Too weak to respond to Zengi's invasion of the county – a reality perhaps contributed to by a reported Byzantine raid, launched on Antiochene territory by Manuel Komnenos in 1144 (in retaliation for the events of 1143) – the principality's northern defences were extremely vulnerable.[63] They were then wiped out, along with possessions east of the Orontes, following Nur al-Din's victory at Inab in 1149.[64] The immediate danger was to some extent eased by the Zengid preoccupation with Damascus, although the threat of attack never truly vanished. Magdalino and others have argued that this increased Jerusalem's influence in northern Syria, allowing King Baldwin III to become 'the emperor's trusted representative and the guarantor for the good behaviour of all the Christian princes in the area': a process which would only have been strengthened by his marriage to Manuel's niece, Theodora, in 1157.[65] In contrast, as will be argued in the next chapter, the Jerusalemite monarch actually faced severe difficulties in asserting influence over Antioch, especially as the 1150s progressed.[66] Relations with Byzantium during this time thus also require re-examination.

Indeed, it is instructive that Prince Raymond reacted to the fall of Edessa not by requesting Jerusalemite support, but by making a personal visit to Constantinople, where he became Manuel's 'liegeman' (λίζιον) in return for gifts and the promise of imperial military aid.[67] In light of the tensions in 1142/1143, and the emperor's military campaign of 1144, this was not without risk. It was also the first

---

60 Cahen, *Syrie*, p. 402. See also Grousset, *Croisades*, II, 380–404.
61 Lilie, *Byzantium*, pp. 175–83; Magdalino, *Manuel*, pp. 67–71; Chalandon, *Jean et Manuel*, II, 438–55; Elisséeff, *Nur ad-Din*, II, 534–5; Phillips, *Defenders*, pp. 132–9.
62 See also pp. 97–100.
63 JK, pp. 35–6; NC, p. 31.
64 See pp. 38–9.
65 Magdalino, *Manuel*, pp. 67–71 (here 70); Chalandon, *Jean et Manuel*, II, 438–55; Cahen, *Syrie*, pp. 399–402; Elisséeff, *Nur ad-Din*, II, 534–5; Lilie, *Byzantium*, pp. 175–83.
66 See pp. 233–5.
67 Kinnamos, *Epitome*, p. 35 (JK, p. 36). See also MS, III, 267.

visit made to the imperial city by a prince of Antioch. When placed alongside the subsequent lack of cohesion with Jerusalem over the course of the Second Crusade, during which the two powers proved unable to support each other, it is evident that the Antiochenes now actively pursued alternative avenues of support against the Zengids.[68] It is of further interest that this coincided with similar calls for aid sent to Europe, as this helps to indicate that the Byzantine emperors were considered a relevant source of succour, despite the Greeks' traditional difficulties with crusading armies.[69]

Positivity towards closer relations with Byzantium was also demonstrated by an envoy sent by Princess Constance to request a husband from Manuel in the early 1150s, perhaps with the complicity of the nobility.[70] As only Kinnamos recorded this, caution must be exercised, especially as, alongside his acceptance that Constance rejected the proffered candidate (the emperor's widowed brother-in-law, Caesar John Roger) on account of his age, the chronicler also claimed that the Antiochenes were 'anxious lest ... they should become subject to the payment of tax to the Romans'.[71] Consequently, this may signify an attempt to showcase Latin duplicity: although historians have accepted it as fact, encouraging the belief that 'there was general rejection of the Greeks in the principality'.[72] Interestingly, this stance also overlooks the fact that Kinnamos recorded that it was Antioch who initially made contact, not Byzantium – just as Raymond had made the decision to go to Constantinople in 1145. Even if it can be trusted, therefore, the Greek account does not so much demonstrate underlying opposition to relations with the empire, rather that Manuel's reaction was considered unfavourable. This may have been influenced by the emperor's failure to retain the last remnants of the county of Edessa, which he purchased around this time: the inability to prevent further Muslim conquests demonstrated Greek military limitations and perhaps provoked the Antiochenes to look elsewhere.[73] Nevertheless, Antioch's continued willingness to co-operate was demonstrated when Constance's new husband, Renaud of Châtillon, acted as Manuel's mercenary in a campaign against the Armenians of Cilicia, who had begun to challenge imperial authority there, in 1154.[74] Once again, it proves important that unsubstantiated assumptions do not prejudice an understanding of the nuanced pragmatism of political relations between Antioch and Byzantium.

There is one event, however, which does point towards enduring difficulties: Renaud's attack on Cyprus in around 1156. Carried out in the wake of the successful completion of the aforementioned mercenary campaign, William of Tyre explained

---

68 Phillips, *Second Crusade*, pp. 207–27.
69 Otto of Freising, *Duabus Civitatibus*, pp. 363–5; *Chronique de Morigny*, p. 85.
70 JK, pp. 96–7. See also pp. 77–80 of this book.
71 JK, pp. 96–7, 136.
72 Lilie, *Byzantium*, pp. 165–6; Phillips, *Defenders*, pp. 124–5; Cahen, *Syrie*, p. 389; Magdalino, *Manuel*, p. 66; Harris, *Byzantium*, pp. 112–13.
73 WT, pp. 781–5; MS, III, 297.
74 WT, p. 824; MS, III, 314.

this action – conducted in conjunction with the Armenian warlord, and enemy of the Greeks, Thoros – by noting that 'it seemed to [Renaud] that [Manuel] was greatly delaying the distinguished recompense for so great an act'.[75] That tensions appeared regarding money was also noted by Kinnamos.[76] Historians have argued, perhaps correctly, that the emperor's refusal to reimburse the prince stemmed from his anger that the Cilician campaign was used to install – or re-install – the Templars into the Amanus Mountains, which is unlikely to have been its initial remit.[77] More significant, though, is that, because there is no evidence for widespread aristocratic involvement, it cannot be securely accepted that this attack represented widely held Antiochene antagonism towards Byzantium, rather than the rash actions of its prince.[78] This would also only have been accentuated by Renaud's apparent need for funds, as he would likely have had to utilise paid forces to carry out these assaults. It is of further interest that, although William of Tyre was appalled by the recklessness and brutality of Renaud's actions, he was also careful to hint that it had been sparked by Manuel reneging on an agreement – a rare occasion of even implicit criticism for this emperor.[79] The raid on Cyprus was certainly an aggressive and inflammatory act, and a highly unwise one in relation to diplomatic ties with the Greeks, but it was not necessarily considered unprovoked by contemporaries. When added to the negative reactions to apparent imperial abuses of agreements in 1138 and 1142, a consistent Latin willingness to defend Antioch's rights, if contracts were not maintained, can therefore be noted. A close reading of the available evidence again hints at great complexities, with sweeping generalisations regarding Antiochene views of Byzantium obscuring the many nuances of reality. As such, despite the events in Cyprus, this period still demonstrates Antioch's proactive participation in diplomatic relations with the empire. This was made clearer when Manuel arrived in northern Syria in 1158.

1158: Manuel at Antioch

Spurred into action by Renaud's attack on Cyprus, Manuel brought a sizeable imperial army into Cilicia with a speed that is reported to have alarmed both Thoros and the Antiochenes.[80] It also elicited a dramatic response from Renaud and his advisors, the effectiveness of which allowed the Franks of the principality to retain a strong and important position in the developing diplomatic situation.

---

75 WT, pp. 823–5 (here 824): honestam pro tanto facto retributionem, videbatur ei differri plurimum. See also MS, III, 314–15; GP, p. 272–5; Sempad, *RHC Arm.* I, 621.
76 JK, pp. 136–7.
77 Chalandon, *Jean et Manuel*, II, 435–8; Cahen, *Syrie*, p. 392; Lilie, *Byzantium*, pp. 168–9; Magdalino, *Manuel*, p. 67; Harris, *Byzantium*, pp. 112–14; Augé, *Byzantins*, pp. 277–80; Chevalier, *Ordres*, pp. 61–8. See also pp. 29–30, 43–4 of this book.
78 See pp. 121–2.
79 The Old French translation of William's chronicle (*Eracles*, II, 209) was even more explicit in accusing Manuel of refusing to pay the promised money. See also Handyside, 'Differing Views', pp. 49–50.
80 The events of this visit are also discussed in Buck, 'Between Byzantium and Jerusalem?', pp. 109–14.

Rather than passive observers, they were at the forefront of events. On this, William of Tyre reported that the prince of Antioch, after a brief exchange of envoys led by the bishop of Latakia, came to Mamistra to intercept the emperor. Here he

> was restored to the emperor's merit with the greatest disgrace and shame of our people, barefoot, it was said, clothed in wool with sleeves cut off all the way to the elbow, a rope tied around his neck. Having [his] sword unsheathed in his hand, holding the sword point he extended the hilt to the lord emperor. He was presented to the lord emperor in the presence of all the legions and having surrendered his sword to the lord emperor there, threw [himself] to the ground before his feet.[81]

An agreement was then forged which recognised Manuel's overlordship, promised to install a Greek patriarch and stipulated that the Latins would provide military service in the imperial armies.[82] This was then solemnised by a procession into Antioch involving the entire breadth of Antiochene society, as well as the king of Jerusalem.[83]

The penance at Mamistra was a startling piece of theatricalised ritual. Considered by most historians to represent the powerlessness and subservience of the Antiochene Franks, its profound diplomatic consequences have been all but overlooked.[84] However, a closer inspection of the influences which lay behind this act can provide a significantly different perspective. Indeed, while Byzantine Christians would not have been unaware of public displays of penance, for example those included in the Bible, or that imposed on Emperor Theodosius by St Ambrose in the fourth century, Renaud's ritual did not draw on any discernible Greek political traditions.[85] Such an act had certainly not been forced on Raymond of Poitiers during his visit to Constantinople in 1145, although he did show humility by praying at John Komnenos' tomb.[86] The events at Mamistra instead followed the Latin ritual of supplicatory penance, in which religious or political sinners would abase themselves at an altar, or to a person, with a cross – in this instance an inverted sword – in front of them or around their neck: an action which served to re-establish the right order of society following a fracture.[87] Jenny Benham has demonstrated

---

[81] WT, pp. 844–5 (here 845): cum summa ignominia et populi nostri confusione imperiali reconciliatus est excellentie. Nudis enim, ut dicitur, pedibus, indutus laneis, manicis usque ad cubitum decurtatis, fune circa collum religato, gladium habens in manu nudum, quem mucrone tenens cuius capulum domino imperatori porrigeret, coram universis legionibus domino imperatori presentatus est ibique ante pedes eius ad terram prostratus, tradito domino imperatori gladio. See also *Eracles*, II, 232–3; JK, pp. 139–42; Manganeios Prodromos, pp. 66–87.

[82] *Ibid.*, pp. 844–7; JK, pp. 137–45; NC, pp. 59–63.

[83] WT, 847–9; JK, pp. 137–45; NC, pp. 59–63; Manganeios Prodromos, pp. 126–43; MS, III, 316; *1234*, II, 119; GP, pp. 272–5; Sempad, 'Armenian Chronicle', pp. 147–9.

[84] Chalandon, *Jean et Manuel*, II, 438–55; Cahen, *Syrie*, pp. 399–402; Lilie, *Byzantium*, pp. 175–83; Magdalino, *Manuel*, pp. 67–71; Harris, *Byzantium*, pp. 112–14; Augé, *Byzantins*, pp. 108–13, 277–86.

[85] S. Hamilton, *The Practice of Penance, 900–1050* (Woodbridge, 2001), pp. 174–5.

[86] Kinnamos, *Epitome*, p. 35 (JK, p. 36); MS, III, 267.

[87] G. Koziol, *Begging Pardon and Favor: Ritual and Political Order in Early Medieval France* (Ithaca, NY, 1992), pp. 181–7; Benham, *Peacemaking*, pp. 96–106; Cheyette, 'Suum', pp. 287–299. See also Y.

that, after the break-up of the Carolingian Empire, and via high-profile cases such as Henry IV of Germany's supplication to Pope Gregory VII at Canossa in 1077, such rituals became part of a political order 'integrated into secular society and no longer performed just on set days before bishops or priests'.[88] This was confirmed in 1169 when Henry II of England abased himself in front of Louis VII of France at Montmirail in order to diffuse tension over the dispute with Thomas Becket and to broker peace.[89] For Benham, 'such a show of penitence and complete submission had to be rewarded with forgiveness and absolution', and that, had Louis refused to comply, 'he would have struck at the very heart of his own office ... [even if] it is unlikely that Henry with his actions actually conceded anything new'.[90] Thus, while Renaud's ritual actively showed subservience, this does not mean that the political power of this act can be overlooked.

Yet, the significance of the penance *has* often been ignored, in part because it has long been held that it was engineered by Manuel and Baldwin III during negotiations for the latter's marriage to the emperor's niece, Theodora Komnena.[91] This is based primarily on Gregory the Priest's suggestion that the principality's ruling elites submitted to Manuel in 1158 lest they 'violate the oath taken at the tomb of the Redeemer and the promise given to the king of Jerusalem when he became allied to Manuel through marriage'.[92] The oath and promise in question was the emperor's apparent statement that he would come to Syria to aid in the fight against the Muslims. Crucially, no explicit mention was made of Antiochene submission forming part of this agreement, and without corroborating evidence it is problematic to place so great an emphasis on this text.[93] Importantly, other sources instead portray Renaud and his advisors as the principal instigators of the meeting at Mamistra, with no input from Baldwin or guidance from Manuel. William of Tyre even lamented that Renaud:

> had not even been willing to await the presence of the lord king, though it was hoped he would be approaching nearby, although he would have certainly known with trust [that], through his intervention and zeal, and by the grace of the powerful new affinity [between Baldwin and Manuel], he would have managed to receive far better conditions.[94]

Friedman, 'Gestures of Conciliation: Peacemaking Endeavours in the Latin East', *In Laudem Hierosolymitani: Studies in Crusades and Medieval Culture in Honour of Benjamin Z. Kedar*, ed. I. Shagrir, R. Ellenblum and J. Riley-Smith (Aldershot, 2007), pp. 31–48.

88   Benham, *Peacemaking*, p. 96.

89   *Ibid.*, pp. 96–7.

90   *Ibid.*, p. 97.

91   Magdalino, *Manuel*, pp. 67–71; Chalandon, *Jean et Manuel*, II, 438–55; Cahen, *Syrie*, pp. 399–402; Elisséeff, *Nur ad-Din*, II, 534–5; Lilie, *Byzantium*, pp. 175–83.

92   GP, pp. 272–3.

93   William of Tyre (p. 845) mentioned discussions but not their content.

94   WT, pp. 844–5 (here 845): ut nec domini regis, quem tamen in proximo venturum sperabat, vellet expectare presentiam, cum tamen certo certius nosse poterat eius interventione et studio, et maxime nove affinitatis gratia, in causa predicta longe meliores se inventurum conditiones.

The *Eracles* continuator of his work, who lacked William's Byzantine sensitivities, even expanded upon this by claiming that the bishop of Latakia had:

> advised [Renaud] to go before the emperor, who was in Cilicia, without delay, and to cry to him most humbly for mercy because he knew how arrogant the Greeks were and that they wanted nothing more than that one should do honour to them under duress.[95]

It seems, therefore, that the initiative for this action came solely from within Antioch, not from Byzantium or Jerusalem. This is likewise supported by Kinnamos' account, as well as the air of shocked surprise detailed in the contemporary poems of Manganeois Prodromos, who was not an eye-witness, rather he reacted to reports returning to Constantinople. He asked of the penance of Renaud and his men: 'what transformation have these warlike men undergone, and what is the innovation and what the strange violence?'[96] For Greek authors, this was not a recognisable performance.

Another crucial element in assessing the impetus behind these events regards Manuel's intentions. A number of historians have explained the emperor's reserved reaction to this display by stating his sensitivity to Western opinion and his understanding of traditional imperial notions of recognition over possession: Manuel preferred to accept overlordship rather than inflict a military defeat.[97] It does seem that Manuel adopted a more favourable policy towards Latin Christendom after 1144, but it cannot be ruled out that he had expected – or had been expected – to make a show of force similar to his earlier campaign and that displayed by his father in 1137.[98] The raid on Cyprus had been an act of war against Byzantium after all. Moreover, given that a vast imperial army had gathered, the reluctance shown in directing it against Muslim Syria in 1159 hints that Manuel had envisaged an alternative target.[99] In fact, he appears to have actually sought to engender positive ties to the Islamic world, as Kinnamos reported that a number of Muslim envoys were present at Mamistra upon Renaud's arrival.[100] Importantly, hopes of bringing Islamic leaders into line would almost certainly have relied on an ability to demonstrate magnanimity. Had Manuel acted aggressively to the prince's voluntary abasement, this may have adversely affected his chances of convincing these powers to trust in an alliance. Whatever Manuel's initial intentions were for Antioch, Renaud's

---

95 *Eracles*, II, 232: li loa que sanz delai il s'en alast encontre l'Empereur qui estoit encore en Cilicie, et li criast merci mout humblement; car il cognoissoit les Grieus de tel maniere que il estoient bobancier, et ne queroient autre chose fors ce que l'en leur feist enneur par dehors.

96 JK, pp. 139–142; Manganeios Prodromos, p. 69.

97 Chalandon, II, 438–55; Cahen, *Syrie*, pp. 399–402; Elisséeff, *Nur ad-Din*, II, 534–45; Lilie, *Byzantium*, pp. 175–83; Magdalino, *Manuel*, pp. 67–71; Harris, *Byzantium*, pp. 113–5; Augé, *Byzantins*, pp. 108–13, 277–86.

98 This is confirmed as the primary motive in WT, pp. 844–5; JK, pp. 136–7.

99 Despite having agreed to attack Nur al-Din, the venture was swiftly cancelled (reportedly due to issues in Constantinople) and an agreement was made with the Sultan to release a number of Latin prisoners. WT, pp. 846–9; JK, pp. 137–45; NC, pp. 59–63; IQ, pp. 353–5; AS, *RHC Or.* I, 102–5; GP, pp. 272–5; Sempad, 'Armenian Chronicle', pp. 147–9; MS, III, 316, *1234*, II, 119.

100 JK, pp. 139–42. See also Lilie, *Byzantium*, pp. 167–8.

arrival at Mamistra left him with few other options than to consent to a peaceful settlement. That this was recognised at the time can perhaps be gleaned from the poems of Manganeios Prodromos, which praised Manuel's magnanimity and Christ-like forgiveness – an exaggeration which hints at a need to save face.[101] Given that the subsequent terms agreed with Renaud were not particularly damaging to the principality, it is clear the emperor valued the benefits of the recognition of his overlordship, but the prominent part played by the Antiochenes in protecting their status requires acknowledgement. Commenting on another of Henry II of England's public penances, this time for the murder of Thomas Becket (in which the monarch had been forced to order the monks of Canterbury to observe his public debasement through the streets of the city and in the cathedral), Nicholas Vincent has noted that 'a king who has to command the observation of his own humility cannot be said to be truly humbled'.[102] By demonstrating that Renaud and his advisors had initiated the penance of Mamistra, the same can be said here. Rather than a result of political impotence, this ritual can instead be viewed as a political masterstroke; one which defused Manuel's wrath and ensured a settlement far less damaging to Antioch than it could have been.

The penance also prevented the involvement of another interested party, one whom historians have long credited with a high degree of influence: the kingdom of Jerusalem.[103] Indeed, Baldwin III appears to have initially struggled to make his authority felt. Although William of Tyre argued that the emperor 'invited [Baldwin] to come without delay ... [as a] most beloved son of the empire', Kinnamos suggested that Manuel actually felt that Baldwin hoped to seize Antioch and so initially refused him an audience.[104] There are nevertheless suggestions that the Byzantines and Antiochenes recognised that the king could not be entirely ignored, as on top of Baldwin's subsequent participation in Manuel's triumph into Antioch, both Kinnamos and Gregory the Priest detailed an approach made to the king by the city's inhabitants in the hope that he might leave for Cilicia and intercede on Renaud's behalf. Once Manuel allowed Baldwin into his presence, this did seemingly lead to a reduction in the principality's military service.[105] The accounts of the emperor and king hunting together, with the former personally administering to the latter's wounds following an accident, also suggest that Manuel was at pains to promote a sense of friendship between the two rulers.[106] It is important to recognise, however, that royal influence was not so great as to convince the emperor to relinquish his demand for a Greek patriarch, even though it was not enforced

---

[101] Manganeios Prodromos, pp. 75–83.
[102] N. Vincent, 'The Pilgrimages of the Angevin Kings of England 1154–1272', *Pilgrimage: The English Experience from Becket to Bunyan*, ed. C. Morris and P. Roberts (Cambridge, 2002), p. 16.
[103] Chalandon, *Jean et Manuel*, II, pp. 438–55; Cahen, *Syrie*, pp. 399–402; Lilie, *Byzantium*, pp. 175–83; Magdalino, *Manuel*, pp. 67–71; Harris, *Byzantium*, pp. 113–5; Augé, *Byzantins*, pp. 108–13, 277–86.
[104] WT, pp. 846–7 (here 846): ut regem moneant et invitent ut ad eum venire non pigritetur ... imperii dilectissimum filium; JK, pp. 139–42.
[105] WT, pp. 846–7; JK, pp. 139–42.
[106] WT, pp. 846–9; JK, pp. 137–45.

until 1165. Meanwhile, the reduction in Antiochene service was only achieved when Baldwin promised to personally cover the shortfall. This implies that Manuel had agreed simply in order to extend his influence over the kingdom. Care should also be taken not to confuse the Antiochenes' request for help with a recognition of the king's suzerainty over the principality, for a number of sources considered Baldwin's role to have been so minimal as to not even be worthy of mention.[107] Manganeios Prodromos even suggested that Manuel had actually forced Baldwin to hold the bridle of his horse – a reality the poet suggested was an honour, but which the king appears to have been displeased by.[108] The corroboration of other accounts allow for an acceptance that Baldwin was involved, at least on the periphery; yet, it is telling that the main negotiations were carried out, and agreed upon, before he could intervene.[109]

Similar doubts emerge in relation to another piece of evidence used to promote belief in Baldwin's influence: a coin supposedly issued by Manuel to commemorate the monarch's role. This coin, which carries a cross and the inscription *XRE*, has been examined by Metcalf, who concluded that it is a badly rendered form of *REX*. He thus presents it as evidence that the emperor promoted Baldwin's role as leader of *Outremer*.[110] Conversely, the poor quality of the cast – which Metcalf posits is Armenian-made – intimates that it was created *after* Manuel's arrival in Cilicia (most likely following Renaud's penance). This contradicts claims that the decision to accept Baldwin's chief position pre-dated the campaign. The presence of the cross, moreover, makes it is more probable that *XRE* is a shortened form of *XR[IST]E*, or Christ, and represented an attempt to portray the emperor as the head of Christendom during his procession into Antioch. That this was seemingly not produced before his departure from Constantinople perhaps again intimates that he had not envisaged a peaceful entrance into the city. Numismatic evidence is often difficult to interpret and must be treated with caution, especially as the survival rate for this coin is exceptionally poor, but Metcalf's conclusions are difficult to substantiate.

This adds to the growing realisation that there is no adequate evidence that Baldwin was recognised as the Frankish figurehead in 1158, either by Manuel or the principality's elites. Although Phillips has agreed that Manuel 'had the strength, authority, and the justification' to act alone, he also argues that the king 'had reason to be content with the outcome' for his position at the head of *Outremer* had been secured.[111] Augé goes further, suggesting that Baldwin's role in the triumph into Antioch (where he rode on horseback whilst Renaud acted as Manuel's groom) was

---

[107] NC, pp. 59–63; *1234*, II, 119.
[108] Manganeios Prodromos, p. 137.
[109] GP, pp. 272–5; MS, III, 316; Sempad, 'Armenian Chronicle', pp. 147–9; Chalandon, *Jean et Manuel*, II, pp. 438–55; Elisséeff, *Nur ad-Din*, II, 534–5.
[110] Metcalf, *Coinage*, pp. 140–2. See also M. O'Hara, 'A Possible Coinage for Alexius II (?), 1180–1184', *Numismatic Circular* 97 (1987), 111–13.
[111] Phillips, *Defenders*, pp. 132–9.

the perfect embodiment of the political status quo.[112] This stretches the evidence too far. Baldwin was allowed some part in proceedings, and a more prominent ceremonial position than Renaud (even if he did not appreciate this), yet this is hardly surprising given that the prince was demonstrating his contrition. In reality, the king was only on the fringes of the truly important developments.

Consequently, while it has long been held that the instabilities of the 1140s and 1150s ensured that the principality of Antioch was an impotent pawn, caught between the rival machinations of Byzantium – a state to which it harboured only hatred – and Jerusalem – the premier Latin power in the Near East; this view overlooks both the fluid nature of power in northern Syria and the activities of the Antiochenes themselves. The years following Zengi's capture of Edessa and the loss of the principality's northern and eastern frontiers were undoubtedly of great significance to Antioch, but there is evidence that rather than cowing the Antiochenes into submission, they retained a strong, guiding hand in their diplomatic relations. This resulted in renewed attempts to welcome imperial overlordship, both through Raymond's visit to Constantinople and a proposed marriage alliance with Constance (even if the rejection of John Roger shows that the terms of a secure relationship were yet to be found), and often came at the expense of ties with Jerusalem. It cannot be overlooked that the suspicion of imperial treachery was still met by force, as is shown by the attack on Cyprus; but, while this suggests Antioch was prepared to defend its position, it does not go so far as to imply that the entire principality perpetuated a monochromatic anti-Greek stance. Moreover, although Manuel seemingly held a more conciliatory attitude towards the Franks than his father, which may have helped to protect Antioch somewhat in 1158, it would be wrong to assume that he would not have wanted to demonstrate his martial superiority following an assault on imperial territory. In this context, interpreting Renaud's penance as a carefully staged act of diplomatic theatre, allows for the identification of an astute level of politicking that deflected a potentially disastrous situation and secured terms of only minor insignificance. That the prince and ruling elites of the principality favoured, rather than begrudgingly accepted, the distant financial benevolence offered by imperial overlordship, has often been disregarded by historians; almost certainly because of an over-reliance on a narrative of conflict which dominates historical coverage of Latin–Greek relations. Although tension remained, the evidence portrays a far more diverse and complicated diplomatic strategy than has hitherto been acknowledged, and over which the elites of the principality retained a strong guiding hand. Rather than becoming mere passengers in the political world around them, the losses of the 1140s and 1150s appear to have spurred Antioch into greater action. By managing the influences of Jerusalem and Byzantium, they were eventually able to secure a highly beneficial agreement to implement imperial overlordship in northern Syria.

---

[112] Augé, *Byzantins*, pp. 277–86.

A *Condominium* in Action? Byzantium and Antioch, 1159–1182

The belief that a *condominium* was created over Antioch, that the principality – so weak that it could no longer guide its own diplomatic policy – now had the kings of Jerusalem acting as its spokesperson and Byzantium as its overlord, thus ignores important evidence to the contrary. Indeed, Antioch retained a strong level of independence. This was also to be demonstrated in the following two decades.

The Marriage of Manuel Komnenos and Maria of Antioch

There are suggestions that a certain level of unity existed between the three powers in the years following Manuel's departure, with Kinnamos' comment that the emperor called upon Baldwin and Renaud to fulfil their military service duties in a campaign against the Turks of Asia Minor in 1159/1160, considered an indication of the *condominium*'s implementation.[113] However, the Greek chronicler also described separate summoning processes for each ruler, and it is unclear that the operation was even enacted – there is evidence of both rulers issuing charters in their domains during this period.[114] Whether Baldwin was to lead a Latin coalition, or if he was just another satellite ruler, is likewise uncertain. Perhaps the most significant indication that the king of Jerusalem did not hold real influence in northern Syria, despite the emperor clearly recognising the potential benefits of amicable ties, is the subsequent marriage between Manuel Komnenos and Maria of Antioch.[115] The events surrounding negotiations for this union, in which Constance willingly cooperated with the emperor in an act of diplomatic subterfuge by pursuing a highly favourable match with Byzantium well away from royal intervention, proved to be a great embarrassment for Baldwin III.

It does appear, though, that following the death of his German wife, Bertha of Salzburg, Manuel initially approached the kingdom in order to open negotiations over a new Frankish bride. William of Tyre duly recorded that an envoy was dispatched from Constantinople to Jerusalem to inform Baldwin III, who had reportedly just returned from Antioch after installing Patriarch Aimery as regent in the wake of Renaud of Châtillon's capture in November 1161, that:

> finally, from the favour and consent of all the princes it pleased [us] that we should unite the empire in marriage [with one] from your bloodline, which our empire loves unparalleled; either of your relations, the illustrious woman [Melisende] sister of the count of Tripoli, or the magnificent

---

[113] JK, pp. 151–2.
[114] Chalandon, *Jean et Manuel*, II, pp. 517–18; Cahen, *Syrie*, pp. 405–7; Elisséeff, *Nur ad-Din*, II, pp. 545–6; Lilie, *Byzantium*, pp. 183–4; Augé, *Byzantins*, pp. 285–6; *Urkunden Jerusalem*, I, 248, 253–6, 258, 260; *CGOH*, I, 265; *Codice Diplomatico*, I, pp. 206–7.
[115] This is also discussed in Buck, 'Between Byzantium and Jerusalem?', pp. 114–17.

woman [Maria] youngest sister of the prince of Antioch, having all faith in the honest option you may choose for us.[116]

After some deliberation, Baldwin proposed Melisende (perhaps in order to prevent increased imperial influence at Antioch), and his decision was relayed to Manuel for agreement. Certain Greek authors support this, particularly Constantine Manasses, a poet who wrote an account – perhaps used later by Kinnamos – of his partic-ipation in the embassy to Jerusalem, as well as a visit to Tripoli. Despite this, both Choniates and Sempad the Constable noted instead that Manuel simply chose Maria during his visit in 1158.[117] Following the king's decision to recom-mend Melisende, a delay ensued in which Manuel's envoys prevaricated. Baldwin was obviously confident, for he allowed Melisende to use the title 'future empress of Constantinople' in a charter of July 1161.[118] However, the embassy eventually returned with the reply that she was unsuitable, either on grounds of illegitimate birth or poor health.[119] After a significant period of delay, Baldwin then appears to have revisited Antioch where, according to William of Tyre, he discovered the Greek envoys in 'daily and intimate discussions' with Constance regarding Maria.[120] Unable to block this, Baldwin, albeit undoubtedly embarrassed, respectfully aided in the princess's departure to Constantinople.[121]

The most thorough examination of these events has been carried out by Hans Mayer, whose careful study of its chronology culminated in the conclusion that, contrary to William of Tyre's account, the initial envoy to Jerusalem was dispatched from Constantinople in the summer of 1161 and so pre-dates both Renaud's capture and Baldwin's visit to Antioch. Accordingly, he argues that Manuel had initially been prepared to accept Baldwin's decision, but that the prince's incarceration altered the dynamics. The emperor now sought to seize an opportunity to increase his influence at Antioch, which could only have occurred, so Mayer suggests, 'after the elimination of the less than pro-Byzantine Renaud'.[122] This view was largely shared by Magdalino, who argued that 'it was fully in the spirit of the settlement of 1159 [sic] that Manuel should use Baldwin as his broker in dealings with the other crusader princes', and that the subsequent delay could only have occurred due to Renaud's capture: at which point 'at the very least, a show of respect for Bald-win's wishes was necessary to divert his attention away from the negotiations with

---

116 WT, pp. 854–6 (here 855): Tandem de universorum principum favore consensu placuit ut de sanguine tuo, quem unice diligit nostrum imperium, nobis in consortium iungamus imperii, et utram consobrinarum tuarum, seu illustris viri Tripolitani comitis sororem sue magnifici viri Antiochem prin-cipis germanam iuniorem, nobis elegeris, nos, pro tua optione sinceritati tue omnem fidem habentes.
117 Constantine Manasses, pp. 165–221; JK, pp. 145–60; NC, pp. 65–6; Sempad, *Chronique*, pp. 45–9.
118 *Urkunden Jerusalem*, I, 263: futurae imperatricis Constantinopolitanae.
119 WT, pp. 856–7; Constantine Manasses, pp. 165–221; JK, pp. 145–60. For interpretation of Baldwin's actions, see Magdalino, *Manuel*, pp. 71–2; WT, pp. 854–7; Chalandon, *Jean et Manuel*, II, 518–24; Cahen, *Syrie*, pp. 405–7; Lilie, *Byzantium*, pp. 182–9; Mayer, *Varia*, pp. 48–54.
120 WT, pp. 856–7 (here 857): cotidianum et familiarem … tractatum.
121 *Ibid.*
122 Mayer, *Varia*, p. 50.

Antioch'.[123] Questions nevertheless remain regarding whether Manuel ever truly intended to accept a Tripolitan empress, especially as Byzantium had shown little interest in the county since the opening years of crusader settlement.[124] Alongside Choniates and Sempad's suggestions that the emperor had chosen Maria during his earlier visit to Antioch, problems also arise with those sources which support traditional opinion. Mayer has correctly pointed to William of Tyre's confused chronology, and it now appears very unlikely that Baldwin had been returning from Antioch when the initial imperial envoy arrived. Yet, his belief that the king still made two trips to northern Syria, first in early 1162 and then again in the summer of that year (at which point he found the Greek embassy in discussions with Constance), is tenuous. More plausible is that Baldwin came only once, staying from the beginning of 1162 until Maria's departure in the summer, during which time he was made aware of the union. That he remained for a considerable period is even suggested by William of Tyre, who chronicled that the king helped to rebuild the fortress of the Iron Bridge during his stay, a not inconsiderable undertaking.[125] Anger over Constance's part in the subterfuge also more readily explains why Baldwin reportedly sought to oust her from government in favour of the patriarch, despite her years of experience and claims to legitimacy.[126] Left with little choice but to acquiesce to Manuel's desires – which even William of Tyre concluded – Baldwin attempted to recover some prestige by exacting revenge on the princess, albeit seemingly without success. Further questions surround the work of Constantine Manasses, on whom Mayer is largely reliant. That the poet took part in the envoy to Jerusalem is undeniable, but he was, by his own admission, poorly informed on the nature of the trip, and was not particularly focused on its finer details.[127] Miroslav Marcovich has even described Constantine as 'a hopelessly lyric and romantic *enfant terrible*' who 'clearly never intended to produce a historical chronicle'.[128] The extent of his knowledge of Manuel's true intentions is, therefore, highly questionable, even if Kinnamos utilised his text.

It is evident that a Byzantine embassy was indeed sent to Jerusalem in 1161. That this represented a genuine recognition of Jerusalemite rights over Antioch is not so secure. Indeed, it seems more likely that Manuel had either expected Baldwin to toe the line by promising not to hinder a marriage alliance with Antioch; or that, even before Renaud's capture, this was little more than a distraction to allow talks with the Antiochenes to progress. Konstantine Horna has argued as such, describing it as a 'double cross', as 'the Byzantine court had once again provided an example of the ambiguous diplomatic skills through which it had so loved to prove its intellectual superiority over the inept Western governments, especially in the era of the

---

[123] Magdalino, *Manuel*, pp. 71–2. See also Chalandon, *Jean et Manuel*, II, pp. 518–24; Cahen, *Syrie*, pp. 405–7; Lilie, *Byzantium*, pp. 182–9.
[124] Augé, 'Une collaboration efficace?', pp. 141–55.
[125] WT, p. 858.
[126] *Ibid.*, pp. 854–7. See also pp. 228–9 of this book.
[127] Constantine Manasses, pp. 179–81.
[128] *Ibid.*, pp. 165–71; Marcovich, '*Itinerary*', pp. 277–91.

crusades'.[129] Antioch's willing acquiescence to this, probably even during Renaud's reign, reveals a great deal about their stance towards Jerusalem and the nature of relations with Byzantium. This has often gone unnoticed by historians, whose belief in the inherent weakness of the principality has shifted the primary focus onto the empire and the kingdom. Yet, Antioch had much to gain from a marriage alliance, as it tied Manuel to the principality's cause even more strongly, and offered the prospect of a half-Antiochene emperor – which was almost realised with Alexios II Komnenos in the early 1180s. Not only would this have promised reliable support, it also altered the dynamic of the relationship: the Latins now held a stake in the imperial succession, whereas Maria was never likely to gain the Antiochene throne. Even if some Latins remained apprehensive about ties to Byzantium, there were few negatives to this. In this context, it is far from surprising that they would have actively pursued such an offer, and it must not be forgotten that Antioch carried out its negotiations entirely separate from Jerusalem, as they had also done in 1158. Belief in a *condominium*, and Baldwin's position within it, is thus undermined; as is the suggestion that the Antiochenes were mere bystanders.

Overlordship Secured, 1163–1180

That Antioch now welcomed a secure form of overlordship which was both highly beneficial and came at little cost, can also be observed over the course of the following seventeen years. This was manifested in a number of ways. It was seen, most obviously, through the military support offered by the Byzantine *dux* of Cilicia, Coloman, against Nur al-Din at Buqay'a Gap in 1163 and at Artah in 1164, after which defeat Manuel's influence was even said to have stayed the Muslim ruler's hand from inflicting further losses.[130] Byzantine support here demonstrated the impact that the threat of imperial power could have on Islamic aggression, albeit not to the extent of preventing it entirely. Likewise, Manuel's decision to pay for Bohemond III's ransom in 1164, granted when the prince made a personal visit to Constantinople in 1165, showed the financial benefits of overlordship – even if it was influenced by the emperor's desire to secure the release of Coloman.[131] It also caused the long-desired installation of a Greek patriarch at Antioch, Athanasius III, at the expense of Aimery Limoges. This fulfilled the promise made in 1158; although, as Athanasius died in the earthquake of 1170, and was not replaced, the consequences were not lasting.[132] Moreover, while it is dangerous to argue *ex nihilo*, the lack of recorded Frankish furore at this appointment could be significant. Hamilton is correct that Bohemond probably had little choice than to accept

---

129 Horna, 'Hodoiporikon', pp. 313–20.
130 IA, II, 148. See also pp. 46–8 of this book.
131 WT, pp. 877–9; MS, III, 326. Antioch's comparative importance to Byzantium is demonstrated by Manuel's refusal to pay Raymond III of Tripoli's ransom after he had also been captured, likely as a result of the latter's sponsorship of attacks on Greek territory following the failure of marriage negotiations regarding Melisende in 1161.
132 MS, III, 326, 332–5, 339.

this demand in 1165, yet the silence of the sources perhaps suggests that the notion of an Orthodox prelate was simply not as divisive as some historians have assumed – especially given the patriarch's limited influence over princely governance after 1136 and the toleration of certain princely abuses of the Church.[133]

Significantly, this also came at a time when King Amalric of Jerusalem dispatched letters to the West inviting support against Byzantine incursions, before requesting an imperial bride – which was granted in the form of another of the emperor's nieces, Maria – and Manuel's recognition of his status as suzerain of Antioch – which was rejected.[134] Amalric even sought to involve himself in the principality following Artah, but is unlikely to have played a major role in securing Bohemond III's release when compared to the emperor's input.[135] However, he eventually recognised the benefits of imperial support in his attempt to capture Egypt, and also allied with Bohemond III and Greek forces to combat Mleh in Cilicia.[136] Nevertheless, the *condominium* – once again – cannot be identified. Manuel can be seen fulfilling the more mundane facets of overlordship, though. In the early 1170s, he married the Antiochene princess, Agnes, to Bela III of Hungary, and he also took Renaud's son, Baldwin, into imperial service (the latter died leading a Latin contingent at the fateful battle of Myriokephalon in 1176).[137] Ties were further strengthened by the union of Bohemond III to Theodora, yet another of Manuel's ample supply of imperial nieces, in around 1177.[138] There is no evidence for the diplomatic processes behind this marriage, although the very fact it occurred argues against any particular opprobrium. Even if the succession of Bohemond's two sons from Orgeuillse, Raymond II and Bohemond IV, would have been protected (just as those of Amalric's first marriage to Agnes of Courtney were before his union with Maria), by allowing this union, the potential eventuality of children born from a marriage to an imperial bride succeeding to the Antiochene throne was considered acceptable.[139] That there was no rebellion against this wedding, contrary to Bohemond's later union with Sybil (see below), is further implicit evidence for this. As is the fact that the level of co-operation was seemingly strong enough to cause disquiet in the West, for Pope Alexander III dispatched a letter to Patriarch Aimery in 1178 calling on the Antiochene Church to oppose the prince – even to the point of excommunication – amid fears he would again supplant the Latin hierarchy with a Greek one.[140] Such pressures clearly did not affect Bohemond's diplomatic

---

133 Hamilton, *Latin Church*, pp. 18–51, 45–6, 175–7; and 'Three Patriarchs', pp. 199–207; Lilie, *Byzantium*, p. 191; Todt, 'The Greek-Orthodox Patriarchate', pp. 33–53. See also pp. 101–9 of this book.

134 Louis VII, 'Epistolae', *RHGF* XVI, 39–40; Lilie, *Byzantium*, pp. 187–211.

135 WT, pp. 877–9. See also pp. 229–30 of this book.

136 See pp. 235–6.

137 On the Louis letter, see *RHGF* XVI, 14–15. On Agnes, see JK, p. 214; NC, p. 96; Alberic of Trois Fontaines, *MGH SS* XXIII, 849–50. On Baldwin, see NC, pp. 96, 102; and p. 83 of this book.

138 The exact date of her arrival is unknown, as the only evidence for the marriage is Bohemond's later rejection of her, but 1177 remains the most likely year given Alexander III's disquiet of 1178. See Cahen, *Syrie*, pp. 419–20; Phillips, *Defenders*, p. 245. Cf. Hodgson, 'Conflict and Cohabitation', p. 93.

139 Hamilton, *Leper King*, pp. 23–43.

140 Hiestand, *Papsturkunden*, pp. 278–9. See also Tessera, *Orientalis ecclesia*, pp. 368–9.

policy, as a joint Byzantine–Antioch envoy was present at the court of Henry II of England in 1179/1180, perhaps in the hope of securing Western acknowledgement of the succession of Manuel's son, Alexios II, or to promote military intervention in the East.[141] In addition to this, William of Tyre admitted to personally delivering a message to the prince from the emperor as he journeyed back from the Third Lateran Council in 1179.[142] Rather than diminishing, ties between Antioch and Byzantium were strengthening.

Bohemond III and the Breakdown of Contact

This changed with Manuel Komnenos' death on 24 September 1180, which left behind a young son, Alexios II, as heir and Maria of Antioch as regent.[143] In reaction, Bohemond, as already noted, abandoned Theodora in favour of Sybil. This resulted in an armed struggle with the Church and nobility, as well as the prince's excommunication – ironically, despite Alexander III's efforts, it was the breaking of the Greek union, not the earlier forming of it, that led Aimery to inflict a religious punishment on the prince.[144] Quite why Bohemond decided to divorce Theodora remains unclear. There was certainly little need to continue with a Greek bride once Andronikos seized power in 1182: he murdered Maria and Alexios II and took the imperial throne abreast a wave of anti-Latin sentiment. However, given that the union with Sybil pre-dated events in Constantinople, it seems likely that genuine affection was its root cause.[145] To forego the alliance with Byzantium at a time when Alexios' accession promised to provide extensive support to the principality nevertheless appears strange, especially as relations appear strong in the months before Manuel's death.[146] Mayer suggests that the decline of Byzantine strength after Myriokephalon left the empire 'so weak that an alliance with them had lost its value for Antioch'.[147] Ohers have questioned the actual impact of this battle, though, and it is hard to see how his view can be substantiated given the rise of Saladin and the decline in Western crusading interest.[148] Yet, this opinion is seemingly shared by Hamilton, who has suggested that Theodora was 'forced' on Bohemond, who took the earliest opportunity to break from her and Byzantium.[149] More probable is Lilie's belief that the prince's motives were not originally political, but that the divorce and the subsequent breakdown of contact during Andronikos'

---

[141] *The Great Roll of the Pipe for the Twenty-Fifth Year of the Reign of King Henry the Second, A.D. 1178–1179*, ed. J. H. Round (London, 1907), p. 125. See also C. Brand, *Byzantium Confronts the West* (Cambridge, MA, 1968), pp. 26–7; Phillips, *Defenders*, pp. 241–5.
[142] WT, pp. 1009–12.
[143] Lilie, *Byzantium*, pp. 222–3.
[144] WT, p. 1012–16. See also Buck, 'Noble Rebellion', pp. 96–102.
[145] NC, pp. 140–9; MS, III, 390; WT, pp. 1020–5.
[146] Phillips, *Defenders*, p. 250.
[147] Mayer, *Varia*, p. 163
[148] Magdalino, *Manuel*, pp. 98–100; Phillips, *Defenders*, pp. 225–45.
[149] Hamilton, *Leper King*, pp. 164–5.

reign should be linked to Bohemond's subsequent incursions into Cilicia.[150] Bohemond was perhaps even influenced by his interest in the kingdom of Jerusalem. While this is discussed in greater depth in the following chapter, it is perhaps no coincidence that the divorce came only a short while after a reported failed attempt to engineer a coup in Jerusalem along with Raymond III of Tripoli. Indeed, the count, along with elements of the kingdom's nobility and the Jerusalemite patriarch, all maintained an anti-Greek viewpoint. Bohemond may thus have considered that his chances of influence would be improved by breaking with the empire. It is of interest, therefore, that by the time Andronikos' actions had broken all ties with the Latins, the prince was able to play a lead role in deposing the unpopular Guy of Lusignan as regent of Jerusalem in 1183.[151]

Moreover, it has been presented here that, contrary to existing opinion that the anti-Greek nobility would not have cared for Theodora's fate, the cause of the extreme aristocratic reaction likely related to the decision to break with Byzantium and to take a new Antiochene bride without proper consultation.[152] The potential eye-witness account of Michael the Syrian supports this, for he commented that the subsequent peace settlement with the rebels ensured that Bohemond and Theodora were reconciled.[153] Likewise, charter evidence demonstrates that Sybil was absent from the Antiochene court between early 1182 and May 1183 – thus implying that she was not in a secure enough position to participate in governance during this period.[154] This was certainly temporary, and Andronikos' murder of Maria and Alexios probably heralded Sybil's return to court in May 1183; but Michael's generally anti-Greek tone makes it unlikely that he would have deliberately lied.[155] Conversely, William of Tyre suggested that Bohemond, who was rarely deemed worthy of his praise, instead chose to continue to live in sin with Sybil. Yet, this may also have been influenced by Andronikos, with the prominent role of Jerusalemite figures in negotiating the settlement at Antioch perhaps prompting William to hide the somewhat embarrassing fact that they had reconciled Bohemond and Theodora only for the empire to descend into chaos (and for the Greeks to end their association with *Outremer*).

Manuel's death clearly heralded a change. It is misleading, though, to rely on traditional conventions which offer a negative and inaccurate portrayal of Antiochene views towards Byzantium. With the exception of the events of 1180–1182, the years following Manuel's departure from Antioch in 1159 were generally characterised by close and productive contact, not conflict.

---

[150] Lilie, *Byzantium*, pp. 223–9. See also Harris, *Byzantium*, pp. 121–36; and pp. 54–5 of this book.

[151] B. Hamilton, 'Manuel I Komnenos and Baldwin IV of Jerusalem', *Kathegetria: Essays Presented to Jean Hussey for her 80th Birthday*, ed. J. Chrysostomides (Camberley, 1988), pp. 353–75; Lilie, *Byzantium*, pp. 206–9, 216–20; Phillips, *Defenders*, pp. 225–45. See also p. 239 of this book.

[152] See Buck, 'Noble Rebellion', pp. 96–102; and pp. 99–100 of this book.

[153] MS, III, 389.

[154] *CGOH*, I, 623, 648; Mayer, *Varia*, pp. 118–21; *Urkunden Venedig*, I, 68.

[155] *CGOH*, II, appendix no. 23.

The Final Years, 1182–1193

There can be little doubt that all hopes of close relations were ended by Andronikos' murder of Maria. Contact was now minimal, and it is instructive that Bohemond now moved on Cilicia and was also said to have aided in the capture and imprisonment of Isaac Komnenos, soon to become 'emperor' of Cyprus, in 1183.[156] There is some evidence that a modicum of friendship endured, with Eustathios of Thessaloniki commenting that the Antiochenes sheltered Greek exiles during Andronikos' reign, which again shows how relations with Byzantium could be influenced by circumstance.[157] Nonetheless, this was limited to the enemies of Andronikos, and an envoy of Emperor Isaac Angelos was reportedly captured at Acre in 1188 having been sent to discuss a union with Saladin.[158] For their part, the Greeks now focused on Leon II of Armenia, whereas the Latins of Antioch looked to the West – in particular Sicily and the German emperor – for help facing Saladin.[159] As a consequence, although Choniates suggested that Isaac Angelos expressed a desire to save Palestine and Lebanon from the Muslims in 1193, such a notion was a mere pipe-dream, and there is no reason to believe imperial involvement would have been welcomed as it once had.[160]

Conclusion

This chapter sought to re-examine the association between Byzantium and Antioch with two key aims: to demonstrate that the Antiochenes were more open to imperial overlordship than has been acknowledged, and that they were far more active in defining the terms of this relationship. It has been argued that, following Bohemond II's death in 1130, the elites and rulers of the principality pursued a more pragmatically pro-Greek diplomatic policy, one in which they sought to find terms agreeable for the implementation of Byzantine suzerainty. This process was fraught with difficulties, especially when John Komnenos' actions provoked aggression; yet, outright resistance to the very notion of co-operation with the emperors – so characteristic of the years before 1130 – was over. With the intensification of Zengid

---

[156] On Isaac, Roger of Howden noted he was captured by Rupen of Armenia and handed to Bohemond III (*Gesta Regis*, I, 254), though Choniates (NC, p. 161) did not mention any Antiochene involvement in this, rather that it was the Templars. See also Lilie, *Byzantium*, p. 224.

[157] Eustathios of Thessaloniki, *The Capture of Thessaloniki*, ed. and trans. J. R. Melville Jones (Canberra, 1988), p. 57. See also Brand, *Byzantium*, p. 27; Phillips, *Defenders*, p. 244.

[158] Magnus of Reichersberg, 'Chronicon', *MGH SS* XVII, 511; Roger of Wendover, *Liber qui dicitur Flores historiarum*, ed. R. Hewlett, 3 vols (London, 1886–98), I, 153. Some, like Lilie (*Byzantium*, pp. 231–9), have dismissed this as anti-Greek propaganda, although Harris (*Byzantium*, pp. 139–41) notes that there was some truth in negotiations, even though there is little chance Isaac hoped to work with Saladin against the Crusade.

[159] Cahen, *Syrie*, pp. 588–90; Hiestand, 'Antiochia', pp. 70–121.

[160] NC, p. 238. See also Harris, *Byzantium*, pp. 139–41.

aggression in the 1140s and 1150s, instability brought relations into sharper focus, and there are indications of a growing desire to extend links with Byzantium (in spite of Renaud's attack on Cyprus). This was achieved after Manuel Komnenos' visit to Antioch in 1158, during which the Antiochenes utilised astute diplomacy to forge an agreement that proved to be of great benefit to the principality over the following two decades. Antioch was now an imperial protectorate, not a political pawn between Byzantium and Jerusalem. Importantly, the principality's elites played an active role in defining the terms of this assimilation. This broke down with Manuel's death in 1180, as Bohemond III's divorce of Theodora somewhat pre-empted Andronikos' successful plot to plunge the empire into anti-Latin chaos, and the relationship never recovered. However, this should not be considered inevitable. Throughout the period 1159–1180, there was close and frequent contact between the two polities, which belies belief in enduring antagonism. Above all, there has been a genuine need to critically examine Antioch's actions, rather than to perpetuate the historiographical trend of dismissing the principality as both anti-Greek and a passive observer to decisions made by Jerusalem and Byzantium. Such a discussion reveals a complex and diverse strategy, in which the Antiochenes were able to deflect abuses while gradually strengthening ties to the imperial throne: perhaps most clearly demonstrated by Renaud's penance in 1158. So nuanced a conclusion again inverts traditional views of Antioch's history.

7

Antioch and the Latin East

As one of four polities created in the wake of the First Crusade, the principality of Antioch was an important part of the Latin East's tumultuous development. With crusade veterans often heading these fledgling states, the social and political bonds that had underpinned the venture's success proved an important catalyst to their cohesion and growth, a process otherwise classed as a 'confraternity' or the *Verband der Kreuzfahrerstaaten* ('association of the crusader states').[1] Thus, Bohemond offered his support to Edessa at Harran in 1104, and even when both Tancred or Roger sought to expand Antioch's influence over Edessa and Tripoli before 1119 (moves which did not prove popular within the latter states), open conflict was largely prevented through intervention from Jerusalem – overlords of at least Edessa – or a shared sense of Latin, or Frankish, identity.[2] After Roger's death at *Ager Sanguinis*, King Baldwin II even stepped in to secure Antioch, over the course of a seven-year regency, until Bohemond II took up his inheritance.[3] Coordination between the states, albeit not continuous, was therefore largely preserved, with common purpose and the leadership of crusade veterans also supplemented by a network of marriage alliances and political connections.[4] This dynamic was altered in 1131, however, as Bohemond II's death was swiftly followed by those of the last two crusaders in power: Baldwin II of Jerusalem and Joscelin I of Edessa. Control of the Latin East now passed entirely to the so-called 'second generation', with Western migrants presiding over Jerusalem and Antioch, and sons of crusaders

---

[1]   Barber, *Crusader States*, pp. 50–97. See also J. Riley-Smith, 'A Note on the Confraternities in the Latin Kingdom of Jerusalem', *The Bulletin of Historical Research* 44 (1971), 301–8; J. Richard, 'La confrérie de la croisade: à propos d'un épisode de la première croisade', *Mélanges offerts à E. R. Labande* (Poitiers, 1974), pp. 617–22; Hiestand, 'Antiochia', p. 82.

[2]   Asbridge, *Creation*, pp. 104–28; and 'The Principality of Antioch and the Early History of the Latin East', *East and West II*, pp. 1–10; Amouroux-Mourad, *Edesse*, pp. 80–4; Richard, *Tripoli*, pp. 30–8. On common identity, see Murray, 'Frankish Identity', pp. 59–73; Kirschberger, *Erster Kreuzzug*, pp. 75–102.

[3]   Asbridge, *Creation*, pp. 77–89, 126–7; and 'How the Crusades Could Have Been Won', pp. 73–94; H. E. Mayer, 'Jérusalem et Antioche au temps de Baudouin II', *Comptes-rendus de l'Académie des inscriptions et belles-lettres, Novembre–Décembre 1980* (Paris, 1981), pp. 717–33.

[4]   Asbridge, *Creation*, p. 104.

ruling Edessa and Tripoli.[5] With these changes, new bonds and allegiances had to be forged.

Despite this, no systematic study has been carried out to outline Antioch's place within this evolving political framework, although studies have examined certain elements of its links to the wider Latin East. In relation to the counties of Edessa and Tripoli, Monique Amouroux-Mourad has noted the principality's growing, but difficult, relationship with Edessa in the 1130s and 1140s, while both Mayer and Jean Richard have inspected the eventual unification of Antioch and Tripoli after 1187.[6] Ties with Jerusalem have been more extensively explored. René Grousset considered Renaud of Châtillon a 'baron' of Baldwin III in 1157, and Bohemond III one of Baldwin IV's '*grand vassaux*' in 1183.[7] In contrast, Martin has maintained that the principality was a sovereign power, not one subject to Jerusalemite vassalage (a viewed shared by Richard, at least for the period before 1183), and Mayer has argued that, despite his efforts, Bohemond III proved an ineffectual player when he sought to intervene in Palestinian politics during the 1170s and 1180s.[8] For the most part, therefore, historiography has focused primarily on relations with Jerusalem, and almost exclusively from the kingdom's perspective. This has ensured that Cahen (among others) relegated Antioch to a minor role in the Near East, arguing that Antioch became a *condominium* divided between Jerusalem and Byzantium by 1158.[9] In spite of his aforementioned caution in accepting the notion of royal overlordship, even Richard has presented the king of Jerusalem as 'president of the confederation of Christian states in Syria'.[10] Not all have gone this far: Marshall Baldwin argued that 'the Latin states were at best a loose federation', while Hamilton has described Antioch as 'wholly independent' of Jerusalem by the late 1170s.[11] Nevertheless, the pervading notion that the Holy City's supreme political and spiritual importance ensured the kingdom was the premier power in *Outremer*, with Antioch a politically weak and ineffectual neighbour, remains prominent. This is best represented in Malcolm Barber's recent study, in which has notes that 'although the Latins ... governed the lands independently, at the same time they were part of a wider Christian community, for Jerusalem and the holy places ... belong[ed] to all Christians'.[12] The wider crusader states were thus defined, first and foremost, by their proximity to Jerusalem.

5   Barber, *Crusader States*, p. 149.
6   Amouroux-Mourad, *Edesse*, pp. 80–4; Mayer, *Varia*, pp. 184–202; J. Richard, 'Les comtes de Tripoli et leurs vassaux sous la dynastie antiochénienne', *Crusade and Settlement*, ed. P. Edbury (Cardiff, 1985), pp. 213–24.
7   Grousset, *Croisades*, II, 371, 660.
8   Martin, 'Structures', p. 231; J. Richard, *The Kingdom of Jerusalem*, trans. J. Shirley, 2 vols (Amsterdam, 1979), II, 55, 83; Mayer, *Varia*, pp. 123–37, 184–202.
9   Cahen, *Syrie*, p. 402; Phillips, *Defenders*, pp. 134–5; Lilie, *Byzantium*, p. 175.
10   Richard, *Kingdom of Jerusalem*, II, 55, 83.
11   M. Baldwin, 'The Latin States under Baldwin III and Amalric I, 1143–1174', *A History of the Crusades vol.1: The First Hundred Years*, ed. K. Setton *et al.* (Madison, WI, 1963), p. 529; Hamilton, *Leper King*, p. 44.
12   Barber, *Crusader States*, p. 3.

This chapter seeks to offer a more detailed examination of Antioch's position within the Latin East, exploring themes of Jerusalemite regency, Antioch's interaction with royal claims to the position as head of *Outremer* and the principality's place within the so-called 'confraternity' of the East. It is contended that, although the Antiochenes appear to have continued to recognise the need for confraternal collaboration in times of difficulty, there are indications that the kingdom of Jerusalem no longer enjoyed the same level of political influence over northern Syria – due in part to the emerging relationship with Byzantium. Furthermore, that the princes of Antioch, albeit not always successfully, were seemingly willing to challenge Jerusalem's position as head of the association.

Jerusalemite Regency

One of the principality of Antioch's most characteristic features was the frequency with which its leaders were either killed or captured in battle. It was in these instances that the kings of Jerusalem most noticeably sought to exert their influence in northern Syria. This was especially prominent before 1130, as Baldwin II implemented a seven-year regency of the principality following Roger's death at *Ager Sanguinis* in 1119. Having been warmly welcomed by the Antiochenes, the king took his role seriously, leading various offensive campaigns against the Muslims, including an attempt to capture Aleppo in 1124/1125.[13] His extended absences even caused tension in Jerusalem.[14] Baldwin also appears to have asserted his position as the supreme ruler of Antioch, as Walter the Chancellor believed 'he obtained the rank of prince', which Fulcher of Chartres extended to 'king of the Antiochenes'.[15] The *Historia Nicaena vel Antiochena*, a source probably produced for Baldwin III of Jerusalem in 1146 or 1147, similarly noted that Baldwin II had 'enlarged the realm of the Jerusalemites with that of the realm of the Antiochenes'.[16] Asbridge has suggested these may have been exaggerations, stating that 'we possess no ... documentary, numismatic or sigillographic evidence to suggest [Baldwin] ever used the title of ... prince ... in connection with Antioch'.[17] However, Roberto Pesant has identified a coin bearing the inscription ΒΑΛΔΟΥΙΝΟC ΔΕCΠΟΤΗΕ, or 'Baldwin, despot': a Greek title, which translates as 'Lord', often used on the coins

---

[13] Asbridge, *Creation*, pp. 81–9, 126–8; and 'How the Crusades Could Have Been Won', pp. 73–94; Mayer, 'Jérusalem et Antioche', pp. 717–33.

[14] A. V. Murray, 'Baldwin II and his Nobles: Baronial Factionalism and Dissent in the Kingdom of Jerusalem, 1118–1134', *Nottingham Medieval Studies* 38 (1994), 60–85.

[15] WC, p. 98: principatus dignitatem adeptus est; Fulcher of Chartres, p. 635: Antiochenorum rex.

[16] *Historia Nicaena vel Antiochena, RHC Occ.* V, 184: regnum Jerosolymorum regno Antiochenorum ampliavit. See also D. Gerish, 'The *Historia Nicaena vel Antiochena* and Royal Identity', *The Second Crusade: Holy War on the Periphery of Latin Christendom*, ed. J. Roche and J. Jensen (Turnhout, 2015), pp. 51–90.

[17] Asbridge and Edgington, *The Antiochene Wars*, pp. 32–4, 143, n. 163; Asbridge, *Creation*, pp. 143–6.

of Byzantine emperors.[18] The use of Greek text on coins was known in the county of Edessa, as well as in the principality of Antioch, but in the former this tended to be accompanied by inscriptions like 'count' or 'servant of the cross'; not despot.[19] As such, although John Porteous has argued that this coin may instead date from the period between Baldwin II's accession as king of Jerusalem in 1118 and Joscelin I's appointment as count of Edessa in 1119, it remains possible that it instead reflects Baldwin's attempt to establish himself as ruler of Antioch.[20] This is supported by a letter sent by Baldwin to Abbot Bernard of Clairvaux in the 1120s, in which he styled himself *princeps Antiochie*.[21] Such evidence appears to place Baldwin on a par with both Tancred and Roger vis-à-vis the position of prince-regent, and while Asbridge is undoubtedly correct that he did not claim Antioch for himself in the long term, the strength of royal influence is clear.[22]

As will be examined below, the grand welcome enjoyed by Baldwin in 1119 was not repeated after Bohemond II's death in 1130. Consequently, whereas historians appear to have credited the kings with the power to extract military service from the Antiochenes, to portion out lands following disaster and to dictate in matters of succession and foreign policy, an examination of these events, and those of the subsequent interregnums of 1149–1153 and 1161–1163, point instead towards an emerging shift in the dynamic of relations between Antioch and Jerusalem.

Baldwin II, Fulk of Anjou and the Interregnum of 1130–1136

When Baldwin II arrived at Antioch in 1130, accompanied by his son-in-law and future king, Fulk of Anjou, he faced immediate difficulties. According to William of Tyre, Princess Alice, in alliance with Zengi and in opposition to the general Antiochene support for Jerusalem, had 'devised an evil plan', and 'sought, against the will of the chief men and all the common people, to claim Antioch for herself in perpetuity', thus 'disinheriting her daughter [Constance]'.[23] As already noted, accusations of Alice's collusion with Zengi cannot be securely substantiated, and although she certainly acted as a figurehead against royal intervention, Asbridge has convincingly demonstrated that William's account overlooks the implicit non-opposition of the patriarch and key noble figures, such as Renaud I Masoir – with Baldwin only gaining entrance into Antioch thanks to the help of two minor figures.[24] It is of

---

[18]   R. Pesant, 'A Coin of Baldwin II, King of Jerusalem, as Regent of Antioch', *Spink Numismatic Circular* 96:8 (1988), p. 245.

[19]   J. Porteous, 'Crusader Coinage with Greek or Latin Inscriptions', *A History of the Crusades vol. 6: the Impact of the Crusades on Europe*, ed. H. W. Hazard and N. Zacour (Madison, WI, 1989), pp. 362–6. See also Metcalf, 'Six Unresolved Problems', pp. 298–9.

[20]   Porteous, 'Crusader Coinage', pp. 365–6.

[21]   *Cartulaire général de l'ordre du temple (1119–1150)*, ed. Marquis d'Albon (Paris, 1913), 1.

[22]   Asbridge, *Creation*, pp. 143–6. See also pp. 68–9 of this book.

[23]   WT, pp. 623–5 (here 623–4): rem concepit nefariam … invitis patribus et plebe universa, Antiochiam sibi in perpetuum vendicare posse … exheredata filia. See also MS, III, 320; al-Azimi, pp. 125–6; KD, *RHC Or.* III, 660–1.

[24]   Asbridge, 'Alice', pp. 33–4.

further interest that Michael the Syrian, who lacked William's pro-Jerusalem stance, suggested that the cause of the division was not the lone ambition of Alice, rather the Antiochenes' general disapproval of Baldwin's apparent intention to install Count Joscelin I of Edessa as regent – a move probably made unpopular by an earlier conflict between the count and Bohemond II.[25]

Whatever the underlying cause, Baldwin was clearly unable to re-assert the authority he had in 1119, or to resume his previous titles. Even once the dispute was settled, rather than gain promises from the nobles that they would abide by *his* rule, William of Tyre noted that the king simply 'obtained the fidelity and bodily oath, from the major men as from the minors, that both during his life, and after his death, they would faithfully conserve Antioch, with its appurtenances, for Constance'.[26] When compared to William's terminology for similar events, such as Bohemond II's initial arrival in Antioch or Raymond of Poitiers' submission to John Komnenos in 1137, it is significant that, in this instance, he deployed the simpler *fidelitatibus*, not the stronger *fidelitatem ligiam*.[27] It is unclear whether Michael the Syrian was correct that the king did eventually appoint Joscelin I as regent, as the count's death soon after made the situation moot: although it is evident that the latter's son, Joscelin II, did not assume this role.[28] Instead, control of the principality was seemingly left to the Antiochene nobility.[29] The events of 1130 thus marked an important diminution to Baldwin's position, as well as an important shift in the political dynamic of the Latin East. Though the king secured an oath recognising Constance's succession, this was actually of greater benefit to Antioch, for it placed the princess' future in aristocratic hands, not Jerusalem's. It is noteworthy that, as a consequence, this period subsequently saw a diplomatic approach made towards Byzantium for a marriage alliance.[30] Phillips' suggestion that Baldwin was recognised *bailli* of the principality cannot therefore be securely accepted, especially as it is based more on the later title of his successor, Fulk of Anjou (see below), than explicit evidence.[31]

Nevertheless, relations with Jerusalem were not actively opposed in the longer term, as, soon after Baldwin II's death in August 1131, Fulk was called upon to provide political guidance and military support in northern Syria. He proved an able mediator and military leader, and was described as 'bailiff' of the principality – although he too was unable to fully recover the prestige of Baldwin's earlier position. The context for Fulk's first independent incursion into Antiochene affairs was the series of inter-Latin conflicts which arose in 1132.

---

[25] MS, III, 320. See also WT, pp. 614–15.

[26] WT, p. 624: sumptis tamen prius tam maiorem quam minorum fidelitatibus et corporaliter iuramentis, quod vel eo vivente vel post eius obitum Antiochiam cum suis pertinentiis Constantie.

[27] *Ibid.*, pp. 613, 671. William (pp. 560–2) did not describe an act of liege homage when Baldwin II came in 1119, but his account of 1130 is certainly much less positive regarding the powers given to the king.

[28] MS, III, 230. This is accepted by Cahen (*Syrie*, p. 350) and Phillips (*Defenders*, p. 45).

[29] See pp. 69–76.

[30] See pp. 191–2.

[31] Phillips, *Defenders*, p. 45.

On this, Ibn al-Qalanisi noted that 'a dispute had risen amongst the [Franks] – though a thing of this kind was not usual with them – and fighting had taken place between them in which a number of them were killed'.[32] William of Tyre considered this the result of Alice's desire to seize power in Antioch with the help of her allies, Pons of Tripoli (who garrisoned Arzghan and *Chastel Rouge* by right of his marriage to Tancred's widow, Cecilia), Joscelin II of Edessa and William of Saone.[33] There are some problems in trusting this account, though; not only due to William of Tyre's clear dislike of Alice, but also because Michael the Syrian offered an alternative explanation, stating merely that the Antiochenes turned on Joscelin II of Edessa (and so called on Fulk) after the count attempted to enforce his regency over them.[34] The death of William of Saone, meanwhile, was reportedly the result of Turcoman raids, or an assassination, in 1133, and was not demonstrably described as a direct result of his participation in the Latin civil war – a reality supported by the fact that neither William, nor any of his kinsmen, appeared in the independent charters issued by Alice during this period.[35] Caution must therefore be urged in accepting William of Tyre's portrayal of the princess's involvement, as well the level of Antiochene antagonism towards Fulk – whose power at this point had probably not been so established as to warrant opposition. Asbridge has nonetheless argued that the disputes of 1132 represented a 'full-scale challenge to Jerusalem's pre-eminence among the Latin powers in the east'.[36] Outside of Antioch, a possible catalyst for this could be that, unlike Baldwin I and Baldwin II, Fulk had not originally been a count of Edessa; neither was he a crusade veteran or related the now-ruling Courtenay family. Joscelin II, especially, but also Pons (who had earlier sought to oppose royal supremacy during Baldwin II's reign), are thus unlikely to have automatically considered him their overlord, or even worthy of their loyalty.[37] Perhaps realising that their own autonomy could not be achieved if the kingdom could re-establish its influence within Antioch, Pons and Joscelin rebelled and sought to exert their own power over the principality. Whether Alice or William of Saone were actually involved in this is far less clear. Moreover, that the majority of Antioch's nobility seemingly opposed the counts' actions – a fact reiterated by both Michael the Syrian and William of Tyre, with the latter recording that the 'nobles of the region' requested Fulk's aid – shows that the notion of royal involvement was much preferred to a potential alliance with, or perhaps subservience to, Tripoli and Edessa.[38] This was almost certainly related to the balance of power in Frankish northern Syria, which would have

---

[32] IQ, p. 215.

[33] WT, pp. 635–7.

[34] MS, III, 233.

[35] IQ, p. 215; al-Azimi, p. 130; KD, *RHC Or.* III, 664–5. See also Mallett, *Popular Muslim Reactions*, p. 83.

[36] Asbridge, 'Alice', p. 37. See also Cahen, *Syrie*, p. 350; Phillips, *Defenders*, pp. 46–9; Barber, *Crusader States*, pp. 152–3; Jotischky, *Crusading*, p. 76.

[37] Amouroux-Mourad, *Edesse*, p. 79; Richard, *Tripoli*, p. 32–6; Lewis, *Rule and Identity*, pp. 100–13.

[38] MS, III, 233; WT, pp. 635–6 (here 635): magnates illius regionis.

been irrevocably altered had the rebels succeeded, but a move to repair ties with Jerusalem was also made worthwhile by the decision to reject John Komnenos' marriage offer, as well as the growing Zengid threat – the *atabeg* used the instabilities of 1132 to launch powerful raids on the principality.[39]

Fulk swiftly demonstrated his value as an ally, and qualities as a military leader, by quashing Pons and the rebels, before eventually departing having 'entrusted the care of the principality to the noble and industrious man Renaud, surnamed Masoir'.[40] Whether this was a royally imposed appointment is unknown, and there are no suggestions of an oath of allegiance to Fulk.[41] As such, despite the move towards closer cooperation, the Antiochene aristocracy's role was seemingly undiminished: the king's mediatory and military position cannot be seen to extend to, or upon, that afforded to Baldwin II after *Ager Sanguinis*. In fact, it appears reduced. Renaud I Masoir was evidently willing to work with Fulk, though, as he witnessed two charters issued by the king at Antioch before 1136.[42] The lack of demonstrable support from the other great families in these documents could indicate some internal fractures, especially as the Sourdevals appeared in a number of Alice's charters at Latakia-Jabala.[43] However, the aristocracy often remained in their lordships (an impulse that would only have been strengthened by increased Zengid activity), and there is no clear evidence for conflict at this time between the princess, Fulk or the principality's other elites.[44] There was certainly enough of a willingness to work alongside Jerusalem in 1133/1134, as a coalition of Latin forces led by the king defeated Zengid forces at Qinnasrin and then captured Qusair.[45]

It is also significant that Fulk, in the first of his Antioch documents, issued in either January 1133 or 1134, was ascribed the title 'protector and bailiff of the principality of Antioch and of the daughter of Bohemond the younger'.[46] The role of bailiff was not as prestigious as Baldwin's earlier regency, and implies his position was more of a military protectorate; yet, it does represent an acknowledgement of his influence.[47] In spite of this, William of Tyre's comment that 'from then on, the lord king captivated all of the Antiochenes, whether they were nobles or common people, [being] fully reconciled to their hearts and having the favour of

---

[39] See pp. 24–5.

[40] WT, pp. 636–7 (here 637): cura principatus nobili et industrio viro Rainaldo cognomento Masuer commissa.

[41] William preferred to use the perfect passive participle (entrusted) over the more explicit third-person singular (he entrusted).

[42] *CCSSJ*, 73–4.

[43] Mayer, *Varia*, pp. 113–14; *CGOH*, I, 109.

[44] See pp. 95–101.

[45] WT, p. 639; al-Azimi, p. 132; IQ, pp. 222–3; IA, I, 299–300; MS, III, 233–4.

[46] *CCSSJ*, 73: rector ac bajulus Antiocheni principatus filieque Boamundi junioris. That Fulk was 'governing' (*moderante*) is also shown by Patriarch Bernard's charter, loosely dated to before September 1134. See *CGOH*, I, 102.

[47] The notion of a military protectorate can also be seen from the fact that both charters related to the possessions of the Holy Sepulchre, and to gifts made by religious figures (not secular). Moreover, that Raymond of Poitiers was made to initiate an inquest and reconfirmation of this church's rights in 1140 suggests Fulk's rulings were not considered definitive.

all', is somewhat counterbalanced by al-Azimi's observation that 'the king returned to Antioch, annoyed the population of this city and named a new duke'.[48] This may explain why Fulk was no longer given the role of Constance's protector in his second charter, issued in August 1135.[49] Such a shift in title has gone unnoticed by historians, but indicates that his standing was subject to change. The reasons for this are not immediately apparent. A total fracture is unlikely given that Fulk actively supported the nobles in their decision to approach Raymond of Poitiers as a suitable husband for Constance.[50] Royal prestige was also still such that the 1135 document was witnessed by the patriarch, the bishop of Mamistra and Renaud I Masoir. That this charter appears to have coincided with Alice's reported move from Latakia to Antioch – a move that coincided with a devastating Zengid raid on the coastal city, but which William of Tyre described as a successful bid to seize power aided by Queen Melisende's prohibition of Fulk's intervention – could be indicative.[51] That William disliked Alice, and would have been mindful of presenting any diminishing of Jerusalemite prestige in as positive light as possible, means caution must be taken in following his account.[52] It is not implausible, though, that she returned because the nobles, now hopefully awaiting Raymond's arrival, allowed her to take responsibility for her daughter's upbringing in order to prepare her for marriage. This is made all the more plausible given that even William was reluctant to point to any specific opposition to Alice's return. It would be wrong to see in this the existence of a wider anti-Jerusalem bias in Antioch, but it does appear that, by the end of 1135, the Antiochenes had strengthened their own hand at the expense of royal influence; albeit not to the extent of making a complete break.[53] In fact, any opposition to the kingdom could have impacted upon Raymond's decision to accept the offer to take the princely throne, and was made militarily dangerous by Zengi's seizure of a number of key sites on the eastern frontier in 1135.[54]

Fulk had thus been able to recover some of the prestige lost by Baldwin II in 1130, as he was afforded the position of mediator, military leader and even bailiff. Yet, it would be misleading to ascribe him too much power, particularly when compared to Baldwin II's regency of 1119–1126. Indeed, certain tensions may have existed when the king tried to exert too much administrative influence (as seen by al-Azimi's aforementioned comments regarding the duke), while there are suggestions that his role as Constance's protector was relinquished by August 1135. Although the Antiochenes appear to have supported some royal involvement

48   WT, p. 639: extunc cepit dominus rex omnium Antiochenorum, indifferenter tam procerum quam popularium, corda plenius reconciliata et omnium habere favorem; al-Azimi, p. 132.
49   *CCSSJ*, 74: bajulus et tutor Antiocheni principatus.
50   See pp. 70–3.
51   WT, p. 658; IQ, pp. 238–9; KD, *RHC Or.* III, 672; IA, I, 327; MS, III, 245.
52   William's account has still been readily accepted. See Phillips, *Defenders*, pp. 53–67; Cahen, *Syrie*, pp. 356–8; Hamilton, 'Ralph of Domfront', p. 1–21. Cf. Asbridge, 'Alice', pp. 44–6; and pp. 70–1 of this book.
53   This is also evidenced by the frequent interaction between Antioch and Jerusalem once Raymond acceded to the throne (see below).
54   See pp. 25–6.

in the principality, primarily in a military setting, a diminution in the kingdom's status had occurred, one which instead placed greater responsibility in the hands of the nobility.

Baldwin III and Amalric at Antioch, 1149–1153 and 1161–1165

The issue of Jerusalemite regency again emerged following Raymond's death at Inab in 1149. William of Tyre noted that Baldwin III, upon 'hearing of the perils in those parts, and having learned of the death of the lord prince, was greatly concerned', and so 'hastened to the Antiochenes' lands' – seemingly accompanied by a force of Templars.[55] The king thence carried out an inconclusive campaign against Nur al-Din before the latter agreed to a truce and retired.[56] Although the Zengid ruler's withdrawal is unlikely to have directly resulted from Baldwin's intervention, the king had made an important contribution to the city's defence. However, it is of interest that William of Tyre did not explicitly state that the Antiochenes had called the king north, as he had done in relation to the earlier ventures of Baldwin II and Fulk. Michael the Syrian even reported that internal divisions had initially emerged after Inab over whether to approach Jerusalem or simply surrender to Nur al-Din.[57] This was perhaps the result of Raymond's oath of homage given to Manuel Komnenos in 1145, which recognised Byzantium's position as overlord, or even tension over the Second Crusade's decision to ignore northern Syria – an eventuality which, as will be examined below, Baldwin may have contributed to.[58] It may also have been influenced by the apparent absence of the greater aristocracy at Inab, with the probable exception of Renaud of Marash, who are unlikely to have abandoned their lordships while Nur al-Din raided the principality.[59] Given that the nobles had earlier acted as the driving force behind approaching Jerusalem, as well as setting the terms of royal power within Antioch, their non-attendance perhaps led to uncertainty over whether to approach Baldwin, even if his offer to help is unlikely to have been rejected once he arrived.

The king was reportedly able to gain some prominence, though. William of Tyre noted that Baldwin 'delayed at Antioch, conducting the care of the destitute regions; whereby, having organised the affairs according to the place and time, [and] having restored tranquillity for a certain time … he returned into his kingdom'.[60] It was

---

[55]   WT, pp. 772–4 (here 773): audiens illarum partium pericula et morte domini principis cognita mente plurimum consternatus … celer ad partes convolat Antiochenas; Louis VII, 'Epistolae', *RHGF* XV, 540–1.

[56]   WT, pp. 772–4; Louis VII, 'Epistolae', *RHGF* XV, 540–1; William of Newburgh, I, 67–8; 'Sigeberti Gemblacensis, Continuatio Praemonstratensis', *MGH SS* VI, 454–5; IQ, pp. 294–5; KD, *ROL* 3, 522–3; IA, II, 36; AS, *RHC Or.* IV, 63.

[57]   MS, III, 290.

[58]   WT, pp. 756–69.

[59]   *Ibid.*, p. 772–4.

[60]   *Ibid.*, p. 774: apud Antiochiam, destitute regionis curam agens, adhuc moram faciens; ubi compositis pro loco et tempore negociis, tranquilitate aliquatenus restituta … in regnum suum est reversus.

also added that the principality was now under Baldwin's protection.[61] Although Barber has pointed to the king's limited resources, as well as the distraction of the regnal crisis with his mother, Queen Melisende, both Cahen and Jotischky have argued that Baldwin thus had the status of regent.[62] Baldwin may indeed have sought to install Joscelin II of Edessa as governor, with William of Tyre reporting that the count was called to Antioch by Patriarch Aimery and the *1234 Chronicle* noting that Joscelin hoped to seize Antioch (albeit not after having been invited to do so).[63] Yet, the Antiochenes proved unprepared to hand over administration to an external power, which would have been all the more pertinent in relation to Joscelin, who had earlier fallen into dispute with Raymond. As such, the reports of other non-Latin sources which simply state that Joscelin was in the vicinity of Antioch to raid or to meet a ship are probably more accurate.[64] There is also a need to be more careful in assuming Baldwin had such authority, as Constance remained to lead the principality's administration – issuing two independent charters in this period as *Antiochenorum principissa*; while the lack of disruption to the composition of the aristocracy ensured that local military leadership remained.[65] A power vacuum similar to that which had provided Baldwin II with strong influence after *Ager Sanguinis* certainly cannot be identified.

Barber's claim that Baldwin was unable to attempt to intervene due to financial and political limitations nevertheless overlooks this king's frequent incursions into northern Syria over the following years. During this time, he presided over the sale of the final remnants of the county of Edessa to Manuel Komnenos and led an armed withdrawal of refugees from the region with the support of Antiochene aristocratic forces under Robert II of Sourdeval, which demonstrates royal influence in the county and the continued prominence of military alliances.[66] However, when he sought to impose a new husband on Constance at a hastily called general Council of the Latin East at Tripoli in around 1151, the first of its kind since Baldwin I's intervention to halt Tancred's attempts to become involved in the succession of the county of Tripoli in 1109 and 1110, he was less successful.[67] As Hodgson has rightly noted, the king followed here the established Western protocol for overlords when seeking to intervene in the inheritance of a female heir by offering three suitors from which to choose.[68] This lays bare the status Baldwin III hoped to claim. Yet, whereas earlier kings had effectively enforced their will on Antioch and had helped to establish unity through marriage alliances, Constance obstinately refused to accept any of the proposed candidates, preferring instead to request

[61] *Ibid.*, pp. 795–7 (here 796): sub … protectione principatus.
[62] Barber, *Crusader States*, pp. 194–6; Cahen, *Syrie*, pp. 384–91; Jotischky, *Crusading*, pp. 91–2.
[63] WT, p. 774; *1234*, II, 116; Phillips, *Defenders*, pp. 118–25.
[64] IA, II, 39; KD, *ROL* 3, 523; MS, III, 295; GBE, I, 276.
[65] *CGOH*, I, 190, 198. See also pp. 115–17 of this book.
[66] WT, pp. 780–5.
[67] *Ibid.*, pp. 785–6. On the earlier councils, see Asbridge, *Creation*, pp. 115–23.
[68] Hodgson, *Women*, pp. 73–4.

a husband from Manuel Komnenos.[69] This clearly established the limits of royal interference: military aid was welcome, political intervention was not. Even when Constance married Renaud of Châtillon, a knight in Baldwin's service, there is no secure evidence that the king imposed this union. William of Tyre did comment that the princess had decided upon her new husband in private and had 'refused to publicise her decision until she [had] the consensus of the lord king, who was her cousin and under whose protection the principality seemed to remain, lest she seem to intervene in [his] authority'.[70] Unsurprisingly, the Jerusalemite William sought to portray Baldwin as Antioch's regent, whose permission had to be gained before a husband could be found for Constance – a reality which has not truly been questioned by historians.[71] Significantly, this view of royal influence is in stark contrast to the events at Tripoli in 1151, and there are no indications that the king's assent was sought, or needed to be gained, when approaching Byzantium for a husband. Baldwin's permission would have been needed to release Renaud from an oath of fealty, however, while the comment in *Eracles* that '[Baldwin] was pleased that he would not have to defend a land which was so far away' is likely quite accurate.[72] It cannot be accepted, though, that Constance needed royal assent to marry, nor that the king had enough political influence, either to force a suitor or to be considered a regent. The implementation of Jerusalemite supremacy during this particular interregnum thus proved difficult, with indications that underlying tensions emerged when attempts were made at political interference, as opposed to providing military aid. Royal involvement was clearly less favourable than the king may have hoped, perhaps as a result of Constance's age – she was now old enough to rule in her own name – and the survival of the majority of the principality's internal power structures after Inab.

Despite this, Baldwin III renewed his interest in northern Syria after the incarceration of Renaud of Châtillon in November 1161. Indeed, William of Tyre observed that:

> with the prince thus captured, the provinces of Antioch were devoid of leadership [and] solace. The people of those regions were again fearful and anxious lest they be carried away ... and [so], at length, they looked to have recourse to their usual source of aid ... They therefore sent a legation to confer tearful distress to the lord king of the Jerusalemites.[73]

---

69   WT, pp. 785–6; JK, pp. 96–7.

70   WT, p. 796: noluit autem verbum publicari quoadusque domini regis, cuius erat consobrina et sub cuius protectione principatus videbatur consistere, interveniret auctoritatis et consensus.

71   Cahen, *Syrie*, p. 391; Schlumberger, *Renaud*, p. 21; Phillips, *Defenders*, p. 126; Barber, *Crusader States*, p. 206; Hamilton, 'Elephant of Christ', pp. 97–108.

72   *Eracles*, II, pp. 179–81 (here 180): volentiers de décharja de garder la terre qui estoit loing. Baldwin's relief is also noted in Phillips, *Defenders*, p. 126; Barber, *Crusader States*, p. 206; Cahen, *Syrie*, p. 391.

73   WT, p. 854: capto igitur principe et Antiochia provincia rectoris solatio destitute, populus iterum regionis timore et anxietate corripitur ... tandemque visum est ad solitum recurrere auxilium ... missis ergo legatione et adiunctis precibus lacrimosis, dominum regem Ierosolimorum.

The events surrounding this were examined in the previous chapter, where it was argued that Constance and Manuel Komnenos willingly worked together to undermine the king's hopes of preventing increased imperial involvement at Antioch by negotiating a marriage between the emperor and Maria of Antioch.[74] Consequently, Baldwin sought to place Patriarch Aimery in charge of governance instead of the princess, likely in punishment for her part in this subterfuge.[75] As such, Marshall Baldwin suggested that in spite of Constance's actions, the king's arrival heralded the creation of a bailliage, similar to that exercised by Fulk in the 1130s. There is no actual evidence Baldwin ever had this title, though, and it is unlikely that either Constance (who retained her prominence until at least 1163) or the emperor were prepared to afford the king too much power in northern Syria.[76] With imperial overlordship securely implemented after 1158, Jerusalem's ability to interfere at Antioch was severely limited, especially regarding the notion of regency. In this context, it is significant that when the dispute arose over Bohemond III's succession in 1163, there were no suggestions that Jerusalem was asked, or sought, to intervene. Baldwin III's death that year perhaps accounted for this, although it may also serve to explain William of Tyre's decision not to report on these events.[77]

Nevertheless, this did not preclude King Amalric from potentially attempting to intervene at Antioch. In 1163, he dispatched letters to the West calling for aid against imperial designs in Antioch, and then, in 1164, he came north following Bohemond III's capture at the battle of Artah.[78] William of Tyre noted that, when Amalric received word of this disaster, he immediately withdrew from a campaign in Egypt – which had likely prompted Nur al-Din's desire to strike at Antioch – and

> having been called so that he would come by the Antiochenes, who hoped that he might provide solace for their afflictions, for their affairs were almost desperate, [and] being taken by fraternity, he [Amalric] called his men and hastened with speed on the road to Antioch along with the count of Flanders. Arriving promptly, he therefore carried out of the affairs of the lord prince with as much diligence and concern as he had become accustomed to manage his own lands with.[79]

Having reportedly placed each of the principality's cities in the hands of 'wise men', Amalric returned south, continuing to seek Bohemond's release, which was eventu-

---

[74] See pp. 209–12.
[75] WT, pp. 854–5.
[76] Baldwin, 'Latin States', p. 546. See also Cahen, Syrie, pp. 405–6; Mayer, Varia, p. 48.
[77] See pp. 80–4.
[78] Louis VII, 'Epistolae', RHGF XVI, 39 –40, 60–1; WT, pp. 874–5; 'Sigeberti Gemblacensis, Continuatio Aquicinctina', MGH SS VI, 411; Robert of Torigny, I, 223–4; KD, ROL 3, 538–41; IA, II, 145–9; AS, RHC Or. IV, 108–9; MS, III, 324–6; 1234, II, 121–2.
[79] WT, pp. 877–9 (here 877–8): vocatus ab Antiochenis ut rebus eorum pene desperatis subveniret, vocantibus eis fraterna assumpto secum comite Flandrense maturatis itineribus Antiochiam properat, eorum afflictioni optata solatis prestiturus. Adveniens ergo presensque factus negocia domini principis tanta diligentia tantaque sollicitudine, quanta vix propria tractare consueverat. See also Louis VII, 'Epistolae', RHGF XVI, 79; 'Continuatio Aquicinctina', MGH SS VI, 411.

ally secured due to 'the pressing of the *fideles* and friends of the same [Prince Bohemond]'.[80] The extent of his influence here can be questioned, for it was not Amalric who paid for Bohemond's ransom, rather Manuel: to whom the prince made a personal visit upon his release in 1165 and who had clear motives for intervening in the release of an Antiochene ruler, as well as the imperial *dux* of Cilicia.[81] Historians have nevertheless ascribed the king with a key role in negotiations, with Barber suggesting Amalric may even have 'advised' Bohemond to go to Constantinople to gain funds – although Yvonne Friedman has demonstrated that royal involvement in paying ransoms was not established practice in the kingdom of Jerusalem.[82] This cannot be securely accepted, particularly because Amalric had only recently urged Louis VII of France to support him in combating imperial encroachment, making it unlikely that the king would have promoted such an action (even if the scale of the defeat at Artah possibly heralded a change in his stance). While it does appear that Amalric's defensive support was welcomed, caution must again be urged in accepting that this acted as recognition of his authority in Antioch. Indeed, Amalric may simply have acted out of concern for the security of the kingdom, with Nur al-Din offered a freer hand to attack Jerusalem and Egypt if the principality was neutralised.[83] The difference between military ally and political overlord may be subtle, but it reflects a clear differentiation in the dynamics of power.

In the decades following Bohemond II's death in 1130, therefore, the kings of Jerusalem faced strong challenges when attempting to recover the position of regent, which Baldwin II had so securely held in the 1120s. This did not preclude influence, as can be seen by Fulk's involvement before Raymond of Poitiers' accession and the frequent courting of military aid, but there are significant indications that the monarchs found their path to authority blocked by staunch Antiochene opposition whenever an effort was made to assert control over administration or politics. This led to embarrassing political situations, such as the failed council of Tripoli or the negotiations for Maria of Antioch's marriage to Manuel, and ties to the Byzantines now frequently accounted for Jerusalem's reduced status. It should be noted that, in contrast to Amalric's attempts to intervene in Bohemond III's release from captivity in 1164, when the prince was released from his Armenian imprisonment at the hands of Leon in 1195, it was said to have happened through the intervention of the then king of Jerusalem, Henry of Champagne.[84] However, this was not as part of a regency and came at a time when Greek influence had entirely dissipated. For most of the twelfth century, as the relationship between Antioch and Byzantium had shifted, so had the dynamic between the principality and the kingdom of Jerusalem.

---

80   WT, p. 878: prudentibus viris ... cum eiusdem fidelibus et amicis satagens.
81   See pp. 212–13.
82   Cahen, *Syrie*, p. 411; Richard, *Kingdom of Jerusalem*, I, 47; Barber, *Crusader States*, pp. 240–1; Elisséeff, *Nur ad-Din*, II, 598–9; Friedman, *Encounter between Enemies*, p. 83.
83   Asbridge, *Crusades*, pp. 259–61.
84   *CGT*, pp. 128–32; MS, III, 411; Sempad, *Chronique*, pp. 68, 71–2; IS, pp. 256–7.

Jerusalem as the Head of *Outremer*

Nevertheless, the kingdom of Jerusalem continues to be traditionally viewed as the premier Latin power in *Outremer*. Even those historians who argue against formalised legal bonds accept that the kingdom was the leader of an association of polities in the Latin East. Yet, the diminishing of the king's role as regent of the principality during periods of crisis after 1130 has now been established: replaced with a greater preference for closer ties with Byzantium and an opposition to overbearing Jerusalemite political interference. It will be contended here, moreover, that this not only also appears to have been the case when Antioch was not in danger, but that there are also suggestions that the principality's rulers sought to mount their own challenge to become head of *Outremer*.

Antioch, Jerusalem and the County of Edessa

Before 1130, the kingdom of Jerusalem and the county of Edessa shared a powerful bond, resulting from the fact that the Holy City's first two kings were also formerly counts. This ensured Edessa's lords were vassals of the kingdom, despite attempts by Tancred and Roger to assert their own influence there.[85] Ties between the two powers continued even into the early 1130s, as Joscelin I accompanied Baldwin II to Antioch in the wake of Bohemond II's death, with Michael the Syrian reporting that he was the king's vassal.[86] However, as shown above, the elder count's heir, Joscelin II, demonstrated his unwillingness to follow in his father's political footsteps by assuming a prominent part in the aforementioned upheavals of 1132. Importantly, there are indications that this shift in the dynamics of the Latin states subsequently presented Raymond of Poitiers with the chance to replace the king as the county's overlord.

Indeed, when William of Tyre accused Joscelin II of deliberately undermining John Komnenos' attack on Shaizar in 1138 by leading Raymond astray, it was suggested that the count had done so 'against his lord, the said prince [of Antioch]'.[87] When the Edessan then issued a charter in favour of the Hospitallers in 1141, he dated his document with reference to Raymond's position as prince, which Amouroux-Mourad considered 'irrefutable proof' of the principality's suzerainty over Edessa.[88] This is perhaps too definitive a statement, but there is some further corroboration for an evolving relationship in the account of Gregory the Priest. The Armenian author wrote that, when Joscelin II fell into dispute with a certain Simon, who seized Aintab, this would have incited an extended period of open civil war had peace not been restored 'through the intervention of the prince of Antioch'.[89]

[85] Amouroux-Mourad, *Edesse*, pp. 80–4; Asbridge, *Creation*, pp. 104–28.
[86] WT, pp. 623–5; MS, III, p. 230.
[87] WT, p. 676: adversus dominum suum, principem videlicet.
[88] *CGOH*, I, 137; Amouroux-Mourad, *Edesse*, p. 112, n. 18.
[89] GP, p. 242. Kamal Salibi argued that this Simon was a Maronite, although this is not particularly clear. See *Maronite Historians of Mediaeval Lebanon* (Beirut, 1959), pp. 50–1.

By recognising Raymond's right to adjudicate over such a dispute, it would certainly appear that the Antiochene ruler now enjoyed a certain level of political influence within Edessa, perhaps having replaced the king of Jerusalem as its overlord.[90] The reason for this apparent change has not been recorded. William of Tyre's failure to comment on Edessa's shift in allegiance away from Jerusalem – despite his usual vociferous dislike of the county's ruling Courtenay family – suggests it was either so embarrassing as to warrant suppression, or that it was not a particularly controversial matter.[91] His comments regarding Joscelin II's ties to Raymond recommend it was not a matter of ignorance, and William's conversations with the count's half-sister, Abbess Stephany, probably ensured he was well informed.[92] Given that close indications of a growing bond between Edessa and Antioch appear to have emerged early in Raymond's reign through Joscelin's involvement in the campaigns against Leon in 1136 and at Montferrand in 1137, it is possible that growing Armenian and Zengid power provided an impetus for an alliance – even if the count's presence in Cilicia is said to have resulted from his desire to forge a friendly agreement between the prince and the Rupenids (to whom he was related by marriage).[93] Perhaps a more likely context is John Komnenos' arrival in northern Syria in 1137. Indeed, the reality of imperial involvement in *Outremer* was a threat to both polities, and so it may have been considered prudent to show subservience to Antioch in order that the county would be protected through Raymond's treaty with the emperor. Fulk was in no position to resist Byzantine incursions, with Zengi's growing interest in Damascus meaning that it benefitted the kingdom that matters in the county would not demand royal interest. In this context, it is unsurprising that the king seemingly showed no opposition to this move.

Regardless, demonstrations of Raymond's active overlordship are not always so forthcoming. Alongside John Komnenos' apparently unopposed move on Tell Bashir in 1142, designed seemingly to prevent Joscelin II from intervening at Antioch, this is also shown by the events surround the fall of Edessa in 1144.[94] William of Tyre reported that, on the eve of Zengi's capture that city, the situation in northern Syria

> had become exceedingly dangerous because of the hatred that had arisen between Raymond, prince of the Antiochenes, and Joscelin, count of the same city [Edessa] … [as] there was enmity between the prince of the Antiochenes and the count, which was no longer secret but had proceeded all the way to open hatred.[95]

90 On mediation more generally, see W. Davis and P. Fouracre, 'Conclusion', *The Settlement of Disputes in Early Medieval Europe*, ed. W. Davis and P. Fouracre (Cambridge, 1986), pp. 207–40; Benham, *Peacemaking*.
91 Hamilton, 'Titular Nobility', pp. 197–203.
92 See pp. 8–9.
93 Sempad, *RHC Arm.* I, 616; WT, pp. 665–7.
94 WT, pp. 700–1.
95 *Ibid.*, pp. 718–20 (here 718): simultatibus, que inter principem Antiochenum Raimundum et eiusdem comitem civitatis Ioscelinum exorte fuerant nimis periculose … erant autem … inter princ-ipem Antiochenum et comitem inimicite, non iam occulte, sed que iam usque ad odium processerant manifestum.

The Latin author then accused Raymond of taking joy in seeing Edessa's fall, a criticism potentially supported by the Armenian *Lament on Edessa* authored by Nerses Snorhali.[96] Jotischky has even suggested that Zengi's success was a direct consequence of 'the inability of Joscelin II and Raymond of Poitiers to recreate the vigorous, if stormy, partnership between Count Baldwin and Tancred in the early period of Frankish settlement'.[97] Phillips has urged more caution, noting that Manuel Komnenos' attack on the principality earlier in 1144 would have weakened Raymond and hampered his ability to react, while Ibn al-Qalanisi's report of reinforcements gathering at Antioch – only to be defeated by Zengi – intimates that some efforts were made at relief.[98] Raymond proved reluctant to personally intervene in Edessa's military problems, though, as he refused to aid Joscelin II and Baldwin of Marash in their fateful attempt to recover Edessa in 1146.[99] It might be argued that this was so that more time could be given to awaiting either Byzantine or Latin reinforcements, but it is perhaps significant that in 1148 Raymond subsequently attempted to direct the forces of the Second Crusade against Aleppo, not Edessa – the city the venture had been launched to save.[100]

While Edessa's fall ended the need for formal relations, enduring bonds can still be discerned after this point in the figure of Joscelin III. The titular count, later seneschal of the kingdom of Jerusalem, was involved in Antiochene raiding in 1159/1160 and perhaps contributed to the castellany of Harim.[101] Furthermore, Bohemond III described this same Joscelin as his 'liegeman' when donating a fief to him in 1179.[102] Thus, while Antioch's relationship to the county of Edessa was complicated, it does nonetheless represent a challenge to royal intervention in the northern crusader states, which can again be viewed in the context of the pervading influence of Byzantium. Jerusalem's position as the head of the Latin East was clearly being undermined.

Renaud of Châtillon and Baldwin III

This can also be discerned from the relationship between Renaud of Châtillon and Baldwin III. It was noted earlier that Baldwin would likely have initially favoured Renaud's appointment as prince, not simply because it helped to strengthen the security of the principality, but he may also have expected his former vassal to prove a more favourable ally than Raymond of Poitiers. This was not to be the case.

In summer 1157, a coalition of Christian forces laid siege to Shaizar under the leadership of Renaud, Baldwin III, Thierry of Flanders and Thoros of Armenia. It

---

[96] *Ibid.*, pp. 718–20; T. M. Van Lint, 'Seeking Meaning in Catastrophe, Nerses Snorhali's Lament on Edessa', *East and West in the Crusader States II*, ed. K. Ciggaar and H. Teule (Leuven, 1999), p. 53.

[97] Jotischky, *Crusading*, p. 78.

[98] Phillips, *Defenders*, pp. 73–4; IQ, p. 269.

[99] WT, pp. 734–8; IQ, pp. 274–5; KD, *ROL* 3, 514–15; IA, II, 8; MS, III, 270–1; *1234*, II, 104–9; GP, pp. 244–5.

[100] WT, pp. 754–7. See also pp. 37–8 of this book.

[101] See pp. 143–6.

[102] *Tabulae Theutonici*, 9: hominio ligio.

was a particularly opportune moment to strike, as Muslim Syria was still reeling from a devastating earthquake which had destroyed fortifications near to Aleppo, as well as Hama and Homs, while a potentially life-threatening illness had struck Nur al-Din. The Christian forces enacted a swift and effective attack which soon promised to ensure the fortress's capture, but the siege broke down when Baldwin noted his preference to place Thierry in control of Shaizar.[103] William of Tyre recorded that, in response to this, 'Prince Renaud embroidered quibbles, saying that this city, with its appurtenances, had been part of the inheritance of the principality of Antioch from the beginning, and therefore required that whomsoever should possess it shall have to swear fealty to the prince of Antioch.'[104] Thierry was reportedly taken aback by this request, insisting 'never to have sworn fealty except to kings', with Renaud accused of 'carelessness and insolent temerity' in one Flemish monastic account.[105] The siege thus dispersed in failure, and although it is true that a subsequent attack on Harim was successful, it cannot be ignored that the prince of Antioch had resolutely repudiated Baldwin's claim as head of *Outremer*.[106] Phillips has plausibly suggested that this was in response to the potential threat to the principality which might have emerged through the creation of a rival Latin power in northern Syria.[107] Likewise, Renaud may also have opposed the move for fear that he would have been called upon to take some responsibility for Shaizar's defences in the likely eventuality that Thierry returned to the West – a duty made increasingly difficult by the loss of the eastern frontier and growing Isma'ili power.[108] Steven Runciman once pointedly remarked of these events that 'Baldwin could only solve the difficulty by abandoning the disputed territory', and it certainly seems that, in opposition to Grousset's belief that Renaud was Baldwin's 'baron', the king actually displayed a level of ineffectual authority here which belies suggestions of even notional suzerainty.[109]

Significantly, the same is also true for Manuel Komnenos' visit to Antioch in 1158, for Renaud and the emperor carried out the mainstay of negotiations entirely separate of the king, whose influence over proceedings was minimal. There are indications amongst the Greek sources that Baldwin sought to take Antioch under his sway – perhaps having grown disillusioned by the prince's stubborn actions at Shaizar – but historiographical belief in a *condominium* proves inaccurate. The king was not ignored, and, by accepting Baldwin's request to lighten the principality's

---

[103] WT, pp. 834–6; IQ, pp. 328–9, 341–4; KD, *ROL* 3, 528–31; IA, II, 87–9; AS, *RHC Or.* IV, 92–6; MS, III, 315–16; *1234*, II, 118–19; GP, pp. 267, 270–1.

[104] WT, p. 836: Princeps Rainaldus ambages intexuit, dicens urbem illam cum suis pertinentiis ab initio hereditatis Antiocheni principis portionem esse ideoque oportere ut quicumque eam possideat, Antiocheno principi fidelitatem exhibeat.

[105] *Ibid.*, p. 837: nunquam nisi regibus fidelitatem exhibuisse; 'Auctarium Affligemense', *MGH SS* VI, 403: incuria et insolenti temeritate.

[106] WT, pp. 838–40.

[107] Phillips, *Defenders*, pp. 270–81.

[108] See pp. 38–43.

[109] S. Runciman, *A History of the Crusades*, 3 vols (Cambridge, 1951–1954), II, 349; Grousset, *Croisades*, II, 370–1. See also Richard, *Kingdom of Jerusalem*, I, 45.

military service and allowing him a role in the procession into Antioch, Manuel demonstrated his appreciation that Jerusalem was a useful ally. Nevertheless, it would be wrong to confuse the emperor's hopes of securing the kingdom as a satellite state with recognition of Baldwin's place as head of an association of *Outremer*. This was most evidently demonstrated in 1161/1162, when Constance and Manuel (and potentially also Renaud) allied to embarrass Baldwin over the marriage of Maria of Antioch.[110]

The period of Renaud's tenure was thus one of great difficulty for Jerusalem, as Baldwin's right to intervene was continually called into question – just as it had been during the interregnum following Raymond's death. Through the rise of imperial influence in northern Syria, hopes that royal influence might be increased during a period of instability, or through the presence of a former Jerusalemite vassal on the princely throne, were dashed. Contrary to the traditional belief that the kingdom held sway within Antioch as a result of its participation in a *condominium*, implemented in conjunction with Byzantium, it appears rather that the princely house rejected such attempts by taking a more active and independent stance. This did not preclude joint military action, nor did it mean that the Antiochenes and Byzantines ignored the need to court Jerusalem's goodwill, yet it would be misleading to see in this genuine regnal authority.

Bohemond III and the Kingdom of Jerusalem

Indeed, over the longer term, secure Byzantine overlordship over the principality distinctly restricted Jerusalemite influence in northern Syria. As noted above, Amalric does not appear to have immediately recognised this, dispatching letters to the West in 1163 which called for aid against imperial designs in Antioch, and also attempting to intervene after Artah.[111] However, his impact was limited and there is no sense of a formal recognition of his position as suzerain of *Outremer*, as opposed to a military ally.

Instances of royal intervention in the principality became even more minimal after this point. The exception to this is Amalric's support against Mleh in the early 1170s, during which the king, having heard of the Armenian warlord's actions against the Templars and Byzantine forces in Cilicia, 'descended into the regions of Antioch with [his] household escort, hoping to insert into this region the peace which he had in his'.[112] With Jerusalem's forces combined to those of Bohemond III, and potentially also the Greeks, Mleh was brought to heel; and Lilie has therefore posited that Manuel had requested that the king carry out this venture during the latter's visit to Constantinople in 1171.[113] Amalric had certainly proved largely disinterested in Antioch before 1172, focused as he was on the struggle for Egypt;

[110] See pp. 209–12; and Buck, 'Between Byzantium and Jerusalem?', pp. 109–18.
[111] See pp. 229–30.
[112] WT, pp. 948–50 (here 949): *partes suas in his que ad pacem sunt interponere cupiens, cum familiari comitatu ad partes descendit Antiochenas.*
[113] WT, pp. 948–50; JK, pp. 214–17; MS, III, 337; Lilie, *Byzantium*, p. 205.

yet there were factors which ensured that he could not simply ignore Nur al-Din's alliance with Mleh. As suggested in Chapter 1, this *détente* undermined the king's earlier efforts to promote Armenian emigration into the kingdom. Importantly, it also provided the Zengid ruler with enough security in northern Syria to push his claims to Egypt.[114] Chevalier has argued that the king may also have been pressed to intervene by the Templars, although this is perhaps unlikely given the Order's refusal to participate in Amalric's Egyptian campaign of 1168.[115] Consequently, while the propensity for military alliance amongst the Latin states again appears prominent, enough mitigating factors exist to ensure that it cannot be accepted that these events reflect Antiochene recognition of Jerusalemite supremacy, rather than a simple recognition of mutual benefit.

These severe limitations to Jerusalem's political influence were to be compounded during the reign of the leprous King Baldwin IV. It is true that he provided indirect military support for Bohemond III's joint venture against Harim with Count Phillip of Flanders and Raymond III of Tripoli in 1177, as well as in response to the prince's request for knights against Saladin in 1183.[116] Nevertheless, the king's illness meant he could not personally participate, nor was he able to properly intervene in the noble rebellion of 1180–1182, despite the suggestion that, in 'bearing the appropriate concern', he dispatched a high-profile embassy from the kingdom in the hope of mediating a settlement.[117] Cahen, along with the modern translators of William of Tyre, wrongly interpreted *sollicitudinem* as 'responsibility', which led to the assumption that it was the king's *duty* to intervene in the internal disputes of the principality – in turn implying overlordship.[118] However, 'concern' is far more appropriate translation, and it seems instead that Baldwin simply understood the gravity of the situation: a civil war in Antioch threatened to provide Saladin with the chance to again intervene at Aleppo, while Barber has posited that there may even have been fears it would put off Western aid.[119] William of Tyre acknowledged the limits of Baldwin's influence, noting that the king 'hesitated to use force, lest, wishing to resist, [Bohemond] would call on the assistance of enemy strength'.[120] Even though this was probably an attempt to denounce Bohemond III in a similar fashion to the accusations levelled at Alice in 1130, such an admission regarding the bounds of Jerusalemite authority was rare.[121] Baldwin evidently felt the need to

---

[114] Dédéyan, 'Un projet de colonisation', pp. 101–40; Cahen, *Syrie*, p. 441; Barber, *Crusader States*, pp. 231–61. See also pp. 48–51 of this book.

[115] Chevalier, *Ordres*, p. 110; Barber, *New Knighthood*, pp. 95–7.

[116] On 1177, see WT, pp. 979–86; MS, III, pp. 375–6; *1234*, II, 142–3. For 1183, see WT, pp. 1046–8.

[117] WT, pp. 1012–15 (here 1014): debitam gerentes sollicitudinem. See also MS, III, pp. 388–9; and Buck, 'Noble Rebellion', pp. 105–6.

[118] William of Tyre, *A History of Deeds Done Beyond the Sea*, 2 vols, trans. E. W. Babcock and A. C. Krey (New York, 1943), II, 455; Cahen, *Syrie*, p. 423.

[119] Barber, *Crusader States*, p. 277. See also pp. 51–4 of this book.

[120] WT, p. 1015: vim inferre dubitant, ne forte, hostium viribus et rogatis auxiliis volens resistere.

[121] The weakness of Baldwin's position has been accepted by historians. See Mayer, *Varia*, p. 130, 166–7; Cahen, *Syrie*, p. 423; Hamilton, *Leper King*, p. 165.

act to prevent disastrous consequences, but the extent to which his influence was formally recognised in Antioch is far less clear.

Perhaps of greater significance to an understanding of the balance of power in the Latin East at this point are the allied efforts of Bohemond III and Raymond III to intervene in Jerusalem.[122] As a leper, Baldwin was unable to marry or produce an heir, and so the succession passed to his sister, Sybil. She was originally married to William of Montferrat in 1176, but he soon died, albeit not before impregnating his new wife. This created the need to find a new husband for Sybil, who could act as regent until her son, the future Baldwin V, came of age. It was in the context of this problem that Bohemond and Raymond now seemingly sought to intervene.[123] The prince and count, who were both descendants of King Baldwin II of Jerusalem and perhaps considered the kingdom's succession part of their familial duty, appear to have initially forged a close relationship during the former's struggle for accession. As such, Raymond witnessed a document issued by Bohemond at Latakia in 1163, and was only prevented from future support by his incarceration after the battle of Artah.[124] The pair nevertheless reunited following Raymond's release in 1174 and soon turned their collective attentions onto Jerusalem.[125] Indeed, both were present at Jerusalem in 1177 for discussions with Count Philip of Flanders over Baldwin IV's succession, the appointment of Renaud of Châtillon as regent and also whether to utilise a Byzantine fleet gathered at Acre for a joint venture against Egypt.[126] That Philip decided to oppose the campaign in North Africa, and to instead fight along- side Bohemond and Raymond in northern Syria, could indicate some amount of subterfuge. William of Tyre certainly suggested so with his barbed comment that:

> there were some who claimed that it was because of the lord prince of Antioch, who was present, and the count of Tripoli, that the count [of Flanders] was so opposed to the campaign in Egypt. Moreover, it was said, they strove to drag him to their regions, hoping in any way to accost him for his help, caring [only] for the growth of their own lands.[127]

Hamilton and Mayer have accepted the validity of this, and it certainly hints at a lack of responsibility for Jerusalem's safety given that Saladin had already gath- ered a sizeable force to meet the planned invasion.[128] However, it should also be noted that Philip appears to have been a disruptive presence in Jerusalem, while

[122] This is also examined in Mayer, *Varia*, pp. 123–37.

[123] Hamilton, *Leper King*, pp. 109–19.

[124] *CGOH*, I, 311.

[125] Mayer (*Varia*, p. 126) argued that stylistic indications suggest Constantine (eventually an Anti- ochene cleric) drafted a charter issued by Raymond III at Jerusalem in December 1174, and thus hypothesised that Bohemond III was also present, but this remains somewhat speculative.

[126] WT, pp. 979–86.

[127] *Ibid.*, p. 985: Erant nonnulli qui domino principi Antiocheno, qui presens erat, et domino comiti Tripolitano imputabant quod comes ita erat adversus profectioni in Egyptum: nitebantur enim, ut dicitur, ad suas eum partes trahere, sperantes eius auxilio aliquid adoriri ad incrementum regionem suarum respiciens.

[128] Hamilton, *Leper King*, pp. 119–31; Mayer, *Varia*, pp. 127–8. See also Cahen, *Syrie*, p. 419.

the king's support for the venture in northern Syria argues against strong tension between the rulers of the Latin East – a view also adopted by Phillips.[129] Likewise, the *Continuatio Aquicinctina*, a contemporary French source usually well informed on the affairs of the counts of Flanders, suggested that Bohemond had only invited Philip once the count had fallen into dispute with the Templars and could no longer remain in Jerusalem.[130] It remains possible that Bohemond and Raymond *had* opposed the attack on Egypt, perhaps remembering that Nur al-Din had earlier used a similar venture to inflict a chastening assault on the principality in 1164, or fearing that Saladin might use this as a way of uniting Muslim Syria to him under the banner of *jihad*. As a consequence, they promoted a campaign in northern Syria instead. Of greater importance, though, is that both were evidently looking to increase their involvement in Jerusalemite affairs.

This came to a head in 1179/1180, when, not long after both offered support to Baldwin IV by helping to preside over an agreement between the Templars and Hospitallers, it is reported that:

> the lord Bohemond, prince of the Antiochenes, and the lord Raymond, count of Tripoli, entering the kingdom with soldiers, terrified the lord king, who feared lest they attempt to undertake a revolution, namely they wished to claim the kingdom for themselves by stealing the throne from the king.[131]

Baldwin's response was to hastily marry Sybil to Guy of Lusignan, a Poitevin nobleman who proved to be a divisive character.[132] Hamilton, among others, has thus interpreted Bohemond and Raymond's actions as no less than an attempted coup, aimed at imposing their chosen suitor for Sybil – who Asbridge suggests was Baldwin of Ibelin (Raymond's stepson).[133] The validity of this is difficult to ascertain, as even William of Tyre was cautious to reserve comment on whether the king was correct to be frightened. Nonetheless, these events at least indicate that the two rulers were considered both interested and powerful enough to claim an influence over the Jerusalemite succession. This almost certainly stems from their aforementioned mutual descent from Baldwin II, as this made them kinsmen of Baldwin IV and, by want of their age, senior.

Bohemond took a less active role in Palestine following Guy's appointment as regent, probably as a result of the distractions caused by the noble rebellion at

---

129 Phillips, *Defenders*, pp. 225–38.

130 'Continuatio Aquicinctina', *MGH SS* VI, p. 416.

131 *CGOH*, I, 558; WT, p. 1007: dominus Boamundus Antiochenorum princeps et dominus Raimundus comes Tripolitanus cum militia in regnum ingredientes dominum regeum terruerunt, timentem ne res novas moliri attemptarent, videlicet ne rege regno privato sibi regnum vellent vendicare.

132 WT, pp. 1007–8. On Guy's reign, see P. Edbury, 'Propaganda and Faction in the Kingdom of Jeru-salem: The Background to Hattin', *Crusaders and Muslims in Twelfth-Century Syria*, ed. M. Shatzmiller (Leiden, 1993), pp. 172–89; Hamilton, *Leper King*, pp. 211–34.

133 Hamilton, *Leper King*, pp. 150–5; Mayer, *Varia*, pp. 128–9; Phillips, *Defenders*, pp. 242–3; Cahen, *Syrie*, p. 427; Asbridge, *Crusades*, p. 323.

Antioch and his attempts to assert authority over Cilicia.[134] Princely interest in the kingdom was not over, however, as Bohemond returned to aid the forces of Jerusalem at Kerak, which was threatened by Saladin, in 1183. The prince was also an influential voice within a group that successfully pushed Baldwin IV to depose Guy following the failure to meet the invading Muslim force in battle.[135] Bohemond also came to the kingdom in either April 1185 or 1186.[136] Mayer has noted that it is unknown why this journey was made, for although Hiestand believed – wrongly, so the former argues – it to be in response to Baldwin IV's deteriorating health, this is ruled out by the fact that the document issued by Bohemond during this visit is dated to 1186.[137] In this context, it is not unfeasible that Bohemond came south to visit the new king, the young Baldwin V, and his regent, Raymond III of Tripoli. While there were no recorded political summits or joint military ventures, and it is unlikely the prince stayed very long, Jerusalemite issues clearly continued to draw his attention. Indeed, once the unpopular Guy became king following Baldwin V's death in 1186, Antioch became a haven for disaffected Palestinian nobles, with the aforementioned Baldwin of Ibelin witnessing two Antiochene documents in early 1187, and perhaps receiving lands within the principality, after refusing to pay homage to the new king.[138] The strength of internal factionalisation within Jerusalem was not so strong as to preclude Antiochene involvement at the battle of Hattin later in 1187 (see below), but Guy's coronation appears to have ended Bohemond III's desire for pro-active involvement against him and in Jerusalemite politics.

In examining the entire span of Bohemond III's attempts to influence affairs in the kingdom of Jerusalem, Mayer has described the prince's efforts as a failure: arguing that in reality it was only through the auspices of Raymond III that the prince could have hoped to exert any authority.[139] While there is some truth to this, his case is perhaps made too vehemently, for it also overlooks the wider implications of Antiochene actions in altering the balance of power in the Latin East. Indeed, although the kings of Jerusalem appear to have retained an interest in promoting their position at the head of the association of crusader states throughout this period, their involvement in northern Syria was largely reduced to military alliances. There was certainly little of the authority wielded by earlier kings, particularly once Byzantine interference increased. Moreover, it is clear that Antioch had grown willing to challenge Jerusalem's position as leader of *Outremer*, in relation to both its authority over the other states and also the kingdom's internal politics.

---

[134] See pp. 54–5, 99–101; and Buck, 'Noble Rebellion', pp. 93–121.

[135] WT, pp. 1046–58. See also R. C. Smail, 'The Predicaments of Guy of Lusignan, 1183–1187', *Outremer: Studies in the History of the Crusading Kingdom of Jerusalem*, ed. B. Z. Kedar, H. E. Mayer and R. C. Smail (Jerusalem, 1982), pp. 159–76.

[136] Mayer, *Varia*, pp. 121–2.

[137] Mayer, *Varia*, pp. 132–3; R. Hiestand, 'Chronologisches zur Geschichte des Königreichs Jerusalem', *Deutsches Archiv* 35 (1979), 542–55.

[138] CGOH, I, 782–3; *Ernoul*, p. 139.

[139] Mayer, *Varia*, pp. 136–7.

The Creation of a New State: Antioch-Tripoli

Significantly, Bohemond's influence was soon to be felt within the county of Tripoli. Like Edessa, Tripoli had often come to feel the weight of Jerusalemite influence in the twelfth century, even to the point whereby Amalric acted as its regent during Raymond III's incarceration from 1164 to 1174.[140] Yet, when the heirless Raymond lay dying at Tripoli in 1187, having escaped the battle of Hattin, he faced a dilemma over his succession. The author of *Eracles* thus reported that the count 'decided to entrust Tripoli to the prince of Antioch so that he would guard both lands as one'.[141] Given the close relationship between Raymond and Bohemond III over the previous two decades, as well as their familial bonds, the Antiochene prince was perhaps the obvious choice; but, it cannot be denied that this placed a great deal of power into latter's hands, for he now controlled two crusader states. Indeed, it promised to stretch Antiochene authority as far south as Jubail, at least until the campaigns of Saladin decimated the extent of the Frankish domains. A messenger was subsequently dispatched to Antioch, whereby it was requested that Bohemond allow his eldest son, Raymond – who had fought with his Tripolitan namesake at Hattin – to rule over the county, perhaps as the prince's proxy.[142] Mayer has argued that the princeling did enact a short-lived, potentially titular tenure, although the evidence on which this is based – a later description of a now-lost charter seal – remains tenuous.[143] It appears rather that Bohemond III himself took temporary control, for a charter of April 1189 lists the prince at Tyre with Tripolitans amongst his retinue.[144] Nevertheless, power soon passed to the prince's other son, Bohemond IV, as fragmentary evidence survives for a charter he may have issued as count in March 1189.[145] Given the apparent crossover of these documents, it is possible that, while Bohemond III had installed his youngest son, he retained a guiding hand over Tripolitan matters to ensure stability. As the most senior ruler remaining in the Latin East, Bohemond III had been able to extend his authority south with more success than he had managed in the kingdom of Jerusalem. While his efforts perhaps had greater significance in the thirteenth century, as Bohemond IV, proving himself his father's son, united these two polities into one state (the principality of Antioch-Tripoli), this remained an important extension of Antiochene influence.[146]

---

[140] Richard, *Tripoli*, pp. 30–8.

[141] 'Eracles', *RHC Occ.* II, pp. 71–2 (here 72): si se pensa que il laisseroit Triple en la main dou prince d'Antioche, que il porroit garder l'une par l'autre. On relations between Jerusalem and Tripoli, see Richard, *Tripoli*, pp. 30–8.

[142] Roger of Howden, *Chronica magistri*, II, 322; William of Newburgh, I, 264; Robert of Auxerre, 'Chronicon', *MGH SS* XXVI, 251; 'Eracles', *RHC Occ.* II, pp. 71–2; *Lignages d'Outremer*, p. 94; IA, II, 353–4. For Hattin, see *Ernoul*, pp. 153–4; *CGT*, p. 42.

[143] Mayer, *Varia*, pp. 184–202.

[144] *Libri Iurium*, I/2, 342.

[145] *CGOH*, I, 871.

[146] Richard, *Tripoli*, pp. 42–3; and 'Comtes de Tripoli', pp. 213–24; Cahen, *Syrie*, pp. 590–652.

Antioch and the 'Confraternity' of the East

Although it has become apparent that the principality of Antioch grew steadily less supportive of Jerusalem's efforts to impose its suzerainty over northern Syria, it would be misleading to assume that this caused a wider malaise towards the notion of confraternal action. There were instances when political fractures hindered Antiochene involvement in common military activity in support of the other crusader states, but there were also numerous occasions when martial and political assistance was offered. The most prominent form of involvement in the so-called confraternity was the provisioning of military aid to the neighbouring crusader states. Such occasions rarely saw the convocation of the principality's full military strength, as the instability of northern Syria ensured mass absence could have heralded attacks from Aleppo or Cilicia.[147] However, there are important examples which demonstrate that Antioch – particularly its prince – was prepared to offer support to the rest of the Latin East.

The earliest case was the siege of Montferrand in 1137, which occurred after Fulk of Jerusalem and Raymond II of Tripoli were first defeated in battle by Zengi, and then chased into the aforementioned fortress.[148] William of Tyre noted that envoys were duly dispatched to Antioch and Edessa, and that Prince Raymond considered it

> inhumane not to come to the help of the lord king [when] placed in such necessity and hardship beyond measure … He judged it better to put up with whatever evils with his brothers than to withdraw so as to abound in prosperity and rejoice in tranquillity in any way.[149]

Though this is undoubtedly a fabricated speech deliberately exaggerated in order to promote the notion of Latin unity, the corroboration of various other texts demonstrates that the prince did indeed go to Montferrand, despite John Komnenos' presence in Cilicia.[150] He may even have forged an agreement with the Byzantine emperor in order to allow his forces to ride to the aid of the beleaguered Franks.[151] That the prospect of allowing Zengi to kill half of *Outremer*'s rulership was considered unfavourable is unsurprising, and it is significant that William's account does not imply that Raymond's presence was a result of a formal summons to military service, as would be expected if Jerusalem was Antioch's overlord. Rather, he used this event to promote the importance of Latin unity in the face of Muslim aggression. This also underpinned William's account of Raymond's subsequent presence

---

[147] See pp. 119–21.

[148] WT, pp. 663–5.

[149] *Ibid.*, p. 666: iterum domino regi in tanta necessitate posito durum nimis et inhumanum reputat non subvenire … satius iudicat cum fratribus quantumlibet adversa sustinere quam eis sic deficientibus habundare prosperis et qualibet tranquillitate gaudere.

[150] Orderic Vitalis, VI, 502, 506–8; al-Azimi, pp. 138; KD, *RHC Or.* III, 673; IQ, pp. 241–4; IA, I, 335–6; JK, p. 23; MS, III, 245–6; *1234*, II, 80.

[151] See p. 193.

at Fulk's siege of Banyas in 1140.[152] This castle, which helped to govern an important strategic and economic plain between Damascus and Jerusalem, had been promised to the king by Unur, the Burid ruler of Damascus, in return for help against Zengi.[153] As such, this probably represented an attempt to provide coordinated Latin opposition to Zengid hopes of unifying northern and southern Syria.[154] William of Tyre's use of the term *convocent* in describing the summons dispatched to Antioch and Tripoli nonetheless appears to imply that one or both of these rulers owed service to Fulk. Although this is perhaps possible in the case of Raymond II, it is highly unlikely to be true for Raymond of Poitiers, who had already done homage to John Komnenos in 1137.[155] Additionally, the author's subsequent comment that the rulers had been 'excited' (*exciti*) by the legates to participate, suggests rather that they had again been roused by common purpose, not 'feudal' duty.[156]

It is clear that such unity was not infallible. Alongside the aforementioned dispute between Raymond and Joscelin II of Edessa, during which the Antiochene prince seemingly failed to offer any meaningful support to the count following the fall of Edessa in 1144, there is the debacle of the Second Crusade. This venture, launched in the West to recover Edessa and stem the tide of Zengid aggression, notably saw the Antiochenes absent themselves from the Jerusalemite-crusader siege of Damascus in 1148 after Louis VII of France had refused to commit to an assault on Aleppo. William of Tyre even suggested that Prince Raymond deliberately sought to sabotage the attack in retaliation for this rejection and for Baldwin III's apparent role in turning the Western forces away from northern Syria.[157] Phillips has recently challenged belief in Jerusalemite duplicity, but there can be no denying that Antioch was an inactive participant in the confraternity during the mid-1140s.[158] This could perhaps help to explain why Raymond took the extreme step of travelling to Constantinople in 1145 in order seek renewed contact with Byzantium.

Importantly, these divisions did not put an end to Antiochene support of the other crusader states. In addition to the involvement of Antioch's nobles during Baldwin III's armed withdrawal from Edessa in the early 1150s, Renaud of Châtillon is also said to have gathered forces to aid in the defence of Banyas in 1157.[159] In both instances, these ventures were instigated in opposition to the expansionism of Nur al-Din, whose growth after Inab – which included the capture of Damascus in 1154 – now threatened the whole of *Outremer*. Despite this, there are again no indications of 'feudal'-style military service; rather an

---

[152] *Ibid.*, pp. 685–8; KD, *RHC Or.* III, 681–2; IQ, pp. 256–62; IA, I, 352–3.
[153] WT, pp. 684–5; al-Azimi, p. 147; KD, *RHC Or.* III, 681–2; IQ, pp. 256–62; IA, I, 352–3. See also Schenk, 'Nomadic Violence', pp. 39–55; El-Azhari, *Zengi*, pp. 83–6.
[154] Cahen, *Syrie*, p. 364; El-Azhari, *Zengi*, pp. 84–5.
[155] Richard, *Tripoli*, pp. 30–8.
[156] WT, 684–5.
[157] WT, pp. 756–69.
[158] *Ibid.*; Phillips, *Second Crusade*, pp. 207–12; M. Hoch, 'The Choice of Damascus as the Objective of the Second Crusade', *Autour de la Première Croisade*, ed. M. Balard (Paris, 1996), pp. 359–69; A. Forey, 'The Second Crusade: Scope and Objectives', *Durham University Journal* 86 (1994), 165–75.
[159] WT, pp. 780–5, 832–3.

acceptance that a united front was beneficial. As outlined earlier, though, Renaud's refusal to acquiesce to the demands made by Baldwin III at Shaizar later in 1157, indicate that this did not go beyond martial co-operation. The threat of Nur al-Din nevertheless appears to have initiated further Antiochene involvement outside of the principality, such as at the battle of Buqay'a Gap in 1163.[160] This victory had no long-term consequences for the Muslims due to the Zengid ruler's victory at Artah the following year; yet, it did prevent him from gaining easy access to the southern coastal road into the principality via Margat.[161] Mutual strategic concerns, as well as the greater unification of the Muslim world, thus ensured military co-operation between the crusader states was renewed.

This was further reinforced by the support offered to the kingdom of Jerusalem by Bohemond III during the 1180s. As already noted, when Baldwin IV's regent, Guy of Lusignan, gathered forces to oppose Saladin's siege of Kerak at the Springs of Sephorie in 1183, Bohemond was in attendance with his household retinue.[162] Grousset argued that the prince appeared because he was one of the king's *grand vassaux*, but there are no suggestions this was done out of formal obligation, nor is there any evidence that Bohemond ever did homage to Baldwin.[163] Moreover, in spite of the apparently strained relations between the prince and Guy after the latter became king in 1186, when Raymond III advised him to send to Bohemond for help in the lead up to Hattin in 1187, 'the king did as the count had advised him to do', and the prince duly 'dispatched to him his eldest son [Raymond], along with fifty knights'.[164] While not a particularly large force, it included the heir to the principality. It is also likely that there would have been soldiers other than knights to accompany this detachment. There are even suggestions that Bohemond utilised his remaining military strength in an effort to prevent northern reinforcements from reaching Saladin's army, as Baha al-Din ibn Shaddad noted that 'the troops of Aleppo were delayed because they were occupied with the Franks in the territory of Antioch' – which perhaps alluded to Bohemond III's defeat of a large band of Turcomans.[165] It appears, therefore, that the prince provided both direct and indirect support to Jerusalem against Saladin. This endured beyond Hattin, for Bohemond reportedly harboured a large number of refugees from Jerusalem and offered aid to Guy while he prepared for the siege of Acre.[166] It is significant, nonetheless, that he did not choose to participate in the Third Crusade, either by contributing to the military ventures or offering guidance in the dispute between

---

[160] WT, pp. 873–4.
[161] Cahen, *Syrie*, pp. 173–4.
[162] WT, pp. 1046–59.
[163] Grousset, *Croisades*, II, 660.
[164] *Ernoul*, pp. 153–4 (here 154): Li rois fist chou que li quens li consella ... là li envoia li princes d'Antioce un sien fil, à tout .LX. chevaliers. See also *CGT*, p. 42.
[165] BD, p. 71. See also p. 54 of this book.
[166] *CGT*, pp. 88–9; *Itinerarium Peregrinorum et Gesta Regis Ricardi*, ed. W. Stubbs, *Chronicles and Memorials of the Reign of Richard I*, 2 vols (London, 1864–1865), I, 60.

Richard I and Conrad of Montferrat; preferring instead to pursue his own policy of raiding northern Syria, which successfully brought him Arzghan and Amuq.[167]

With the exception of the mid-to-late 1140s, Antiochene rulers – and occasionally also the nobles – showed a genuine willingness to provide confraternal military support to the neighbouring crusader states. This was undoubtedly a response to the growing unity of the Muslim world, as the lords of *Outremer* could not have hoped to match Zengid and Ayyubid forces without a united front. This was not always successful, and it cannot be ignored that the Antiochenes never successfully co-operated with Jerusalem during a major crusading expedition – they even caused troubles during minor ones, such as that of Thierry of Flanders in 1157. In spite of this, martial confraternity often remained strong during times of great crisis, even if the political association did not.

Conclusion

This chapter has sought to examine the principality of Antioch's position within the Latin East's political and military landscape by identifying three key themes: Jerusalemite regency, Jerusalem as the head of *Outremer* and Antioch's engagement with the so-called 'confraternity of the East'. It has been argued that, in contrast to the existing historiographical consensus regarding the supremacy of Jerusalem and the relative weakness of the principality, the Antiochenes frequently acted in ways which invert this traditional view of *Outremer*'s political framework. This not only ensured resistance to royal efforts at imposing regencies during the frequent interregnums, thus leading to a clear diminution from the status enjoyed by Baldwin II between 1119 and 1126; there also appears to have been a willingness on behalf of Antioch's ruling elites, when faced with attempts at political intervention, to outwardly oppose the kingdom. Military alliances remained prominent, so Jerusalem's monarchs were able to enjoy some support during times of crisis. Nevertheless, embarrassing diplomatic reverses, such as the council of Tripoli and the marriage negotiations over Maria of Antioch, attest to the real limitations of royal authority. The growing interest of Byzantium was an undoubted catalyst for this, as increased ties with the Greeks were often used as a tool to undermine Jerusalem. There are even suggestions that Antioch sought to increase its own standing in *Outremer* by implementing suzerainty over Edessa, by becoming embroiled in the complex politics in the kingdom of Jerusalem during the 1170s and 1180s and, finally, by uniting with Tripoli after 1187. While these moves were not always successful or, in the case of Tripoli, came only at the very end of this period, the level of willingness to claim independence, and to intervene elsewhere in the Latin East, demonstrates that the principality of Antioch can no longer be considered a complicit puppet of Jerusalem. The 'confraternity' or 'association' endured, but it was much changed.

---

[167] See pp. 56–7.

Conclusion

As a result of modern trends in the fields of power, authority, frontiers and inter-cultural contact, a growing need has arisen to re-assess the history of the Latin East. The unique – and, at times, not so unique – challenges faced by the Frankish inhabitants of *Outremer*, due to their physical and social surroundings, provide significant insights into how Latin Christians interacted with their frontiers and neighbours. It has been argued here that this is especially so for the principality of Antioch, as the military, political and cultural pressures placed upon its rulers and settlers were of an intensity, and variety, unknown elsewhere in the medieval world. In response to this, the Frankish elites adopted the sort of fluidity of action also characteristic of western borderlands, with internal power structures and foreign policies shaped to meet the localised needs of security and stability. Although testament to the diversity of socio-political relationships which could emerge on medieval frontiers, that this has gone almost entirely unnoticed by historians demonstrates the need to re-examine Antioch's history.

An undoubted impetus for Frankish reactivity was the principality's fluctuating territorial extent. During the twelfth century, various strategic hotspots emerged which helped to shape the balance of power and the strategies pursued by Antioch's ruling elites. This was influenced, first and foremost, by the increased external scrutiny exerted on the principality after Bohemond II's death in 1130, as well the declining vigour with which princes were able to recover lost territory. As Zengid power on the eastern frontier developed, therefore, earlier attempts at isolating and subduing Antioch's nearest threat, the city of Aleppo, began to falter, and Frankish power east of the Orontes diminished. This was compounded by large-scale reverses, such as Inab in 1149 and Artah in 1164, as well as the rise of the Ayyubids under Saladin, whose devastating invasion in 1188 reduced the principality to its capital and immediate environs. This final loss did not entirely preclude Frankish military or political activity, but it was now severely inhibited. Coupled to this were evolving relations with the Christian powers of Byzantium and Armenian Cilicia, with both serving as allies and enemies at various points – a complication unique to Antioch in *Outremer*. Indeed, it was the return of Byzantium to Cilicia in the 1130s that destroyed Antiochene power there for most of the twelfth century, and while an attempt was made to restore Latin authority in the 1180s, this served only to isolate the Armenians and nurture an enmity that had far-reaching consequences. Yet, the principality's territorial decline was not a simple process, with the support of the aforementioned Eastern Christian powers, as well as the other crusader states, the military orders and crusading forces, at times stemming the tide of losses, if only temporarily. Situated within such a complicated patchwork of interests, the diplomatic and military strategies employed by the Antiochenes thus had to be finely balanced. As a consequence, the important role played by specific strategic pressure points is unsurprising. In particular, the key river crossings, like Jisr ash-Shughur and the Iron Bridge, the sites which overlooked and helped to protect these bridges, such as Arzghan and Darkush, positions of surveillance facing Aleppo, such as Harim and al-Atharib, and even the mountain passes to the north and south of the principality, proved to be of great significance to the balance of power in the region. Control over these sites could not halt an invasion, but an ability to prevent a surprise attack, or to launch counter-assaults, helped to preserve Antioch's existence. The manipulation of northern Syria's topography – by Franks and non-Franks alike – therefore significantly moulded the region's political climate, with the alliances and tactics pursued by both the Latins and their enemies often centring on possession of a single fortress or zone, with Harim proving a particularly prominent military hub. Precise strategic concerns likewise provided the catalyst for joint ventures with external powers: Cilicia frequently proved a facilitator for links to Byzantium, while territorial instability throughout the region prompted closer links to the military orders, to whom much of the principality had been surrendered by 1187. As historians have so far largely failed to show sensitivity to these unique and divergent concerns, key matters in the principality's history have either been overlooked or misunderstood. In truth, however, a detailed understanding of events here in the twelfth century also requires a thorough examination of the region's topography and the influence it had over the main protagonists.

The dynamism of the principality's frontiers also had an impact on its internal power structures. Indeed, whereas Cahen argued – along with most other historians, including Mayer and to some extent Asbridge and Martin – that Antioch was subject to autocratic rulership and unlimited 'feudal' service, it appears instead that the reality was far more fluid and much less weighted in favour of the prince. It is not always possible to relate this directly to specific losses or defeats (though at times it is), and there is some evidence which points towards a move to limit princely power even before Bohemond II's death, but it is undeniable that the latter event afforded the nobility with an unparalleled position, as they were now placed in charge of seeking a suitable husband for an heiress, Constance. This allowed for an alteration in the internal dynamics of power: for the first time, an Antiochene ruler – as opposed to a prince-regent – based their authority not on right of conquest or familial ties, but on aristocratic election. Raymond of Poitiers perhaps used this opportunity to have the succession of his progeny protected, ensuring Renaud of Châtillon should be considered a prince-regent; yet, Bohemond III's difficulties when securing the throne in 1163 demonstrate that establishing control in the principality was no simple process. Rather, it was subjected to a number of influences. With this shift also came a move away from the propagation of ties to the dynasty of Antioch's Norman founders in the opening clauses of princely titles and the numismatic evidence, as well as the significant development that Bohemond III claimed his authority through his Poitevin blood. In naming his eldest son, and heir-apparent, Raymond, Bohemond III (at least temporarily) interrupted the tradition of ascribing the name of the principality's founder to the prince's first-born son.

Just as the form in which power was legitimised evolved, so too did the way in which it was manifested, with the extent of princely power in some cases distinctly reduced. This did not necessarily mean a strong level of aristocratic or ecclesiastical supervision over centralised princely governance through the *haute cour*, as the ruler retained primary control over both the composition of the princely household, including the offices of state and the *familiares*, and the general practice of administration. As such, the nobility – differentiated here from a series of individuals carrying toponymic surnames – and the formerly influential Antiochene Church, now only infrequently attended court, and, with the exception of some chancellor-bishops, never as officers of state. Significant aristocratic influence can nevertheless be noted for matters of great importance, such as prestigious donations, the succession and the visits of powerful foreign rulers, while the Church also retained at least some diplomatic and symbolic value. Accordingly, relations with Byzantium were characterised by the Frankish nobility's overriding intervention, as they frequently led negotiations and represented the principality in an ambassadorial capacity. In this regard, the nobles appear to have supplanted the ecclesiastical hierarchy, which had earlier been so influential under the leadership of its first patriarch, Bernard of Valence. Churchmen could still be called upon politically and diplomatically, as attempts to promote Western sympathy for northern Syria often involved religious figures, but this was certainly to a diminished extent. There are suggestions, however, that this did not extend to increased noble involvement when Antioch's princes made foreign visits, almost certainly because the concerns of local defences precluded the large-scale absence of the principality's ruling elites. This may also have influenced the sporadic nature of noble attestation of princely charters, as well as the apparent lack of defined military service. Indeed, the noticeable absence of regulation for 'feudal' dues, especially when compared to the growing impetus for quotas seen in the West and in Jerusalem by the end of the twelfth century, is especially revealing. While aristocratic involvement in princely ventures can occasionally be identified, for instance during the campaign of John Komnenos in 1138, and it would be misleading to deny that some form of service existed, it was certainly not unlimited. For the most part, the available evidence instead implies that the mainstay of Antioch's armed capacity was formed from the ruler's household, paid forces, political allies or the military orders – not its fief-holders.

These changes also impacted upon the administration of the principality's major lordships. Consequently, Cahen's influential argument that the prince kept a tight control over the nobility cannot be substantiated, although neither (truly) can Asbridge's more revisionist belief in marcher-style holdings, or Martin's proposal for the relaxation in central administration over the principality's 'feudality'. Rather, while those families which can be considered actual lords (or *domini*), which may include the previously unknown county of al-Atharib, developed local bases of power according to the concerns of their locality, there is a lack of uniform regulation –

more so, perhaps, than in the West – which argues against consistent marcher-style rights. Moreover, although the presence of seigneurial officers and retainers suggests a strong level of independence, examples such as the seneschal of Marash imply that princely interference – theoretical or otherwise – was not entirely void. Despite clear instances of familial descent, there remains a wealth of complications which hint both at the regulated protection of inheritance rights, as well as the prince's willingness to intervene, particularly in times of crisis or in the extinction of a noble line. Single possessions within fiefs may thus have required frequent reconfirmation and the ruler perhaps retained the right to appoint Marash's lord (or at the very least the duty consistently fell upon him). The example of Harim, meanwhile, suggests that rights of wardship existed, even if an extant noble family could not be disinherited if their possessions were no longer in Frankish hands. Significantly, though, the matter of land alienation demonstrates a far stronger level of independent seigneurial donation rights than can be found elsewhere in the Latin East. This is complicated by the matter of princely reconfirmations, which show that the ruler retained the ability, or at least the desire, to intervene; but it cannot be accepted that Antiochene lords actually recognised the validity of such claims. Instead, the concerns of benefactors were likely to have been a far more prominent catalyst for the production of such documents. This further establishes the complexity and dynamism of Antiochene custom, as well as the pervading influence of security concerns on political activities. Existing historiographical trends, which have focused on distinct rules, are therefore not adequately supported. Lordship and landholding in the principality was evidently as divergent, if not more so, as on other medieval borderlands. Whereas the nobles had forged important powers, both locally and centrally, so fluid a frontier was not conducive to rigid custom.

The picture to emerge is one in which the princes retained control over central governance and some aspects of lordly administration, but the nobles secured a greater involvement in matters of importance, initiated limitations to 'feudal' services (both military and administrative) and increased their local power. Bohemond II's premature death in 1130 thus appears to have exacerbated concerns which had arisen earlier in the wake of the disaster at *Ager Sanguinis*, with a change now enacted to ensure that Antioch's future, and its stability, was not dependent on the lifespan of its prince. That the principality survived so many disasters in the twelfth century suggests that this policy was broadly successful. Yet, there were problems. It is likely that the prince's standing diminished somewhat, and it is certainly clear that they were subject to severe financial limitations, whether as a result of their inability to properly harness trade, or the difficulties presented by severe land losses and the growing alienation from the major fief-holders. Moreover, open tensions with the Church, seen at various points, as well as the noble rebellion of 1180–1182 (and the issues which lay behind it), show that the balance of power at Antioch was not always harmonious. As the period progressed, therefore, it seems that Antiochene cohesion was undermined by internal divisions. Sales to the military orders, although inevitable, likewise served to further fragment this delicate political patchwork. With Bohemond III seemingly unable to prevent the alienation of Margat and most of its surrounding area by 1187, much of the principality had now passed into the hands of an external power more interested in preserving its own status, not Antioch's. It is highly likely that these factors, when combined, greatly facilitated Saladin's widespread gains in 1188 – an invasion which further altered Frankish internal frameworks, for it destroyed noble landholding networks and left only the princely *demesne*. Nevertheless, the principality had survived significant disasters up to this point: more so than most other contemporary states could have endured. This is testament to the reactivity and adaptability of its ruling elites.

The same can also be said for the forms of intercultural contact witnessed in the principality. Given the existence of various religious communities in northern Syria and Cilicia, the methods by which the Franks governed and treated these peoples can help to further reveal the dynamism of custom that was required to ensure stability. As such, it is evident that, although Eastern Christians and Muslims were involved in administration, the extent of this, and the methods by which positions were received, is not so clear cut. Some indigenous figures may have been provided with long-term protected status, perhaps at a price, while others – for example the *qadi* of Jabala, Mansur ibn Nabil – probably rose to prominence due to changing political circumstances and a need to establish control. Whatever the case, the available examples are not discernibly widespread. Likewise, despite evidence for religious freedom, at least for Eastern Christians, as well as opportunities for land-holding and military contributions, there is also evidence for slavery, conversion and limitations to social liberties. Even trade and inter-marriage, so often viewed as facilitators and signifiers of cross-cultural contact in the Latin East and elsewhere, are not hugely prominent (if known at all). Yet, to have imposed uniform regulation onto a polity of so diverse and dispersed communities – subject, as it was, to drastic political and geographical fluctuations – would have been highly difficult, perhaps even impossible. It may even have been politically inexpedient given the variability of relations with external powers such as Byzantium, the Armenians and the Muslim world, as well as the (albeit rare) possibility for local collusion with invading forces. This would certainly help to explain the silence of the *Assises d'Antioche* on these groups, and it also helps to demonstrate the need to refrain from superimposing generalised models of behaviour onto the crusader states as a whole. Consequently, suggestions of oppressive colonialism prove just as difficult to support as the defined hierarchies, or 'rough tolerance', proposed by other historians. Despite this, a certain level of distrust towards non-Latins can be detected, which belies suggestions of cultural harmony. These relationships, like the principality's power structures, could be messy, complicated and subject to variations based on time and place. In looking to define intercultural contact, therefore, historians have perhaps overlooked the necessary dynamism of Antioch's frontier character, as well as the limitations imposed upon a Frankish minority when dealing with such diverse populations.

It was not only internal communities who could challenge the Franks, for another important concern for Antioch was its political and diplomatic dealings with Byzantium. With tension arising over the principality's conception due to imperial claims to the city and its surrounding area, the Antiochenes' relationship with the Byzantines was to have a distinct influence on their actions during this period. While historians have long recognised the importance of contact between these two powers, opinion has collected around two main beliefs: that the Antiochenes retained a deep-seated and endemic hatred of the Greeks (which permeated all of their actions), and that political developments over the course of the twelfth century left the principality a mere passenger to the diplomatic activities which occurred – even to the point whereby, from 1158 onwards, it formed a *condominium* divided between Byzantium and Jerusalem. These arguments can no longer be sustained. While it is undeniable that a level of antagonism continued from the opening decades of Frankish rule, there was a clear increase in direct contact after 1130, instigated, at least in part, by the Latins. This included proposed, and enacted marriage alliances, an agreement to surrender Antioch in 1137 and the eventual acceptance of imperial overlordship in 1158 – which brought with it significant military and financial support. Direct contact with the empire proved a realistic, and often even a preferable, option for the Antiochenes in their diplomatic policy. This is in stark contrast to the period before 1130, which was characterised by frequent conflict. Difficulties continued, as both parties sought to find the most suitable terms of a union, but those instances in which negative engagements emerged were regularly the result of Byzantine abuses of concords, rather than intractable Frankish hatred. This can even be detected in the events surrounding Bohemond III's divorce of Theodora Comnena in 1180, as although this was a provocative act, and many have seen in this a signifier long-held antagonism towards the Greeks, it seems rather to have been driven by non-political motives – at least until Andronikos' actions ended ties. It also elicited a response from the nobility which belies suggestions of a deep-seated and widespread opposition to Byzantium. The same need for re-evaluation is also true for the assumption that the principality was an impotent power. Instead, Antioch was repeatedly the driving force behind opening, and maintaining, contacts: it was certainly not subject to guiding directives, particularly those of the kings of Jerusalem. In 1158, this even led to a theatrically staged penance, in which Renaud of Châtillon deflected a potentially harmful situation and in the process secured imperial overlordship, as well as long-term political, military and social benefits. Importantly, like the subsequent negotiations for Manuel's marriage to Maria of Antioch, the deal of 1158 was made without Jerusalemite intervention. The kings were occasionally afforded a position of prominence, but historians have often misinterpreted diplomatic nicety for actual influence.

This did not preclude positive Antiochene relations with the wider Latin East, though, even if certain traditional tropes stand in need of revision. Consequently, although the kingdom of Jerusalem has long been classified as the supreme Frankish power in *Outremer*, with the principality subject to its will, this does not appear to have been the case. Antioch's ruling elites did remain active participants in the defence of the crusader states, and in the maintenance of its political stability, yet the external interference of Jerusalem over northern Syria was eroded, and at times actively opposed. Instances of Jerusalemite regency in this period thus never recovered the status enjoyed by Baldwin II from 1119 to 1126. Rather, even if military support was often welcome, there was a clear diminution in influence – frequently to the point of embarrassing reverses for Jerusalem, most prominently during the reign of Baldwin III. Kings did not stop in their attempts to exert power, but none ever achieved a similar level of control, especially as Byzantine involvement in northern Syria increased. Even when a prince was *in situ*, the pattern of military support and opposition to political intervention continued – with the exception of the 1140s and 1150s – as Antiochene rulers frequently attended joint ventures, despite preventing Jerusalemite monarchs from imposing their will over the principality. There are even suggestions that the princes sought to subvert the Latin East's traditional political order by exerting their authority over Edessa and Tripoli, as well as intervening in the kingdom. This manifested itself in a brief and perhaps fractious period of suzerainty over the county of Edessa, the unification of Antioch and Tripoli at the end of the twelfth century and Bohemond III's active participation in the factionalism of the kingdom of Jerusalem during the 1170s and 1180s. Although levels of success were variable, and it cannot be argued that the princes ever truly became the recognised heads of *Outremer*, pre-existing assumptions about the importance of the principality to the political framework of the crusader states require revision. The 'confraternity' of the Frankish states in the East continued to provide an impetus for military co-operation, but the power dynamics between these polities had evidently evolved.

What, then, was the principality of Antioch during the twelfth century? Owing to its position on the easternmost edge of Latin Christendom, it was a polity subject to a significant level of military, political and social dynamism. This fluidity was almost certainly a key requirement for Frankish settlers to maintain their presence and retain control. While this approach was similar to other Western or Near Eastern borderlands (at least in terms of its variability), it was also the product of uniquely intense external interests, which were focused on the principality from a myriad of competing powers, as well the highly diverse collection of non-Latin internal communities. The Antiochenes' willingness to adapt, usually overlooked by historians, was vital to ensuring the principality's survival through frequent disasters and reverses. However, the structural changes engendered by Saladin's conquests in 1188, and the capture of Bohemond III at Baghras by the Armenian ruler Leon II in 1193, perhaps proved too great to continue along this line. The nobility's independent strength was broken and the opportunity for an alliance with Eastern Christian neighbours had dissipated now that Byzantium was no longer a present force and the Armenians sought to exert their own independent authority. The principality endured into the thirteenth century, but it was much altered. Nevertheless, for most of the twelfth century, the Frankish presence in northern Syria and Cilicia had been predicated on their (largely effective) ability to react to military and political challenges (some fairly disastrous), and to manage divergent interests and peoples. That the principality survived these at all, is testament both to the underlying success of this approach and to the dynamism of the medieval frontier.

Bibliography

Manuscripts

Arras AD Pas-de-Calais 12H (Fonds Cercamp) Carton 3 piece no. 182

Primary Sources

Abu Shama, 'Le livre des deux jardins', *RHC Or.* IV, 3–522; V, 3–206

Abu'l Fida, 'Tire des annales d'Abou 'l-Feda', *RHC Or.* I, 1–165

Aerts, W., 'A Byzantine Traveller to One of the Crusader States', *East and West in the Crusader States III*, ed. K. Ciggaar and H. Teule (Leuven, 2003), pp. 165–221

Alberic of Trois Fontaines, 'Chronica', *MGH SS* XXIII, 631–950

Albert of Aachen, *Historia Hierosolimitana*, ed. and trans. S. Edgington (Oxford, 2007)

Al-Dahabi, *Kitab Duwal al-Islam (Les dynasties de l'islam)*, trans. A. Nègre (Damascus, 1979)

Anonymi auctoris Chronicon ad A. C. 1234 pertinens, ed. and trans. A. Abouna, J.-M. Fiey and J.-B. Chabot, 4 vols (Louvain, 1916–1974)

Arnold of Lübeck, 'Chronica Slavorum', *MGH SS* XXI, 100–250

Assises d'Antioche, ed. and trans. L. Alishan (Venice, 1876)

Baha al-Din Ibn Shaddad, *The Rare and Excellent History of Saladin*, trans. D. S. Richards (Aldershot, 2002)

Bar Ebroyo, Gregory, *The Chronography: Being the First Part of his Political History of the World*, trans. E. A. Wallis Budge, 2 vols (London, 1932)

Benjamin of Tudela, *The Itinerary of Benjamin of Tudela*, ed. and trans. M. Adler (London, 1907)

Caffaro di Caschifellione, 'Annali genovesi di Caffaro e de' suoi continuatori', ed. L. Belgrano, *Fonti per la storia d'Italia*, 118 vols (Rome, 1887–1993), XI–XIV

—— *Caffaro, Genoa and the Twelfth-Century Crusades*, trans. M. Hall and J. Phillips (Aldershot, 2013)

Carte dell'Archivio Capitolare di Pisa, ed. M. Carli, 4 vols (Rome, 1969–1977)

Cartulaire général de l'ordre des hospitaliers de S. Jean de Jérusalem (1100–1300), ed. J. Delaville Le Roulx, 4 vols (Paris, 1894–1906)

Cartulaire général de l'ordre du temple (1119–1150), ed. Marquis d'Albon (Paris, 1913)

Chartes de Terre Sainte provenant de l'Abbaye de N.-D de Josaphat, ed. H.-F. Delaborde (Paris, 1880)

Choniates, Niketas, *Historia*, ed. I. van Dieten (Berlin, 1975)

—— *O City of Byzantium, Annals of Niketas Choniates*, trans. H. Magoulias (Detroit, MI, 1984)

Chronique d'Ernoul et de la Bernard Le Trésorier, ed. L. de Mas Latrie (Paris, 1871)

Codice diplomatico del Sacro Militare Ordine Gerosolimitano oggi di Malta, ed. S. Paoli, 2 vols (Lucca, 1733–1737)

De Oorkonden der Graven van Vlaanderen (Juli 1128–September 1191): II. Uitgrave – Band I (Juli 1128–17 January 1168), ed. T. de Hemptinne, A. Verhulst and L. de Mey (Brussels, 1988)

Delaville Le Roulx, J., *Les archives la bibliothèque et le trésor de l'Ordre de Saint-Jean de Jérusalem a Malte* (Paris, 1883)

—— 'Inventaire de pièces de Terre Sainte de l'Ordre de l'Hopital', *ROL* 3 (1885), 36–106

Die Register Innocenz' III, ed. O. Hageneder and A. Haidacher, 12 vols (Graz, 1964–2012)

Die Urkunden der lateinischen Könige von Jerusalem, ed. H. Mayer and J. Richard, 4 vols (Hannover, 2010)

Documenti sulle Relazione delle citta Toscane: Coll' Oriente Cristiano e coi Turchi fino all'anno MDXXI, ed. G. Müller (Rome, 1966)

'Epistolae A. Dapiferi Militiae Templi', *RHGF* XV, 540–1

Eustathios of Thessaloniki, *The Capture of Thessaloniki*, trans. R. Melville Jones (Canberra, 1988)

Fulcher of Chartres, *Historia Hierosolymitana*, ed. H. Hagenmeyer (Heidelberg, 1913)

Gesta Francorum et aliorum Hierosolymitanorum, ed. and trans. R. Hill (Oxford, 1962)

'Gregory the Priest: Continuation of Matthew of Edessa', trans. A. E. Dostourian, *Armenia and the Crusades: Tenth to Twelfth Centuries* (New York, 1993), pp. 241–80

Guiragos of Kantzag, 'L'histoire d'Arménie', *RHC Arm.* I, 411–30

Hagenmeyer, H., *Epistulae et chartae ad historiam primi belli sacri spectantes. Die Kreuzzugsbriefe aus den Jahren 1088–1100* (Innsbruck, 1901)

Hiestand, R., 'Antiochia, Sizilien und das Reich am Ende des 12. Jahrhunderts', *Quellen und Forschungen aus italienischen Archiven und Bibliotheken* 73 (1993), 70–121

—— 'Ein neuer Bericht über das Konzil von Antiochia 1140', *Annuarium historiae conciliorum* 20 (1988), 314–50

—— 'Ein unbekanntes Privileg Fürst Bohemunds II. von Antiochia für das Hospital vom März 1127 und die Frühgeschichte der antiochenischen Fürstenkanzlei', *Archiv für Diplomatik Schriftgeschichte Siegel- und Wappenkunde* 43 (1997), 27–46

—— *Papsturkunden für kirchen im Heiligen Lande* (Göttingen, 1985)

Historia Nicaena vel Antiochena, RHC Occ. V, 139–85

Ibn al-Athir, *The Chronicle of Ibn al-Athir for the Crusading Period from al-Kamil fi'l-Ta'rikh*, ed. and trans. D. S. Richards, 3 vols (Aldershot, 2005–2008)

Ibn al-Furat, *Ayyubids, Mamlukes and Crusaders*, trans. U. Lyons, M. Lyons and J. Riley-Smith, 2 vols (Cambridge, 1987)

Ibn al-Qalanisi, *The Damascus Chronicle of the Crusades*, trans. H. A. R. Gibb (London, 1932)

Imad al-Din al-Isfahani, *Conquête de la Syrie et de la Palestine par Saladin*, trans. H. Massé (Paris, 1972)

I Libri iurium della Repubblica di Genova, ed. D. Puncuh, 8 vols (Rome, 1992–2002)

Italia Sacra, ed. F. Ughelli, 10 vols (Venice, 1719–1722)

Italikos, Michael, *Lettres et discours*, ed. and trans. P. Gautier (Paris, 1972)

Itinerarium Peregrinorum et Gesta Regis Ricardi, ed. W. Stubbs, *Chronicles and Memorials of the Reign of Richard I*, 2 vols (London, 1864–1865), I, 3–450

Izz al-Din ibn Shaddad, *Description de la Syrie du Nord*, trans. A.-M. Eddé-Terrasse (Damascus, 1984)

Jacques de Vitry, *Historia Orientalis*, ed. and trans. J. Donnadieu (Turnhout, 2008)

Jeffreys, E., and M. Jeffreys, 'A Constantinopolitan Poet Views Frankish Antioch', *Crusades* 14 (2015), 49–152

John of Ibelin, *Le Livre des Assises*, ed. P. Edbury (Leiden, 2003)

Kemal al-Din, 'La chronique d'Alep', *RHC Or.* III, 577–690

—— Blochet, E., 'L'histoire d'Alep', *ROL* 3 (1895), 509–65; 4 (1896), 145–225; 5 (1897), 37–107; 6 (1898), 1–49

Kedar, B. Z., 'The *Tractatus de locis et statu sancte terre ierosolimitane*', *The Crusades and Their Sources: Essays Presented to Bernard Hamilton*, ed. J. France and W. G. Zajac (Aldershot, 1998), pp. 111–33

Kinnamos, John, *Epitome: Rerum ab Ioanne et Alexio Comnenis Gestarum*, ed. A. Meineke (Bonn, 1836)

—— *Deeds of John and Manuel Comnenus*, trans. C. Brand (New York, 1976)

Kohler, C., 'Chartes de l'abbaye de Notre-Dame de Josaphat', *ROL* 7 (1890), 108–222

Komnene, Anna, *The Alexiad*, trans. E. Sewter and P. Frankopan (London, 2009)

La chronique de Morigny, ed. L. Mirot (Paris, 1912)

La continuation de Guillaume de Tyr (1184–1197), ed. M. R. Morgan (Paris, 1982)

Le cartulaire du chapitre du Saint-Sépulchre de Jérusalem, ed. G. Bresc-Bautier (Paris, 1984)

Les registres de Grégoire IX, ed. L. Auvray, 4 vols (Paris, 1896–1955)

'L'estoire de Eracles empereur et la conqueste de la terre d'Outremer', *RHC Occ.* II, 1–638

'L'estoire de Eracles empereur et la conqueste de la terre d'Outremer', ed. M. Paulin Paris, *Guillaume de Tyr et ses continuateurs*, 2 vols (1879–1880)

Lignages d'Outremer, ed. M.-A. Nielen (Paris, 2003)

Louis VII, 'Epistolae', *RHGF* XVI, 1–170

Magnus of Reichersberg, 'Chronicon', *MGH SS* XVII, 439–523

Comté Marsy, 'Fragment d'un cartulaire de l'ordre de Saint-Lazare, en Terre Sainte', *AOL* 2B (1884), 121–57

'Matthew of Edessa: Chronicle', trans. A. E. Dostourian, *Armenia and the Crusades: Tenth to Twelfth Centuries* (New York, 1993), pp. 1–239

Mayer, H. E., 'Das syrische Erdbeben von 1170: Ein unedierter Brief König Amalrichs von Jerusalem', *Deutsches Archiv* 45 (1989), 474–84

Memorie storico-diplomatiche dell'antica città e ducato di Amalfi, ed. M. Camera (Salerno, 1876)

Michael the Syrian, *Chronique de Michel le Syrien, patriarche jacobite d'Antioche (1166–1199)*, ed. and trans. J.-B. Chabot, 4 vols (Paris, 1916–1920)

—— 'Extrait de la chronique de Michel Syrien, traduit de l'arménien', *RHC Arm.* I, 309–409

Monot, F., 'La chronique abrégée d'al-Azimi années 518–538/1124–1144', *Revue des études islamique* 59 (1991), 101–64

Odo of Deuil, *De Profectione Ludovici VII in Orientem*, ed. and trans. V. G. Berry (New York, 1948)

Orderic Vitalis, *The Ecclesiastical History of Orderic Vitalis*, ed. and trans. M. Chibnall, 6 vols (Oxford, 1969–1980)

Otto of Freising, *Chronica sive Historia de Duabus Civitatibus*, ed. A. Hofmeister (Hannover, 1912)

Patrologiae cursus completus: series Latina, ed. J.-P. Migne, 221 vols (Paris, 1844–1904)

Pringle, D., 'Wilbrand of Oldenburg's Journey to Syria, Lesser Armenia, Cyprus, and the Holy Land (1211–1212): A New Edition', *Crusades* 11 (2012), 109–37

Ralph of Caen, 'Gesta Tancredi in Expeditione Hierosolymitana', *RHC Occ.* III, 599–716

Raymond d'Aguilers, *Historia Francorum qui ceperunt Iherusalem*, ed. J. H. Hill and L. L. Hill (Paris, 1969)

Recueil des actes de Henri II roi d'Angleterre et duc de Normandie concernant les provinces françaises et les affaires de France, ed. L. Deslisle and É. Berger, 4 vols (Paris, 1909–1927)

Recueil des chartes de l'abbaye de Clairvaux au XIIe Siècle, ed. J. Waquet, J.-M. Roger and L. Veyssière (Paris, 2004)

Regesta Regni Hierosolymitani (MCVII–MCCXCI), ed. R. Röhricht, 2 vols (Innsbruck, 1893–1904)

Rey, E., *Recherches geographiques et historiques sur la donations des latins en Orient* (Paris, 1877)

Richard, J., 'Le comté de Tripoli dans les chartes du fonds des Porcellet', *Bibliothèque de l'école des chartes* 130:2 (1972), 339–82

Robert of Auxerre, 'Chronicon', *MGH SS* XXVI, 219–76

Robert of Torigny, 'The Chronicle of Robert of Torigni, Abbot of the Monastery of St. Michael-in-Peril-of-the-Sea', ed. R. Howlett, *Chronicles of the Reigns of Stephen, Henry II, and Richard I*, 4 vols (London, 1884–1889), IV, 81–315

Roger of Howden, *Chronica magistri Rogeri de Houedene*, ed. W. Stubbs, 4 vols (London, 1868–1871)

—— *Gesta Regis Henrici Secundi*, ed. W. Stubbs, 2 vols (London, 1867)

Roger of Wendover, *Liber qui dicitur Flores historiarum*, ed. R. Howlett, 3 vols (London, 1886–1898)

Sempad the Constable, 'Chronique du royaume de la Petite Armenie', *RHC Arm.* I, 605–80

—— Der Nersessian, S., 'The Armenian Chronicle of the Constable Smpad or of the "Royal Historian"', *Dumbarton Oaks Papers* 13 (1959), 141–68

—— *La chronique attribuée au connétable Smbat*, trans. G. Dédéyan (Paris, 1980)

'Sigeberti Gemblacensis, Auctarium Affligemense', *MGH SS* VI, 398–405

'Sigeberti Gemblacensis, Continuatio Aquicinctina', *MGH SS* VI, 405–38

'Sigeberti Gemblacensis, Continuatio Preamonstratensis', *MGH SS* VI, 447–56

Suger of Saint Denis, 'Epistolae', *RHGF* XV, 483–532

—— *La vie de Louis de Gros*, ed. A. Molinier (Paris, 1887)

Tabulae Ordinis Theutonici, ed. E. Strehlke (Berlin, 1869, rep. 1975)

The Great Roll of the Pipe for the Twenty-Fifth Year of the Reign of King Henry the Second, A.D. 1178–1179, ed. J. H. Round (London, 1907)

Thompson, R., 'The Historical Compilation of Vardan Arewelts'i', *DOP* 43 (1989), 125–226

Urkunden zur älteren Handels- und Staatsgeschichte der Republik Venedig: mit besonderer Beziehung auf Byzanz und die Levante vom neunten bis zum Ausgang des fünfzehnten Jahrhunderts, ed. G. Tafel and G. Thomas, 2 vols (Vienna, 1856)

Usamah ibn Munqidh, *The Book of Contemplation: Islam and the Crusades*, trans. P. Cobb (London, 2008)

Van Lint, T. M., 'Seeking Meaning in Catastrophe, Nerses Snorhali's Lament on Edessa', *East and West in the Crusader States II*, ed. K. Ciggaar and H. Teule (Leuven, 1999), pp. 49–105

Walter the Chancellor, *Bella Antiochena*, ed. H. Hagenmeyer (Innsbruck, 1896)

—— *Walter the Chancellor's The Antiochene Wars*, trans. T. Asbridge and S. Edgington (Aldershot, 1999)

William of Newburgh, 'Historia Rerum Anglicarum', ed. R. Howlett, *Chronicles of the Reigns of Stephen, Henry II, and Richard I*, 4 vols (London, 1884–1889), I, 1–408

William of Tyre, *Chronicon*, ed. R. B. C. Huygens, 2 vols (Turnhout, 1986)

—— *A History of Deeds Done Beyond the Sea*, trans. E. W. Babcock and A. C. Krey, 2 vols (New York, 1943)

Secondary Sources

Abel, F., 'Lettre d'un templier récemment trouvée à Jérusalem', *Revue biblique* 35 (1926), 288–95

Abulafia, D., 'Introduction: Seven Types of Ambiguity, c.1100–c.1500', *Medieval Frontiers: Concepts and Practices*, ed. D. Abulafia and N. Berend (Aldershot, 2002), pp. 1–34

Ailes, A., 'The Knight's Alter Ego: From Equestrian to Armorial Seal', *Good Impressions: Image and Authority in Medieval Seals*, ed. N. Adams, J. Cherry and J. Robinson (London, 2008), pp. 8–11

Albu, E., 'Antioch and the Normans', *Crusading and Pilgrimage in the Norman World*, ed. K. Hurlock and P. Oldfield (Woodbridge, 2015), pp. 159–76

Amouroux-Mourad, M., *Le Comté d'Edesse 1098–1150* (Paris, 1988)

Andrews, T., 'The New Age of Prophecy: The Chronicle of Matthew of Edessa and its Place in Armenian Historiography', *The Medieval Chronicle* 6 (2009), 105–23

Asbridge, T., 'Alice of Antioch: a Case Study of Female Power in the Twelfth Century', *The Experience of Crusading vol. 2: Defining the Crusader Kingdom*, ed. P. Edbury and J. Phillips (Cambridge, 2003), pp. 29–47

—— 'How the Crusades Could Have Been Won: King Baldwin II of Jerusalem's Campaigns against Aleppo (1124–5) and Damascus (1129)', *Journal of Medieval Military History* 11 (2013), 73–94

—— *The Creation of the Principality of Antioch, 1098–1130* (Woodbridge, 2000)

—— 'The "Crusader" Community at Antioch: The Impact of Interaction with Byzantium and Islam', *TRHS* 6th Series 10 (1999), 305–25

—— *The Crusades: The War for the Holy Land* (London, 2010)

—— 'The Principality of Antioch and the Early History of the Latin East', *East and West II*, pp. 1–10

—— 'The Principality of Antioch and the Jabal as-Summaq', *The First Crusade: Origins and Impact*, ed. J. Phillips (Manchester, 1997), pp. 142–52

—— 'The Significance and Causes of the Battle of the Field of Blood', *JMH* 23 (1997), 301–16

—— 'William of Tyre and the First Rulers of the Latin Principality of Antioch', *Deeds Done Beyond the Sea*, pp. 35–42

Augé, I., *Byzantins, Arméniens et Francs au temps de la croisade: politique religieuse et reconquête en Orient sous la dynastie des Comnènes (1081–1185)* (Paris, 2007)

—— 'Les Comnènes et le comté de Tripoli: une collaboration efficace?', *Le comté de Tripoli: état multiculturel et multiconfessionnel (1102–1289)*, ed. G. Dédéyan and K. Rizak (Paris, 2010), pp. 141–55

Bachrach, B., 'A Study in Feudal Politics: Relations between Fulk Nerra and William the Great, 995–1030', *Viator* 7 (1976), 111–22

Baldwin, B., 'Classicism, Content, and Contemporaneity in Michael Italicus', *Byzantion* 62 (1992), 109–17

Baldwin, M., 'The Latin States under Baldwin III and Amalric I, 1143–1174', *A History of the Crusades vol.1: The First Hundred Years*, ed. K. Setton *et al.* (Madison, WI, 1963), pp. 528–61

Barber, M., *The Crusader States* (New Haven, CT, 2012)

——, *The New Knighthood: A History of the Order of the Temple* (Cambridge, 1994)

Barber, M., and K. Bate, *Letters from the East: Crusaders, Pilgrims and Settlers in the 12th–13th Centuries* (Farnham, 2013)

Barbero, A., 'Noblesse et chevalerie en France au Moyen Age: une réflexion', *Le Moyen Âge* 97.3 (1991), 431–49

Barthélemy, D., 'Castles, Barons and Vavassors in the Vendômois and Neighboring Regions in the Eleventh and Twelfth Centuries', *Cultures of Power: Lordship, Status, and Process in the Twelfth-Century Europe*, ed. T. Bisson (Philadelphia, PA, 1995), pp. 56–68

Bartlett, R., *The Making of Europe: Conquest, Colonization and Cultural Change 950–1350* (London, 2003)

Barton, T., 'Lords, Settlers and Shifting Frontiers in Medieval Catalonia', *JMH* 30 (2010), 1–49

Beech, G., 'A Little-Known Armenian Historian of the Crusading Period: Gregory the Priest (1136–1162)', *Truth As Gift: Studies in Medieval Cistercian History in Honor of John R. Sommerfeldt*, ed. M. Dutton, D. La Corte and P. Lockey (Kalamazoo, MI, 2004), pp. 119–43

—— 'The Crusader Lordship of Marash in Armenian Cilicia, 1104–1149', *Viator* 27 (1996), 35–52

—— 'The Ventures of the Dukes of Aquitaine into Spain and the Crusader East in the Early Twelfth Century', *Haskins Society Journal* 5 (1993), 61–75

Benham, J., *Peacemaking in the Middle Ages: Principles and Practice* (Manchester, 2011)

Berend, N., *At the Gate of Christendom: Jews, Muslims and 'Pagans' in Medieval Hungary, c.1000–c.1300* (Cambridge, 2001)

Besançon, J., and B. Geyer, 'Le cuvette du Rug (Syrie du Nord): les conditions naturelles et les étapes de a mise en valeur', *Syria* 72 (1995), 307–55

Billy, P.-H., 'A Sociology of First Names in the Late Middle Ages', *Name and Naming: Synchronic and Diachronic Perspectives*, ed. O. Felecan (Cambridge, 2012), pp. 53–64

Birk, J., 'The Betrayal of Antioch: Narratives of Conversion and Conquest during the First Crusade', *Journal of Medieval and Early Modern Studies* 41:3 (2011), 463–85

Bisson, T., *The Crisis of the Twelfth Century: Power, Lordship, and the Origins of European Government* (Princeton, NJ, 2009)

Boas, A. J., *Archaeology of the Military Orders* (London, 2006)

Boase, T. S. R., 'The History of the Kingdom', *The Cilician Kingdom of Armenia*, ed. T. S. R. Boase (Edinburgh, 1978), pp. 1–33

Bossina, L., 'Niketas Choniates as a Theologian', *Niketas Choniates: A Historian and a Writer*, ed. A. Simpson and S. Efthymiadis (Geneva, 2009), pp. 165–84

Boyle, L., 'Diplomatics', *Medieval Studies: An Introduction*, 2nd edn, ed. J. Powell (New York, 1992), pp. 82–113

Bozoyan, A., 'Armenian Political Revival in Cilicia', *Armenian Cilicia*, ed. R. Hovannisian and S. Payaslian (Costa Meza, CA, 2008), pp. 67–78

Brand, C., *Byzantium Confronts the West* (Cambridge, MA, 1968)

Brands, G., 'Prokop und das Eiserne Tor. Ein Beitrag zur Topographie von Antiochia am Orontes', *Syrien und seine Nachbarn von der Spätantike bis in die islamische Zeit*, ed. I. Eichner and V. Tsamakda (Wiesbaden, 2009), pp. 9–20

Brasse, C., 'Von der Stadtmauer zur Stadtgeschichte. Das Befestigungssystem von Antiochia am Orontes', *Neue Forschungen zu antiken Stadtbefestigungen im östlichen Mittelmeerraum und im Vorderen Orient (Byzas 10)*, ed. J. Lorentzen, F. Pirson *et al.* (Istanbul, 2010), pp. 261–82

Browning, R., 'The Death of John II Comnenus', *Byzantion* 31 (1961), 229–35

Buck, A. D., 'Between Byzantium and Jerusalem? The Principality of Antioch, Renaud of Châtillon, and the Penance of Mamistra in 1158', *Mediterranean Historical Review* 30:2 (2015), 107–24

—— 'The Castle and Lordship of Harim and the Frankish-Muslim Frontier of Northern Syria in the Twelfth Century', *Al-Masaq* 28:2 (2016), 113–31

—— 'The Noble Rebellion at Antioch, 1180–82: A Case Study in Medieval Frontier Politics', *Nottingham Medieval Studies* 60 (2016), 93–121

Buckley, P., *The Alexiad of Anna Komnene: Artistic Strategy in the Making of a Myth* (Cambridge, 2014)

Burgtorf, J., 'Der Antiochenische Erbfolgekrieg', *Ordines Militares* 18 (2013), 219–39

—— 'Die Herrschaft der Johanniter in Margat im Heiligen Land', *Die Ritterorden als Träger der Herrschaft: Territorien, Grundbesitz und Kirche*, ed. R. Czaja and J. Sarnowsky (Toruń, 2007), pp. 27–57

—— 'The Antiochene War of Succession', *The Crusader World*, ed. A. Boas (Abingdon, 2016), pp. 196–211

—— 'The Hospitaller Lordship of Margat', *East and West II*, pp. 11–50

—— 'The Military Orders in the Crusader Principality of Antioch', *East and West I*, pp. 217–46

Burnett, C., 'Antioch as a Link between Arabic and Latin Culture in the Twelfth and Thirteenth Centuries', *Occident et Proche-Orient: contacts scientifiques au temps des croisades*, ed. A. Tihon, I. Draelants and B. van den Abeele (Louvain-la-Neuve, 2000), pp. 1–78

—— 'Stephen, the Disciple of Philosophy, and the Exchange of Medical Learning in Antioch', *Crusades* 5 (2006), 113–29

Burns, R., *Monuments of Syria: A Guide* (London, 2009)

Burns, R., 'The Significance of the Frontier in the Middle Ages', *Medieval Frontier Societies*, ed. R. Bartlett and A. MacKay (Oxford, 1996), pp. 307–30

Buyukasik, T., 'A Survey of the Measurements of the Castles, Villages and Cities that are Situated in the Kingdom of the Just King Nur al-Din Abu al-Qasim Mahmud ibn Zangi ibn Aqsunqur in the year 564/1168–9, as described in MS

Arabe 2281 (BN Paris) (Introduction, Translation and Arabic Text)', *East and West II*, pp. 79–200

Buzás, G., 'The Two Hospitaller Chapter Houses at al-Marqab: a Study in Architectural Reconstruction', *The Military Orders 5: Power and Politics*, ed. P. Edbury (Farnham, 2012), pp. 49–64

Cahen, C., *La Syrie du nord a l'époque des croisades et la principauté franque d'Antioche* (Paris, 1940)

—— 'La chronique abrégée d'al-Azimi', *Journal Asiatique* 230 (1938), 353–448

—— 'Note sur les seigneurs de Saone et de Zerdana', *Syria* 12 (1931), 154–9

—— 'Un document concernant les Melkites et les Latins d'Antioche au temps des Croisades', *Revue des etudes byzantines* 29 (1971), 285–92

Carrier, M., 'Ordéric Vital sur les rapports entre Latins et Grecs à la veille de la deuxième croisade', *Memini: Travaux et documents* 11 (2007), 131–50

Castellana, P., and E. Hybsch, 'Il castello del Roudj o Chastel de Ruge dei Crociati', *Studia Orientalia Christiana Collectanea* 23 (1990), 309–23

Cavell, E., 'Aristocratic Widows and the Medieval Welsh Frontier: the Shropshire Evidence', *TRHS* 6th Series 17 (2007), 57–82

Chalandon, F., *Jean II Comnène (1118–1143) et Manuel I Comnène (1143–1180)*, 2 vols (Paris, 1912)

Chandon de Brialles, F., 'Lignages d'Outre-Mer, les seignors de Margat', *Syria* 25 (1946), 231–58

Cheney, C. R., and B. Jones, *English Episcopal Acta II: Canterbury 1162–1190* (London, 1986)

Chevalier, M.-A., *Les ordres religieux-militaires en Arménie cilicienne: Templiers, hospitaliers, teutoniques et Arméniens à l'époque des croisades* (Paris, 2010)

Cheyette, F., 'Suum cuique tribuere', *French Historical Studies* 6 (1970), 287–99

Cheynet, J.-C., 'The Duchy of Antioch during the Second Period of Byzantine Rule', *East and West I*, pp. 1–16

Christie, N., 'Ibn al-Qalanisi', *Medieval Muslim Historians and the Franks in the Levant*, ed. A. Mallett (Leiden, 2015), pp. 7–28

Church, S., 'The 1210 Campaign in Ireland: Evidence for a Military Revolution?', *Anglo-Norman Studies* 20 (1998), 45–57

Ciggaar, K., 'Adaptation to Oriental Life by Rulers in and around Antioch: Examples and Exempla', *East and West I*, pp. 261–82

—— 'Northerners in Antioch and Environs in History and in Northern Literature', *East and West II*, pp. 323–44

Ciggaar, K., and M. Metcalf (ed.), *East and West in the Medieval Eastern Mediterranean I: Antioch from the Byzantine Reconquest Until the End of the Crusader Principality* (Leuven, 2006)

Ciggaar, K., and V. van Aalst (ed.), *East and West in the Medieval Eastern Mediterranean II: Antioch from the Byzantine Reconquest Until the End of the Crusader Principality* (Leuven, 2013)

Clanchy, M., *From Memory to Written Record: England 1066–1307*, 2nd edn (Oxford, 1993)

Claverie, P.-V., *Honorius III et l'Orient (1216–1227)* (Leiden, 2013)

Constable, G., 'The Crusading Project of 1150', *Montjoie; Studies in Crusade History in Honour of Hans Eberhard Mayer*, ed. B. Z. Kedar, J. Riley-Smith and R. Hiestand (Aldershot, 1997), pp. 67–75

Crouch, D., *The Image of Aristocracy in Britain* (London, 1992)

—— *The Reign of King Stephen 1135–1154* (Harlow, 2000)

Daftary, F., *The Isma'ilis: Their History and Doctrines*, 2nd edn (Cambridge, 2007)

Dangles, P., 'Afamiya – Qal'at al-Mudiq. Die Mittelalterliche Wiederbefestigung der Antiken Zitadelle von Apamea am Ende des 12. bis Mitte des 13. Jahrhunderts', *Burgen und Städte der Kreuzzugszeit*, ed. M. Piana (Petersberg, 2008), pp. 221–33

Davies, R., 'Kings, Lords and Liberties in the March of Wales, 1066–1272', *TRHS* 5th Series 29 (1979), 41–61

—— *The Age of Conquest: Wales, 1064–1415* (Oxford, 1991)

Davis, W., and P. Fouracre, 'Conclusion', *The Settlement of Disputes in Early Medieval Europe*, ed. W. Davis and P. Fouracre (Cambridge, 1986), pp. 207–40

Dédéyan, G., 'Les listes "féodales" du pseudo-Smbat', *Cahiers de civilisation médiévale* 125 (1989), 25–42

—— 'Un projet de colonisation Arménienne dans le Royaume Latin de Jérusalem sous Amaury Ier (1162–1174)', *Le partage du monde: échanges et colonisation dans la Méditerranée médiévale*, ed. M. Balard and A. Ducellier (Paris, 1998), pp. 101–40

Dédéyan, G., and K. Rizk (ed.), *Le comté de Tripoli: état multiculturel et multiconfessionnel (1102–1289)* (Paris, 2010)

Deschamps, P., 'Le château de Saone et ses premiers seigneurs', *Syria* 16 (1935), 73–88

—— *Les châteaux des croisés 3: la défense du comté de Tripoli et de la principauté d'Antioche* (Paris, 1973)

Duggan, A., 'Henry II, the English Church and the Papacy, 1154–76', *Henry II: New Interpretations*, ed. C. Harper-Bill and N. Vincent (Woodbridge, 2007), pp. 154–83

Dussaud, R., *Topographie historique de la Syrie antique et médiéval* (Paris, 1927)

Ebels-Hoving, B., 'William of Tyre and his Patria', *Medi Latinitas: A Collection of Essays to Mark the Occasion of the Retirement of L. J. Engels*, ed. R. Nip, H. van Dijk *et al.* (Turnhout, 1996), pp. 211–16

Edbury, P., 'Fiefs and Vassals in the Kingdom of Jerusalem: from the Twelfth Century to the Thirteenth', *Crusades* 1 (2002), 49–62

—— *John of Ibelin and the Kingdom of Jerusalem* (Woodbridge, 1997)

—— 'New Perspectives on the Old French Continuations of William of Tyre', *Crusades* 9 (2010), 107–14

—— 'Propaganda and Faction in the Kingdom of Jerusalem: The Background to Hattin', *Crusaders and Muslims in Twelfth-Century Syria*, ed. M. Shatzmiller (Leiden, 1993), pp. 172–89

—— 'The *Assises d'Antioche*: Law and Custom in the Principality of Antioch', *Norman Expansion: Connections, Continuities and Contrasts*, ed. K. Stringer and A. Jotischky (Farnham, 2013), pp. 241–8

—— 'The French Translation of William of Tyre's *Historia*: the Manuscript Tradition', *Crusades* 6 (2007), 69–106

—— *The Kingdom of Cyprus and the Crusades, 1191–1374* (Cambridge, 1991)

—— 'The Lyon *Eracles* and the Old French Continuations of William of Tyre', *Montjoie; Studies in Crusade History in Honour of Hans Eberhard Mayer*, ed. B. Z. Kedar, J. Riley-Smith and R. Hiestand (Aldershot, 1997), pp. 139–54

Edbury, P., and J. Rowe, *William of Tyre: Historian of the Latin East* (Cambridge, 1988)

Eddé, A.-M., 'Kamal al-Din 'Umar Ibn al-'Adim', *Medieval Muslim Historians and the Franks in the Levant*, ed. A. Mallett (Leiden, 2015), pp. 109–35

—— *Saladin*, trans. J. Todd (Cambridge, MA, 2011)

Edgington, S., 'Albert of Aachen Reappraised', *From Clermont to Jerusalem: The Crusades and Crusader Societies 1095–1500*, ed. A. V. Murray (Turnhout, 1998), pp. 55–68

—— 'Antioch: Medieval City of Culture', *East and West I*, pp. 247–59

Edgington, S., and H. Nicholson (ed.), *Deeds Done Beyond the Sea: Essays on William of Tyre, Cyprus and the Military Orders Presented to Peter Edbury* (Farnham, 2014)

Edgington, S., and C. Sweetenham, *The Chanson d'Antioche: An Old French Account of the First Crusade* (Farnham, 2011)

El-Azhari, T., *Zengi and the Muslim Response to the Crusades: The Politics of Jihad* (Abingdon, 2016)

Elisséeff, N., *Nur ad-Din: un grande prince musulman de Syrie au temps des croisades*, 3 vols (Damascus, 1967)

Ellenblum, R., *Crusader Castles and Modern Histories* (Cambridge, 2007)

—— *Frankish Rural Settlement in the Latin Kingdom of Jerusalem* (Cambridge, 1998)

Enzensberger, H., 'Chanceries, Charters and Administration in Norman Italy', *The Society of Norman Italy*, ed. G. Loud and A. Metcalfe (Leiden, 2002), pp. 117–50

Epp, V., *Fulcher von Chartres: Studien zur Geschichtsschreibung des ersten Kreuzzuges* (Düsseldorf, 1990)

Favreau-Lilie, M.-L., *Die Italiener im Heiligen Land vom Ersten Kreuzzug bis zum Tode Heinrichs von Champagne 1098–1197* (Amsterdam, 1999)

Forey, A., 'The Second Crusade: Scope and Objectives', *Durham University Journal* 86 (1994), 165–75

Fourdrin, J.-P., 'La fortification de la seigneurie épiscopale latine d'El Bara dans le patriarcat d'Antioche (1098–1148)', *Pèlerinages et croisades*, ed. L. Pressouyre (Paris, 1995), pp. 351–406

—— 'Qastun et Chastel de Ruge', *Syria* 72 (1995), 415–26

France, J., *Western Warfare in the Age of the Crusades 1100–1300* (London, 1999)

Friedman, Y., *Encounter between Enemies Captivity and Ransom in the Latin Kingdom of Jerusalem* (Leiden, 2002)

—— 'Gestures of Conciliation: Peacemaking Endeavours in the Latin East', *In Laudem Hierosolymitani: Studies in Crusades and Medieval Culture in Honour of Benjamin Z. Kedar*, ed. I. Shagrir, R. Ellenblum and J. Riley-Smith (Aldershot, 2007), pp. 31–48

Froment, Lieutenant, 'Carte touristique et archéologique du Caza de Harim', *Syria* 11 (1930), 280–92

Gabrieli, F., *Arab Historians of the Crusades*, trans. E. Costello (Berkeley, CA, 1969)

Ganshof, F., *Feudalism* (London, 1952)

Gates, M.-H., '1992 Excavations at Kinet Höyük (Dortyl/Hatay)', *Kazi Sonuçlari Toplantisi* 15:1 (1993), 193–200

Gelichi, S., 'Die Burg Harim', *Burgen und Städte der Kreuzzugszeit*, ed. M. Piana (Petersberg, 2008), pp. 211–20

—— 'Pottery from Ḥarim Castle (Northern Syria): Crusader and Muslim Period', *Çanak: Late Antique and Medieval Pottery and Tiles in Mediterranean and Archaeological Contexts*, ed. B. Böhlendorf-Arslan, A. O. Uysal and J. Witte-Orr (Istanbul, 2007), pp. 457–68

—— 'The Citadel of Harim', *Muslim Military Architecture in Greater Syria: From the Coming of Islam to the Ottoman Period*, ed. H. Kennedy (Leiden, 2006), pp. 184–200

Gerish, D., 'The *Historia Nicaena vel Antiochena* and Royal Identity', *The Second Crusade: Holy War on the Periphery of Latin Christendom*, ed. J. Roche and J. Jensen (Turnhout, 2015), pp. 51–90

Goodman, A., 'Introduction', *War and Border Societies in the Middle Ages*, ed. A. Goodman and A. Tuck (London, 1992), pp. 1–29

Grandin, T., 'Introduction to the Citadel of Salah al-Din', *Syria: Medieval Citadels between East and West*, ed. S. Bianca (Turin, 2007), pp. 139–80

Grecu, V., 'Nicétas Choniatès a-t-il connu l'histoire de Jean Cinnamos?', *Revue des Études Byzantines* 7 (1949), 194–204

Green, J., *Henry I: King of England and Duke of Normandy* (Cambridge, 2009)

—— *The Government of England under Henry I* (Cambridge, 1986)

Greenwood, T., 'Armenian Sources', *Byzantines and Crusaders in Non-Greek Sources 1025–1204*, ed. M. Whitby (Oxford, 2007), pp. 221–52

Grousset, R., *Histoire des Croisades et du Royaume Franc de Jérusalem*, 3 vols (Paris, 1934–1936, new edn 2006)

Hamilton, B., 'Aimery of Limoges, Patriarch of Antioch: Ecumenist, Scholar and Patron of Hermits', *The Joy of Learning and the Love of God: Studies in Honor of Jean Leclercq*, ed. E. R. Elder (Kalamazoo, MI, 1995), pp. 269–90

—— 'Aimery of Limoges, Patriarch of Antioch (c.1142–c.1196), and the Unity of the Churches', *East and West in the Crusader States II*, ed. K. Ciggaar and H. Teule (Leuven, 1999), pp. 1–12

—— 'Manuel I Comnenus and Baldwin IV of Jerusalem', *Kathegetria: Essays Presented to Jean Hussey for her 80th Birthday*, ed. J. Chrysostomides (Camberley, 1988), pp. 353–75

—— 'Ralph of Domfront, Patriarch of Antioch (1135–1140)', *Nottingham Medieval Studies* 18 (1984), 1–21

—— 'The Elephant of Christ: Reynald de Châtillon', *Studies in Church History* 15 (1978), 97–108

—— 'The Growth of the Latin Church of Antioch and the Recruitment of its Clergy', *East and West I*, pp. 171–84

—— 'The Old French Translation of William of Tyre as an Historical Source', *The Experience of Crusading vol. 2: Defining the Crusader Kingdom*, ed. P. Edbury and J. Phillips (Cambridge, 2003), pp. 93–112

—— *The Latin Church in the Crusader States: The Secular Church* (London, 1980)

—— *The Leper King and his Heirs: Baldwin IV and the Crusader Kingdom of Jerusalem* (Cambridge, 2005)

—— 'The Titular Nobility of the Latin East: the Case of Agnes of Courtenay', *Crusade and Settlement*, ed. P. Edbury (Cardiff, 1985), pp. 197–203

—— 'Three Patriarchs at Antioch, 1165–1170', *Dei gesta per Francos: études sur les croisades dédiées à Jean Richard*, ed. M. Balard, B. Z. Kedar and J. Riley-Smith (Aldershot, 2001), pp. 199–207

—— 'William of Tyre and the Byzantine Empire', *Porphyrogenita: Essays on the History and Literature of Byzantium and the Latin East in Honour of Julian Chrysostomides*, ed. C. Dendrinos, J. Harris *et al.* (Aldershot, 2003), pp. 219–33

Handyside, P., 'Differing Views of Renaud de Châtillon', *Deeds Done Beyond the Sea*, pp. 43–52

Hamilton, S., *The Practice of Penance, 900–1050* (Woodbridge, 2001)

Harari, Y., 'The Military Role of the Frankish Turcopoles: A Reassessment', *Mediterranean Historical Review* 12:1 (1997), 75–116

Harris, J., *Byzantium and the Crusades*, 2nd edn (London, 2014)

Harrison, T., 'The 1998 Amuq Valley Regional Project Survey', *Araştirma Sonuçlari Toplantisi* 17:2 (1999), 127–32

Harrison, T., and S. Batiuk, 'The 1999 Amuq Valley Regional Project Survey', *Araştirma Sonuçlari Toplantisi* 18:2 (2000), 181–6

Harvey, P., and A. McGuinness, *A Guide to British Medieval Seals* (London, 1996)

Hiestand, R., 'Chronologisches zur Geschichte des Königreichs Jerusalem', *Deutsches Archiv* 35 (1979), 542–55

—— 'Un centre intellectual en Syrie du Nord? Notes sur la personalité d'Aimery d'Antioche, Albert de Tarse et *Rorgo Fretellus*', *Le Moyen Age* 100 (1994), 7–36

—— 'Zum Problem des Templerzentralarchiv', *Archivalische Zeitschrift* 76 (1980), 17–37

Hilkens, A., 'The Anonymous Syriac Chronicle Up to the Year 1234 and its Sources' (unpublished PhD thesis, Universiteit Gent, 2014)

Hillenbrand, C., '"Abominable Acts": the Career of Zengi', *The Second Crusade: Scope and Consequences*, ed. J. Phillips and M. Hoch (Manchester, 2001), pp. 111–32

—— 'Sources in Arabic', *Byzantines and Crusaders in Non-Greek Sources 1025–1204*, ed. M. Whitby (Oxford, 2007), pp. 283–340

—— *The Crusades: Islamic Perspectives* (Edinburgh, 1999)

Hirschler, K., *Medieval Arabic Historiography: Authors as Actors* (London, 2006)

Hitti, P., *An Arab-Syrian Gentleman and Warrior in the Period of the Crusades* (New York, 1929)

Hoch, M., 'The Choice of Damascus as the Objective of the Second Crusade', *Autour de la Première Croisade*, ed. M. Balard (Paris, 1996), pp. 359–69

—— 'The Price of failure: the Second Crusade as a Turning-Point in the History of the Latin East?', *The Second Crusade: Scope and Consequences*, ed. J. Phillips and M. Hoch (Manchester, 2001), pp. 180–200

Hodgson, N., 'Conflict and Cohabitation: Marriage and Diplomacy between Latins and Cilician Armenians, c.1097–1253', *The Crusades and the Near East: Cultural Histories*, ed. C. Kostick (Abingdon, 2011), pp. 83–106

—— *Women, Crusading and the Holy Land in Historical Narrative* (Woodbridge, 2007)

Holmes, C., 'Byzantium's Eastern Frontier in the Tenth and Eleventh Centuries', *Medieval Frontiers: Concepts and Practices*, ed. D. Abulafia and N. Berend (Aldershot, 2002), pp. 83–104

Holt, J., 'The Introduction of Knight-Service in England', *Colonial England, 1066–1215*, ed. J. Holt (London, 1997), pp. 81–101

Horna, K., 'Das Hodoiporikon des Konstantin Manasses', *Byzantinische Zeitschrift* 13 (1904), 313–55

Hunyadi, Z., '*Maiores, Optimates, Nobiles*: Semantic Questions in the Early History of the Hungarian Nobility', *Annual of Medieval Studies at the CEU* 4 (1996/1997), 204–11

Huygens, R. B. C., 'Editing William of Tyre', *Sacris Erudiri* 27 (1984), 461–73

—— 'La campagne de Saladin en Syrie du Nord 1188', *Colloque Apamée de Syrie: Bilan de recherches archéologiques* (Brussels, 1974), pp. 273–83

Jacoby, D., *Commercial Exchange Across the Mediterranean* (Aldershot, 2005)

Jamil, N., and J. Johns, 'An Original Arabic Document from Crusader Antioch (1213 AD)', *Texts, Documents and Artefacts: Islamic Studies in Honour of D.S. Richards*, ed. C. F. Robinson (Leiden, 2003), pp. 157–90

Jeffreys, E., *Four Byzantine Novels* (Liverpool, 2012)

Jiménez, M., 'Frontier and Settlement in the Kingdom of Castile (1085–1350)', *Medieval Frontier Societies*, ed. R. Bartlett and A. MacKay (Oxford, 1996), pp. 49–76

John, S., 'Historical Truth and the Miraculous Past: The Use of Oral Evidence in Twelfth-Century Latin Historical Writing on the First Crusade', *EHR* 543 (2015), 263–301

Johns, J., *Arabic Administration in Norman Sicily: The Royal Diwan* (Cambridge, 2002)

Jotischky, A., *Crusading and the Crusader States* (Harlow, 2004)

—— 'Ethnographic Attitudes in the Crusader States: The Franks and the Indigenous Orthodox People', *East and West in the Crusader States III*, ed. K. Ciggaar and H. Teule (Leuven, 2003), pp. 1–19

——— *The Perfection of Solitude: Hermits and Monks in the Crusader States* (University Park, PA, 1995)

Kaniewski, D., *et al.*, 'Medieval Coastal Syrian Vegetation Patterns in the Principality of Antioch', *The Holocene* 21 (2010), 251–62

Kaufhold, H., 'Notizen zur Späten Geschichte des Barsaumo-Klosters', *Hugoye: Journal of Syriac Studies* 3:2 (2000), 223–46

Kazhdan, A., *The Oxford Dictionary of Byzantium*, 3 vols (Oxford, 1991)

Kazhdan, A., and S. Franklin, *Studies on Byzantine Literature of the Eleventh and Twelfth Centuries* (Cambridge, 1984)

Kedar, B. Z., 'Convergences of Oriental Christian, Muslim, and Frankish Worshippers: The Case of Saydnaya', *De Sion exibit lex et verbum domini de Hierusalem: Essays on Medieval Law, Liturgy and Literature in Honour of Amnon Linder*, ed. Y. Hen (Turnhout, 2001), pp. 59–69

——— *Crusade and Mission: European Approaches towards the Muslims* (Princeton, NJ, 1984)

——— 'Gerard of Nazareth, a Neglected Twelfth-Century Writer in the Latin East: A Contribution to the Intellectual and Monastic History of the Crusader States', *DOP* 37 (1983), 55–77

——— 'On the Origins of the Earliest Laws of Frankish Jerusalem: The Canons of the Council of Nablus, 1120', *Speculum* 74:2 (1999), 310–35

——— 'Some New Light on the Composition Process of William of Tyre's *Historia*', *Deeds Done Beyond the Sea*, pp. 3–12

——— 'The Subjected Muslims of the Frankish Levant', *Muslims under Latin Rule, 1100–1300*, ed. J. Powell (Princeton, NJ, 1990), pp. 135–74

Kedar, B. Z., and E. Kohlberg, 'The Intercultural Career of Theodore of Antioch', *Intercultural Contacts in the Medieval Mediterranean*, ed. B. Arbel (London, 1996), pp. 164–76

Kennedy, H., *Crusader Castles* (Cambridge, 1994)

Kirschberger, T., *Erster Kreuzzug und Ethnogenese: In novam formam commutatus – Ethnogenetische Prozesse im Fürstentum Antiochia und im Königreich Jerusalem* (Göttingen, 2015)

Köhler, M., *Alliances and Treaties between Frankish and Muslim Rulers in the Middle East*, trans. P. Holt and K. Hirschler (Leiden, 2013)

Kostick, C., 'William of Tyre, Livy, and the Vocabulary of Class', *Journal of the History of Ideas* 65:3 (2004), 353–68

Kováts, I., 'Meat Consumption and Animal Keeping in the Citadel at al-Marqab: a Preliminary Report', *The Military Orders 5: Power and Politics*, ed. P. Edbury (Farnham, 2012), pp. 65–74

Koziol, G., *Begging Pardon and Favor: Ritual and Political Order in Early Medieval France* (Ithaca, NY, 1992)

Kuehn, E., 'Melchizedek as Exemplar for Kingship in Twelfth-Century Political Thought', *History of Political Thought* 31:4 (2010), 557–75

La Monte, J. L., *Feudal Monarchy in the Latin Kingdom of Jerusalem, 1100–1291* (Baltimore, MD, 1932)

Lapina, E., 'Gambling and Gaming in the Holy Land: Chess, Dice and Other Games in the Sources of the Crusades', *Crusades* 12 (2013), 121–32

Lawrence, A., 'The Castle of Baghras', *The Cilician Kingdom of Armenia*, ed. T. S. R. Boase (Edinburgh, 1978), pp. 34–83

Lewis, B., *The Assassins: A Radical Sect in Islam* (London, 1967)

Lewis, K., 'Medieval Diglossia: The Diversity of the Latin Christian Encounter with Written and Spoken Arabic in the "Crusader" County of Tripoli, with a Hitherto Unpublished Arabic Note from the Principality of Antioch (MS, AOM 3, Valletta: National Library of Malta, no. 51v)', *Al-Masaq* 27:2 (2015), 119–52

—— 'Rule and Identity in a Diverse Mediterranean Society: Aspects of the County of Tripoli during the Twelfth Century' (unpublished PhD thesis, University of Oxford, 2014)

Lieberman, M., *The Medieval March of Wales: The Creation and Perception of a Frontier, 1066–1283* (Cambridge, 2010)

Lilie, R.-J., *Byzantium and the Crusader States 1096–1204*, trans. J. C. Morris and J. E. Ridings (Oxford, 1993)

Loud, G., 'Norman Italy and the Holy Land', *The Horns of Hattin: Proceedings of the Second Conference of the Society for the Study of the Crusades and the Latin East*, ed. B. Z. Kedar (Jerusalem, 1992), pp. 49–62

—— *The Crusade of Frederick Barbarossa: The History of the Expedition of the Emperor Frederick and Related Texts* (Farnham, 2013)

Lyons, M., and D. Jackson, *Saladin: the Politics of the Holy War* (Cambridge, 1982)

MacEvitt, C., *The Crusades and the Christian World of the East: Rough Tolerance* (Philadelphia, PA, 2008)

Magdalino, P., *The Empire of Manuel I Komnenos 1143–1180* (Cambridge, 1993)

—— 'The Pen of the Aunt: Echoes of the Mid-Twelfth Century in the *Alexiad*', *Anna Komnene and Her Times*, ed. T. Gouma-Peterson (New York, 2000), pp. 15–43

Major, B., 'Crusader Towers of the *Terre de Calife* and its Vicinity', *The Arabist* 19–20 (1998), 211–28

—— *Medieval Rural Settlements in the Syrian Coastal Region (12th and 13th Centuries)* (Oxford, 2015)

—— 'Muslim Towers in the Medieval Syrian Countryside', *Continuity and Change in the Realms of Islam: Studies in Honour of Professor Urbain Vermeulan*, ed. K. D'Hulster (Leuven, 2008), pp. 423–8

—— 'Observations on Crusader Settlements between the Nahr al-Kabir and the Nahr as-Sinn', *Le comté de Tripoli: état multiculturel et multiconfessionnel (1102–1289)*, ed. G. Dédéyan and K. Rizak (Paris, 2010), pp. 119–52

—— 'The Fortified Caves of the Jabal Wastani Region', *Château Gaillard* 22 (2006), 251–7

—— 'The Medieval Mill of Banyas and Some Notes on the Topography of the Town of Valania', *East and West II*, pp. 367–90

Major, B., and E. Galambos, 'Archaeological and Fresco Research in the Castle Chapel at al-Marqab: a Preliminary Report on the Results of the First Seasons',

The Military Orders 5: Power and Politics, ed. P. Edbury (Farnham, 2012), pp. 23–48

Mallett, A., 'Islamic Historians of the Ayyubid Era and Muslim Rulers from the Early Crusading Period: A Study in the Use of History', *Al-Masaq* 24:3 (2012), 241–52

—— *Popular Muslim Reactions to the Franks in the Levant, 1097–1291* (Farnham, 2014)

—— 'The Battle of Inab', *JMH* 39:1 (2013), 48–60

Marcovich, M., 'The *Itinerary* of Constantine Manasses', *Illinois Classical Studies* 12:1 (1987), 277–91

Marshall, C., *Warfare in the Latin East, 1192–1291* (Cambridge, 1992)

Martin, J.-M., 'Les structures féodales normanno-souabes et la Terre Sainte', *Il Mezzogiorno normanno-svevo e le Crociate: Atti delle quattordicesime giornate normanno-sveve Bari, 17–20 Octobre 2000*, ed. G. Musca (Bari, 2002), pp. 225–50

—— 'Settlement and the Agrarian Economy', *The Society of Norman Italy*, ed. G. Loud and A. Metcalfe (Leiden, 2002), pp. 17–46

Matthew, D., *The Norman Kingdom of Sicily* (Cambridge, 1992)

Mayer, H. E., 'Angevins *versus* Normans: The New Men of King Fulk of Jerusalem', *Proceedings of the American Philosophical Society* 133:1 (1989), 1–25

—— 'Die antiochenische Regentschaft Balduins II. von Jerusalem im Spiegel der Urkunden', *Deutsches Archiv* 47 (1991), 559–66

—— *Die Kanzlei der lateinischen Könige von Jerusalem* (Hannover, 1996)

—— 'Die Register der Secrète des Königreichs Jerusalem', *Deutsches Archiv* 57 (2001), 165–70

—— 'Die Seigneurie de Joscelin und der Deutsche Orden', *Die geistlichen Ritterorden Europas*, ed. J. Fleckenstein and M. Hellman (Sigmaringen, 1980), pp. 171–216

—— 'Guillaume de Tyr á l'École', *Mémoires de l'Académie des sciences, arts et belles-lettres de Dijon* 127 (1988), 257–65

—— 'Jérusalem et Antioche au temps de Baudouin II', *Comptes-rendus de l'Académie des inscriptions et belles-lettres, Novembre–Décembre 1980* (Paris, 1981), pp. 717–33

—— 'Latins, Muslims and Greeks in the Latin Kingdom of Jerusalem', *History* 63 (1978), 175–92

—— 'Studies in the History of Queen Melisende of Jerusalem', *DOP* 26 (1972), 93–182

—— 'The Double County of Jaffa and Ascalon: One Fief or Two?', *Crusade and Settlement*, ed. P. Edbury (Cardiff, 1985), pp. 181–90

—— 'The Wheel of Fortune: Seignorial Vicissitudes under Kings Fulk and Baldwin III of Jerusalem', *Speculum* 65 (1990), 860–77

—— 'Une lettre de sauf conduit d'un roi croisé de Jérusalem à un marchand musulman (1156/1163)', *La présence latine en Orient au Moyen Âge*, ed. G. Brunel *et al.* (Paris, 2000), pp. 27–35

—— *Varia Antiochena: Studien zum Kreuzfahrerfürstentum Antiochia im 12. und frühen 13. Jarhundert* (Hannover, 1993)

Mesqui, J., 'Bourzey, une forteresse anonyme de l'Oronte', *La fortification au temps des croisades*, ed. N. Faucherre, J. Mesqui and N. Prouteau (Rennes, 2004), pp. 95–133

—— 'Die Burg Saone (Sahyun, Qal'at Salah ad-Din)', *Burgen und Städte der Kreuzzugszeit*, ed. M. Piana (Petersberg, 2008), pp. 356–66

Metcalf, D., 'Billon Coinage in the Crusading Principality of Antioch', *Numismatic Chronicle* 9th Series 7 (1969), 247–67

—— *Coinage of the Crusades and the Latin East in the Ashmolean Museum* (Oxford, 1983)

—— 'Monetary Questions Arising out of the Role of the Templars as Guardians of the Northern Marches of the Principality of Antioch', *The Crusades and the Military Orders: Expanding the Frontiers of Medieval Latin Christianity*, ed. Z. Hunyadi and J. Laszlovsky (Budapest, 2001), pp. 77–87

—— 'Six Unresolved Problems in the Monetary History of Antioch, 969–1268', *East and West I*, pp. 283–318

Metcalfe, A., 'The Muslims of Sicily under Christian Rule', *The Society of Norman Italy*, ed. G. Loud and A. Metcalfe (Leiden, 2002), pp. 289–317

Michaudel, B., 'Burzaih', *Burgen und Städte der Kreuzzugszeit*, ed. M. Piana (Petersberg, 2008), pp. 178–87

—— 'Le château de Saône/Sahyûn en Syrie, creuset de l'architecture médiévale en Orient', *Chronos* 23 (2011), 1–39

—— 'Le château de Saône/Qal'at Salah-al-Din', *Archéologie Islamique* 11 (2001), 201–6

Micheau, F., 'De l'Occident a l'orient: Claude Cahen, historien des croisades', *Arabica* 43:1 (1996), 71–88

—— 'Ibn al-Athir', *Medieval Muslim Historians and the Franks in the Levant*, ed. A. Mallett (Leiden, 2015), pp. 52–84

Morillo, S., *Warfare under the Anglo-Norman Kings, 1066–1135* (Woodbridge, 1994)

Morray, D., 'A Rock-Working at Cursat Castle', *Anatolian Studies: Journal of the British Institute of Archaeology at Ankara* 40 (1990), 199–204

Morris, C., *The Papal Monarchy: The Western Church from 1050 to 1250* (Oxford, 1991)

Morton, N., *The Medieval Military Orders, 1120–1314* (Harlow, 2013)

Mourad, S., and J. Lindsay, 'A Muslim Response to the Second Crusade: Ibn Asakir of Damascus as a Propagandist of Jihad', *The Second Crusade: Holy War on the Periphery of Latin Christendom*, ed. J. Roche and J. Møller Jensen (Turnhout, 2015), pp. 91–111

Murray, A. V., 'Baldwin II and His Nobles: Baronial Factionalism and Dissent in the Kingdom of Jerusalem, 1118–1134', *Nottingham Medieval Studies* 38 (1994), 60–85

—— 'Ethnic Identity in the Crusader States: the Frankish Race and the Settlement of Outremer', *Concepts of National Identity in the Middle Ages*, ed. S. Forde, L. Johnson and A. V. Murray (Leeds, 1995), pp. 59–73

—— 'Franks and Indigenous Communities in Palestine and Syria (1099–1187): A Hierarchical Model of Social Interaction in the Principalities of Outremer', *East and West in the Middle Ages and Early Modern Times: Transcultural Experiences in the Premodern World*, ed. A. Classen (Berlin, 2013), pp. 289–307

—— 'How Norman was the Principality of Antioch? Prolegomena to a Study of the Origins of a Crusader State', *Family Trees and the Roots of Politics: The Prosopography of Britain and France from the Tenth to the Twelfth Century*, ed. K. Keats-Rohan (Woodbridge, 1997), pp. 349–59

Mutafian, C., 'The Brilliant Diplomacy of Cilician Armenia', *Armenian Cilicia*, ed. R. Hovannisian and S. Payaslian (Costa Meza, CA, 2008), pp. 93–110

Nasrallah, J., 'Syriens et Suriens', *Symposium Syriacum 1972: célebré dans les jours 26–31 octobre 1972 à l'Institut Ponitifical Oriental de Rome: Rapports et Communications* (Rome, 1974), pp. 487–503

Nicholson, R., *Joscelyn III and the Fall of the Crusader States 1134–1199* (Leiden, 1973)

—— 'The Growth of the Latin States, 1118–1144', *A History of the Crusades vol.1: The First Hundred Years*, ed. K. Setton *et al.* (Madison, WI, 1963), pp. 410–48

O'Hara, M., 'A Possible Coinage for Alexius II (?), 1180–1184', *Numismatic Circular* 97 (1987), pp. 111–13

Ouzounian, A., 'Les Assises d'Antioche ou la langue en usage: remarques à propos du texte arménien des Assises d'Antioche', *La Méditerranée Arméniens: XII–XV siècle*, ed. C. Mutafian (Paris, 2014), pp. 133–62

Pahlitzsch, J., *Graeci und Suriani im Palästina der Kreuzfahrerzeit* (Berlin, 2001)

Parnell, D., 'John II Comnenus and Crusader Antioch', *Crusades – Medieval Worlds in Conflict*, ed. T. Madden, J. Naus and V. Ryan (Aldershot, 2010), pp. 149–57

Paul, N., *To Follow in their Footsteps: The Crusades and Family Memory in the High Middle Ages* (Ithaca, NY and London, 2012)

Peña, I., P. Castellana and R. Fernández, *Inventaire du Jébel Baricha: Recherches archéologiques dans la région des Villes Mortes de la Syrie du Nord* (Milan, 1987)

—— *Inventaire du Jebel el-A'la: Recherches archéologiques dans la région des Villes Mortes de la Syrie du Nord* (Milan, 1990)

—— *Inventaire du Jébel Wastani: Recherches archéologiques dans la région des Villes Mortes de la Syrie du Nord* (Milan, 1999)

—— *Inventaire du Jébel Doueili: Recherches archéologiques dans la région des Villes Mortes de la Syrie du Nord* (Milan, 2003)

Pesant, R., 'A Coin of Baldwin II, King of Jerusalem, as Regent of Antioch', *Spink Numismatic Circular* 96:8 (1988), 245

—— 'St. George and the Dragon on the Coinage of Roger of Antioch', *Spink Numismatic Circular* 100:3 (1992), 79

Phillips, J., 'A Note on the Origins of Raymond of Poitiers', *EHR* 418 (1991), 66–7

—— *Defenders of the Holy Land: Relations between the Latin East and the West, 1119–1187* (Oxford, 1996)

—— *The Second Crusade: Extending the Frontiers of Christendom* (New Haven, CT, 2007)

Porteous, J., 'Crusader Coinage with Greek or Latin Inscriptions', *A History of the Crusades vol. 6: the Impact of the Crusades on Europe*, ed. H. W. Hazard and N. Zacour (Madison, WI, 1989), pp. 354–87

Power, D., *The Norman Frontier in the Twelfth and Early Thirteenth Centuries* (Cambridge, 2004)

Powers, J., *A Society Organized for War: the Iberian Municipal Militias in the Central Middle Ages, 1000–1284* (Berkeley, CA, 1987)

Prawer, J., *Crusader Institutions* (Oxford, 1980)

—— *The Crusaders' Kingdom: European Colonialism in the Middle Ages* (New York, 1972)

Prestwich, J., 'The Military Household of the Norman Kings', *Anglo-Norman Warfare: Studies in Late Anglo-Saxon and Anglo-Norman Military Organization and Warfare, ed. M. Strickland (Woodbridge, 1992), pp. 93–127*

Prestwich, M., 'The Military Household of the Norman Kings', *EHR* 378 (1981), 1–35

Pringle, D., 'Castles and Frontiers in the Latin East', *Norman Expansion: Connections, Continuities and Contrasts*, ed. K. Stringer and A. Jotischky (Farnham, 2013), pp. 227–38

Pryor, J., *Commerce, Shipping and Naval Warfare in the Medieval Mediterranean* (London, 1987)

—— *Geography, Technology and War: Studies in the Maritime History of the Mediterranean, 649–1571* (Cambridge, 1988)

Pryor, J., and M. Jeffreys, 'Alexios, Bohemond, and Byzantium's Euphrates Frontier: A Tale of Two Cretans', *Crusades* 11 (2012), 31–86

Redford, S., *The Archaeology of the Frontier in the Medieval Near East: Excavations at Gritille, Turkey* (Boston, MA, 1998)

—— 'Trade and Economy in Antioch and Cilicia in the Twelfth and Thirteenth Centuries', *Trade and Markets in Byzantium*, ed. C. Morrisson (Washington, DC, 2012), pp. 297–309

Reilly, B., *The Medieval Spains* (Cambridge, 1993)

Reynolds, S., *Fiefs and Vassals: the Medieval Evidence Reinterpreted* (Oxford, 1994)

—— 'Fiefs and Vassals in Twelfth-Century Jerusalem: a View from the West', *Crusades* 1 (2002), 29–48

Rheinheimer, M., 'Tankred und das Siegel Boemunds', *Schweizerische Numismatische Rundschau* 70 (1991), 75–93

Richard, J., 'Aux origins d'un grand lignage: des Paladii à Renaud de Châtillon', *Recueil de melanges offerts a Karl Ferdinand Werner à l'occasion de son 65e anniversaire* (Maulévrier, 1989), pp. 409–18

—— 'La confrérie de la croisade: à propos d'un épisode de la première croisade', *Mélanges offerts à E. R. Labande* (Poitiers, 1974), pp. 617–22

—— *Le comté de Tripoli sous la dynastie toulousaine* (Paris, 1945)

—— 'Les comtes de Tripoli et leurs vassaux sous la dynastie antiochénienne', *Crusade and Settlement*, ed. P. Edbury (Cardiff, 1985), pp. 213–24

—— 'Sainte-Croix d'Antioche: un monastère feminine de tradition érémitique au temps des croisades?', *Chronos. Revue d'Histoire de l'Université de Balamand* 13 (2006), 29–35

—— *The Kingdom of Jerusalem*, trans. J. Shirley, 2 vols (Amsterdam, 1979)

Richter-Bernburg, L., "Imad al-Din al-Iṣfahani', *Medieval Muslim Historians and the Franks in the Levant*, ed. A. Mallett (Leiden, 2015), pp. 29–51

Riis, T., 'Die Übernahme Marqabs durch die Johanniter (1186)', *Werkstatt des Historikers der mittelalterlichen Ritterorden. Quellenkundliche, Probleme und Forschungsmethoden*, ed. Z. Nowak (Toruń, 1987), pp. 151–6

—— 'The Medieval Period', *Topographical Studies in the Gabla Plain*, ed. P. J. Riis *et al.* (Copenhagen, 2004), pp. 85–115

Riley-Smith, J., 'A Note on the Confraternities in the Latin Kingdom of Jerusalem', *The Bulletin of Historical Research* 44 (1971), 301–8

—— 'Further Thoughts on Baldwin II's établissement on the Confiscation of Fiefs', *Crusade and Settlement*, ed. P. Edbury (Cardiff, 1985), pp. 176–80

—— 'Government and the Indigenous in the Latin Kingdom of Jerusalem', *Medieval Frontiers: Concepts and Practices*, ed. D. Abulafia and N. Berend (Aldershot, 2002), pp. 121–31

—— 'Some Lesser Officials in Latin Syria', *EHR* 87 (1972), 1–26

—— *The Feudal Nobility and the Kingdom of Jerusalem, 1174–1277* (London, 1973)

—— *The Knights of St. John in Jerusalem and Cyprus, c.1050–1310* (London, 1967)

—— 'The Templars and the Teutonic Knights in Cilician Armenia', *The Cilician Kingdom of Armenia*, ed. T. Boase (London, 1978), pp. 92–117

Rowe, J., 'The Papacy and the Ecclesiastical Province of Tyre', *Bulletin of the John Rylands Library* 43 (1960–1961), 160–89

Rubin, J., 'The Debate on Twelfth-Century Frankish Feudalism: Additional Evidence from William of Tyre's *Chronicon*', *Crusades* 8 (2009), 53–62

Rudt de Collenberg, W.-H., 'A Fragmentary Copy of an Unknown Recension of the "Lignages d'Outre-Mer" in the Vatican Library', *EHR* 387 (1983), 311–27

Runciman, S., *A History of the Crusades*, 3 vols (Cambridge, 1951–1954)

—— 'The Greeks in Antioch at the Time of the Crusades', *Proceedings of the International Congress of Byzantine Studies, Thessalonica, 1953* (Athens, 1956), pp. 583–91

Russo, L., *I Normanni del Mezzogiorno e il movimento crociato* (Bari, 2014)

Saadé, G., 'Histoire du château de Saladin', *Studii Medievali* 3rd Series 9:2 (1968), 980–1016

Salibi, K., *Maronite Historians of Mediaeval Lebanon* (Beirut, 1959)

Sanders, I. J., *English Baronies: A Study of their Origin and Descent, 1086–1327* (Oxford, 1960)

Sanjian, A., 'The Armenians in Bilad al-Sham', *Proceedings of the First International Conference on Bilad al-Sham* (Amman, Jordan, 1974), pp. 195–221

Schenk, J., 'Nomadic Violence in the First Latin Kingdom of Jerusalem and the Military Orders', *Reading Medieval Studies* 36 (2010), 39–55

Schlumberger, G., 'Monnaies et sceaux des Croisades', *Mélanges Numismatiques* 2 (1877), 168–96

—— *Numismatique de l'Orient latin* (Paris, 1878)

—— *Renaud de Châtillon, prince d'Antioche, seigneur de la terre d'Outre-Jourdain* (Paris, 1923)

Schlumberger, G., F. Chalandon and A. Blanchet, *Sigillographie de l'Orient latin* (Paris, 1943)

Schwinges, R. C., *Kreuzzugsideologie und Toleranz: Studien zu Wilhelm von Tyrus* (Stuttgart, 1977)

Simpson, A., *Niketas Choniates: A Historiographical Study* (Oxford, 2013)

Sivan, E., *L'Islam et la Croisade: idéologie et propagande dans les réactions Musulmanes aux Croisades* (Paris, 1968)

Skottki, K., 'Of "Pious Traitors" and Dangerous Encounters. Historiographical Notions of Interculturality in the Principality of Antioch', *Journal of Transcultural Medieval Studies* 1:1 (2014), 75–115

Smail, R. C., *Crusading Warfare, 1097–1193*, 2nd edn (Cambridge, 1995)

—— 'The Predicaments of Guy of Lusignan, 1183–1187', *Outremer: Studies in the History of the Crusading Kingdom of Jerusalem*, ed. B. Z. Kedar, H. E. Mayer and R. C. Smail (Jerusalem, 1982), pp. 159–76

Smarandache, B., 'The Franks and the Nizari Isma'ilis in the Early Crusader Period', *Al-Masaq* 24:3 (2012), 221–40

Sourdel-Thomine, J., 'Le peuplement de la region des "villes-mortes" (Syrie du Nord) à l'époque ayyūbide', *Arabica* 1 (1954), 187–200

Stephenson, P., 'John Cinnamus, John II Comnenus and the Hungarian Campaign of 1127–1129', *Byzantion* 66 (1996), 177–87

Stone, M. E., 'A Notice about Patriarch Aimery of Antioch in an Armenian Colophon of 1181', *Crusades* 3 (2004), 125–9

Takayama, H., 'Familiares Regis and the Royal Inner Council in Twelfth-Century Sicily', *EHR* 441 (1989), 357–72

Talmon-Heller, D., 'Arabic Sources on Muslim Villagers under Frankish Rule', *From Clermont to Jerusalem: The Crusades and Crusader Societies 1095–1500*, ed. A. V. Murray (Turnhout, 1998), pp. 103–17

Tessera, M. R., *Orientalis ecclesia: Papato, Chiesa e regno latino di Gerusalemme (1099–1187)* (Milan, 2010)

——, '*Prudentes homines…qui sensus habebant magis exercitos*: a Preliminary Inquiry in William of Tyre's Vocabulary of Power', *Crusades* 1 (2002), 63–71

Thompson, K., *Power and Border Lordship in Medieval France: The County of the Perche, 1000–1226* (Woodbridge, 2002)

—— 'Robert of Bellême Reconsidered', *Anglo-Norman Studies* 13 (1991), 263–86

Tibble, S., *Monarchy and Lordships in the Latin Kingdom of Jerusalem, 1099–1291* (Oxford, 1989)

Todt, K.-P., 'The Greek-Orthodox Patriarchate of Antioch in the Period of the Renewed Byzantine Rule and in the Time of the First Crusades (969–1204)', *The History of the Greek Orthodox Church. What Specificity? Papers Given at a Conference in the University of Balamand (Tripolis/Lebanon) 11–14 January 1999* (Balamand, 1999), pp. 33–53

Tonghini, C., and N. Montevecchi, 'The Castle of Shayzar: The Fortification of the Access System', *Muslim Military Architecture in Greater Syria: From the Coming of Islam to the Ottoman Period*, ed. H. Kennedy (Leiden, 2006), pp. 201–24

Urban, W., 'The Frontier Thesis and the Baltic Crusade', *Crusade and Conversion on the Baltic Frontier, 1150–1500*, ed. A. V. Murray (Aldershot, 2001), pp. 45–71

Van Houts, E., 'Genre Aspects of the Use of Oral Information in Medieval Historiography', *Gattungen mittelalterlicher Schriftlichkeit*, ed. B. Frank, T. Haye and D. Tophinke (Tübingen, 1997), pp. 297–311

Van Luyn, P., 'Milites et Barones', *Cahiers de civilisation médiévale* 36e année 143 (1993), 281–95

Van Nerom, C., 'Un fragment de trésor: 129 deniers de Bohémond III prince d'Antioche (1149–1201)', *Revue belge de numismatique et de sigillographie* 131 (1985), 163–84

Vessey, D., 'William of Tyre and the Art of Historiography', *Mediaeval Studies* 35 (1973), 433–55

Vincent, N., 'The Court of Henry II', *Henry II: New Interpretations*, ed. C. Harper-Bill and N. Vincent (Woodbridge, 2007), pp. 278–334

—— 'The Pilgrimages of the Angevin Kings of England 1154–1272', *Pilgrimage: The English Experience from Becket to Bunyan*, ed. C. Morris and P. Roberts (Cambridge, 2002), pp. 12–45

Vorderstrasse, T., *Al-Mina: A Port of Antioch from Late Antiquity to the End of the Ottomans* (Oosten, 2005)

—— 'Archaeology of the Antiochene Region in the Crusader Period', *East and West I*, pp. 319–36

—— 'Medieval Encounters between China, Mongolia, Antioch and Cilicia', *East and West II*, pp. 345–66

Weltecke, D., 'A Renaissance in Historiography? Patriarch Michael, the Anonymous Chronicle ad a.c. 1234, and Bar 'Ebroyo', *The Syriac Renaissance*, ed. H. Teule, T. Fotescu *et al.* (Leuven, 2010), pp. 95–111

—— *Die 'Beschreibung der Zeiten' von Mor Michael Dem Grossen (1126–1199): Eine Studie zu ihrem historischen und historiographiegeschichtlichen Kontext* (Louvain, 2003)

—— 'Contacts between Syriac Orthodox and Latin Military Orders', *East and West in the Crusader States III*, ed. K. Ciggaar and H. Teule (Leuven, 2003), pp. 53–77

—— 'On the Syriac Orthodox in the Principality of Antioch during the Crusader Period', *East and West I*, pp. 95–124

—— 'Originality and Function of Formal Structures in the Chronicle of Michael the Great', *Hugoye: Journal of Syriac Studies* 3:2 (2000), 173–202

—— 'The World Chronicle by Patriarch Michael the Great (1126–1199): Some Reflections', *Journal of Assyrian Academic Studies* 11 (1997), 6–30

Wilkinson, T., and K. Yener, 'Amuq Interim Report 1995/1196', *Araştirma Sonuçlari Toplantisi* 14:2 (1996), 413–31

Witakowski, W., 'Syriac Historiographical Sources', *Byzantines and Crusaders in Non-Greek Sources 1025–1204*, ed. M. Whitby (Oxford, 2007), pp. 253–82

Yener, K. *et al.*, 'The Amuq Valley Regional Project, 1995–1998', *American Journal of Archaeology* 104:2 (2000), 162–220

Index

Abd al-Massie, *rayyis* of Margat 170, 180, 185
'Abd al-Rahim al-Atharibi 185
Abu Shama 14, 37, 53, 168, 177
Adana 27, 54, 102, 167, 193
Afis 41, 167–8
Ager Sanguinis, battle of 1, 21, 24, 27, 69, 73,
    77, 101, 112–13, 118, 130, 174, 192,
    218, 220, 224, 227, 248
Agnes, daughter of Renaud of Châtillon and
    Constance of Antioch 99, 213
Agnes of Courtenay, daughter of Count
    Joscelin II of Edessa 147–8, 151, 213
Agnes of Tripoli, daughter of Count Pons of
    Tripoli 148–9, 155
Aimery, bishop of Tripoli 108
Aimery of Limoges, patriarch of Antioch 9,
    51–3, 103–9, 117, 153, 165, 209,
    212–14, 227, 229
al-Atharib (Cerep) 17, 24–7, 30–1, 33, 36,
    185, 196, 246–7
    lordship of 132–3, 143, 157, 163
al-Azimi 13, 25–6, 31, 35, 141–2, 175–6,
    193, 225
al-Bab 30–1
al-Bara 37–8
    bishopric of 101
al-Salih, sultan of Aleppo 51–3, 55
Alan of al-Atharib 132, 185
Albert, archbishop of Tarsus 108, 125
Albert of Aachen 8, 68, 167
Aleppo 1, 13, 17, 21, 24–7, 30–8, 41–2, 48,
    51–3, 60, 94, 120, 131–2, 173, 192, 194,
    196, 220, 233–4, 236, 241–3, 245–6
Alexander III, pope 107–8, 213–14
Alexios I Komnenos, emperor of Byzantium
    189, 192, 195
Alexios II Komnenos, emperor of Byzantium
    51, 100, 212, 214–15
Ali ibn Wafa, Isma'ili leader 38, 116

Alice, princess of Antioch 4, 22, 24–5, 70–1,
    73, 89, 96–7, 121, 132–9, 141, 143,
    191–2, 221–6, 236–7
Alice of Armenia, wife of Raymond II of
    Antioch 59, 182
Amalric, king of Jerusalem 7, 49–50, 114–15,
    118, 151, 213, 229–30, 235–6, 240
Amalric of Nesle, patriarch of Jerusalem 81
Amanus (mountains) 5, 22, 27, 29, 39, 43–4,
    49, 54, 60, 158, 202
Amuq (plain) 39–40, 57, 59, 86, 244
Anazarba 22, 27–8
Andronikos Komnenos, emperor of
    Byzantium 54, 100, 190, 214–17, 250
Anna Komnene 195
Ansarriyah (mountains) 17, 26–7, 37, 60,
    173, 175
Anterius, bishop of Valania 106, 108
Antioch, city of 1, 3, 22, 30, 34–6, 38, 41,
    45–6, 49, 51, 56, 75, 167–73, 175,
    181–6, 192–9, 206–8, 210–15, 218, 221
    –2, 224–9, 232, 234–6, 239–40
    governance of 62–3, 69–73, 86–92,
        97–109, 175–6, 179–80, 220–1,
        224–9
Apamea (Affamiyah) 37–9, 43, 46, 93, 167
    archbishopric of 101, 106, 153
Armenaz 92–3
Armenians
    internal community of 1, 100, 137, 164–
        9, 172–4, 181–2, 184
    of Cilicia 1, 12, 16–17, 22, 27, 29–31,
        35, 41, 43–6, 48–50, 54–5, 59–61,
        70, 81, 87, 108–9, 113–14, 191–2,
        195, 201–2, 230, 232, 235–6, 245,
        249, 251
Artah 25, 37–8, 93, 169
    battle of 46, 48–9, 84, 91, 94, 106, 112,
        117–18, 122, 176, 212–13, 229–30,

235, 237, 243, 245
bishopric of 101–2
Arzghan 33, 45–6, 48, 57, 59–60, 65, 86,
 93–4, 148–9, 155, 223, 244, 246
Asbridge, Thomas 4, 16, 24, 41, 62, 70, 72–3,
 78, 88, 92, 110, 118, 128–9, 131–4, 136–
 7, 139–41, 147, 150–3, 159, 165, 177–8,
 195, 220–1, 223, 238, 246–7
Assises d'Antioche 5, 14–15, 63–6, 87–9, 95,
 106–7, 111, 117, 128, 140, 142, 146–7,
 150, 152, 155, 157–9, 174, 184, 188, 249
Athanasius III, Greek Patriarch of Antioch
 105–6, 212

Baghras (Gaston) 29–30, 39–41, 44, 55–8,
 108, 158, 172, 251
Baha al-Din ibn Shaddad 13, 177, 243
Balatanos 26, 56, 130, 173, 175, 185
Baldwin I, king of Jerusalem 68, 223
Baldwin II, king of Jerusalem 22, 69–70,
 73–4, 118, 148, 167, 192, 218–25,
 230–1, 233, 237–8, 244, 251
Baldwin III, king of Jerusalem 38–9, 43, 45,
 74, 77–8, 80–2, 97, 104–5, 114, 120,
 199–200, 204, 206–12, 219–20, 226–9,
 233–5, 242–3, 251
Baldwin IV, king of Jerusalem 9, 51–2, 117,
 120, 146, 215, 219, 236–9, 243
Baldwin V, king of Jerusalem 239
Baldwin, lord of Marash 27, 35, 39, 103, 113,
 132, 134, 143, 148, 151, 162
Baldwin, son of Renaud of Châtillon and
 Constance of Antioch 83, 213
Baldwin of Ibelin 238–9
Banyas 34, 42, 120, 145, 153, 241–1
Barsutah 35, 121
Bartholomew, archbishop of Mamistra 108
Basarfut 37–46
Beatrice, widow of William of Saone and wife
 of Joscelin II of Edessa 145, 147–8
Bernard of Valence, patriarch of Antioch 70,
 101–3, 107, 109, 224, 247
Bertrand Masoir, lord of Margat 54, 65–6,
 154, 156–8, 161, 185
Bikisrail (Vetule) 26–7, 52, 55–6, 93–4, 141–
 2, 154, 158, 173, 175, 177–8, 185
Black Mountain 181
Bohemond I, prince of Antioch 1, 3, 68–9,
 73–4, 76, 119, 183, 189, 192, 218

Bohemond II, prince of Antioch 3, 16–17,
 22, 24–7, 29, 60, 62–3, 65, 68–77, 84,
 88, 90, 94–5, 101–2, 113, 117, 119, 123,
 132, 134, 148, 150–1, 183, 189, 191,
 216, 218, 221–2, 224, 230–1, 245–6, 248
Bohemond III, prince of Antioch
 accession to the throne 77, 79–84, 96,
  229, 247
 captivity of
  1164–5 48, 91, 94, 176, 212–13,
   229–30
  1193–5 16, 59, 108, 172, 182, 230,
   251
 marriages of 51, 54, 99–100, 107, 131,
  146, 149, 213–15, 217, 250
 military activities of 46, 49, 51–61, 112,
  186, 213, 216, 235–6, 243
 relationship with the Church 105–9,
  152–3
 rule of 46, 51–2, 54, 63–5, 74, 76, 89–91,
  93–4, 96, 99, 106–8, 111, 136, 141–2,
  145, 149–50, 154–8, 170, 172, 177–9,
  184–5, 213–14, 219, 233, 235–40,
  243, 246–9, 251
 services owed to 64–6, 99, 114–15, 117–
  18, 120–1
 succession of his sons 14, 59, 100
Bohemond IV, prince of Antioch and count of
 Tripoli 14, 100, 147, 170, 213, 240
Bokebais (Abu Qubais) 33, 43, 46, 52–3, 178
Bonable Baufre 89
Bonable, lord of Sarmin and Kafartab 89
Bourzey 33, 56, 89, 99, 149
Buqay'a Gap, battle of 46, 48, 155–6, 212,
 243
Butler of Antioch, office of 88, 91, 124–5
Buza'a 30–1, 33, 35, 113–14, 183
Byzantium, empire of 1, 24, 27–31, 35–6, 39,
 43–4, 46, 48–51, 53–4, 70–2, 76–8,
 80–3, 87, 91, 94–5, 97–102, 105–9,
 113–15, 117, 121, 144–5, 172, 176,
 189–217, 221–2, 226–30, 232–5, 237,
 239, 241–2, 244–7, 249–51

Cahen, Claude 3–6, 14, 16, 62, 64, 66,
 88–90, 94, 96, 100, 106, 112, 122, 128,
 130, 139–42, 145, 153–4, 159, 165–6,
 168, 171, 175, 178–9, 186, 188, 192,
 198–9, 219, 227, 236, 246–7

Castellan of Antioch, office of 88, 90–1, 116, 126

Chancellor of Antioch, office of 88, 107–8, 125, 247

Coinage 4, 7, 14, 68–9, 75–6, 79, 83–4, 171, 176, 186, 207, 220–1, 246

Coloman, *dux* of Cilicia 48, 117, 212, 230

Commune of Antioch 59, 109, 172–3

Constable of Antioch, office of 26, 88–91, 116, 123, 129, 142

Constance, princess of Antioch
marriages of 24, 27, 42, 69–80, 84, 102, 191–2, 201, 208
regency for 22, 69–72, 95, 221–9, 246
role in governance 64, 69, 74–5, 77–85, 91, 104–5, 132, 141, 181, 198, 201, 209–12, 226–229, 235

Constantine Manasses 11, 210–11

Conversion 182–3, 187, 249

Crusading
First Crusade 1, 26, 51, 76, 96, 166–7, 169, 171, 183, 189, 193–5, 218
Second Crusade 37–9, 41, 79, 103, 201, 226, 233, 242
Third Crusade 56–7, 99, 243–4
Fourth Crusade 11

Cyprus 44, 57, 114, 121, 201–2, 205, 208, 216–17

Damascus 13, 26, 33–4, 38–9, 41–3, 51, 119, 174, 196, 200, 232, 242

Danishmend Turks 1, 22, 29, 35, 39

Darbsak (Trapesac) 41, 44, 56, 59

Darkush (*Caveam*) 46, 65, 89, 91–4, 246

Duke (*dux*) of Antioch, office of 65, 88–91, 126, 172, 175–6, 224–5

Duke (*dux*) of Jabala, office of 88, 127, 137

Duke (*dux*) of Latakia, office of 88–91, 93, 127, 137

Edbury, Peter 5, 8, 14, 67, 110, 128, 174,

Edessa, county of 27–9, 33, 36, 39, 97, 101, 113–14, 119–20, 132, 147–8, 197–8, 200, 218–19, 222–4, 227, 231–3, 242, 244, 251
overlordship of 231–3

Ellenblum, Ronnie 33, 133, 164–5

Eracles 9–10, 78, 173, 205, 228, 240

Ernoul 10

Familiares 67–8, 88–90, 92–5, 110–11, 114, 121, 141–2, 149, 158, 247

Frederick, duke of Swabia 57

Fulcher of Chartres 7–8, 65, 68, 182, 220

Fulk of Anjou, king of Jerusalem 24–5, 34, 69–74, 77, 90, 97–8, 102, 113, 119–120, 130, 146, 175–6, 192, 221–6, 229–30, 232, 241–2

Garenton I of Saone 96–7, 116, 141, 162

Genoa 15, 86, 104–5, 186

Geoffrey the Monk, lord of Marash 132, 134–5, 142–3

Gerald, archbishop of Apamea 106

Gerard, bishop of Latakia 104–5, 144–5

Greeks, internal community of 164–5, 169–73

Gregory Bar Ebroyo 11–12, 53, 184

Gregory the Priest 12, 35, 44–6, 116, 132, 167, 196, 204, 206, 231

Gumushtegin, emir of Harim 51–2

Guy of Lusignan, king of Jerusalem 215, 238–9, 243

Hab 37

Hama 24, 26, 30, 37, 194, 196, 234

Hamilton, Bernard 5, 78, 90, 100, 104, 165, 212–14, 219, 237–8

Harim (Harenc) 17, 25–6, 34–9, 42–6, 48, 51–5, 57, 60, 66, 92, 96, 115–17, 122, 155, 170, 186, 234, 236, 246
lordship of 83, 96, 99, 118, 122, 131, 138, 142–7, 149, 157, 159, 161–2, 233, 248

Harran, battle of 1, 21, 27, 36, 112–13, 119, 218

Henry I, king of England 69–70, 73, 90, 94–5, 143

Henry II, king of England 88, 97, 108, 144, 204, 206, 213–14

Henry of Champagne, king of Jerusalem 230

Henry, brother of Raymond of Poitiers 143

Hisn ad-Dair 132

Homs 24, 30, 194, 196, 234

Hospitallers, order of 5, 17, 45–6, 52–5, 74–5, 106–7, 110, 130–2, 136, 141–2, 151–3, 155–8, 170, 172, 178–80, 182, 184–5, 231, 238

Ibn al-Athir 13–14, 25–6, 46, 79, 145, 177, 183
Ibn al-Furat 38, 45
Ibn al-Qalanisi 13, 113, 145, 167, 196, 223, 233
Il-Ghazi of Mardin 24, 173–5
'Imm 171
Imad al-Din al-Isfahani 13, 177
Inab, battle of 37–9, 41, 45, 75, 77–8, 90–1, 103–4, 112, 116–18, 122, 148–9, 175, 200, 226, 228, 242, 245
Iron Bridge (Jisr al-Hadid) 33–5, 42, 44–5, 51, 53, 56, 65, 92, 115, 121, 211, 246
Isaac Angelos, emperor of Byzantium 216
Isaac Komnenos, emperor of Cyprus 216
Isma'ilis (Assassins) 1, 26–7, 30, 33, 37–8, 43, 46, 53–4, 60, 116, 138, 158, 173, 175, 178, 185, 196, 234
Izz al-Din ibn Shaddad 14, 168
Izz al-Din of Mosul 51, 53

Jabala 24, 26, 49, 55, 57, 59, 65–6, 81–2, 86, 88–9, 94, 96–7, 105, 127, 131–2, 134, 137–9, 141–2, 155–6, 170, 172–3, 175–7, 181, 184–6, 224, 249
  bishopric of 101, 103–4, 108
Jabal as-Summaq 24–7, 35, 37, 39, 52, 60, 131
Jabal Talat (Belus Hills) 25–6, 33–5, 37, 39, 42, 60–1
Jacobites, internal community of 1, 9, 11, 81–2, 107, 165, 168–73, 179, 181
Jisr ash-Shughur 25, 33, 37–8, 44–6, 48, 56, 60, 130, 139, 158
Jerusalem, kingdom of
  intervention from 22, 24–5, 38–9, 43, 45, 49–51, 69–73, 77–8, 84–5, 105, 190–2, 199–201, 204–13, 216–17, 220–30, 233–6, 250–1
  intervention in 34, 94–5, 120, 145, 215, 235–44, 250–1
Jews, internal community of 165, 173, 182, 184
John II Komnenos, emperor of Byzantium 10, 24, 27–31, 35–6, 65, 70–2, 75, 80, 87, 95, 97–9, 102, 113–14, 132–3, 183–4, 186, 190–9, 203, 222, 224, 231–2, 241–2, 247
John, bishop of Tripoli 107–8, 125

John Kinnamos 10–11, 30, 70–1, 99, 191, 198, 201–2, 205–6, 209–11, 216
Josaphat, abbey of 89, 102, 136, 152, 170
Joscelin I, count of Edessa 9, 25, 117, 148, 218, 221–2, 231
Joscelin II, count of Edessa 24–5, 27, 35–6, 39, 97, 113–14, 147–8, 197, 222–3, 227, 231–3, 242
Joscelin III, count of Edessa 65, 111, 117, 131, 143–6, 233
Jotischky, Andrew 79–80, 164–5, 168–9, 227, 233

Kafarbasil (Kafar Rum) 35
Kafarlatha 37
Kafartab 25–6, 30, 33, 43, 52, 89, 113, 121, 129
Kafar Dubbin 168
Kemal al-Din (Ibn al-Adim) 13, 26, 33–4, 59, 177
Kesoun 12, 29, 35–6, 39, 101, 116, 132, 167
Köhler, Michael 12, 21, 24, 42, 48, 56

La Roche de Roissel 41, 44, 56, 92–4
La Roche Guillaume 41, 44, 56
Laitor 65, 131
Lake of Antioch 86
Latakia 24, 30, 45, 49, 55, 57, 59, 64–5, 81–2, 86, 88–9, 91–4, 96–7, 118, 127, 131–2, 134, 137–9, 141–2, 156, 167, 170–3, 177, 181, 184–6, 224–5, 237
  bishopric of 101, 104–5, 144–5, 203, 205
Leon I of Armenia 22, 24, 27, 29–30, 43, 113, 232
Leon II of Armenia 16, 55, 57–9, 109, 172, 182, 216, 230, 251
Liege homage 64–6, 146, 156, 194, 200, 222, 233
Lilie, Ralph-Johannes 29, 71–2, 75, 98, 190, 195–6, 214–15, 235
Louis VII, king of France 37–8, 81, 99, 103, 204, 230, 242

Ma'arrat an-Nu'man 25–6, 30–1, 33, 35, 41, 43, 52, 167–8
Ma'arrat Mesrin 24–5
Mabula (Mamulah) 37
MacEvitt, Christopher 1, 9, 164, 166–8, 170, 174–5, 177, 179, 184

Magdalino, Paul 49, 195, 198–200, 210–11
Mallett, Alex 37–8, 41, 116, 174–5, 183
Mamistra 22, 27–9, 54–55, 105, 129, 152, 167, 193, 199,
    archbishopric of 101–3, 108, 225
    penance of 202–9
Manganeios Prodromos 11, 99, 205–7
Mansur ibn Nabil, *qadi* of Jabala 55–6, 176–9, 187, 249
Manuel I Komnenos, emperor of Byzantium 10–11, 18, 24, 36, 38–9, 43–4, 46, 48–51, 53–5, 65, 77–8, 80, 82, 91, 94, 99–100, 105–6, 144–5, 176, 189–191, 195, 198–217, 226–30, 233–5, 250
Marash 22, 29, 35–6, 48, 137, 139, 167, 233
    bishopric of 101
    lordship of 5, 27, 29, 35, 38–9, 96, 103, 113, 116, 132–9, 142–3, 147–8, 151, 157, 159, 162, 226, 233, 248
Margat (Marqab) 54–5, 93, 96, 107–8, 129–30, 139, 157–8, 167, 178, 185, 243, 248–9
    lordship of 5, 26, 51, 54, 65–6, 93, 96, 111, 129–30, 134–6, 138–9, 141–2, 150–2, 154–8, 170, 175, 180, 185
Maria of Antioch, daughter of Raymond of Poitiers and Constance of Antioch 48, 51, 99–100, 105, 209–12, 214–16, 229–30, 235, 244, 250
Marshal of Antioch, office of 88–91, 93, 116–17, 124
Martin, Jean-Marie 4–5, 62, 64, 66, 87–8, 95, 100, 111, 128, 133, 140, 147, 150–2, 159, 219, 246–7
Masyaf 26, 43
Mayer, Hans Eberhard 3–4, 15, 62, 80–1, 88, 93, 100, 128, 132, 134–5, 140–2, 144, 150, 152, 154–9, 178, 210–11, 214, 219, 237, 239–40, 246
Melisende, queen of Jerusalem 69, 74, 77, 80–81, 119–20, 225, 227
Melisende, sister of Raymond III of Tripoli 209–12
Melkites, internal community of 1, 165, 168–172, 179, 181
Mercenaries 112
Michael the Syrian 9, 11–12, 22, 39, 45, 54, 80–2, 100, 105, 118, 167, 170–2, 175, 181, 215, 221–3, 226, 231

Mleh of Armenia 48–51, 114, 213, 235–6
Montferrand (Ba'rin) 25–6, 30, 97, 119, 121, 193, 232, 241
Mosul 1, 13, 24, 27, 30–1, 37, 42, 51, 174
Mt Hingron 92–3
Muslims, internal community of 26–7, 165, 173–80, 182–7

Niketas Choniates 10–12, 113, 167, 169, 186, 210–11, 216
Nobility
    independence of 68–9, 77, 128–60
    marriages of 147–9
    military service of 94–5, 110–23
    relationship with the prince 64–75, 99–101, 140–7, 149–60, 214–15
    role in governance 68–73, 77–85, 87–9, 94–101
Normandy 39, 61, 134–5, 141, 143, 160
Normans
    Antiochene identity with 15, 70–6, 83–4
Nur al-Din, ruler of Aleppo and Damascus 13–14, 36–52, 60, 80, 82, 94, 103–4, 114, 116–17, 120, 131, 143–6, 148, 153, 158, 167–8, 175, 186, 200, 205, 212, 226, 229–30, 234–6, 238, 242–3

Orderic Vitalis 9, 71, 94–5, 134
Orgeuillse Fresnel, princess of Antioch 83, 99–100, 131, 146, 149, 162, 213
Orontes (river) 1, 17, 25–7, 33, 37–9, 41–6, 56, 60, 93–4, 130, 158, 168, 196, 200, 245

Papacy 1, 8, 30, 72, 103, 107–8, 167, 170, 172–3, 183, 193, 204, 213
Paschal of Saone 147, 163
Patriarch of Antioch 8–9, 25, 51–3, 56, 70–2, 99–109, 117, 153, 157–8, 165, 173, 181–2, 196, 209–11, 213–15, 221, 224–5, 227, 229, 247
Patriarchate and Church of Antioch 4–5, 17, 22, 51, 63, 70–1, 88, 99–109, 118, 143, 153, 165, 172–3, 181–2, 196, 213–14, 247–8
    wealth of 86–7, 104
Peter of Angoûleme, patriarch of Antioch 109
Peter of Ivrea, patriarch of Antioch 109
Philip, count of Flanders 52, 115, 144, 237–8

Pisa 15, 86, 186
Pons, count of Tripoli 24, 148–9, 223–4
Princely house of Antioch
  demesne of 66, 75, 81, 86, 88–90, 92–93,
    95, 98–9, 109, 122, 128, 141–2, 148,
    155, 249
  household of 88–95, 107–8, 141–2,
    175–80
  marriages of 22, 27, 42, 51, 69–73, 77–8,
    83, 99–100, 107, 131, 146, 149,
    191–2, 201, 209–15, 225, 227–9
  powers of 87–95, 97–100, 106–7,
    110–27, 135–9, 141–3, 145–7,
    149–60, 197–8, 231–40, 246–9, 251
  title of 69, 73–6, 79–81, 83–4, 114, 120
  wealth of 86–7, 104, 121–2, 185–7
Principality of Antioch
  eastern frontier of 24–7, 30–1, 33–9,
    41–8, 51–5, 57, 59–61, 245–6
  northern frontier of 22–4, 27–31, 35–6,
    39–41, 43–4, 48–51, 54–5, 57–61,
    245–6
  southern frontier of 26–7, 52–3, 55–6, 60,
    245–6

Qadmus 26, 54
Qinnasrin, battle of 25–6, 192, 224
Quorchiya 92–3
Qusair (Cursat) 25, 56, 104, 106–8, 224

Ralph II, patriarch of Antioch 108–9
Ralph of Caen 7, 68, 169, 171
Ralph of Domfront, patriarch of Antioch
  70–2, 102–3, 109
Raymond II, count of Tripoli 119, 148–9,
  241–2
Raymond III, count of Tripoli 49, 52, 115,
  117, 120, 149, 212, 215, 236–7, 239–40,
  243
Raymond II, son of Raymond of Poitiers and
  Constance of Antioch 59, 100, 182, 213,
  240
Raymond of Poitiers, prince of Antioch
  accession of 27, 69–79, 84–5, 102, 143,
    191–2, 225, 230, 246
  death of 38–9, 45, 77, 103, 226, 235
  military activities of 27–31, 34–9, 92, 113,
    115–17, 119–20
  relationship with the Church 102–3, 107,

196
  rule of 5, 39, 48, 65, 73–8, 87–8, 90–2,
    97–9, 103, 107, 110, 130, 132, 143,
    148, 152, 169–70, 175–6, 179, 182,
    193–201, 203, 208, 222, 224, 226–7,
    231–3, 241–2
  services owed to 97, 99, 113–17, 119–20
Raymond-Rupen, prince of Antioch 14, 59,
  109
Rayyis, office of 138, 170, 179–80, 185
Rebellions
  1130–1131/1136: Alice of Antioch 22,
    70–1, 191, 221–6
  1132: civil war 24–5, 96–7, 117, 130–1,
    139, 222–4, 231
  1180–1182: noble revolt 51, 53–4, 91,
    99–101, 107–8, 123, 130, 154, 156–7,
    160, 214–15, 236, 238–9, 248, 250
  Indigenous uprisings 26–7, 174–5, 177–9
Redford, Scott 5, 86–7, 186–7
Renaud I Masoir, lord of Margat 26, 89, 123,
  129, 141–2, 160, 221, 224–5
Renaud II Masoir, lord of Margat 51, 66, 91,
  99–100, 105, 111, 116, 130–1, 134, 136,
  141, 148–9, 152, 154–6, 160, 180
Renaud, lord of Marash 38–9, 116, 132, 134,
  143, 147–8, 162, 226
Renaud of Châtillon, prince of Antioch
  accession of 42, 77–80, 83–4, 104, 149,
    228
  capture of 45, 48, 80–1, 105, 118, 209–
    11, 228–9
  Jerusalemite baron 237
  military activities of 42–5, 48, 114, 116–
    17, 120–2, 145, 201–2, 209, 217, 242
  relationship with the Church 104–5, 107
  rule of 76, 79, 90–1, 94, 99, 104–105,
    134, 143, 145–6, 154, 199, 201–11,
    217, 219, 233–5, 242–3, 246, 250
  services owed to 89, 94, 96, 99, 114,
    116–17, 120–2, 145
Renaud of Saint Valery 131, 143–6
Richard I, king of England 57, 82, 243–4
Richard of Salerno, lord of Marash 132, 142
Riley-Smith, Jonathan 29–30, 175, 179–80
Robert II of Sourdeval 81, 120, 131, 161, 227
Robert fitz-Fulk the Leper, lord of Saone,
  Balatanos and Zardana 130
Robert of Torigny 9, 42, 143–5

Roger II, king of Sicily 71–2, 75, 83

Roger of Salerno, prince of Antioch 9, 69, 76, 79, 89, 107, 112, 119, 132, 142, 152–3, 218, 220–1, 231

Roger of Saone 106, 152–3, 162

Roger of Sourdeval 95, 161

Rugia (*Chastel Rouge*) 46, 148–9, 154–5

Ruj (valley) 46, 130, 154–5

Rupen II of Armenia 49

Rupen III of Armenia 50, 54–5, 216

Saif al-Din, son of Zengi and lord of Mosul 37

Saint George 76

Saint Peter 76, 101

Saone (Qal'at Salah al-Din) 24, 26, 56, 92, 96, 130, 139, 158, 168

    lordship of 24–6, 45, 78, 95–7, 106, 116, 130–1, 133–5, 138–9, 141, 145, 147–8, 151–4, 162–3, 223

Saladin, sultan of Egypt and Syria 3, 10, 13–14, 36, 51–7, 59–61, 66, 99–100, 108, 112, 114, 117–18, 120, 123, 130, 141, 158, 160, 167–8, 173, 175, 177–9, 214, 216, 236–40, 243, 245, 249, 251

Salda 37

Salqin 92–3

Santiago di Compostella, order of 52, 56, 93, 107–8, 141–2, 157, 178, 185

Sarmada 26, 37

Sarmenia 89

Sarmin 26, 33–4, 121, 129, 185

Sawar, lieutenant of Aleppo 24, 34–5

Seals 14, 68, 75–6, 133–5, 240

Secreta, office of 62, 87, 128, 140, 175–6, 180

Seljuk Turks 1, 39, 44, 53–4

Sempad the Constable 12, 14, 22, 54, 81, 106–7, 210–11

Seneschal of Antioch, office of 88–91, 124

Shaizar 25, 30, 34, 43, 52–3, 89, 94, 97, 112, 114–15, 183, 194, 196–7, 231, 233–4, 243

Shih al-Hadid 57

Shughur-Bakas 33, 56

Sicily, kingdom of 6, 57, 71–3, 75, 83, 96, 128, 139, 150, 176, 179, 193–4, 216

Slavery 183–4

St George's, monastery of Antioch 105, 136

St Lazarus, order of 105

St Mary's, church of Antioch 103

St Paul's, monastery of Antioch 102, 106, 108

St Peter's, cathedral chapter of Antioch 102, 106

St Simeon 86, 186

Stephany of Courtenay, abbess of St Mary the Major 8–9, 232

Surhak, governor of Harim 53

Sybil, princess of Antioch 51, 59, 100, 107–8, 149, 156, 213–15

Sybil, queen of Jerusalem 120, 237–8

Symeon II, patriarch of Antioch 170

Tancred Fresnel, lord of Harim 116, 118, 122, 131, 143–6, 162

Tancred of Hauteville, prince of Antioch 21, 69, 79, 115, 129, 142, 148, 189, 191–2, 218, 223, 227, 213, 233

Tarsus 22, 27–8, 48, 54–5, 129, 137, 150–1, 167, 170–1, 193

    archbishopric of 101–2, 108, 125

Tell Aghda 25

Tell Bashir 35, 39, 232

Tell Khalid 33

Templars, order of 5, 15, 17, 29–30, 38–40, 43–4, 49, 52–4, 56, 60, 94, 106, 114–18, 142, 146, 154, 158, 162, 175, 202, 216, 226, 235–6, 238

Theodora Komnena, wife of Baldwin III 200, 204

Theodora Komnena, wife of Bohemond III 51, 99, 107, 213–17, 250

Thierry, count of Flanders 43, 114, 233–4, 244

Thomas of Jabala 66, 155

Thoros of Armenia 41, 43–4, 48–9, 80, 114, 117, 181, 201–2, 233–4

Trade 5, 86–7, 104, 185–7, 248–9

Treaties

    Devol 101, 189, 194–6

    1137 30, 190, 193–8, 232

Tripoli, county of 18, 21, 24, 26, 30, 46, 49, 52, 72, 74, 77, 84, 101, 108, 113, 115, 117, 119–20, 130, 148–9, 151, 155, 157–8, 165, 174–5, 179, 189, 209–12, 215, 218–19, 223, 227–8, 230, 236–42, 244, 251

    unification with 18, 108, 218, 240, 251

Turcomans 25–6, 34, 54, 142, 175, 223, 243

Turcopoles 112, 185
Tyre 8, 101, 105, 167, 240

Usamah ibn Munqidh 14, 179, 182–4, 186

Valania (Baniyas) 104, 130, 154, 172
　bishopric of 101, 104, 106, 108, 154, 167,
　175
Venice 15, 86, 186
Viscount of Antioch, office of 66, 88, 91, 126,
　137, 176

Walter I of Sourdeval 89, 116, 136, 161
Walter II of Sourdeval 65, 86, 95, 142, 161
Walter the Chancellor 7–8, 66–9, 89, 112,
　131, 167, 169, 171, 174–5, 184, 220
Welsh Marches 6, 34, 61, 128, 136–7, 140–1,
　147–8, 159–60
Wilbrand of Oldenburg 169, 172–3, 182
William II, king of Sicily 57, 176
William Bucellus 92–4, 141–2, 158

William Fresnel, lord of Harim 143, 161
William of Saone 25, 130, 145, 147–8, 162,
　223
William of Tyre 7–10, 12, 36, 43, 46, 54,
　64–8, 70–2, 75, 78–9, 81, 89, 91, 94,
　97–8, 100, 112–21, 130–1, 134, 143,
　167, 169, 171, 191, 193–8, 201–6,
　209–11, 214–15, 221–9, 231–2, 234,
　236–8, 241–2

Yaghra 38, 171

Zardana 25–6, 31, 33–4, 36–7, 130
Zengi, *atabeg* of Mosul and Aleppo 24–7,
　29–31, 33–7, 70–1, 113, 115–16, 119,
　133, 148, 192–3, 195–7, 199–200, 208,
　216–17, 221, 224–5, 232–3, 241–2

1234 Chronicle 11–12, 25–6, 81–2, 118,
　144, 170, 193, 196, 227

Lightning Source UK Ltd.
Milton Keynes UK
UKOW06n1322290817
308180UK00002B/165/P